BEATING CANCER
WITH NUTRITION

clinically proven and easy-to-follow strategies to
dramatically improve quality and quantity of life
and chances for a complete remission

Patrick Quillin, PhD,RD,CNS

with Noreen Quillin

NutritionTimesPress,Inc.
Tulsa, Oklahoma

Other books & products by Patrick Quillin, PhD,RD,CNS
available at your local bookstore or health food store, or Bookworld at 1-800-444-2524, or on the Internet at www.amazon.com
-BEATING CANCER WITH NUTRITION, audiotape, NTP, 1998
-IMMUNOPOWER, Nutrition Times Press, Tulsa, 1998
-KITCHEN HEALTH TIPS, 56 minute videotape, Nutrition Times, 1997
-HEALING SECRETS FROM THE BIBLE, Nutrition Times Press, Tulsa, 1996
-HONEY, GARLIC & VINEGAR, Leader Co., N. Canton, OH, 1996
-HEALTH TIPS, Nutrition Times Press, Tulsa, 1996
-HEALING POWER OF WHOLE FOODS, Vitamix, Cleveland, 1994
-ADJUVANT NUTRITION IN CANCER TREATMENT, Cancer Treatment Research Foundation, Arlington Heights, IL, 1994
-AMISH FOLK MEDICINE, Leader Co., N.Canton, OH, 1993
-SAFE EATING, M.Evans, NY, 1990
-LA COSTA BOOK OF NUTRITION, Pharos Books, New York, 1988
-HEALING NUTRIENTS, Contemporary Books, Chicago, 1987, in paperback by Random House, NY, 1988; also published in paperback in Europe and Australia through Penguin Press, London
-THE LA COSTA PRESCRIPTION FOR LONGER LIFE, Ballantine Books, NY, 1985

Revised edition copyright 1998 Patrick Quillin
ISBN 0-9638372-4-9
Copyright 1994, additional printings March & Sept. 1994, June & Oct. 1995, August 1996, March & July 1997

Printed in the United States of America

How to order this book:
BOOKWORLD 1-800-444-2524

Quantity discounts may be available from:
Nutrition Times Press, Inc., Box 700512, Tulsa, OK 74170-0512
phone & fax 918-495-1137

TELL US YOUR STORY
We want to hear about your experiences using nutrition as part of your cancer treatment. Please send us your personal experience with an address or phone number on how to contact you. Your story may provide hope and inspiration for others suffering from the same condition. Thank you.

CONTENTS

Preface: What is new in this revised version   5
Shortcut, executive summary: 13
If you are too sick to read much

SECTION ONE: THE PROBLEM
We have lost the war on cancer
1-What causes cancer? How can we beat cancer?   15
2-Progress report in the war on cancer   22
3-Treatments currently used for cancer   33
4-Note to the oncologist: nutrition helps   47

SECTION TWO: THE SOLUTION
Cancer treatment must include nutrition
5-Nutrition can improve outcome in cancer treatment   51
6-Malnutrition among cancer patients   63
7-Why nutrition can beat cancer   70
     Nutrients as biological response modifiers
     Power of nutritional synergism

SECTION THREE: ACTION PLAN
Beating cancer with a combined attack
8-Food: Nutritious & Delicious   85
SUPPLEMENTS AGAINST CANCER
9-Botanicals, glandulars, lipids, minerals, enzymes   128
10-Vitamins   154
11-Food extracts & accessory factors   185
12-Changing the underlying causes of cancer   211
13-Rational comprehensive cancer treatment   239
14-Beating cancer symptoms   241
15-Parting comments   243

APPENDIX
Referral agencies & other information   246
Mail order nutrition products   254
Nutrition & cancer books   255
Nutritionally oriented doctors   257
INDEX   277

Dedication

To the many cancer patients that I was privileged to work with. Though, for your privacy, you are anonymous here, your names and faces are permanently etched in the gallery of my mind. Thank you for sharing your courage, your wisdom, your insight on priorities and your souls with me.

Acknowledgements

To my lovely wife, Noreen, for your smile, your enthusiastic assistance and your empowering camaraderie for the past quarter of a century. To the many skilled physicians and scientists who sacrificed their careers in order to advance the knowledge base in the area of nutrition and cancer. My most sincere appreciation and admiration for Linus Pauling, PhD and Abram Hoffer, MD, PhD. Nobody ever said that being an ice breaker is an easy job. But the world is better off because you assumed the task.

IMPORTANT NOTICE!!! PLEASE READ!!!

CAUTION!! Cancer is a life-threatening disease. The program and products outlined in this book are designed to be used in conjunction with, not instead of, your doctor's program. All of the foods and supplements described in this book will work synergistically with your oncologist's program. Do not use this information as sole therapy against cancer. If you cannot agree to these terms, then you may return this book in new condition for a full refund. This information has not been evaluated by the Food and Drug Administration.

PREFACE

"I have been wrong. The germ is nothing. The 'terrain' is everything." Louis Pasteur on his deathbed in 1895

Cancer is the best thing that ever happened to me. The words almost knocked me over. I was listening to the testimonials from several cancer survivors who had gathered in a class reunion to celebrate life. These people later went on to explain this strange statement. "My life wasn't working. I didn't take care of my body. I didn't eat right. I didn't get enough rest. I didn't like my job, or myself or those around me. I didn't appreciate life. I rarely stopped to smell the roses along the way. My life was a mess. Cancer was a great big red light flashing on the dashboard of my car saying 'pull this vehicle over and fix it now'".

These cancer victors had shown the ultimate courage by turning adversity into a major victory. In Oriental language, "crisis" is written by two characters, one meaing "danger" and the other meaning "opportunity". Cancer is a crisis of unparalleled proportions, both for the individual and humanity. For a minority of cancer patients, cancer has become an extraordinary opportunity to convert their lives into a masterpiece.

Since the original version of this book was first published in January of 1994, much water has passed underneath the bridge of nutritional oncology. There have been significant changes in the critical mass of data which endorses the use of nutrition for cancer patients. I have organized 3 international scientific symposia, complete with continuing medical education (CME) units offered, on the subject of "Adjuvant Nutrition in Cancer Treatment". A textbook by the same title sprang from the seminal work reported in those conferences. More oncologists are receptive to the theory that nutrition may be valuable for their patients.

Over 2.5 million Americans are currently being treated for cancer. Each year over 1.3 million more Americans are newly diagnosed with cancer. Half of all cancer patients in general are alive after five years. Europe has an even higher incidence of cancer. For the past four decades, both the incidence and age-adjusted death rate from cancer in America has been steadily climbing. Ironically, amidst the high tech wizardry of modern medicine, at least 40% of cancer patients will die from malnutrition, not the cancer itself. This book highlights proven scientific methods use nutrition to:

⇒Prevent or reverse the common malnutrition that plagues cancer patients.

⇒Make the medical therapies of chemotherapy and radiation more of a selective toxin to the cancer while protecting the patient from damage.

⇒Bolster the cancer patient's immune system to provide a microscopic army of warriors to fight the cancer throughout the body, because when the doctor says: "We think we got it all" that's when we are relying on a well-nourished immune system to locate, recognize and destroy the inevitable remaining cancer cells.

⇒Help to selectively starve sugar-feeding tumor cells by altering intake of sugar, blood glucose levels and circulating insulin.

⇒Slow down cancer with high doses of nutrients that make the body more resistant to invasion from tumor cells.

All of this good news means that cancer patients who use the comprehensive therapies described in this book may expect significant improvement in quality and quantity of life and chances for a complete remission--by changing the underlying conditions that brought about the cancer; because no cancer patient is suffering from a deficiency of adriamycin, a common chemotherapy drug. Cancer is an abnormal growth, not just a regionalized lump or bump. Chemo, radiation and surgery will reduce tumor burden but do nothing to change the underlying conditions that allowed this abnormal growth to thrive. In a nutshell, this book is designed to change the conditions in the body that favor tumor growth and return the cancer victor to a healthier status. More wellness in the body means less illness which means unfavorable conditions for cancer to thrive.

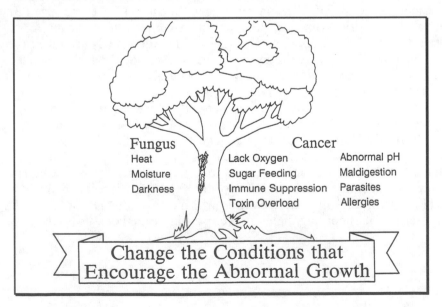

Fungus   Cancer

Fungus	Cancer	
Heat	Lack Oxygen	Abnormal pH
Moisture	Sugar Feeding	Maldigestion
Darkness	Immune Suppression	Parasites
	Toxin Overload	Allergies

Change the Conditions that Encourage the Abnormal Growth

Fungus grows on a tree because of warmth, moisture and darkness. You can cut, burn and poison fungus off the tree but the fungus will return as long as the conditions are favorable. Similarly, there are conditions that favor the growth of cancer. My extensive work with cancer patients shows that the cancer patient will thrive or wither, live or die based upon the ability to change the conditions which favor cancer growth.

SHIFTING PARADIGMS

Once Louis Pasteur discovered how to kill bacteria by heat processing (pasteurization), he embarked upon an energetic but ultimately frustrating career to eliminate all bacteria from the planet earth. Didn't work. And a century later, after the development of numerous "super drugs" to kill bacteria, Americans now have infections as the third leading cause of death, right after heart disease and cancer. Many bacteria are now drug resistant and virtually unstoppable. Similarly, after spending the last half century trying to poison the insects out of our fields with potent pesticides, we now have "super bugs" that are chemically resistant to all poisons and a net INCREASE in crop loss to insects. Same goes for cancer. We thought that we could poison the cancer out of the patient. But many cancers develop a drug resistance or hormone independence, while the toxic drugs compromise our immune systems and leave us "naked" in the battle with the cancer.

There is a new philosophy emerging in science and medicine. According to several articles in major cancer journals, oncologists are asking the question: "Must we kill to cure?". In the prestigious Journal of Clinical Oncology (April 1995, p.801), Drs. Schipper, Goh, and Wang provide a compelling argument that curing the cancer patient need not include killing the cancer cells with potent cytotoxic therapies. In many ways, from our fields to our bacterial infection patients to our cancer patients, we need to re-examine Dr. Pasteur's grand deathbed epiphany: "The terrain is everything." The terrain is your human body. Nourish it properly with

SCIENCE & HEALING ARTS

problem	allopathy	naturopathy-improve terrain
bacteria	antibiotics	immune system
insects	pesticides	natural predators, prevention
weeds	herbicides	exploit, crowd with useful
cancer	chemotherapy	host defense mechanisms

nutrients, oxygen, good thoughts and exercise and it will perform miraculous feats of disease recovery. We don't necessarily fully understand these "host defense mechanisms", but we need to respect and utilize them. That is how we will win the "war on cancer."

WHY ME AND WHY NOW?

You may ask, "What qualifies Patrick Quillin to write such a book on nutrition and cancer?" I have earned my bachelor's, master's, and doctorate degrees in nutrition, taught college nutrition for 9 years, have been a consultant to the Office of Alternative Medicine of the National Institutes of Health, the U.S. Army Breast Cancer research project, Scripps Clinic and La Costa Spa in southern California, am a registered and licensed dietitian, am one of only a thousand people in America who have earned my Certified Nutrition Specialist (CNS) status with the American College of Nutrition, have written 12 books, organized the first three international symposia on the subject of "Adjuvant (helpful) nutrition in cancer treatment", edited the textbook by the same name, written numerous articles and contributed a chapter to a medical textbook. I am a member of the American College of Nutrition and New York Academy of Sciences, as well as being listed in WHO'S WHO IN SCIENCE. I have my own access code to computer search the 8 million scientific documents in the National Library of Medicine and the 500 other computer accessed data bases around the world through Dialog and other services.

More importantly, I have studied the subject of nutrition in cancer as intensively as anyone. Even more critical, I have been privileged to use nutrition in a formal clinical setting for 8 years with hundreds of cancer patients. The scientific studies are important, but even more crucial is what is happening to the patients in front of me. This stuff works. You will read a few patient profiles from patients that I have worked with.

Some critics might say,"The evidence is very preliminary for you to be making any recommendations." I disagree. The evidence is substantial and points toward an inexpensive and low-risk method for extending the quality and quantity of life for cancer patients, many of whom have no options left. As poetically stated by Arthur Janov, PhD: "Research is a necessity for scientists, but a luxury for suffering humanity who cannot wait for final statistical proofs. For them, waiting may be a fatal disease." It can be an absurdly long wait for this or any field to become "politically correct", which requires people overcoming their reluctance to change. Traditional cancer therapies alone offer almost no hope for many cancer patients, especially lung, pancreas, liver, bone, and advanced colon and breast cancer. These people need supportive therapies to dovetail with traditional therapies. They need options and hope. There are too many lives at stake, and nothing to lose in implementing the nutrition program presented in this book.

In the 1970s, amidst heavy criticism, two Canadian physicians, the Shute brothers, began writing about their clinical success using vitamin E supplements to reverse heart disease and relieve the symptoms of angina and leg pain. A multi-nation study was begun in Europe to examine this issue. As reported at the University of California, Berkeley conference on Antioxidants and Free Radicals in 1989 by Dr. Fred Gey, the best predictor of developing heart disease was low vitamin E levels in the blood. The Shute brothers were right. Since then, other work has shown that a low intake of vitamin E can also lead to suppressed immune functions, cancer, Alzheimer's disease and cataracts. How many people suffered and died needlessly while the authorities tried to make up their minds about whether to endorse non-toxic and inexpensive nutrients? Where is the down side to this equation?

In the early 1980s, I would ask scientists at professional meetings "how many of you are taking supplements?". The answer was about 5%, with the remainder being sarcastic about the subject. At a recent meeting, 90% of the scientists polled admitted to taking therapeutic levels of supplements to protect their health. Free radicals were discovered to be the cause of degenerative diseases by Denom Harmon, MD, PhD of the University of Nebraska in the 1940s. This crucial area was then popularized by Dirk Pearson and Sandy Shaw in their 1982 book, LIFE EXTENSION, and fully supported by the world's most prestigious group of nutrition scientists in the American Journal of Clinical Nutrition conference held in 1990. A half century had produced more evidence and explanations, but had wasted many lives in the process.

America is a consumer driven society. You will create the momentum for change. Don't wait for some government organization, or new law, or general endorsement from one of the major health care organizations to implement nutrition as part of comprehensive cancer treatment.

It has been said that all truth must go through three stages: first, it is rejected, second, it is violently opposed, third, it is accepted as self-evident. Nutrition in cancer treatment currently resides on stage two, and is moving swiftly toward stage three. When is the evidence enough? Right now.

HOW IS THIS BOOK DIFFERENT?

Attacking cancer on many levels. A hammer, pliers and screwdriver belong in any good tool box, just as chemo, radiation and surgery have their place in cancer treatment. But that tool box is far from complete. There are many alternative cancer therapies which can be valuable assets in cancer treatment. This book offers other "tools" to support the basic but incomplete toolbox that we currently use against cancer.

There are a number of books on the market that offer alternative advice for cancer patients. Many of these books have served a valuable purpose and have helped cancer patients to be aware of cancer treatment options. This book offers a unique multi-disciplinary approach to treating cancer that is based on both scientific studies and actual clinical experience. My basic strategy is a two-pronged attack on cancer:

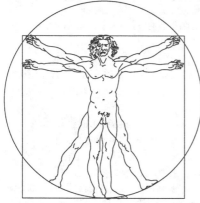

1) External medicine. Traditional and innovative oncology. To reduce cancer burden and symptoms with non-toxic and sometimes selectively toxic approaches.
2) Internal medicine. Naturopathic means of improving "non-specific host defense mechanisms" which prevent and reverse disease. To use nutrition, exercise, attitude and detoxification to elevate the body's own internal healing abilities.

Avoid tunnel vision. It is important to avoid the mistakes of the past; which is to focus on one aspect of cancer treatment and forget the other potentially valuable therapies. Avoid mono-mania, or obsession with one "magic bullet" idea. This book pays homage to the complexities of the human body and mind and draws on many fields to provide maximum firepower against cancer. We need all the weapons we can muster, for cancer is no simple beast to kill.

Individualize treatment plans. I recognize the diversity of the human population. There are nearly 6 billion people on the planet earth. We are as different as we are alike. There is no one perfect diet. The macrobiotic diet is truly a major improvement over the typical American diet, yet was developed by a Japanese physician who was drawing heavily on his ancestral Oriental diet. Eskimos eat 60% of their calories from high fat animal food, with very little vitamin C, fiber, fruit or vegetables in their diet. Yet they have a very low incidence of cancer and heart disease. There are groups of people in Africa and Asia that rely on their dairy herds for their dietary staples and others that are vegans, or pure vegetarians. Each of these groups has adapted to a unique diet that strongly influences their health. Rather than give you one set diet to follow, I am going to work with you to find a diet that reflects your ancestral heritage and your unique biochemical needs.

Also, we need to fix the problem(s) that may have triggered the cancer. If low thyroid and milk allergies were the initial problems, then you will never really resolve the cancer until the problems have been fixed. I will present a logical flow later in the book that will help you to detect common problems that can be the original insult which triggered the cancer.

RE-ENGINEERING CANCER TREATMENT

American health care is nearing a financial "meltdown". We spent $1.2 trillion in 1997 on disease maintenance, which is 14% of our gross national product--twice the expense per capita of any other health care system on earth. Notice that I said "disease maintenance", because we certainly do not support health care in America, and "health insurance" is neither related to health nor solid actuarial insurance. Just to put that into perspective, 10% of the cost of that new car you bought was for health insurance for factory workers. And Richard Lamm, visiting professor at Dartmouth College, has estimated that inefficient and unnecessary health care expenditures add $100 billion annually to the cost of American goods and services, which jeopardizes our ability to compete in the emerging global economy.

The most expensive disease in America is cancer, which cost Americans $110 billion in 1992, which is greater than 11% of the total spent on all diseases. These opulent expenses would be easier to swallow if we were obtaining impressive results. But many experts argue that we have made limited progress in the costly and lengthy "war on cancer". Annually in America, there are more than 50 million cancer-related visits to the doctor; one million cancer operations and 750,000 radiation treatments.

By 1971, cancer had become enough of a nuisance that President Richard Nixon launched the long awaited "war on cancer", confidently proclaiming that we would have a cure within 5 years, before the Bicentennial celebration in 1976. Twenty seven years later, with over $39 billion spent on research, $1 trillion spent on therapy, 7 million casualties, and no relief in sight from traditional therapies--it is blindingly obvious that we must re-examine some options in cancer prevention and treatment.

As of 1998, experts estimate that 45% of males and 39% of females living in America will develop cancer in their lifetime. Breast cancer has increased from one out of 20 women in the year 1950 to one out of 8 women in 1995. With some cancers, notably liver, lung, pancreas, bone and advanced breast cancer; our five year survival rate from traditional therapy alone is virtually the same as it was 30 years ago. In 1992, there were 547,000 deaths in America from cancer, which is 1500 people per day, which is the equivalent of 5 loaded 747 airplanes killing all occupants on board.

This book is about options. If our current results from traditional cancer treatment were encouraging, then there would be no need for alternative therapies against cancer. Unfortunately, traditional cancer therapies have plateaued--some might say that they hit a dead end brick wall. In many instances, the treatment is worse than the disease, with chronic nausea and vomiting, hair loss, painful mouth sores, extreme fatigue and depression as common side effects of therapy and minimal improvements in lifespan. Long term complications include toxicity to the heart, kidneys and bone marrow. While many children may recover from cancer, they are placed at much higher risk for getting cancer later in life from their cancer therapy. And if the cancer patient recovers from the disease, which is no small task; then recovering from the therapy may be even more challenging. Obviously, if what we are doing isn't working, then we need to look at some sensible, scientific, non-toxic and cost effective options that can amplify the tumor-killing abilities of traditional therapies. Nutrition is at the top of that list.

The best selling cancer drug in the world is a mushroom extract, PSK, manufactured in Japan and sold throughout Europe and Japan. Only 30% of cancer therapy in Japan is from the "big three" of radiation, chemo and surgery. The bark of the yew tree, Taxol, holds promise as a potent cancer drug. Digestive enzymes and mistletoe (Iscador) are government approved prescription cancer drugs in Germany. Evening primrose oil is an accepted cancer therapy in England. Do not discount any possibilities in this "war on cancer". While America is considered one of the world's heavy weight champions at developing new industrial technologies and patents, we are lagging well behind the rest of the world in cancer treatment.

The recommendations provided in this book are scientifically-backed, time tested, logical, and supported by my clinical observations in working with hundreds of cancer patients over the course of 8 years. Follow the program outlined in this book and you, the cancer patient, will greatly surpass the recovery predictions of your oncologist.

PATIENT PROFILE: BEAT COLON CANCER

S.B. is a 52 year old male who was diagnosed in August of 1996 with stage 2 colon cancer. Chemotherapy was administered in October of 1996 and produced severe reactions. Patient ceased therapy. He was then told by his surgeon to spend 2 months getting his white cell count (immune system) elevated prior to having surgery to remove the golf ball size tumor mass in his colon. Began nutrition therapy in August of 1997 for 2 months as sole therapy. Upon surgical removal of 17 cm (6.5 inches) mass in colon and 10 lymph nodes, there were no living cancer cells found in the pathology report. All of the cancer cells had become a calcified necrotic mass. When the body begins to destroy a cancer, this is the process. Hence, CAT scan X-rays may show the tumor mass to be the same size. Yet, either cancer is growing or dying. It rarely sits in a state of dormancy, unless being blasted by chemotherapy. Physicians were so surprised at this patient's outcome, that he was highlighted in a hospital tumor board presentation. As of December 1997, he is still in remission.

SHORTCUT: EXECUTIVE SUMMARY
IF YOU ARE TOO SICK TO READ MUCH,
THEN READ THIS SECTION

"Progress is impossible without change, and those who cannot change their minds cannot change anything."
George Bernard Shaw

A well nourished cancer patient can better manage and beat the disease. And today's cancer patient needs more help than ever before. After spending $39 billion in research in the 28 year "war on cancer" at the National Cancer Institute and over $1 trillion in therapy at hospitals around the country, we now have a 13% increase in the incidence and 7% increase in the death rate from cancer. Five year survival is virtually unchanged at around 50%. The reason for this lack of progress in beating cancer is our inability to use good judgment in both research and treatment. Blasting the cancer with the cytotoxic therapies of chemotherapy, radiation, and surgery can reduce tumor burden INITIALLY; but they do not change the underlying causes of the disease. And when the cancer returns, it is much more ferocious the second time, now having developed "drug resistance" or "hormone independence" to make medical intervention ineffective.

We need to re-think the cancer battle plan. Fungus grows on the bark of a tree because of the underlying conditions of heat, moisture and darkness. You could cut on the fungus with an axe, or burn with a blow torch, or poison with bleach; yet the fungus would return as long as the underlying conditions of heat, moisture and darkness are present. Similarly, cancer grows in a human body because of one or more underlying conditions; including lack of oxygen (cancer is an anaerobic organism), sugar feeding, immune suppression, toxin overload, and so on. If all you do is "cut, burn and poison" with surgery, radiation and chemotherapy; then there is a very good chance that the cancer will return and the patient's defense mechanisms, like the immune system, will be so compromised that the patient will be consumed by the cancer.

In order to improve outcome in cancer treatment, it is essential that the patient and physician address the underlying causes of the cancer.

If you have been recently diagnosed with cancer

and are too tired to read much, then please do the following. You may also wish to order the audiotape synopsis of this book from the publisher. Send $20 to the Nutrition Times Press address in the front of the book.

⇒ **Bolster your spirits**. Millions before you have beaten cancer. So can you.

⇒ **Get educated**. Find out all of your options for cancer treatment. Unless you have an extremely aggressive form of cancer, you can take 2 weeks to get a second opinion and do some serious investigation before you leap into a therapy that may be irreversible or, worse yet, ineffective.

⇒ **Avoid any sweet foods**. Sugar feeds cancer. Don't eat any white sugar. Seriously curtail your intake of anything that tastes sweet, including fruit, or any foods with a high glycemic index, including carrot juice and rice cakes.

⇒ **Go for the color in vegetables**. Eat all the colorful and fresh vegetables that your bowels can tolerate. Leafy greens (like spinach and collards), beets, tomatoes, peppers, squash, carrots and broccoli are some examples.

⇒ **Get adequate protein**. While the average healthy adult can subsist on 30-50 grams of protein each day, the cancer patient needs more protein; maybe 80-120 grams per day, depending on patient size and potential for weight loss. The backbone of your immune system is built from dietary protein. Without adequate protein, your immune system becomes the Three Stooges trying to round up King Kong.

⇒ **Work with your health care professional** to change the underlying causes of your cancer. This can be an easy or complex process, but it usually requires professional guidance.

⇒ **Take some form of restrained cancer-killing therapy**. The most common traditional therapies are chemotherapy, radiation, and surgery. There are many other useful cancer therapies which are more selectively toxic to cancer, including Cell Specific Cancer Therapy, Ukrain, intravenous vitamin C and much more.

⇒ **Take ImmunoPower, a complex mixture of supplemental nutrients**. If you ignore the first 7 guidelines just mentioned, then ImmunoPower will be much less effective against your condition. Use all of these guidelines and you are bringing maximum force to reverse the cancer.

Chapter 1

CANCER AND ITS CAUSES
KNOW YOUR ENEMY

"Nature, to be commanded, must be obeyed." Francis Bacon

In the terrifying film, "The Predator", a chameleon-like beast from outer space descends upon the sweltering jungles of Central America to hunt humans, including Arnold Schwartzenager. If you sweated through this film, then you have an idea of how hard it is to kill cancer. The Predator wore a shield which allowed it to blend into the surrounding environment, making it almost invisible. Cancer mimics the chemistry of a fetus, and hence becomes invisible to the human immune system. Cancer also mutates by changing its DNA composition almost weekly, which is a major reason why many cancers develop a drug resistance that often limits the value of chemotherapy. Cancer also weakens its host by installing its own abnormal biochemistry, including:

-changes in the pH, or acid base balance, making the environment more favorable for cancer growth and less favorable for host recovery

-creation of anaerobic (oxygen deprived) pockets of tissue which resist radiation therapy like someone hunkered into a bomb shelter

-blunting the immune system, which is the primary means of fighting cancer

-elevating metabolism and calorie needs while simultaneously lowering appetite and food intake to slowly starve the host

-ejecting by-products that create weakness, apathy, pain and depression in the host

-siphoning nutrients out of the bloodstream like a parasite.

With its invisible, predatory and every-changing nature, cancer is truly a tough condition to treat. Cancer is essentially an abnormal cell growth. It is a piece of the cancer patient that was once normal, but somehow developed altered DNA blueprints and began growing wildly. Its unchecked growth tends to overwhelm other functions in the body until death comes from:

1) organ failure, i.e., the kidneys shut down

2) infection, i.e., pneumonia because the immune system has been blunted

3) malnutrition, because the parasitic cancer shifts the host's metabolism into high gear through inefficient use of fuel while also inducing a loss of appetite.

SUBDUE SYMPTOMS OR DEAL WITH THE UNDERLYING CAUSE OF DISEASE?

There is a basic flaw in our thinking about health care in this country. We treat symptoms, not the underlying cause of the disease. Yet, the only way to provide long-lasting relief in any degenerative disease, like cancer, arthritis and heart disease, is to reverse the basic cause of the disease. For example, let's say that you developed a headache because your neighbor's teenager is playing drums too loudly. You take an aspirin to subdue the headache, then your stomach starts churning. So you take some antacids to ease the stomach nausea, then your blood pressure goes up. And on it goes. We shift symptoms with medication, as if in a bizarre "shell game", when we really need to deal with the fundamental cause of the disease.

Let me give you another example. What if, the first thing I do every morning when I arrive at my office is to slam my thumb in the desk drawer. Boy that hurt, yet I keep doing the same masochistic act of slamming my thumb in the desk drawer every morning for a week. And by then, my thumb is swollen, painful, discolored and bleeding. So I go to Dr. A who recommends analgesics to better tolerate the pain. Dr. B suggests an injection of cortisone to reduce the swelling in my thumb. And Dr. C recommends surgery to cut off the finger because it looks defective. Of course, the real answer is to "stop slamming my thumb in the desk drawer."

What's that?? You say that my example has no relevance in American health care? Let's look at the millions of Americans with rheumatoid arthritis, such as Mrs. Smith whose condition is caused by eating too much sugar, plus an allergy to milk protein, and a deficiency of fish oil, vitamin C and zinc. Mrs. Smith goes to Dr. A who recommends analgesics to better tolerate the pain. Dr. B suggests cortisone to reduce the swelling. And Dr. C recommends hip replacement surgery to cut off the defective parts. The real answer is to change the underlying cause of the disease.

A more common example is heart disease. There are over 60,000 miles of blood vessels in the average adult body. When a person develops blockage in the arteries near the heart, open heart bypass surgery will probably be recommended. In this procedure, a short section of vein from the leg is used to replace the plugged up vessels near the heart. But what has been done to improve the other 59,999 miles left that are probably equally obstructed? A Harvard professor, Dr. E. Braunwald, investigated the records from thousands of bypass patients in the Veteran's Administration Hospitals and found no improvement in lifespan after this expensive and risky surgery.[1] Why? Because the underlying cause, which could be a complex array of diet, exercise, stress, and toxins, has not been resolved. Bypass surgery treats the symptoms of heart disease like chemo and radiation treat the symptoms of cancer. Each provide temporary relief, but no long term cure.

Meanwhile, Dr. Dean Ornish was working as a physician doing bypass surgery in the early 1970s and watching some patients come back for their second bypass operation. Ornish reasoned: "Obviously, this procedure is not a cure for heart disease." At the time, there was convincing data that a low fat diet, coupled with exercise and stress reduction could lower the incidence for getting heart disease. Ornish wondered if we took that same program and cranked it up a notch or two, making it more therapeutic, might it reverse heart disease? And it did. His program recently was found effective in a clinical study. While the American Cancer Society was violently opposed to Dr. Max Gerson's nutritional program to treat cancer patients in the 1950s, the ACS then released in the 1980s their dietary guidelines for the prevention of cancer, which--was very similar to the Gerson program. Note the chart comparing nutrient requirements to prevent versus to treat versus to maintain once in remission. The names of nutrients are the same, but the numbers change depending on what you are trying to achieve.

When you deal with the underlying causes of a degenerative disease, you are more likely to get long term favorable benefits. When you allow the fundamental causes to continue and merely treat the symptoms that surface, then the outlook for the patient is dismal. In dozens of diseases and millions of patients, this obvious law holds true.

The crucial missing link in most cancer therapy is stimulating the patient's own healing abilities. Because the best medical equipment cannot detect one billion cancer cells. Imagine leaving behind only one billion dandelion seeds on your lawn after you thought you got them all.

The "war on cancer" is an internal microscopic war that can only be won by working within the laws of nature: stimulating the patient's own abilities to fight cancer while changing the abnormal conditions that allow cancer to grow. All other therapies are doomed to disappointing results. Combined together, these treatments of restrained external medicine coupled with stimulating the cancer patient's internal healing abilities hold great promise for dramatically improving your chances of success against cancer.

WHAT CAUSES CANCER?

Most degenerative diseases, including cancer, do not have a readily identifiable enemy. In a bacterial infection, you can attack the "cause" of the disease with an antibiotic. Cancer seems to be caused by a collection of lifestyle and environmental factors that accumulate over the years. Since success against any degenerative disease requires getting to the root of the problem, let's examine the accepted causes of cancer.

-**Toxic overload.** Of the 5 million registered chemicals in the world, mankind comes in contact with 70,000, of which at least 20,000 are known carcinogens, or cancer-causing agents. Each year, America alone sprays 1.2 billion pounds of pesticides on our food crops, dumps 90 billion pounds of toxic waste in our 55,000 toxic waste sites, feeds 9 million pounds of antibiotics to our farm animals to help them gain weight faster and generally bombards the landscape with questionable amounts of electromagnetic radiation.

What Causes Cancer?

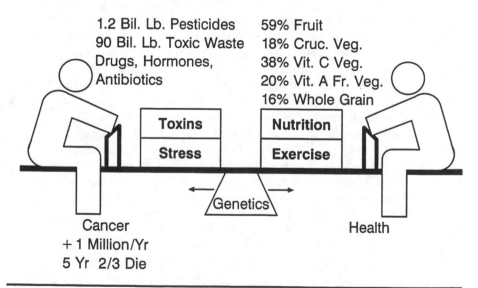

1.2 Bil. Lb. Pesticides
90 Bil. Lb. Toxic Waste
Drugs, Hormones,
Antibiotics

59% Fruit
18% Cruc. Veg.
38% Vit. C Veg.
20% Vit. A Fr. Veg.
16% Whole Grain

Toxins   **Nutrition**

Stress   **Exercise**

Genetics

Cancer
+ 1 Million/Yr
5 Yr 2/3 Die

Health

Bruce Ames, PhD of the University of California at Berkeley has estimated that each of the 60 trillion cells in your body undergoes from 1,000 to 10,000 DNA "hits" or potentially cancer-causing breaks every day. Yet somehow for most of us, our DNA repair mechanisms and immune system surveillance are able to keep this storm of genetic damage under control. Wallowing in our own high tech waste products is a major cause of cancer in modern society, since carcinogens add to the fury of the continuous assault on the DNA. Noted authority, Samuel Epstein, MD of the University of Illinois, says that a major thrust of cancer prevention must be detoxifying our earth. Toxins not only cause DNA breakage, which can trigger cancer, but also subdue the immune system, which then allows cancer to become the "fox in the chicken coop", with no controlling force.

Early research indicated that once cancer has been upregulated, or " the lion is out of the cage", then no amount of detoxification is going to matter. Newer evidence says otherwise. Cancer growth can both be slowed and even reversed under the right conditions. According to the National Cancer Institute, there are 7 million Americans alive today who have lived 5 or more years after their cancer diagnosis. Cancer is reversible. If toxins caused the problem, then detoxification is the solution. For more on detoxification, see the chapter on changing the underlying causes of cancer.

-**Distress**. It was the Canadian physician and researcher, Hans Selye, MD, who coined the term "the stress of life" as he could document the physiological changes that took place in lab animals when exposed to noise, bright lights, confinement and electric shocks. The thymus gland is a pivotal organ in immune system protection against infections and cancer. Dr. Selye noted that stress would induce thymus gland shrinkage, increases in fats in the blood (for the beginnings of heart disease) and erosion of the stomach lining (ulcers).

Since the 1920s, scientific evidence has been advancing the theory that emotional stress can depress the immune system and make that individual more vulnerable to infections and cancer. It was Norman Cousins' book, ANATOMY OF AN ILLNESS, which thrust this mind-body principle in front of the public. After 10 years of lecturing and researching at the University of California at Los Angeles, Cousins' theories held valid under scientific scrutiny.

Carl Simonton, MD, a radiation oncologist, found that his mental imagery techniques seemed to produce better results with fewer side effects for his cancer patients. Bernie Siegel, MD a Yale surgeon, found that certain mental characteristics helped his cancer patients to recover. Candace Pert, PhD a celebrated researcher at the National Institutes of Health, discovered endorphins in human brains and led the charge toward unravelling the chemical mysteries of the mind. Dr. Pert says that the mind is a pharmacy and is continuously producing potent substances that either improve or worsen health. Since the mind can create cancer, it should seem a logical leap that the mind can help to prevent and even subdue cancer. Noted physician and researcher at the University of California San Francisco, Kenneth Pelletier, MD, PhD, wrote his ground breaking book, MIND AS HEALER, MIND AS SLAYER, to show that certain personalities are more prone to certain diseases. Many alternative therapists use a wide variety of psychological approaches to help rid the body of cancer.

Clearly, there is some mental link in the development of cancer for many patients.[2] I have worked with many cancer patients whose major hurdle was spiritual healing. While dietary changes are difficult for many people, it is far easier to change the diet or take some nutrient pills than change the way we think. Pulling emotional splinters are an essential and painful experience. Not only is there a metaphysical link to cancer, but the site of the cancer may provide clues regarding how to fix the problem. Many breast cancer patients have experienced a recent divorce, which results in the loss of a feminine organ. One patient of mine suffered from cancer of the larynx, which began one year after his wife left him with the thought "there's nothing you can say that will make me stay." If spiritual wounds started the cancer, then spiritual healing is an essential element for a cure.

-Nutrition. The human body is built from, repaired by and fueled by substances found in the diet. In the most literal sense, "we are what we eat...and think, and breathe, and do." Nutrition therapy merely tries to re-establish "metabolic balance" in the cancer patients. Medical doctors Gerson, Moerman and Livingston have each provided their own nutrition programs to treat cancer. Other schools of thought include macrobiotics, vegetarianism, acid/alkaline balancing, fasting, fruit and vegetable juicing and others. I will assess all of these therapies in more detail later. After decades of living outside the accepted realm of cancer therapies, nutrition therapy has found a new level of scientific acceptance with the 1990 report from the Office of Technology Assessment, an advisory branch of Congress, whose expert scientific panel wrote in UNCONVENTIONAL CANCER TREATMENTS:

"It is our collective professional judgment that nutritional interventions are going to follow psychosocial interventions up the ladder into clinical respectability as adjunctive and complementary approaches to the treatment of cancer."[3]

-Exercise. While 40% of Americans will eventually develop cancer, only 14% of active Americans will get cancer. A half hour of exercise every other day cuts the risk for breast cancer by 75%. Exercise imparts many benefits, including oxygenation of the tissues to thwart the anaerobic needs of cancer cells. Exercise also helps to stabilize blood glucose levels, which can restrict the amount of fuel available for cancer

cells to grow. Exercise improves immune function, lymph flow and detoxification systems. Exercise helps us better tolerate stressful situations. For cancer patients who can participate, exercise improves tolerance to chemotherapy. Some therapists use hydrogen peroxide or ozone to oxygenate the tissue. Humans evolved as active creatures. Inactivity is an abnormal under-oxygenated metabolic state--so is cancer.

PATIENT PROFILE:
BEAT UNTREATABLE LUNG CANCER

P.S. is a 50 year old female diagnosed in April of 1992 with adenocarcinoma of the lungs. Surgery (lobectomy) & radiation eliminated the measurable tumor mass. Recurrence of the lung cancer in August of 1995 was considered inoperable, metastatic and untreatable. The patient was told "there is nothing more that we can do for you". She was given the anticipated life expectancy of 2 months. She began nutrition therapy as sole therapy in January of 1996. As of January, 1998, she has had no growth of tumors and no progression of disease. She works 40 hours/week, walks 3 miles per night & feels great. Remember, if cancer is not growing, then it is most likely being destroyed and calcified by the body.

ENDNOTES

[1]. Braunwald, E., New England Journal Medicine, vol.309, p.1181, Nov.10, 1983
[2]. Newell, GR, Primary Care in Cancer, p.29, May 1991
[3]. Office of Technology Assessment, UNCONVENTIONAL CANCER TREATMENTS, p.14, IBID

Chapter 2

PROGRESS REPORT IN THE WAR ON CANCER

What do you think of the war on cancer?
"...largely a fraud." Linus Pauling, PhD, twice Nobel laureate
"...a qualified failure." John Bailar, MD, PhD, former editor of
the Journal of the National Cancer Institute
"A medical Vietnam." Donald Kennedy, former President of
Stanford University
"A bunch of sh_t." James Watson, PhD, Nobel laureate, co-
discoverer of the DNA code

C ancer is not a new phenomenon. Archeologists have discovered tumors on dinosaur skeletons and Egyptian mummies. From 1600 B.C. on, historians find records of attempts to treat cancer. In the naturalist Disney film, "Never Cry Wolf", the biologist sent to the Arctic to observe the behavior of wolves found that the wolves would kill off the easiest prey, which were sometimes animals suffering from leukemia. Cancer is an abnormal and rapidly growing tissue which, if unchecked, will eventually smother the body's normal processes. Cancer may have been with us from the beginning of time, but the fervor with which it attacks modern civilization is unprecedented.

President Richard Nixon declared "war on cancer" on December 23, 1971. Nixon confidently proclaimed that we would have a cure for cancer within 5 years, by the 1976 Bicentennial. However, by 1991 a group of 60 noted physicians and scientists gathered a press conference to tell the public "The cancer establishment confuses the public with repeated claims that we are winning the war on cancer... Our ability to treat and cure most cancers has not materially improved."[1] The unsettling bad news is irrefutable:

⇒ newly diagnosed cancer incidence continues to escalate, from 1.1 million Americans in 1991 to an anticipated 1.3 million in 1993

⇒ deaths from cancer in 1992 were 547,000, up from 514,000 in 1991

⇒ since 1950, the overall cancer incidence has increased by 44%, with breast cancer and male colon cancer up by 60% and prostate cancer by 100%

⇒ for decades, the 5 year survival has remained constant for non-localized breast cancer at 18% and lung cancer at 13%

⇒ only 5% of the $1.8-2.4 billion annual budget for the National Cancer Institute is spent on prevention

⇒ grouped together, the average cancer patient has a 50/50 chance of living another five years; which are the same odds he or she had in 1971

⇒ claims for cancer drugs are generally based on tumor response rather than prolongation of life. Many tumors will initially shrink when chemo and radiation are applied, yet tumors often develop drug-resistance and are then unaffected by therapy.

⇒ by the turn of the century, cancer is expected to eclipse heart disease as the number one cause of death in America. It is already the number one fear.

LOSING THE WAR ON CANCER
BETWEEN 1975 AND 1989, U.S. CANCER

INCIDENCE UP 13%

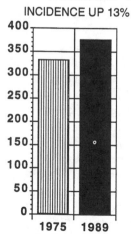

1975   1989

incidence increased
from 332 to 376 per 100,000

DEATH RATE UP 7%

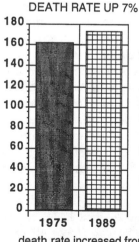

1975   1989

death rate increased from
162 to 173 per 100,000

5 YEAR SURVIVAL RATE
ALMOST UNCHANGED

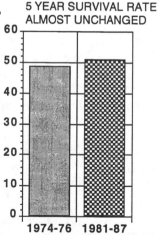

1974-76   1981-87

percent surviving cancer
(all types) for 5 years
increased from 49 to 51

HAVE WE MADE ANY PROGRESS?

Depending on which expert you subscribe to, the war on cancer has been either "a qualified failure" or "is progressing slowly". No one is willing to spread the propaganda that it has been a victory. According to the National Cancer Institute (NCI), five year survival rates (definition of a cure) have increased from 20% of cancer patients in 1930 to 53% of adults and 70% of children today.[2] Critics of the NCI claim that living 5 years after diagnosis has nothing to do with being cured, and that earlier diagnosis alone could account for the improvement in survival.

There are 7 million Americans living today who have been cured of cancer. Twenty years ago, surgery for breast cancer routinely removed the entire breast, lymph nodes and chest muscles in a procedure called radical mastectomy. New methods favor a "lumpectomy" or removal of merely the lump, followed by radiation and/or chemotherapy. In other words, surgeons are becoming more rational and restrained in their efforts to surgically remove the cancer.

Richard Adamson, PhD, Chief of Cancer Etiology at the National Cancer Institute, says that progress has been made against cancer as death rates from colon and rectal cancer have fallen 15-20% in the last 20 years; and other death rates have dropped, including 20% for ovarian, 30% for bladder and 40% for cervical cancer.

TIME FOR EXAMINING OPTIONS

The purpose of this section is not to blast the National Cancer Institute, but rather to make it blatantly obvious that our current cancer treatment methods are inadequate and incomplete and that we need to examine some options--like nutrition. A growing body of dissidents cite data to refute the NCI's confident numbers. Among the skeptics is John Bailar, MD, PhD of Harvard University, whose outspoken article in the prestigious New England Journal of Medicine ushered in a champion for the many strident critics of the National Cancer Institute[3]. Bailar, as a member of the National Academy of Sciences and former editor of the Journal of the National Cancer Institute, cannot be ignored. Dr. Bailar confronts the NCI's unfounded enthusiasm with "We are losing the war against cancer" and has shown that the death rate, age-adjusted death rate and both crude and age-adjusted incidence rate of cancer continues to climb in spite of efforts by the NCI. Non-whites are excluded from the NCI statistics for vague reasons. Blacks, urban poor, and the 11 million workers exposed to toxic substances have all experienced a dramatic increase in cancer incidence and mortality. Less than 10% of patients with cancer of the pancreas, liver, stomach and esophagus will be alive in five years.[4] Bailar wrote a followup article "Cancer Undefeated" published in the May, 1997 edition of the New England Journal of Medicine with similar news. The exception and thin shaft of sunlight in this article indicated a 1% decline in age-adjusted mortality from all cancers from 1991 to 1994. Bailar felt that this almost insignificant improvement may have been due to earlier detection of cancer, not better treatment techniques.

As a percentage of total annual deaths in America, cancer has escalated from 3% in 1900 to 22% of today's deaths. Many experts have been quick to explain away this frightening trend by claiming that our aging population is responsible for the increase in cancer incidence--older people are more likely to get cancer. But aging does not entirely explain our epidemic proportions of cancer in America.

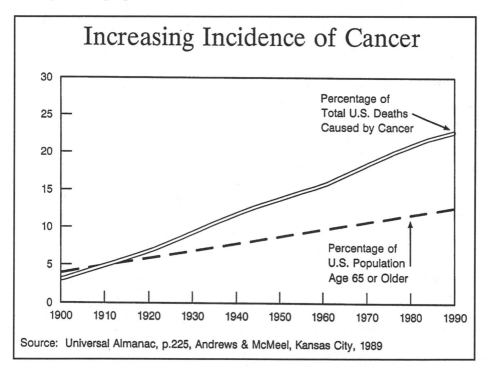

Increasing Incidence of Cancer

Percentage of Total U.S. Deaths Caused by Cancer

Percentage of U.S. Population Age 65 or Older

Source: Universal Almanac, p.225, Andrews & McMeel, Kansas City, 1989

Perhaps the most tragic "pawns" in this game are the children. The NCI admits to a 28% rise in the incidence of childhood cancers from 1950 through 1987, much of which is due to the ubiquitous presence of environmental pollutants.[5] On the other side of the coin, progress in pediatric oncology has produced cure rates in some forms of childhood cancer of up to 90%, which makes chemotherapy for childhood cancers an NCI victory, of sorts. However, while these patients do survive longer, they have a much higher risk for developing bone cancer later in life as a result of the chemo and/or radiation therapy.[6]

Not that money should be a top priority when health and life are at stake, but our health costs are out of control. We spend about $1.2

trillion per year or 14% of our Gross National Product on health care, compared to Sweden at 8%, a socialistic country with free health care for all, and our former American level of 3% in the year 1900. Even after adjusting for inflation, we spend twice as much money on health care for the elderly as we did prior to the inauguration of Medicare.[7] Cancer care is the most expensive of all diseases, costing Americans about $110 billion annually.

Albert Braverman, MD, a full professor of oncology at the State University of New York, has published in the prominent medical journal, Lancet, a biting review of chemotherapy as sole therapy against cancer: "Many medical oncologists recommend chemotherapy for virtually any tumor, with a hopefulness undiscouraged by almost invariable failure."[8] And if Bailar started all this rancor, then Ulrich Abel, PhD of the Heidelberg Tumor Center in Germany has brought the issue to a fever pitch. Abel, a well-respected biostatistics expert, published a controversial 92 page review of the world's literature on survival of chemotherapy-treated cancer patients; showing that chemotherapy alone can help only about 3% of the patients with epithelial cancer (such as breast, lung, colon and prostate) which kills 80% of total cancer patients. "...a sober and unprejudiced analysis of the literature has rarely revealed any therapeutic success by the regimens in question."[9]

A prominent scientist from the University of Wisconsin, Johan Bjorksten, PhD, has shown that chemotherapy alone destroys the immune system beyond a point of return, which increases the risk for early death from infections and other cancers in these immunologically-naked people.[10] Ralph Moss, PhD, former assistant director of public affairs at Sloan Kettering cancer hospital in New York, has written a thoroughly documented analysis of the history of chemotherapy showing its troublesome beginning as mustard gas for warfare and current questionable status as the prevailing treatment for the majority of cancer patients.[11] Critics of American cancer treatment point out that the therapy may sometimes be worse than the condition. Researchers reported in the New England Journal of Medicine that the risk of developing leukemia from chemotherapy treatment of ovarian cancer outweighs the benefits of the therapy.[12]

Breast and prostate cancer have recently surfaced in the press as "forgotten cancers" due to their intimate nature. While one out of 20 women in 1950 were hit with breast cancer, today that number is one in nine. Even with early detection and proper treatment, a "cured" breast cancer patient will lose an average of 19 years of lifespan. Breast cancer kills about 45,000 women each year.[13] Lack of faith in cancer treatment has led a few physicians to recommend that some women with a high incidence of breast or ovarian cancer in their family undergo "preventive surgery" to remove these high risk body parts.[14] Life and health insurance companies now refer to healthy intact women as "with organs" and at high risk, therefore forced to pay higher health insurance premiums.

And while breast cancer is tragic, prostate cancer is equally prevalent in men and even more lethal. The NCI spends one fourth the amount on prostate cancer research as on breast cancer research. There are no good early screening procedures for prostate cancer, which means that in 85% of the prostate cancers found, the cancer has spread beyond the prostate gland and is difficult to treat. Comparing the outcome of 223 patients with untreated prostate cancer to 58 patients who underwent radical prostatectomy, the 10 year disease-specific survival was 86.8% and 87.9% respectively. There was essentially no difference in survival between the treated and untreated groups.[15]

While tamoxifen is an estrogen binder that can be of benefit in short term use for breast cancer patients and it has been touted as a chemo-preventive agent for millions of high risk breast cancer patients, other data shows that long term tamoxifen use elevates the risk for heart attack [16] eye[17] and liver damage[18] and INCREASES the risk of endometrial cancer. [19]

According to an extensive review of the literature, there has been no improvement in cancer mortality from 1952 through 1985.[20] These authors state: "Evidence has steadily accrued that [cancer therapy] is essentially a failure." There are no good screening tests for colon cancer. Meanwhile, we spend millions researching molecular biology in a futile quest for a "magic bullet" against cancer.[21] A London physician and researcher has provided statistical backing for his contention that breast cancer screenings in women under age 50 provides no benefit in 99.85% of the premenopausal women tested.[22] The average cancer patient still has only a 40-50% chance of surviving the next five years, same odds as 30 years ago. A gathering chorus of scientists and clinicians proclaim that success from chemo and radiation therapy has plateaued and we need to examine alternative therapies.[23]

A 1971 textbook jointly published by the American Cancer Society and the University of Rochester stated that biopsy of cancer tissue may lead to the spread of cancer.[24] Although encapsulated cancer can be effectively treated with surgery and 22% of all cancer can be "cured" through surgery[25], 30% or more of surgery patients with favorable prognosis still have cancer recurrences.[26] A study of 440,000 cancer patients who received chemotherapy or radiation showed that those treated with radiation had a significantly increased risk for a type of leukemia involving cells other than the lymphocytes.[27] Long term effects of radiation include: birth defects and infertility. Short term effects include: mouth sores and ulcers which can interfere with the ability to eat, rectal ulcers, fistulas, bladder ulcers, diarrhea and colitis.

HEALTH IS THE SUM TOTAL OF "VECTORS"
(or forces) FROM LIFESTYLE

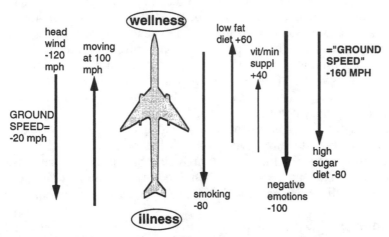

In a survey of 79 Canadian oncologists, all of them would encourage patients with non-small cell lung cancer to participate in a chemotherapy protocol, yet 58% said that they themselves would not participate in such a therapy and 81% said they would not take cisplatin (a chemo drug) under any circumstances.[28]

Analysis of over 100 clinical trials using chemotherapy as sole treatment in breast cancer patients found no benefits and significant damage from the chemotherapy in post-menopausal patients.[29] Dr. Rose Kushner pointed out that toxic drugs are "literally making healthy people sick" and are "only of marginal benefit to the vast majority of women who develop breast cancer."[30] Some evidence indicates that chemotherapy actually shortens the life of breast cancer patients.[31]

According to a psychologist writing in the American Cancer Society Journal, "the side effects of cancer chemotherapy can cause more anxiety and distress than the disease itself."[32] A well-recognized side effect of chemotherapy is suppression of bone marrow, which produces the white blood cells that fight infection. This common immune suppression leads to the all-too-common death from infection.[33]

According to the literature which comes with each chemotherapeutic agent, methotrexate may be "hepatotoxic" (damaging to the liver) and suppresses immune function. Adriamycin can cause "serious irreversible myocardial toxicity (damage to heart) with delayed congestive heart failure often unresponsive to any cardiac supportive therapy." Cytoxan can cause "secondary malignancies" (cancer from its use). It is widely known among health care professionals that just working around chemotherapy agents can cause birth defects.[34]

In spite of $39 billion in research at the NCI and billions more spent in private industry, there have been no new chemotherapy drugs discovered in the past 20 years.[35] Not even NCI official, Dr. Daniel Ihde, can conjur up any enthusiasm for the failure of chemotherapy drugs against lung cancer.[36] Given the limited successes in traditional cancer treatment, it is not surprising that 50% of all American cancer patients seek "alternative therapies".

Biological therapies, such as interferon and interleukin, are extremely toxic, with treatment requiring weeks of hospitalization, usually in intensive therapy, with multiple transfusions, severe bleeding, shock, and confusion as common side effects.[37] Interferon causes rapid onset of fever, chills, and severe muscle contractions that may require morphine. [38]

WHERE DID WE GO WRONG?

There is a lot of finger pointing since the war on cancer has been so heavily criticized. For starters, it would be easy to blame bread mold, from which springs penicillin, which was discovered by Alexander Fleming in 1928 and gave us hope that there was a "magic bullet" against every disease. We could rest equal blame on Jonas Salk, inventor of the polio vaccine in 1952, for such a tremendous show from his medicine bag. With a simple vaccine, one of the most tragic pandemic plagues of history was felled. Again, more reasons to believe that a "magic bullet" against every disease must exist.

Another scapegoat is good old patriotic pride. After all, it was the Americans who rode in to World Wars I and II to rescue the world. Americans stepped in to finish the Panama Canal after the French had failed. Americans threw enough money at the Manhattan Project to develop a war-ending nuclear bomb and again bought our way to the moon in a massive and expensive effort from NASA scientists. Americans have more patents and Nobel laureates than any other nation on earth. We had good reasons to be confident of buying a cure for cancer.

Some of our problems lie in scientific research models. Using animals with induced leukemia, a non-localized disease of the blood-forming organs, is not a realistic representation of how well a cancer drug will work against a solid human tumor. We have also made the erroneous assumption that "no detectable cancer" means no cancer. A million cancer cells are undetectable by even the most sensitive medical equipment. A billion cancer cells become a tiny and nearly undetectable "lump".[39] When the surgeon says,"We think we got it all."--that is when the war on cancer must become an invisible battle involving the patient's well-nourished immune system.

We also have wrongly guessed that "response rate", or shrinkage of the tumor, is synonymous with cure. As mentioned, chemotherapy works on cancer cells like pesticides work on insects. Spraying pesticides on a field of plants may kill 99% of the bugs in the field, but the few insects that survive this baptism of poison have a unique genetic advantage to resist the toxicity of the pesticide. These "super bugs" then reproduce even more rapidly without competition, since the pesticides killed off biological predators in the field and reduced the fertility of the soil for an overall drop in plant health. Similarly, blasting a typically malnourished cancer patient with bolus (high dose once per week) injections of chemotherapy alone may elicit an initial shrinkage of the tumor, but the few tumor cells that survive this poison become resistant to therapy and may even accelerate the course of the disease in the now immune-suppressed patient. Meanwhile, the once marginally malnourished patient becomes clinically malnourished since nausea becomes a prominent symptom in bolus chemo usage. An expert in cancer at Duke University, Dr. John Grant, has estimated that 40% or more of cancer patients actually die from malnutrition.[40]

We also made the mistake of becoming enamored with a few tools that we thought could eradicate cancer. We focused all of our energies in these three areas and ridiculed or even outlawed any new ideas. Because the real reason for our failure lies in our error in thinking. The wellness and illness of our bodies is almost entirely dependent on what we eat, think, drink, move, and breathe. These forces shape our general metabolism, which is the sum total of bodily processes. Our metabolism then either favors or discourages the growth of both infectious and degenerative diseases. Cancer is a degenerative disease of abnormal metabolism throughout the body--not just a regionalized lump or bump.

Our health is composed of a delicate interplay of nutrients consumed, and toxins expelled, coupled with mental and spiritual forces that influence metabolism. We are a product of our genes, lifestyle and environment. We are not dumb automobiles to be taken to the mechanic and fixed. We are physical and metaphysical beings who must become part of the cure, just as surely as we are a part of the disease process. Healing is a joint effort between patient, clinician, and that mysterious and wonderful Force which most of us take for granted. The days of "magic bullet" cures are over. The days of cooperative efforts between patient and clinician are here to stay.

ONLY TEAMWORK WILL BEAT CANCER

Shortly after the turn of the millenia, cancer will become the number one cause of death in Western society[41]. Cancer is a cruel disease that infiltrates the body with abnormal tissue growth and finally strangles its victims with malnutrition, infections or multiple organ failure. We need teamwork in cancer treatment because of the formidable "Predator" that we face. We cannot discard any cancer therapy, no matter how strange or perpendicular to medical theories, unless that therapy does not work. There are no "magic bullets" against cancer, nor can we anticipate such a development within our lifetime. We need to join the forces of traditional oncology along with non-toxic means of selectively killing cancer cells coupled with the naturopathic fields of bolstering "host defense mechanisms" in the cancer patient through nutrition, psychology, detoxification, exercise physiology, botanical extracts and others to develop a more complete arsenal against cancer.

Chemotherapy has its role, especially for certain types of cancer and when administered in fractionated dose or via intra-arterial infusion to a therapeutically nourished patient. Radiation therapy has its place, especially as the highly targeted brachytherapy. Surgery has its place, especially when the tumor has been encapsulated and can be removed

without bursting the collagen envelope. Hyperthermia can be extremely valuable in about 4% of all cancer cases. Combinations of these traditional therapies are becoming better accepted in medical circles. Later in this book, you will see the synergism in creative combinations of conventional and unconventional cancer therapies, like quercetin (a bioflavonid) and heat therapy or niacin with radiation therapy. The take home lesson here is: "Just because traditional medicine has failed to develop an unconditional cure for cancer, doesn't mean that we should categorically reject all traditional approaches."

Our reigning allopathic medical system has maintained a philosophy that most diseases have a readily identifiable enemy that can be surgically removed or blasted into submission with chemo and radiation. Comprehensive cancer treatment uses traditional cancer therapies to reduce the tumor burden, while concurrently building up the "terrain" of the cancer patient to fight the cancer on a microscopic level. That is the "one-two punch" that will eventually bring the Predator of cancer to its knees. Given the dismal results of using cytotoxic therapies to cure cancer, we need to heed the words of Rudyard Kipling:

"Insanity is doing the same thing over and over and expecting a different   result."

PATIENT PROFILE: NO RECURRENCE OF SARCOMA

G.B. is a 48 year old male with multiple recurrent sarcoma in his abdomen. Each year for 5 years in a row, he was forced to have a surgical excision of a "football size" tumor from his abdominal region. He began nutrition therapy as sole therapy in October of 1996 following surgery. He has had no recurrence of a tumor as of June 1997.

ENDNOTES

[1]. Ingram, B., Medical Tribune, vol.33, no.4, p.1, Feb.1992
[2]. Mayo Clinic Health Letter, vol.10, no.2, , p.1, Feb.1992
[3]. Bailar, JC, New England Journal of Medicine, vol.314, p.1226, May 1986
[4]. Squires, S, Washington Post, p.Z19, Dec.3, 1991
[5]. Epstein, SS, and Moss, RW, The Cancer Chronicles, p.5, Autumn 1991
[6]. Weiss, R., Science News, p.165, Sept.12, 1987
[7]. Stout, H, Wall Street Journal, p.B5, Feb.26, 1992
[8]. Braverman, AS, Lancet, vol.337, p.901, Apr.13, 1991
[9]. Abel, U., CHEMOTHERAPY OF ADVANCED EPITHELIAL CANCER: A Critical Survey, Hippokrates Verlag Stuttgart, 1990
[10]. Bjorksten, J, LONGEVITY, p.22, JAB Publ., Charleston, SC, 1987
[11]. Moss, RW, QUESTIONING CHEMOTHERAPY, Equinox Press, NYC, 1995
[12]. Kaldor, JM, et al., New England Journal of Medicine, vol.322, no.1, p.1, Jan.1990
[13]. Neuman, E, New York Times, Insight, p.7, Feb.9, 1992
[14]. Bartimus, T., Tulsa World, p.B3, Dec.22, 1991
[15]. Johansson, JE, et al., Journal American Medical Association, vol.267, p.2191, Apr.22, 1992
[16]. Nakagawa, T., et al., Angiology, vol.45, p.333, May 1994
[17]. Pavlidis, NA, et al., Cancer, vol.69, p.2961, 1992
[18]. Catherino, WH, et al., Drug Safety, vol.8, p.381, 1993
[19]. Seoud, MAF, et al., Obstetrics & Gynecology, vol.82, p.165, Aug.1993
[20]. Temple, NJ, et al., Journal Royal Society Medicine, vol.84, p.95, 1991
[21]. Temple, NJ, et al., Journal Royal Society of Medicine, vol.84, p.95, Feb.1991
[22]. Shaffer, M., Medical Tribune, p.4, Mar.26, 1992
[23]. Hollander, S., et al., Journal of Medicine, vol.21, p.143, 1990
[24]. Rubin, P., (ed), CLINICAL ONCOLOGY FOR MEDICAL STUDENTS AND PHYSICIANS: A MULTI-DISCIPLINARY APPROACH, 3rd edition, Univ. Rochester, 1971
[25]. American Cancer Society, "Modern cancer treatment" in CANCER BOOK, Doubleday, NY, 1986
[26]. National Cancer Institute, Update: Primary treatment is not enough for early stage breast cancer, Office of Cancer Communications, May 18, 1988
[27]. Curtis, RE, et al., Journal National Cancer Institute, p.72, Mar.1984
[28]. Ginsberg, RJ, et al., Cancer of the lung, in: DeVita, CANCER PRINCIPLES AND PRACTICES OF ONCOLOGY, Lippincott, Philadelphia, p.673, 1993
[29]. New England Journal Medicine, Feb.18, 1988; see also Boffey, PM, New York Times, Sept.13, 1985
[30]. Kushner, R., CA-Cancer Journal for Clinicians, p.34, Nov.1984
[31]. Powles, TJ, et al., Lancet, p.580, Mar.15, 1980
[32]. Redd, WH, CA-Cancer Journal for Clinicians, p.138, May1988
[33]. Whitley, RJ, et al., Pediatric Annals, vol.12, p.6, June 1983; see also Cancer Book, ibid.
[34]. Jones, RB, et al., California Journal of American Cancer Society, vol.33, no.5, p.262, 1983
[35]. Hollander, S., and Gordon, M., Journal of Medicine, vol.21, no.3, p.143, 1990
[36]. Ihde, DC, Annals of Internal Medicine, vol.115, no.9, p.737, Nov.1991
[37]. Moertel, CG, Journal American Medical Association, vol.256, p.3141, Dec.12, 1986
[38]. Hood, LE, American Journal Nursing, p.459, Apr.1987
[39]. Dollinger, M., et al., EVERYONE'S GUIDE TO CANCER THERAPY, p.2, Somerville House, Kansas City, 1990
[40]. Grant, JP, Nutrition, vol.6, no.4, p.6S, July 1990 supl
[41]. Meyskens, FL, New England Journal of Medicine, vol.23, no.12, p.825, Sept. 1990

Chapter 3

TREATMENTS CURRENTLY USED FOR CANCER

"If everyone is thinking alike, then no one is thinking."
Benjamin Franklin

In order to know where we are going in cancer treatment, it is important to know where we have been and how we got where we are. This chapter looks at both conventional and alternative cancer treatment methods to give you a better understanding of our "roots" in cancer treatment options. For a more thorough discussion of conventional therapies, read:
CANCER THERAPY by Mallin Dollinger, MD
PRACTICAL ONCOLOGY by Robert Cameron, MD
        For alternative therapies, read:
CANCER THERAPY by Ralph Moss, PhD
ALTERNATIVE CANCER THERAPIES by Ron Falcone
ALTERNATIVES IN CANCER THERAPY by Ross Pelton, R Ph, PhD
CANCER AND NATURAL MEDICINE by John Boik
THIRD OPINION by John Fink
THE ALTERNATIVE CANCER THERAPY BOOK by Richard Walters.

CONVENTIONAL THERAPIES
        Chemotherapy is a spin-off product from the chemical warfare of World Wars I and II and is now given to 75% of all American cancer patients. Yale University pharmacologists who were working on a government project during World War II to develop an antidote for mustard gas noted that bone marrow and lymphoid tissue were heavily damaged by these poisons. That observation led to experiments in which mustard gas was injected into mice with lymphomas (cancer of the lymph glands) and produced remission. In 1943, researchers found that mustard gas had a similar effect on human Hodgkins disease.[1] Chemo has also

become a useful agent against testicular cancer, which is now 92% curable. Most proponents of chemo now recognize the limitations of using chemo as sole therapy against many types of cancer.

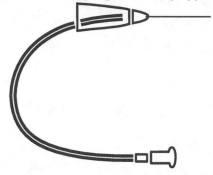

Shortly after these initial exciting discoveries, progress on chemo cures quickly plateaued and forced the innovative thinkers into creative combinations of various chemo drugs, which is now the accepted practice. In the 1980s, oncologists began using chemo by "fractionated drip infusion" in the hospital rather than one large (bolus) injection in the doctor's office. The fractionated method was not only more effective against the cancer but also less toxic on the patient. Think of the difference in toxicity between taking 2 glasses of wine with dinner each night, or guzzling all 14 glasses at one time at the end of the week. Also, fractionated drip infusion is more likely to catch the cancer cells in their growth phase, while bolus injections are a random guess to coincide with the growth phase of cancer. In the next evolutionary step, borrowing from technology developed for heart disease, oncologists began using catheters (thin tubes) that could be inserted into an artery (called intra-arterial infusion) to deliver chemo at the site of the tumor, once again improving response and reducing overall toxicity.

Radiation therapy is given to about 60% of all cancer patients. In 1896, a French physicist, Marie Curie discovered radium, a radioactive metal. For her brilliance, Madam Curie was eventually awarded two Nobel prizes and was considered one of the founders of radiation therapy and the nuclear age. For her unprotected use of radioactive materials, she eventually died while still young of leukemia. Cancer patients were soon being treated with a new technique developed by the German physicist, Wilhelm Roentgen, called radiation therapy. This technique relies on regional destruction of unwanted tissue through ionizing radiation that disrupts the DNA of all bombarded cells. Radiation therapy can be externally or internally originated, high or low dose and delivered with uncanny computer-assisted precision to the site of the tumor. Brachytherapy, or interstitial radiation therapy, places the source of radiation directly into the tumor, as an implanted seed. New techniques use radiation in combination with heat therapy (hyperthermia).

Surgery is the first treatment of choice for about 67% of cancer patients. By 1600 B.C., Egyptian physicians were excising tumors using knives or red-hot irons.[2] By physically removing the obvious tumor, physicians feel that they have the best chance for overall success. Unfortunately, many tumors are so entwined with delicate body organs, such as brain and liver, that the tumor cannot be resected (cut out). Another concern is that partial removal of a cancer mass may open the once-encapsulated tumor to spread, like opening a sack of dandelion seeds on your lawn.

Biological therapies, as with most other discoveries, were the product of accidents being observed by a bright mind. William B. Coley, MD, a New York cancer surgeon scoured the hospital records around 1880 looking for some clue why only a minorty of patients survived cancer surgery. He found that a high percentage of survivors had developed an infection shortly after the surgery to remove the cancer. This observation led Dr. Coley to inject a wide variety of bacteria, known as Coley's cocktail, into his cancer patients, who then underwent the feverish recovery phase, with noteworthy cancer cures produced. Infections were found to induce the immune system into a higher state of activity, which then helped to destroy tumors. From this crude beginning, molecular biologists have found brilliant ways of producing injectable amounts of the immune factors that can theoretically fight cancer.

Biological therapies attempt to fine tune and focus the immune system into a more vigorous attack on the cancer. Lymphokines are basically "bullets" produced by the immune system to kill invading cells, such as cancer. Lymphokine activated killer cells (LAK) are incubated in the laboratory in the presence of a stimulator (interleukin-2) and then injected back into the cancer patient's body for an improved immune response.[3] In some lab tests, LAK cells swarm on the tumor like ants on honey.

Interferon, interleukin, monoclonal antibodies and tumor necrosis factor are among the leading contenders as biological therapies against cancer. The downside of biological therapies is that most forms have extremely toxic side effects, and none can be legally used even in approved experiments unless that patient has been considered untreatable by the other three conventional means. The National Cancer Institute is beginning to place more emphasis on researching biological therapies.

Heat Therapy (hyperthermia). Cancer cells seem to be more vulnerable to heat than normal healthy cells. Since the time of Hippocrates and the Egyptian Pharoahs, heat therapy has been valued. Experts have shown that applying heat to the patient elevates immune responses. Temperatures of 42 degrees Celsius or 107 degrees Fahrenheit will kill most cancer cells, but can be quite stressful on the patient also.

Could it be that exercise induces regular "hyperthermia" to kill off cancer cells before they can become a problem?

Whole body hyperthermia involves a very sophisticated hot tub device, general anesthesia and medical supervision. Regional hyperthermia can involve either a miniature waterbed-like device applied to the tumor or focused microwaves. Major cancer research centers, including Stanford and Duke, have found this therapy useful by itself, or used synergistically to improve the response to chemo and radiation therapy.

ALTERNATIVE THERAPIES

If you need emergency medical care, reconstructive surgery, orthopedic surgery or critical life support, then an American hospital is where you will get the world's best care. That's why alternative emergency care does not exist, because our current system is working just find, thank you very much. Unfortunately, not all areas of American medicine have such an impressive track record of success. Many patients with cancer, Chronic Fatigue Syndrome, arthritis, AIDS, multiple sclerosis, Alzheimer's, mental illness and muscular dystrophy find little help from traditional medicine. When the accepted approach does not work, the grounds are fertile for "alternative" approaches to develop.

Among the many advantages of living in America, we are blessed with abundant individual liberties as guaranteed by the Constitution and Bill of Rights. And we fight viciously to preserve these rights. The controversy of alternative cancer treatment basically centers around the question "Which is more important: the patient's right to chose whatever health care they want, or the responsibility of the government to protect the unwary consumer from fraudulent practices?" This question is heated, polarized and regularly doused with the emotional testimonies of someone who was cured through alternative therapy after conventional therapy told he or she to "go home and get your affairs in order."

Studies now show that up to 50% of all cancer patients use some form of unconventional cancer therapy, with most of these people being of above-average income and education.[4] A study reported in the New England Journal of Medicine from David Eisenberg, MD of Harvard Medical School shows that Americans make more visits to alternative therapists than to family physicians. Since the patient usually pays for alternative therapists while insurance pays for most expenses in a family physician visit, these numbers are quite astonishing. People don't keep going back and paying out of pocket expenses unless they are getting some relief for their health problems. This information somewhat debunks the theory that the government is protecting poor uneducated minority consumers from predatory, dangerous and unproven health care specialists.

While critics brand alternative cancer therapies as "unproven, questionable, dubious, quackery and fraudulent"; proponents prefer the labels "complementary, comprehensive, innovative, nontoxic, holistic, natural and noninvasive." Meanwhile, the American Cancer Society has kept a list of about 100 cancer therapies that the ACS calls "unproven". This blacklist has become the "gatekeeper" in cancer treatment in America. Insurance companies will not reimburse for "unproven or experimental" therapies.

Yet, are we using dual standards in judging our health care options? According to the Office of Technology Assessment, only 10-20% of all surgical procedures practiced in the United States have been "proven" to be effective by controlled clinical trials.[5] Much of what Americans do throughout medicine, law, education and even business are more based on a "Grandfather clause" or tradition, rather than being the best way to do things. We oftentimes "pave cow paths" which are usually inefficient routes from point A to point B, then consider these sacred and inviolable. If 50% of cancer patients this year will seek alternative cancer care, which is non-reimburseable, imagine the stampede toward alternative cancer treatment if people could chose their own therapies.

Improvement in cancer treatment options may be coming soon. Retired Iowa Congressman Berkley Bedell could only find cures for his Lyme disease, then advanced and untreatable prostate cancer from alternative therapists. Mr. Bedell told his powerbroker friends on Capitol Hill of his experiences. Senator Tom Harkin, chairman of the subcommittee on health issues, then convinced his colleagues to allocate $2 million to form the Office of Alternative Medicine as a branch of the National Institutes of Health. Given the $12 billion that goes to the National Institutes of Health each year, $2 million for the OAM has been called a "homeopathic dose", or "token pocket change" to keep the voters happy. Many insurance companies are awakening to the profitability of alternative cancer therapy because: 1) the public wants it and is willing to pay for it, 2) alternative cancer therapy costs about 10% of conventional cancer care and therefore can be more profitable. Some pioneering insurance companies now reimburse for alternative cancer treatment. [6]

The medical freedom advocates argue that a person afflicted with a terminal disease deserves a chance at whatever therapies offer hope. Meanwhile, the Food and Drug Administration cites examples in which premature permission to use newly discovered therapies ended in disaster--like the Thalidomide situation. However, lets compare the risk to benefit ratio of Thalidomide and alternative cancer treatment:

-Thalidomide.
>Benefits: an entirely elective drug used to relieve the mild symptoms of nausea.

>Risks: taken during an extremely vulnerable phase of life, pregnancy. We know, for instance, that small amounts of alcohol will not harm most healthy adults, but the same amount of alcohol could create permanent birth defects when consumed by pregnant women.

The results of Thalidomide use were catastrophic, with thousands of newborn infants suffering irremedial birth defects.

-Alternative cancer therapies.
>Benefits: have been demonstrated to improve quality and quantity of life for many cancer patients; especially for patients who have no hope in conventional cancer treatment.
>Risks: in extremely unprofessional hands they may cause minor side effects. Cost money, but usually less than 10% of standard cancer therapies.

It is unconstitutional to think that protecting the end-stage and otherwise untreatable cancer patient from inexpensive and non-toxic therapies is a government obligation. AIDS patients have become models of political activism and have won this logic debate as the Food and Drug Administration now allows many "compassionate use" variances for otherwise unapproved drugs in AIDS therapy. Cancer patients, also, need a broader scope of treatment options. To quote Hippocrates, the father of modern medicine, 2400 years ago: "Extreme diseases call for extreme measures." Nutrition therapy, surely, is no more extreme than chemo, radiation therapy or surgery.

Alternative cancer therapies would best be categorized as:

-*Physical,* which includes botanicals, nutrition, biochemical vaccinations, anti-neoplastons, biologically guided chemotherapy, eumetabolic, laetrile, DMSO, cellular treatment, oxygen therapy, hydrazine sulfate, immuno-augmentative therapy and more.

-*Metaphysical* (meaning "above physical"), which includes psychoneuroimmunology (PNI), guided imagery, relaxation therapy, primal therapy, faith healing and other methods that use the mind or spirit to elevate the body out of cancer.

It is clear that humans are a complex interplay of physical and metaphysical forces. Many documented cases of paranormal psychology have shown that people can alter autonomic bodily functions by entering suspended animation, walking on hot coals without any burns, reading minds and living outside the laws of nutrition. As humans become more spiritual or metaphysical, we tend to transcend physical laws. Hence, the ultimate cancer cure may come from this relatively untapped area of healing.

PIONEERS AND ALTERNATIVE CANCER THERAPIES
The alternative therapists are at a serious disadvantage in the battle of documentation. Even after $39 billion spent on government-funded research and thousands of researchers working for decades,

scientists are hard pressed to prove efficacy in the assortment of conventional cancer treatment. Alternative therapists don't publish results for a number of reasons:
>poorly financed and cannot support research efforts
>poorly organized and shy away from cooperative pooled data
>outlawed in the U.S. and ineligible for government research grants
>leery of reporting their data in the U.S. for fear of medical license revocation and/or imprisonment.

In spite of minimal funding, there are over 20,000 peer-reviewed scientific studies showing the merits of nutrition therapy to prevent or reverse many common diseases. There are several thousand studies demonstrating the irrefutable link between optimal nutrition and optimal outcome in cancer treatment.

> All of the following alternative cancer therapies are practiced somewhere in the world. My most humble apologies to the pioneers or therapies that have been left out of this brief overview.

-**Max Gerson, MD** emigrated from Europe to the United States in 1936 and began practicing medicine in New York. Gerson was labeled by the famous missionary doctor, Albert Schweitzer, as "I see in Gerson one of the most eminent geniuses in medical history." Gerson was treating cancer patients with a diet and toxin purgative approach. Gerson's program included a diet that was high in raw unprocessed plant food, low in fat, included raw liver injections, thyroid extract, pancreatin (digestive aids), and supplements of minerals and vitamins, especially high doses of vitamin C.

Dr. Gerson's therapy included many nutritional components that are now considered explainable and clinically effective. Too bad that Gerson was forced to leave the U.S. and bring his clinic to Mexico. Realize that we evolved on a "caveman" diet which was high in potassium from fresh plant food and low in sodium (pre-salt shaker era). Our modern American diet reverses this ratio from an ideal of 4 to 1 (potassium to sodium) to our current 1 to 4, a full 16 fold deterioration in this crucial balance of electrolytes. All of your cells are bathed in a salty ocean water, with higher concentrations of potassium inside the cell to create the "battery of life."

Birger Jansson, PhD at the University of Texas finds a strong link between dietary sodium to potassium ratio and cancer.[7] Stephen Thompson, PhD researcher at the University of California San Diego, found that increasing sodium content could accelerate the metastasis of colon cancer in animals. Maryce Jacobs, PhD, former research director of the American Institute of Cancer Research, has written an extensive technical chapter on the link between the sodium to potassium ratio and cancer progression.[8]

When the National Cancer Institute reviewed Gerson's book which illustrated his 30 years of clinical experience with 50 patients who recovered from end-stage cancer, the NCI felt that the evidence was inadequate.

-**William D. Kelley, DDS** was a dentist who healed himself of pancreatic cancer with his own therapy in 1964. Kelley's program included metabolic typing to provide a patient-specific dietary program, detoxification (coffee enemas, etc.), neurological stimulation through chiropractic adjustment and supplements of vitamins, minerals and enzymes. Until 1977, the MERCK MEDICAL MANUAL, considered the "bible of physicians", included coffee enemas as an accepted means of detoxification and constipation relief. Yet coffee enemas became the focal point of critics who considered the Kelley program unscientific.

Meanwhile, there has been an abundance of scientific studies in Europe showing that enzymes (protease, amylase, lipase) can improve the general course of the cancer patient.[9] Kelley's work is carried on by a Sloan-Kettering trained oncologist, Dr. Nicholas Gonzales, in New York City. In his 1970s trial, Kelley was ordered by a federal judge never to speak or write about cancer again. Kelley has since become a recluse in the American Northwest.

-**Macrobiotics**. This program is based on the writings of a Japanese physician, Sagen Ishizuka (1850-1910) who cured himself of cancer by abandoning the refined diet of affluent Japan and reverting back to the unpurified Japanese diet of brown rice, soybeans, fish, miso soup, sea vegetables and other traditional Oriental foods. When you read the "laws of nutrition" later in this book, you will notice the importance of consuming one's ancestral diet. Some proposed mechanisms why the macrobiotic diet helps some cancer patients:

-low in fat

-high in fiber

-high vegetable intake

-improved sodium to potassium ratio

-ability to change an acid (cancer) environment back toward alkaline (healthy)

-potent anti-cancer agents found in soybeans, sea vegetables and other fresh produce

-thyroid stimulating substances found in sea vegetables.

Macrobiotics includes an Eastern philosophy of balancing yin and yang, which are opposing forces. Michio Kushi established a macrobiotic center in Boston in 1978 and has gained a noteworthy following. Kushi has publicly encouraged cancer patients to continue with conventional care.

There are varying levels of intensity in complying with macrobiotic principles, with the ultimate level (+7) being a diet of 100% whole cereals. An American physician, Anthony Sattilaro, cured himself of advanced prostatic cancer with the macrobiotic diet and wrote a book to further popularize this approach. While the macrobiotic lifestyle is certainly a major improvement over the typical American diet, certain aspects of this program may be counterproductive:

-unlimited access to miso and pickles, which are high in sodium

-limited intake of fruit and fish

-high potential for protein malnutrition.

This program originated with Orientals, who have had thousands of years to adapt to such a diet. I have worked with a number of cancer patients who got worse while on the macrobiotic diet. For many other sub-groups macrobiotics may be inappropriate.

-Herbal therapies. Plant extracts are mankind's oldest medicines. One third of all prescription drugs in the U.S. are based on plant extracts. There is a desperate scramble among drug companies and even the National Cancer Institute to develop patentable variations of the many anti-cancer agents found in plants. Many of the people listed below have staked their claim to herbal cures of cancer, including Caisse, Hoxsey, Winters, and others. Periwinkle plant is now the very acceptable cancer drug, vincristine. Undoubtedly, plant extracts will become a major source of cancer drugs in the future. James Duke, PhD, a well respected botanist with the United States Department of Agriculture, has written textbooks on the anti-cancer ingredients in many plants. If you have seen the movie "Medicine Man", then you can appreciate the complexities of trying to find the active ingredient(s) in plant extracts. Botanicals used to fight cancer include Pau D'Arco (LaPacho), ginseng, green tea, mistletoe, polyphenols, carotenoids, bioflavonoids, echinecea, astragalus, chaparral, blood root, garlic and various mushroom extracts.

-Rene Caisse, a Canadian public health nurse, was told by a patient in 1922 that an Indian herbal tea had saved her life from breast cancer. Caisse obtained the recipe, reportedly used it successfully on a few of her patients and then named the therapy "Essiac", or Caisse spelled backward. Her troubles with the government waxed and waned for the coming decades until 1978, shortly before her death, when she signed over the rights to her secret formula to a Canadian manufacturing firm.

-**Harry Hoxsey** (1901-1974) popularized his great-grandfather's herbal formula which had reputedly cured horses of cancer. Harry Hoxsey's father was a veterinary surgeon who also used the formula on both animals and people with cancer. Yet Harry is the man who made the formula famous. Hoxsey's flamboyant and controversial style led to many encounters with federal officials and the American Medical Association. At his zenith in the U.S., Hoxsey had thousands of very happy cancer patients going to his 17 clinics across the country. After uncountable arrests, he closed his Dallas clinic in the late 1950s and moved to Mexico to continue practicing. Hoxsey's formula included bloodroot, burdock, buckthorn, cascara, barberry, licorice, red clover, pokeroot, zinc chloride and antimony trisulfide. Hoxsey's general formula has ended up in many escharotics, or topically applied ointments that successfully burn away surface cancers.

-**Rudolph Steiner, PhD** popularized the use of mistletoe in the early 20th century. A certain lectin in mistletoe has been found to inhibit the growth of proliferating cells. By the 1980s, about 40,000 patients worldwide were receiving Iscador, a fermented form of mistletoe that is injected. Iscador and its variations are licensed in Germany as drugs.

-**Stanislaw R. Burzynski, MD, PhD** theorized that certain anti-neoplastons, or naturally occurring peptides, could inhibit the growth of tumor cells without interrupting normal cell growth. Burzynski first isolated his anti-neoplastons from human urine and later synthesized these compounds in the laboratory. Dr. Burzynski uses about 10 types of anti-neoplastons in both oral and intravenous fashion. Government authorities have repeatedly harrassed and tried to indict Burzynski. Given the less than 5% long term survival of brain cancer patients using traditional therapies and the 33% cure rate using Burzynski's therapy, the treatment of Dr. Burzynski has been a gross misuse of FDA authority to "protect the American public".

-**Paul Niehans, MD** developed his "cell therapy" techniques in Switzerland in the 1930s. The principle is that "something" in young tissue is able to regenerate old and sick tissue. Hence, injecting cells derived from whole fetuses is supposed to make old people feel younger and sick people get well. Cell therapy has been used for a wide range of otherwise untreatable conditions, most notably for aging wealthy people to feel younger.

-**Joseph Gold, MD** of the Syracuse Cancer Research Institute reported good results in the 1970s using hydrazine sulfate to inhibit the growth of tumors in animals.[10] While there certainly are some less effective approaches among alternative cancer therapies, hydrazine sulfate has been found in human clinical studies at the University of

California at Los Angeles to reduce lean tissue wasting (cachexia) and improve the abnormal glucose and insulin levels which are common among end stage cancer patients.[11] Hydrazine sulfate is neutralized when patients are taking tranquilizers, pain killers (analgesics) or other compounds that conflict with a monoamine oxidase inhibitor. The National Cancer Institute ignored Dr. Gold's protocol guidelines, and, predictably, found hydrazine ineffective as a therapy for cancer.[12] While hydrazine is not a magic bullet cure for all cancer, it is a very effective means of reversing cachexia in wasting cancer patients and slowing cancer growth in others. Its lack of widespread use is a real travesty for millions of cancer patients worldwide.

-Ernst Krebs, Sr., MD, and Ernst Krebs, Jr. were the developers of laetrile, which is amygdalin, a cyanide-containing compound first isolated from the seeds of pit fruit, like apricots. The ancient Egyptians, Chinese, Greeks, and Romans all used seed pits, or amygdalin, as their "sacred seeds" against cancer. Since the 1970s, 70,000 people have used laetrile to treat cancer. Laetrile has become an irrational "head butting contest" between the conventional and unconventional cancer communities.

Ralph Moss, PhD was the science writer for the Sloan-Kettering cancer hospital in New York when research was being conducted by a celebrated scientist, Dr. Kanematsu Sugiura, on laetrile. Dr. Moss writes of a disturbing coverup that basically ended any legitimate assessment of laetrile.[13] Dr. Sugiura found that laetrile did not destroy primary tumors in animals, but did inhibit the growth of tumors and signficantly retarded lung metastases. A San Antonio physician, Dr. Eva Lee Sneak wrote a letter to the editor printed in a publication of the American Medical Association: "Laetrile, properly used, has had, in my hands at least, as good a success as chemotherapy with far fewer side effects."[14]

In 1982, the National Cancer Institute funded a laetrile cancer study conducted by Charles Moertel, MD of the Mayo Clinic. Dr. Moertel's results, published in the prestigious New England Journal of Medicine, played "Taps" for laetrile, claiming that it neither helped cancer nor the symptoms of cancer. About 21 states still allow the use of laetrile in cancer treatment, while other states have revoked medical licenses for the same.

A curious footnote to laetrile is that young plants develop their own naturally occurring pesticides to provide some protection against insects and rodents. This "pesticide" is rich in nitrilosides, which are similar in chemical structure to laetrile. Could it be that a diet high in young fresh plants, like alfalfa sprouts, is like having continuous non-toxic chemotherapy to kill pockets of cancer cells before they can flourish?

-Virginia Livingston-Wheeler, MD felt that cancer was caused by a specific pathogen, Progenitor cryptocides (PC), a cousin of the bacteria that causes leprosy and tuberculosis. Treatment includes immunologic vaccines of PC, pharmacologic therapies and nutritional components. Dr. Livingston helped many cancer patients with her nutritional approaches, which included avoidance of foods that contain PC, like chicken and eggs. However, most cancer patients are immune suppressed and subject to nearly every opportunistic infections that comes along, including PC.

While this bacteria and many others are present in most cancer patients, linking cause and effect is another matter. For instance, fire engines are present at most fires, but they do not cause fires. Yet, other researchers are equally intrigued with the theory that cancer is caused by a bacteria.[15] It is known that older people are at greater risk for both developing cancer and experiencing a reduced output of stomach acid. Since the acid bath of the stomach is supposed to destroy many invading organisms, the theory of "cancer caused by a pathogen" would help to explain the prevalence of cancer in older adults.

-Hans Nieper, MD is a European physician who uses conventional and unconventional drugs, vitamins, minerals (many of his own design), plant and animal extracts, a certain diet, and avoidance of "geopathogenic zones" which may incite disease.

-Otto Warburg, PhD was awarded two Nobel prizes and first discovered the link between low oxygen levels and cancer growth. Other scientists have proven that cancer becomes more resistant to therapy as the tumor mass becomes more acidic and anaerobic.[16] Warburg's theories provided the foundation for ozone and hydrogen peroxide therapies, which are given intravenously, orally and rectally. While the efficacy of these therapies is controversial, experts caution against drinking hydrogen peroxide, since it is such a potent free radical generator.

-Emmanuel Revici, MD based his treatment on correcting an imbalance between fatty acids and sterols in the cancer patient; called "biological dualism". Revici was considered a very dedicated physician and developer of selenium as an anti-cancer agent.

-Ewan Cameron, MD, a Scottish surgeon first popularized the use of high dose vitamin C in terminal cancer patients. Linus Pauling, PhD, twice Nobel laureate, furthered this cause with studies and writings. While vitamin C is far from a "magic bullet" against cancer, many cancer patients have been found to have clinical scurvy.

-J.H. Lawrence, a British scientist during World War II, found that something in urine seemed to have anti-tumor activity in animals. His work has since been refined and carried on by numerous disciples throughout the world.

-Lawrence Burton, PhD developed Immuno-Augmentative Therapy by injecting various blood products into cancer patients to stimulate the immune system. Once a well-respected researcher, Burton was ridiculed by his colleagues and driven out of this country to the Bahamas.

-714X & Gaston Naessens. Naessens was driven out of France in the 1950s when he developed a treatment for leukemia called Anablast. He settled in French Quebec in Canada and developed a microscope that supposedly has a much better resolution than other conventional microscopes. Naessens claims to have found "somatids" or "elementary particles endowed with movement and possessing a variable life cycle of many forms." Pleomorphism is the theory that inanimate objects can change into living pathogens and back again. 714X is a compound of camphor and nitrogen which is injected directly into the lymph system of the cancer patient to bring nitrogen to starving cancer cells.

-Cancell (Entelev) was developed by an analytical chemist and patent attorney, Jim Sheridan. Cancell contains a catechol, a natural chemical that can inhibit respiration. By 1942, Sheridan claimed to be getting better than 70% tumor response in mice studies. In 1953, human clinical trials with Cancell were blocked by the American Cancer Society. In 1961, Sheridan tried proving his theories to the government, which needed to see results in 5 days, while Cancell supposedly takes 28 days to show effect. In 1982, Cancell was put into "handcuffs" when the Food and Drug Administration gave Sheridan an Investigative New Drug (IND) number, then put the project on "clinical hold". By then, Sheridan gave up and turned the formula over to Ed Sopcak, a foundry owner, who has since given away 20,000 bottles of Cancell.

-John Prudden, MD, PhD accidentally discovered in 1954 that ground up cartilage applied topically could accelerate wound healing. Later clinical trials found that bovine cartilage taken internally could cure 35% of cancer patients. There will be more on this topic.

-Rigdon Lentz, MD found that only two stages of life allow a foreign body to exist within them: the cancer patient and the pregnant woman. Both have a "time out" factor, called Tumor Necrosis Factor inhibitor (TNF-i), that tells the immune system not to attack the fetus, and sometimes mistakenly the cancer. Dr. Lentz in Nashville (615-831-1222) has developed a device, like a renal dialysis device for kidney failure patients, that filters the TNF-i out of the blood. He is working with the FDA to clinically test his methods on cancer patients.

-Cell Specific Cancer Therapy (CSCT) is one of the more exciting developments in cancer treatment in this century. This therapy can accurately detect cancer cells in the body and, using pulsed electro-magnetic radiation, can selectively kill cancer cells without harming healthy host tissue. Contact these people in the Dominican Republic at 809-534-2090, fax -3089, or on the Internet via www.csct.com.

WHERE DO WE GO FROM HERE?

Some of these approaches warrant further study, yet they have all been lumped together under the tainted reputation of "fringe" and either discouraged or outlawed. We need to separate the chaff from the grain in these therapies and expose them to some much needed research scrutiny.

It is obvious that no unqualified cure for cancer exists, either in conventional or unconventional circles. Given the disappointing results of traditional cancer therapy, it only makes sense to expand our horizons and look at other possibilities

---

PATIENT PROFILE: STABILIZED DISEASE

W.R. is 71 year old male with primary colon cancer diagnosed in November 1993. He had a colostomy to remove the tumor. He then had lung metastasis discovered in July of 1995 with a thoracotomy, or surgical removal of the tumor. He experienced new lung metastases in November of 1996, which were defined as inoperable. He began using nutrition therapy in December of 1996. His CAT scans as of January 1997, April 1997, and June of 1997 showed no growth of tumor (size 5x6x10 cm). Co-morbidity (other diseases) includes emphesema (quit smoking 1991), atrial fibrillation, tachycardia, and gall stones. He feels very good and has high praises for the value of nutrition.

ENDNOTES

[1]. Romm, S, Washington Post, p.Z14, Jan.9, 1990
[2]. Herman, R., Washington Post, p.Z14, Dec.3, 1991
[3]. Boly, W, Hippocrates, p.38, Jan.1989
[4]. Family Practice News, vol.10, Sept.1990
[5]. Office of Technology Assessment, ASSESSING THE EFFICACY AND SAFETY OF MEDICAL TECHNOLOGIES, U.S. Govt. Printing Office, Washington, DC, 1978
[6]. American Western Life, 100 Foster City Blvd, Foster City, CA 94404-1166; ph. 415-573-8041; see also Sidha National Insurance Group, Box 122, Fairfield, IA 52556; ph. 800-383-9108; see also Alternative Health Insurance, Box 9178, Calabasas, CA 91372; ph. 818-509-5742
[7]. Jansson, B., Cancer Detection and Prevention, vol.14, no.5, p.563, 1990
[8]. Jacobs, MM (ed.), VITAMINS AND MINERALS IN THE PREVENTION AND TREATMENT OF CANCER, CRC Press, Boca Raton, FL, 1991
[9]. Wrba, H., Therapie Woche, vol.37, p.7, 1987
[10]. Gold, J., Nutrition & Cancer, vol.9, p.59, 1987
[11]. Chlewbowski, RT, et al., Cancer Research, vol.44, p.857, 1984
[12]. Herbert, V., J. Clin.Oncology, vol.12, no.6, p.1107, June 1994
[13]. Moss, RW, THE CANCER INDUSTRY, Paragon, NY, 1989
[14]. American Medical News, Jan.15, 1982
[15]. White, MW, Medical Hypotheses, vol.32, no.2, p.111, June 1990
[16]. Newell, K, et al., Proceedings of the National Academy of Science, USA, vol.90, no.3, p.1127, Feb.1990; see also White, MW, Medical Hypotheses, vol.39, no.4, p.323, Dec.1992

Chapter 4

NOTE TO THE ONCOLOGIST

"Our way of life is related to our way of death." The
Framingham Study, Harvard University

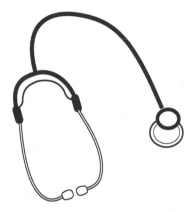

This letter offers some insights regarding the guided use of nutrition therapy to help support your cancer patient while undergoing traditional therapies. You will be spared the onslaught of references in this chapter, though ample scientific documentation is found throughout this book to support the use of nutrition as part of comprehensive cancer treatment. No one is saying that nutrition should be sole therapy in advanced cancer. It is hoped that you will consider using aggressive nutrition to bolster "host defense mechanisms" in your cancer patients.

MISCONCEPTIONS ABOUT NUTRITION & CANCER

The concept of nutrition in cancer treatment comes with a mixed reputation, although its use dates back 2000 years ago to Chinese medical textbooks.

⇒**FALSE HOPE**. You may have heard the undocumented claims regarding cures from advanced cancer using carrot juice. You have also seen more than a few advanced salvageable cancer patients waste precious time "experimenting" with questionable treatment modalities, only to have the patient succumb to the disease.

⇒**QUESTIONABLE PRACTITIONERS**. To be sure, there are a few unsavory characters in the field of nutritional oncology, just as there are in any profession.

⇒**IF YOU FEED THE PATIENT, THEN YOU FEED THE CANCER**. You may have been trained by the founders of chemotherapy, who exploited folic acid antagonists as drugs to slow down neoplasia. It would seem that "if an anti-vitamin (methotrexate) slows down cancer, then a vitamin might accelerate cancer. " In fact, nutrients in general bolster the patient's ability to recover from most diseases. You will see many references throughout this book showing how nutrients improve outcome in cancer treatment. You will also see that some essential nutrients, notably sodium, glucose, iron, copper and the essential fatty acid of linoleic acid can accelerate tumor growth when used in excess or in the absence of other controlling nutrients. This book addresses the concepts of nutrient toxicity and provides guidelines for using nutrition as a positive force in the treatment of your cancer patients.

You may have seen the paper from the American College of Physicians (Annals of Internal Medicine, vol.110, no.9, p.734, May 1989) claiming that Total Parenteral Nutrition is ineffective and may be counterproductive in cancer patients. Paradoxically, malnourished patients were eliminated from this meta-analysis of pooled data. TPN treats malnutrition, not cancer. Also, this collection of studies grouped various TPN protocols together; those that were high in dextrose or low, high in protein or low, with or without fat...all were considered as equal TPN formulas against cancer. Since cancer is an "obligate glucose metabolizer", or sugar feeder, and since the patient needs adequate amounts of protein to re-build lost visceral protein stores and replenish the immune system; it is unwise to group all TPN formulas together. Other studies show that the proper formula of TPN along with proper patient selection criteria can improve the outcome in cancer treatment.

⇒**ANTIOXIDANTS WILL REDUCE THE EFFECTIVENESS OF CHEMO AND RADIATION.**

In basic theory, this statement makes sense. However, in actual human cancer patients, antioxidants have been shown to dramatically improve the tumor kill from pro-oxidative chemo and radiation while protecting the host tissue from damage. Essentially, the proper selection of nutrients taken before and during chemo and radiation can help make the medical therapy more of a selective toxin against the cancer. Cancer cells are primarily anaerobic fermenting cells. Cancer cells do not absorb nor use antioxidants the same way that healthy aerobic cells do. Therefore, we can exploit the differences in biochemistry between healthy and malignant cells by combining aggressive nutrition support with restrained cytotoxic therapies.

⇒**CANCER MUST BE TREATED WITH CYTOTOXIC THERAPY, NOT NOURISHMENT.** That strategy may be changing. An article by an oncologist published in the Journal of Clinical Oncology (vol.13, no.4, p.801, Apr.1995) asks the question: "Must we kill to cure?" Over the past 50 years, we have found that increasing the toxicity and usage of pesticides on insects in the fields has created a net INCREASE in crop loss with some insects developing near total immunity to the most potent insecticides. During the same half century, we have overused antibiotic drugs, with the net effect that infections are now the number three cause of death in America, with some bacteria having become virtually drug resistant. During that same time frame, we have attempted to use potent systemic chemotherapy to eliminate cancer. Initially, the patient often gets a "response", or a shrinkage of the tumor. In many patients, the tumor soon develops a drug resistance which creates a more virulent tumor, yet at that point the chemotherapy may have compromised the patient's host defense mechanisms and ability to recover. Attacking cancer with restrained medical intervention COUPLED with aggressive nutrition is the best strategy. These two therapies combine to create a synergistic response that is better than either therapy could achieve on its own.

⇒**WHY ME?** You might ask, "With all the conflicting information out there regarding nutrition for cancer patients, why is this guy the one to listen to?" In addition to my 3 degrees in nutrition, my certified nutrition specialist status (there are less than a thousand in the country who have passed these rigid criteria), I spent 8 years working with hundreds of cancer patients and know what works and what doesn't. I organized 3 international CME-based scientific symposia on "adjuvant nutrition in cancer treatment" and edited a textbook by the same name. My original release of BEATING CANCER WITH NUTRITION has been translated into Japanese and Chinese and is a home study continuing education course for registered nurses. Please see my complete curriculum vitae at my website: www.4nutrition.com.

The bottom line is that a "well-nourished cancer patient can better manage the disease", has fewer infections, has fewer side effects from chemo and radiation, has a better quality and quantity of life, and improved chances for complete remission. The toxicity of professionally designed nutrition therapies for the cancer patient is near-zero. The risk to benefit to cost ratio of nutrition therapy in cancer treatment warrants its inclusion.

Over the course of 8 years, I worked with hundreds of cancer patients through a nationally recognized cancer treatment group. The oncologists that I worked with were initially skeptical about the use of nutrition in cancer patients for the reasons that I have outlined above. Yet, after a few "miracle patients" and scores of surprisingly good results in patients that would normally be considered "end stage and refractory", these oncologists began to respect the role that nutrition plays as part of comprehensive cancer treatment. Along with your noteworthy intellect and concern for your patients, it is my hope that you will use an open mind to at least try out new possibilities, like nutrition, to help your patients. It was only 2 or 3 decades ago that chemotherapy was considered fringe thinking.

I worked with many cancer patients who came to our centers as the "hospital of last hope" after failing several different chemo and radiation protocols. Many of these patients were in tears as they would tell me about the apathy that their former doctors displayed as the patient asked the doctor: "What about nutrition? Might it help?" As you will see in studies throughout this book, the earlier the cancer patient receives nutrition therapy, the better the outcome. For those patients who are malnourished or have been through extensive cytotoxic therapies without any nutrition support, the recuperative powers of the human body can be exhausted.

By keeping an open mind and the patient's best interests in the forefront, you will make the right decision in using nutrition for your patients. Thank you in advance for your time and consideration.

PATIENT PROFILE: REVERSING PROSTATE CANCER

T.B. is a 69 year old male diagnosed with prostate cancer with metastasis to the bone in June of 1987. Initially, he employed primarily a vegetarian diet as sole therapy. His bone scans in June of 1988 showed no malignancy. "Several years later" he experienced a recurrence of prostate cancer after his dietary relapse. He began using nutrition therapy in November of 1996 with PSA levels dropping from 630 to 2.6, then 5.3. His liver metastasis has been reduced. He says that he feels good.

Chapter 5

NUTRITION CAN IMPROVE
OUTCOME IN CANCER TREATMENT

**"Natural forces within us are the true healers." Hippocrates,
father of modern medicine, 400 BC**

Nutrition is a low cost, non-toxic, and scientifically-proven
helpful component in the comprehensive treatment of
cancer. Adjuvant (helpful) nutrition and traditional
oncology are synergistic, not antagonistic. The advantages in using an
aggressive nutrition program in comprehensive cancer treatment are, in
this critical order of importance:
⇒ 1) avoiding malnutrition
⇒ 2) reducing the toxicity of medical therapy while making
chemotherapy and radiation more selectively toxic to the tumor cells
⇒ 3) stimulating immune function
⇒ 4) selectively starving the tumor
⇒ 5) nutrients acting as biological response modifiers to assist host
defense mechanisms and improve outcome in cancer therapy.

NUTRIENTS AS BIOLOGICAL RESPONSE MODIFIERS
In the early phase of nutrition research, nutrient functions were
linked to classical nutrient deficiency syndromes: e.g., vitamin C and
scurvy, vitamin D and rickets, niacin and pellagra. Today nutrition
researchers find various levels of functions for nutrients. For example,
let's look at the "dose dependent response" from niacin:
⇒20 milligrams daily will prevent pellagra
⇒100 mg becomes a useful vasodilator
⇒2000 mg is a hypocholesterolemic agent endorsed by the National
Institutes of Health. While 10 milligrams of vitamin E is considered the

RDA, 800 iu was shown to improve immune functions in healthy older adults.[1] While 10 mg of vitamin C will prevent scurvy in most adults, the RDA is 60 mg, and 300 mg was shown to extend lifespan in males by an average of 6 years.[2]

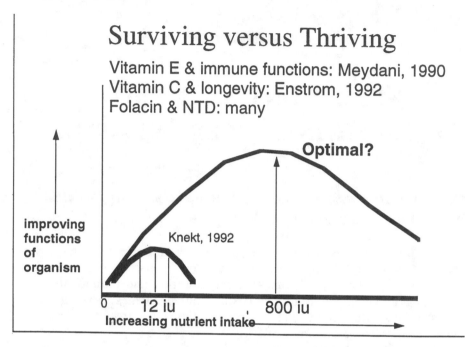

Surviving versus Thriving

Vitamin E & immune functions: Meydani, 1990
Vitamin C & longevity: Enstrom, 1992
Folacin & NTD: many

The dietary requirement of a nutrient may well depend on the health state of the individual and what you are trying to achieve. In animal studies, 7.5 mg of vitamin E per kilogram of body weight was found to satisfactorily support normal growth and spleen to body weight ratio. Yet, consumption at twice that level of vitamin E was essential to prevent deficiency symptoms of myopathy and testis degeneration. Intake at 7 times base level of vitamin E was required to prevent red blood cell hemolysis. Intake of 27 times base level provided optimal T- and B-lymphocyte responses to mitogens.[3]

You can accelerate the rate of a reaction by increasing temperature, surface area, or concentration of substrates or enzymes. Clearly, above-RDA levels of nutrients can offer safe and cost-effective enhancement of metabolic processes, including immune functions. Therapeutic dosages of nutrients may be able to reduce tumor recurrence, selectively slow cancer cells, stimulate the immune system to more actively destroy tumor cells, alter the genetic expression of cancer, and more.

CAN NUTRITION HELP THE MALNOURISHED CANCER PATIENT?

A position paper from the American College of Physicians published in 1989 basically stated that Total Parenteral Nutrition (TPN) had no benefit on the outcome of cancer patients.[4] Unfortunately, this article excluded malnourished patients, which is bizarre, since TPN only treats malnutrition, not cancer.[5] Most of the scientific literature shows that weight loss drastically increases the mortality rate for most types of cancer, while also lowering the response to chemotherapy.[6] Chemo and radiation therapy are sufficient biological stressors alone to induce malnutrition. [7]

In the early years of oncology, it was thought that one could starve the tumor out of the host. Pure malnutrition (cachexia) is responsible for somewhere between 22% and 67% of all cancer deaths. Up to 80% of all cancer patients have reduced levels of serum albumin, which is a leading indicator of protein and calorie malnutrition.[8] Dietary protein restriction in the cancer patient does not affect the composition or growth rate of the tumor, but does restrict the patient's well being.[9]

Parenteral feeding improves tolerance to chemotherapeutic agents and immune responses.[10] Malnourished cancer patients who were provided TPN had a mortality rate of 11% while a comparable group without TPN feeding had a 100% mortality rate.[11] Pre-operative TPN in patients undergoing surgery for GI cancer provided general reduction in the incidence of wound infection, pneumonia, major complications and mortality. [12] Patients who were the most malnourished experienced a 33% mortality and 46% morbidity rate, while those patients who were properly nourished had a 3% mortality rate with an 8% morbidity rate.

In 20 adult hospitalized patients on TPN, the mean daily vitamin C needs were 975 mg, which is over 16 times the RDA, with the range being 350-2250 mg.[13] Of the 139 lung cancer patients studied, most tested deficient or scorbutic (clinical vitamin C deficiency).[14] Another study of cancer patients found that 46% tested scorbutic while 76% were below acceptable levels for serum ascorbate.[15] Experts now recommend the value of nutritional supplements, especially in patients who require prolonged TPN support.[16]

WHY USE NUTRITION AS PART OF COMPREHENSIVE CANCER TREATMENT?

1) Avoiding malnutrition

40% or more of cancer patients actually die from malnutrition, not from the cancer.[17] Nutrition therapy is essential to arrest malnutrition. Among the more effective non-nutritional approaches to reverse cancer cachexia is hydrazine sulfate. Hydrazine sulfate is a relatively non-toxic drug that shuts down energy metabolism in cancer cells. Hydrazine is available through BioTech Labs (800-345-1199) or Great Lakes Metabolics (507-288-2348) or Life Support (209-529-4697) or Life Energy (Vancouver 604-856-0171). Protocol is to take 60 mg capsules: first 3 days 1 cap at brk, day 4-6 take 1 cap at brk & supper, day 7-45 take 3 caps TID (3x/day), off for 1 wk; counterindications are like MAO inhibitor: no aged cheese, yogurt, brewer's yeast, raisins, sausage (tyramine content), excessive B-6, over ripe bananas.

2) Reducing the toxic effects of chemo & radiation

Properly nourished patients experience less nausea, malaise, immune suppression, hair loss and organ toxicity than patients on routine oncology programs. Antioxidants, like beta carotene, vitamin C, vitamin E, and selenium appear to enhance the effectiveness of chemo, radiation, and hyperthermia while minimizing damage to the patient's normal cells; thus making therapy more of a "selective toxin." An optimally nourished cancer patient can better tolerate the rigors of cytotoxic therapy. For a few examples...

VITAMIN K. While in simplistic theory, vitamin K might inhibit the effectiveness of anticoagulant therapy (coumadin), actually vitamin K seems to augment the anti-neoplastic activity of coumadin. In a study with human rheumatoid arthritis patients being given methotrexate, folic acid supplements did not reduce the antiproliferative therapeutic value of methotrexate. [18]

VITAMIN C. Tumor-bearing mice fed high doses of vitamin C (antioxidant) along with adriamycin (pro-oxidant) had a prolonged life and no reduction in the tumor killing capacity of adriamycin.[19] Lung cancer patients who were provided antioxidant nutrients prior to, during, and after radiation and chemotherapy had enhanced tumor destruction and significantly longer life span.[20] Tumor-bearing mice fed high doses of vitamin C experienced an increased tolerance to radiation therapy without reduction in the tumor killing capacity of the radiation.[21]

FISH OIL. A special fat in fish (eicosapentaenoic acid, EPA) improves tumor kill in hyperthermia and chemotherapy by altering cancer cell membranes for increased vulnerability.[22] EPA increases the ability of adriamycin to kill cultured leukemia cells.[23] Tumors in EPA-fed animals are more responsive to Mitomycin C and doxorubicin (chemo drugs).[24] EPA and another special fat from plants (gamma linolenic acid, GLA) were selectively toxic to human tumor cell lines while also enhancing the cytotoxic effects of chemotherapy.[25]

VITAMIN A & BETACAROTENE. There is a synergistic benefit of using vitamin A with carotenoids in patients who are being treated with chemo, radiation and surgery for common malignancies.[26] Beta-carotene and vitamin A together provided a significant improvement in outcome in animals treated with radiation for induced cancers.[27]

VITAMIN E. Vitamin E protects the body against the potentially damaging effects of iron and fish oil. Vitamin E deficiency, which is common in cancer patients, will accentuate the cardiotoxic effects of adriamycin.[28] The worse the vitamin E deficiency in animals, the greater the heart damage from adriamycin.[29] Patients undergoing chemo, radiation and bone marrow transplant for cancer treatment had markedly depressed levels of serum antioxidants, including vitamin E.[30] Vitamin E protects animals against a potent carcinogen, DMBA.[31] Vitamin E supplements prevented the glucose-raising effects of a chemo drug, doxorubicin[32] while improving the tumor kill rate of doxorubicin.[33] Vitamin E modifies the carcinogenic effect of daunomycin (chemo drug) in animals.[34]

VITAMIN K. In one study, patients with mouth cancer who were pre-treated with injections of K-3 prior to radiation therapy doubled their odds (20% vs. 39%) for 5 year survival and disease free status.[35] Animals with implanted tumors had greatly improved anti-cancer effects from all chemotherapy drugs tested when vitamins K and C were given in combination.[36] In cultured leukemia cells, vitamins K and E added to the chemotherapy drugs of 5FU (fluorouracil) and leucovorin provided a 300% improvement in growth inhibition when compared to 5FU by itself.[37] Animals given methotrexate and K-3 had improvements in cancer reversal with no increase in toxicity to the host tissue.[38]

NIACIN. Niacin supplements in animals were able to reduce the cardiotoxicity of adriamycin while not interfering with its tumor killing capacity.[39] Niacin combined with aspirin in 106 bladder cancer patients receiving surgery and radiation therapy provided for a substantial improvement in 5 year survival (72% vs. 27%) over the control group.[40] Niacin seems to make radiation therapy more effective at killing hypoxic cancer cells.[41] Loading radiation patients with 500 mg to 6000 mg of niacin has been shown to be safe and one of the most effective agents known to eliminate acute hypoxia in solid malignancies.[42]

SELENIUM. Selenium-deficient animals have more heart damage from the chemo drug, adriamycin.[43] Supplements of selenium and vitamin E in humans did not reduce the efficacy of the chemo drugs against ovarian and cervical cancer.[44] Animals with implanted tumors who were then treated with selenium and cisplatin (chemo drug) had reduced toxicity to the drug with no change in anti-cancer activity.[45] Selenium supplements helped repair DNA damage from a carcinogen in animals.[46] Selenium was selectively toxic to human leukemia cells in culture.[47]

CARNITINE. Carnitine may help the cancer patient by protecting the heart against the damaging effects of adriamycin.[48]

QUERCETIN. Quercetin reduces the toxicity and carcinogenic capacity of substances in the body[49] YET at the same time may enhance the tumor killing capacity of cisplatin.[50] Quercetin significantly increased the tumor kill rate of hyperthermia (heat therapy) in cultured cancer cells.[51]

GINSENG. Panax ginseng was able to enhance the uptake of mitomycin (an antibiotic and anti-cancer drug) into the cancer cells for increased tumor kill.[52]

⇒In both human and animal studies, nutrients improve the host tolerance to cytotoxic medical therapies while allowing for unobstructed death of tumor cells. Nutrition therapy makes medical therapy more of a selective toxin on the tumor tissue.

---

3) Bolster immune functions

When the doctor says: "We think we got it all." What he or she is really saying is: "We have destroyed all DETECTABLE cancer cells, and now it is up to your immune system to find and destroy the cancer cells that inevitably remain in your body." A billion cancer cells is about the size of the page number at the top of this page. We must rely on the capabilities of the 20 trillion cells that compose an intact immune system to destroy the undetectable cancer cells that remain after medical therapy. There is an abundance of data linking nutrient intake to the quality and quantity of immune factors that fight cancer.[53]

IMMUNE SYSTEM

- Enhanced by:
- Vitamins: A, C, E, B-6
- Minerals: Zn, Cr, Se
- Quasi-vit: CoQ, EPA, GLA
- Amino acids: arg, gluta
- Herbals: astragalus, Cat's claw, Pau D'arco
- Foods: yogurt, cartilage, garlic, enzymes, green leafy, shark oil
- Positive emotions: love

- Reduced by:
- Toxic metals: Cd, Pb, Hg
- VOC: PCB, benzene
- Sugar: glycemic index
- Omega 6 fats: corn, soy
- Stress: depression

4) Selectively starve the tumor

Tumors are primarily obligate glucose metabolizers, meaning "sugar feeders".[54] Americans not only consume about 20% of their calories from refined sucrose, but often manifest poor glucose tolerance curves, due to stress, obesity, low chromium and fiber intake, and sedentary lifestyles.

SUGAR AND CANCER

-average U.S. consumption: 132 lb/year/person
-Paleolithic diet: about 0%, Modern US diet: 19% of kcal
-cancer is a "sugar feeder", obligate glucose metabolizer
-elevated blood glucose lowers immune system
-diets high in sugar have more cancer, DB, CAD, caries, etc.
-glycemic index of foods is crucial: how much sugar in blood
-sugar elevates insulin, changes prostaglandin prod. to "bad"

WHAT TO DO:

1) eat less sweet foods
2) try to avoid refined white sugar
3) never eat anything sweet by itself
4) preferred sweeteners: honey, fructose, molasses, sucanat

5) Anti-proliferative factors

Certain nutrients, like selenium, vitamin K, vitamin E succinate, and the fatty acid EPA, appear to have the ability to slow down the unregulated growth of cancer. Various nutrition factors, including vitamin A, D, folacin, bioflavonoids, and soybeans, have been shown to alter the genetic expression of tumors.

NUTRITION THERAPY IMPROVES OUTCOME IN COMPREHENSIVE CANCER TREATMENT

Finnish oncologists used high doses of nutrients along with chemo and radiation for lung cancer patients. Normally, lung cancer is a "poor prognostic" malignancy with a 1% expected survival at 30 months under normal treatment.. In this study, however, 8 of 18 patients (44%) were still alive 6 years after therapy.[55]

NUTRITION IMPROVES OUTCOME IN MEDICALLY TREATED LUNG CANCER PATIENTS

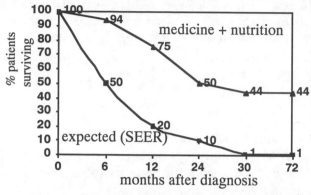

medicine + nutrition

expected (SEER)

% patients surviving

months after diagnosis

STUDY DESIGN:
18 non randomized patients with small cell lung cancer. Therapy: chemo, radiation, & nutrition supplements vs expected (SEER).

"No side effects observed (from nutrients)." "Surviving patients started AOX treatment earlier than those who succumbed." "AOX treatment should start as early as possible in combination with chemotherapy and/or radiation."
Jaakkola, K., et al., Anticancer Research, vol.12, p.599, 1992

Oncologists at West Virginia Medical School randomized 65 patients with transitional cell carcinoma of the bladder into either the "one-per-day" vitamin supplement providing the RDA, or into a group which received the RDA supplement plus 40,000 iu of vitamin A, 100 mg of B-6, 2000 mg of vitamin C, 400 iu of vitamin E, and 90 mg of zinc. At 10 months, tumor recurrence was 80% in the control group (RDA supplement) and 40% in the experimental "megavitamin" group. Five year projected tumor recurrence was 91% for controls and 41% for "megavitamin" patients. Essentially, high dose nutrients cut tumor recurrence in half.[56]

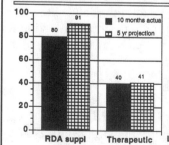

CAN THERAPEUTIC NUTRITION LOWER TUMOR RECURRENCE?

■ 10 months actual
▦ 5 yr projection

65 patients, transitional cell carcinoma of bladder, BCG immun, randomized, double blind, RDA-level suppl 24 of 30 tumor recur, therapeutic suppl (RDA + 40,000 iu A, 100 mg B-6, 2000 mg C, 400 iu E, 90 mg Zn) 14 of 35

Lamm, DL, et al., J. Urol., 151:p.21, Jan.94

In a non-randomized clinical trial, Drs. Hoffer and Pauling instructed patients to follow a reasonable cancer diet (unprocessed food low in fat, dairy, and sugar), coupled with therapeutic doses of vitamins and minerals.[57] All 129 patients in this study received concomitant oncology care. The control group of 31 patients who did not receive nutrition support lived an average of less than 6 months. The group of 98 cancer patients who did receive the diet and supplement program were categorized into 3 groups:

-Poor responders (n=19) or 20% of treated group. Average lifespan of 10 months, or a 75% improvement over the control group.

-Good responders (n=47), who had various cancers, including leukemia, lung, liver, and pancreas; had an average lifespan of 72 months (6 years) or a 1200% improvement in lifespan.

-Good female responders (n=32), with involvement of reproductive areas (breast, cervix, ovary, uterus); had an average lifespan of over 10 years, or a 2100% improvement in lifespan. Many were still alive at the end of the study.

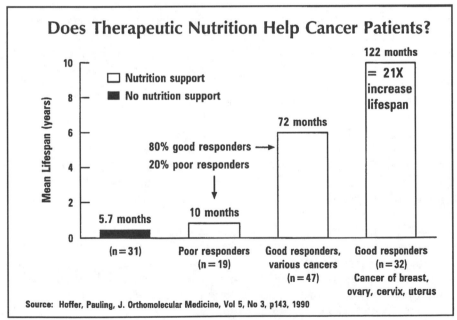

Does Therapeutic Nutrition Help Cancer Patients?

Source: Hoffer, Pauling, J. Orthomolecular Medicine, Vol 5, No 3, p143, 1990

Of the 200 cancer patients studied who experienced "spontaneous regression", 87% made a major change in diet, mostly vegetarian in nature, 55% used some form of detoxification and 65% used nutritional supplements. [58]

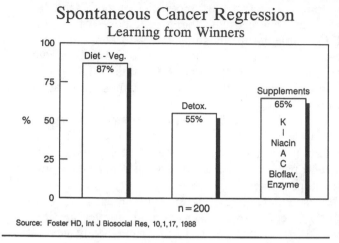

Spontaneous Cancer Regression
Learning from Winners

Source: Foster HD, Int J Biosocial Res, 10,1,17, 1988

Researchers at Tulane University compared survival in patients who used the macrobiotic diet versus patients who continued with their standard Western lifestyle. Of 1467 pancreatic patients who made no changes in diet, 146 (1%) were alive after one year, while 12 of the 23 matched pancreatic patients (52%) consuming macrobiotic foods were still alive after one year.[59] In examining the diet and lifespan of 675 lung cancer patients over the course of 6 years, researchers found that the more vegetables consumed, the longer the lung cancer patient lived.[60]

THE COMPONENTS OF A NUTRITIONAL ONCOLOGY PROGRAM

1) Food. If the gut works and if the patient can consume enough food through the mouth, then this is the primary route for nourishing the patient. The diet for the cancer patient should be high in plant food (grains, legumes, colorful vegetables, some fruit), unprocessed (shop the perimeter of the grocery store), low in salt, fat, and sugar, with adequate protein (1-2 grams/kilogram body weight).

2) Supplements. Additional vitamins, minerals, amino acids, food extracts (i.e. bovine cartilage), conditionally essential nutrients (i.e. fish, flax, and borage oil; Coenzyme Q-10), and botanicals (i.e. echinecea, golden seal, astragalus) can enhance the patient's recuperative powers. ImmunoPower is the most clinically-tested, cost-effective and convenient way to take nutritional supplements.

3) Total parenteral nutrition (TPN) There are many cancer patients who are so malnourished (weight loss of 10% below usual body weight within 1 month period and/or serum albumin below 2.5 mg/dl) that we must interrupt this deterioration with TPN. When the patient cannot or will not eat adequately, TPN can be an invaluable life raft during crucial phases of cancer treatment.

4) Assessment. It is important to determine the patient's general health and nutrient status, which helps the clinician provide patient-specific therapy. Means of assessment include: health history form to detect lifestyle risk factors, physician's examination, anthropometric measurements of height, weight, and percent body fat, calorimeter measurement of basal metabolic needs, and various other laboratory tests.

5) Education. The patient needs a sense of involvement and control in the therapy, which can improve his or her chances for recovery. Just as much as the patient's lifestyle may have contributed to the problem, a pro-active patient can help reverse the underlying causative factors.

6) Research. Those who advance the knowledge base have a responsibility to properly gather data and report their findings to the world.

PATIENT PROFILE: BEAT REFRACTORY COLON CANCER
D.S. is a 45 year old male diagnosed with stage 3 colon cancer in January of 1996 with 3 of 5 lymph nodes positive. He was administered the chemo drug 5FU for 6 months but developed severe toxic reactions. 2 new nodes appeared on his CAT scan in September of 1996, thus he had failed chemotherapy. He began nutrition therapy as sole therapy in January of 1997. His CAT scans showed no malignancy as of April 1997 and again in December 1997. Feels great and praises nutrition.

ENDNOTES

[1]. Meydani, SN, et al, Vitamin supplementation enhances cell-mediated immunity in healthy elderly subjects, Am J Clin Nutr, 52,557-63, 1990
[2]. Enstrom, JE, et al., Vitamin C intake and mortality among a sample of the United States population, Epidem, 3, 3:194-6, 1992
[3]. Bendich, A, et al., Dietary vitamin E requirement for optimum immune response in the rat, J Nutr;116:675-681, 1986
[4]. Meta-analysis of survival in cancer patients using total parenteral nutrition, Ann Intern Med, 110, 9, 735-7, May 1989
[5]. Kaminsky, M. (ed.), Hyperalimentation: a Guide for Clinicians, Marcel Dekker, NY, Oct.1985, p.265
[6]. Dewys, WD, et al., Cachexia and cancer treatment, Amer J Med, 69, 491-5, Oct.1980
[7]. Wilmore, DW, Catabolic illness, strategies for enhancing recovery, N Engl J Med, 1991, 325:10:695-702
[8]. Dreizen, S., et al., Malnutrition in cancer, Postgrad Med, 87, 1, 163-7, Jan.1990
[9]. Lowry, SF, et al., Nutrient restriction in cancer patients, Surg Forum, 28, 143-9, 1977
[10]. Eys, JV, Total parenteral nutrition and response to cytotoxic therapies, Cancer, 43, 2030-7, 1979
[11]. Harvey, KB, et al., Morbidity and mortality in parenterally-nourished cancer patients, Cancer, 43, 2065-9, 1979
[12]. Muller, JM, et al., Nutritional status as a factor in GI cancer morbidity, Lancet, 68-73, Jan.9, 1982
[13]. Abrahamian, V., et al., Ascorbic acid requirements in hospital patients, JPEN, 7, 5, 465-8, 1983
[14]. Anthony, HM, et al., Vitamin C status of lung cancer patients, Brit J Ca, 46, 354-9, 1982
[15]. Cheraskin, E., Scurvy in cancer patients?, J Altern Med, 18-23, Feb.1986
[16]. Hoffman, FA, Micronutrient status of cancer patients, Cancer, 55, 1 sup.1, 295-9, Jan.1, 1985
[17]. Grant, JP, Nutrition, 6, 4, 6S, July 1990 suppl

[18]. Leeb, BF, Clin.Exper.Rheum, 13,459,1995
[19]. Shimpo,K, Am.J.Clin.Nutr.54,1298S,1991
[20]. Jaakkola, K. Anticancer Res., 12, 599, 1992
[21]. Okunieff, P, Am.J.Clin.Nutr.54, 1281S, 1991
[22]. Burns, CP, et al., Nutrition Reviews, vol.48, p.233, June 1990
[23]. Guffy, MM, et al., Cancer Research, vol.44, p.1863, 1984
[24]. Cannizzo, F., et al., Cancer Research, vol.49, p.3961, 1981
[25]. Begin, ME, et al., J.Nat.Cancer Inst., vol.77, p.1053, 1986
[26]. Santamaria, L., et al., Nutrients and Cancer Prevention, p.299, Prasad, KN (eds), Humana Press, 1990
[27]. Seifter, E., et al., J.Nat.Cancer Inst., vol.71, p.409, 1983
[28]. Singal, PK, et al., Mol.Cell.Biochem., vol.84, p.163, 1988
[29]. Singal, PK, et al., Molecular Cellular Biochem., vol.84, p.163, 1988
[30]. Clemens, MR, et al., Am.J.Clin.Nutr., vol.51, p.216, 1990
[31]. Shklar, G., et al., J.Oral Pathol.Med., vol.19, p.60, 1990
[32]. Geetha, A., et al., J.Biosci., vol.14, p.243, 1989
[33]. Geetha, A., et al., Current Science, vol.64, p.318, Mar.1993
[34]. Wang, YM, et al., Molecular Inter Nutr.Cancer, p.369, , Arnott, MS, (eds), Raven Press, NY, 1982
[35]. Krishanamurthi, S., et al., Radiology, vol.99, p.409, 1971
[36]. Taper, HS, et al., Int.J.Cancer, vol.40, p.575, 1987
[37]. Waxman, S., et al., Eur.J.Cancer Clin.Oncol., vol.18, p.685, 1982
[38]. Gold, J., Cancer Treatment Reports, vol.70, p.1433, Dec.1986
[39]. Schmitt-Graff, A., et al, Pathol.Res.Pract., vol.181, p.168, 1986
[40]. Popov, Al, Med.Radiol. Mosk., vol.32, p.42, 1987
[41]. Kjellen, E., et al., Radiother.Oncol., vol.22, p.81, 1991
[42]. Horsman, MR, Radiotherapy Oncology, vol.22, p.79, 1991
[43]. Coudray, C., et al., Basic Res.Cardiol., vol.87, p.173, 1992
[44]. Sundstrom, H., et al., Carcinogenesis, vol.10, p.273, 1989
[45]. Ohkawa, K., et al., Br.J.Cancer, vol.58, p.38, 1988
[46]. Lawson, T., et al.,Chem.Biol.Interactions, vol.45, p.95, 1983
[47]. Milner, JA, et al., Cancer Research, vol.41, p.1652, 1981
[48]. Furitano, G, et al., Drugs Exp.Clin.Res., vol.10, p.107, 1984
[49]. Wood, AW, et al., in PLANT FLAVONOIDS IN BIOLOGY AND MEDICINE, p.197, Cody, V. (eds), Liss, NY, 1986
[50]. Scambia, G., et al., Anticancer Drugs, vol.1, p.45, 1990
[51]. Kim, JH, et al., Cancer Research, vol.44, p.102, Jan.1984
[52]. Kubo, M., et al., Planta Med, vol.58, p.424, 1992
[53]. Bendich, A, Chandra, RK (eds), Micronutrients and Immune Function, New York Academy of Sciences, 1990, p.587
[54]. Rothkopf, M, Fuel utilization in neoplastic disease: implications for the use of nutritional support in cancer patients, Nutrition, supp, 6:4:14-16S, 1990
[55]. Jaakkola, K., et al., Treatment with antioxidant and other nutrients in combination with chemotherapy and irradiation in patients with small-cell lung cancer, Anticancer Res 12,599-606, 1992
[56]. Lamm, DL, et al., Megadose vitamin in bladder cancer: a double-blind clinical trial, J Urol, 151:21-26, 1994
[57]. Hoffer, A, Pauling, L, Hardin Jones biostatistical analysis of mortality data of cancer patients, J Orthomolecular Med, 5:3:143-154, 1990
[58]. Foster, HD, Lifestyle influences on spontaneous cancer regression, Int J Biosoc Res, 10:1:17-20, 1988
[59]. Carter, JP, Macrobiotic diet and cancer survival, J Amer Coll Nutr, 12:3:209-215, 1993
[60]. Goodman, MT, Vegetable consumption in lung cancer longevity, Eur J Ca, 28: 2: 495-499, 1992

Chapter 6

MALNUTRITION AMONG CANCER PATIENTS

"Each patient carries his own doctor inside him. We are at our best when we give the doctor who resides within a chance to go to work." Albert Schweitzer, MD, 1940, Nobel Laureate & medical missionary

Howard Hughes, the multi-billionaire, died of malnutrition. It is hard to believe that there can be malnutrition in this agriculturally abundant nation of ours--but there is. At the time of the Revolutionary War, 96% of Americans farmed while only 4% worked at other trades. Tractors and harvesting combines became part of an agricultural revolution that allowed the 2% of Americans who now farm to feed the rest of us. We grow enough food in this country to feed ourselves, to make half of us overweight, to throw away enough food to feed 50 million people daily, to ship food overseas as a major export, and to store enough food in government surplus bins to feed Americans for a year if all farmers quit today. With so much food available, how can Americans be malnourished?

Malnutrition in typical "healthy" American

average annual consumption of low nutrient foods:

756 doughnuts

60 pounds cakes & cookies

23 gallons ice cream

7 pounds potato chips

22 pounds candy

200 sticks gum

365 servings soda pop

90 pounds fat

134 pounds refined sugar

The answer is: poor food choices. Americans chose their food based upon taste, cost, convenience and psychological gratification--thus ignoring the main reason that we eat, which is to provide our body cells with the raw materials to grow, repair and fuel our bodies. The most commonly eaten foods in America are white bread, coffee and hot dogs. Based upon our food abundance, Americans could be the best nourished nation on record. But we are far from it.

CAUSES OF NUTRIENT DEFICIENCIES:

And there are many reasons for developing malnutrition:

⇒ Don't eat it. Due to poor food choices, loss of appetite, discomfort in the gastro-intestinal region, or consuming nutritionally bankrupt "junk food"; many people just don't get enough nutrients into their stomachs.

⇒ Don't absorb it. Just because you eat it, does not necessarily mean that it will end up in your body. Malabsorption can occur from loss of digestive functions (including low hydrochloric acid or enzyme output), allergy, "leaky gut" or intestinal infections.

⇒ Don't keep it. Increased excretion or loss of nutrients can be due to diarrhea, vomiting or drug interactions.

⇒ Don't get enough. Increased nutrient requirements can be due to fever, disease, alcohol or drug interactions.

MOST POPULAR GROCERY ITEMS IN AMERICA

1. Marlboro cigarettes
2. Coke Classic
3. Pepsi Cola
4. Kraft processed cheese
5. Diet Coke
6. Campbell's soup
7. Budweiser beer
8. Tide detergent
9. Folger's coffee
10. Winston cigarettes

from "1992 Top Ten Almanac"
by Michael Robbins

Anyone who is confused about why we spend so much on medical care with such poor results in cancer treatment might glean some wisdom by reading what sells best in American grocery stores. Overwhelming evidence from both government and independent scientific surveys shows that many Americans are low in their intake of:[1]

-VITAMINS: A, D, E, C, B-6, riboflavin, folacin, pantothenic acid
-MINERALS: calcium, potassium, magnesium, zinc, iron, chromium, selenium; and possibly molybdenum and vanadium. With many common micronutrient deficiencies in the western diet, it makes sense that a major study in Australia found that regular use of vitamin supplements was a protective factor against colon cancer.[2]
-MACRONUTRIENTS: fiber, complex carbohydrates, plant protein, special fatty acids (EPA, GLA, ALA), clean water

Meanwhile, we also eat alarmingly high amounts of: fat, salt, sugar, cholesterol, alcohol, caffeine, food additives and toxins.

This combination of too much of the wrong things along with not enough of the right things has created epidemic proportions of degenerative diseases in this country. The Surgeon General, Department of Health and Human Services, Center for Disease Control, National Academy of Sciences, American Medical Association, American Dietetic Assocation, and most other major public health agencies agree that diet is a major contributor to our most common health problems, including cancer.

Percentage of Americans not meeting 1980 Recommended Dietary Allowances

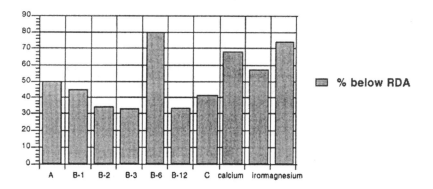

The typical diet of the cancer patient is high in fat while being low in fiber and vegetables--"meat, potatoes, and gravy" is what many of my patients lived on. Data collected by the United States Department of Agriculture from over 11,000 Americans showed that on any given day:

-41 percent did not eat any fruit

-82 percent did not eat cruciferous vegetables

-72 percent did not eat vitamin C-rich fruits or vegetables

-80 percent did not eat vitamin A-rich fruits or vegetables

-84 percent did not eat high fiber grain food, like bread or cereal[3]

The human body is incredibly resilient, which sometimes works to our disadvantage. No one dies on the first cigarette inhaled, or the first drunken evening, or the first decade of unhealthy eating. We misconstrue the fact that we survived this ordeal to mean we can do it forever. Not so. Malnutrition can be blatant, as the starving babies in third world countries. Malnutrition can also be much more subtle.

SEQUENCE OF EVENTS IN DEVELOPING A NUTRIENT DEFICIENCY

⇒ 1) Preliminary. Reduction of tissue stores and depression of urinary excretion.

⇒ 2) Biochemical. Reduction of enzyme activity due to insufficient coenzymes (vitamins). Urinary excretion at minimum levels.

⇒ 3) Physiological. Behavioral effects, such as insomnia or somnolence. Irritability accompanied by loss of appetite and reduce body weight. Modified drug metabolism and reduced immune capabilities.

⇒ 4) Clinical. Classical deficiency syndromes as recognized by the scientific pioneers in the developmental phases of nutrition science.

⇒ 5) Terminal. Severe tissue pathology resulting in imminent death.

It was the Framingham study done by Harvard University that proclaimed: "Our way of life is related to our way of death." Typical hospital food continues or even worsens malnutrition. While many Americans are overfed, the majority are also poorly nourished. If proper nutrition could prevent from 30 to 90% of all cancer, then doesn't it seem foolish to continue feeding the cancer patient the same diet that helped to induce cancer in the first place?

MALNUTRITION AMONG CANCER PATIENTS

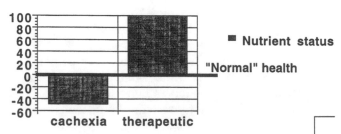

Functions of Nutrition Therapy

Repletion: bring malnourished up to "normal"

Pharmacology/Nutraceutical: therapeutic benefit

From 25-50% of hospital patients suffer from protein calorie malnutrition. Protein calorie malnutrition leads to increases in mortality and surgical failure, with a reduction in immunity, wound healing, cardiac output, response to chemo and radiation therapy, plasma protein synthesis and generally induces weakness and apathy. Many patients are malnourished before entering the hospital and another 10%

become malnourished once in the hospital. Nutrition support, as peripheral parenteral nutrition, has been shown to reduce the length of hospital stay by 30%. Weight loss leads to a decrease in patient survival. Common nutrient deficiencies, as determined by experts at M.D. Anderson Hospital in Houston, include protein calorie, thiamin, riboflavin, niacin, folate and K.

So nutrition therapy has two distinct phases

1) Take the clinically malnourished patient and bring them up to "normal" status.

2) Take the "normal" sub-clinically malnourished person and bring them up to "optimal" functioning. For at least the few nutrients tested thus far, there appears to be a "dose-dependent" response--more than RDA levels of intake provide for more than "normal" immune functions.

Not only is malnutrition common in the "normal" American, but malnutrition is extremely common in the cancer patient. A theory has persisted for decades that one could starve the tumor out of the host. That just ain't so. The tumor is quite resistant to starvation and most studies find more harm to the host than the tumor in either selective or blanket nutrient deficiencies.[4] Pure malnutrition (cachexia) is responsible for at least 22% and up to 67% of all cancer deaths. Up to 80% of all cancer patients have reduced levels of serum albumin, which is a leading indicator of protein and calorie malnutrition.[5] Dietary protein restriction in the cancer patient does not affect the composition or growth rate of the tumor, but does restrict the patient's well being.[6]

A commonly used anti-cancer drug is methotrexate, which interferes with folate (a B vitamin) metabolism. Many scientists guessed that folate in the diet might accelerate cancer growth. Not so. Depriving animals of folate in the diet allowed their tumors to grow anyway.[7] Actually, in starved animals, the tumors grew more rapidly than in fed animals, indicating the parasitic tenacity of cancer in the host.[8] Other studies have found that a low folate environment can trigger "brittle" DNA to fuel cancer metastasis.

There is some evidence that tumors are not as flexible as healthy host tissue in using fuel. A low carbohydrate parenteral formula may have the ability to slow down tumor growth by selectively starving the cancer cells.[9] Overall, the research shows that starvation provokes host wasting while tumor growth continues unabated.[10] Weight loss drastically increases the mortality rate for most types of cancer, while also lowering the response to chemotherapy.[11]

Parenteral feeding improves tolerance to chemotherapeutic agents and immune responses.[12] Of 28 children with advanced malignant disease, 18 received parenteral feeding for 28 days with resultant improvements in weight gain, increased serum albumin, and transferrin and major benefits in immune functions. In comparing cancer patients on TPN versus those trying to nourish themselves by oral intake of food, TPN provided major improvements in calorie, protein, and nutrient intake but did not encourage tumor growth. Malnourished cancer patients who were provided TPN had a mortality rate of 11% while the group without TPN feeding had a 100% mortality rate.[13] Pre-operative TPN in patients undergoing surgery for GI cancer provided general reduction in the incidence of wound infection, pneumonia, major complications and mortality.[14] Patients who were the most malnourished experienced a 33% mortality and 46% morbidity (problems and illness) rate, while those patients who were properly nourished had a 3% mortality rate with an 8% morbidity rate. In 49 patients with lung cancer receiving chemotherapy with or without TPN, complete remission was achieved in 85% of the TPN group versus 59% of the non-TPN group.[15] A TPN formula that was higher in protein, especially branched chain amino acids, was able to provide better nitrogen balance in the 21 adults tested than the conventional 8.5% amino acid TPN formula.[16]

A finely tuned nutrition formula can also nourish the patient while starving tumor cells. Enteral (oral) formulas fortified with arginine, fish oil and RNA have been shown to stimulate the immune system, accelerate wound repair and reduce tumor burden in both animals and humans. Diets with modified amino acid content, low tyrosine (2.4 mg/kg body weight) and low phenylalanine (3.5 mg/kg body weight), were able to elevate natural killer cell activity in 6 of 9 subjects tested.[17]

In 20 adult hospitalized patients on TPN, the mean daily vitamin C needs were 975 mg, which is over 16 times the RDA, with the range being 350-2250 mg.[18] Of the 139 lung cancer patients studied, most tested deficient or scorbutic (clinical vitamin C deficiency).[19] Another study of cancer patients found that 46% tested scorbutic while 76% were below acceptable levels for serum ascorbate.[20] Experts now recommend the value of nutritional supplements, especially in patients who require prolonged TPN support.[21] The Recommended Daily Allowance (RDA) is inadequate for many healthy people and nearly all sick people.

The take-home lesson here is that:

1) at least 20% of Americans are clinically malnourished, with 70% being sub-clinically malnourished (less obvious), and the remaining "chosen few" 10% in good to optimal health.

2) once these malnourished people get sick, the malnutrition oftentimes gets worse through higher nutrient needs and lower intake

3) once at the hospital, malnutrition escalates another notch

4) cancer is one of the more serious wasting diseases known

5) a malnourished cancer patient suffers a reduction in quality and quantity of life, with higher incidences of complications and death

6) the only solution for malnutrition is optimal nutrition

PATIENT PROFILE: STABILIZING MULTIPLE CANCERS

F.J. is a 65 year old male diagnosed in June of 1996 with stage 3 colon cancer. He was given levamisol chemotherapy which produced severe flu-like symptoms. He began nutrition therapy in October of 1996. Doctors and nurses were surprised at how he "sailed through therapy". CAT scans show no colon cancer as of July of 1997. In July of 1997 was given the diagnosis of indolent prostate cancer. He feels greats and works full time. He is very pleased with how nutrition helped him.

ENDNOTES

[1]. Quillin, P., HEALING NUTRIENTS, p.43, Vintage Books, NY, 1989
[2]. Kune, GA, and Kune, S., Nutrition and Cancer, vol.9, p.1, 1987
[3]. Patterson, BH, and Block, G., American Journal of Public Health, vol.78, p.282, Mar.1988
[4]. Axelrod, AE, and Traketelis, AC, Vitamins and Hormones, vol.22, p.591, 1964
[5]. Dreizen, S., et al., Postgraduate Medicine, vol.87, no.1, p.163, Jan.1990
[6]. Lowry, SF, et al., Surgical Forum, vol.28, p.143, 1977
[7]. Nichol, CA, Cancer Research, vol.29, p.2422, 1969
[8]. Norton, JA, et al., Cancer, vol.45, p.2934, 1980
[9]. Dematrakopoulos, GE, and Brennan, MF, Cancer Research, (sup.),vol.42, p.756, Feb.1982
[10]. Goodgame, JT, et al., American Journal of Clinical Nutrition, vol.32, p.2277, 1979
[11]. Dewys, WD, et al., American Journal of Medicine, vol.69, p.491, Oct.1980
[12]. Eys, JV, Cancer, vol.43, p.2030, 1979
[13]. Harvey, KB, et al., Cancer, vol.43, p.2065, 1979
[14]. Muller, JM, et al., Lancet, p.68, Jan.9, 1982
[15]. Valdivieso, M., et al., Cancer Treatment Reports, vol.65, sup.5, p.145, 1981
[16]. Gazzaniga, AB, et al., Archives of Surgery, vol. 123, p.1275, 1988
[17]. Norris, JR, et al., American Journal of Clinical Nutrition, vol.51, p.188, 1990
[18]. Abrahamian, V., et al., Journal of Parenteral and Enteral Nutrition, vol.7, no.5, p.465, 1983
[19]. Anthony, HM, et al., British Journal of Cancer, vol.46, p.354, 1982
[20]. Cheraskin, E., Journal of Alternative Medicine, p.18, Feb.1986
[21]. Hoffman, FA, Cancer, vol.55, 1 sup.1, p.295, Jan.1, 1985

Chapter 7

WHY NUTRITION CAN BEAT CANCER
☆
NUTRIENTS AS BIOLOGICAL RESPONSE MODIFIERS
&
POWER OF NUTRITIONAL SYNERGISM

**"The doctor of the future will give no medicine, but will involve the patient in the proper use of food, fresh air, and exercise."
Thomas Edison, celebrated inventor**

The following is a very brief overview of how nutrients affect the body's ability to recover from cancer. For more detailed information and references, please see the section "OTHER GOOD SOURCES OF INFORMATION ON NUTRITION AND CANCER".

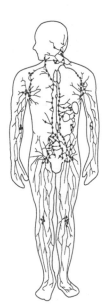

IMMUNE STIMULANTS

A healthy adult body includes around 60 trillion cells, of which nearly a third, or 20 trillion cells are immune factors. Among the primary aspects of the immune system are:

⇒ **Birth place**. The bone marrow generates most immune cells, primarily in the long bones, especially the ribs.

⇒ **Maturation**. Bone immune cells (B-cells) move into the thymus gland for maturation and activation, and are then called "T" cells.

⇒ **Gastro-intestinal tract**. 40% of the immune system surrounds the GI tract as lymph nodes, not only to absorb fat soluble nutrients (like essential fatty acids), and to protect against bacterial translocation (crossing of the intestinal barrier into the bloodstream by disease-causing bacteria) but also to stimulate the production of various immunoglobulins (IgA etc.) A healthy gut is a critical aspect of a healthy immune system.

⇒ **Filtering**. The immune cells move through the lymphatic ducts, not unlike the blood moving through the arteries and veins. Dead immune cells and invaders are filtered out of this "freeway" system in the spleen and lymph nodes.

⇒ **Quantity**. There are many factors that can influence the sheer numbers of immune warriors. Factors that will improve quantities of immune cells are discussed on pages 226 and 249.

⇒ **Quality**. Not all immune cells have the same level of ferocity against an invading tumor cell. Some immune cells become confused about "who to shoot at" and end up creating an autoimmune response (often called an allergic response), which imbalances the immune system and detracts from the critical task of killing cancer cells. Some nutrients provide the immune warriors with a protective coating, like an asbestos suit, so that the immune cell is not destroyed in the process of killing a cancer cell with some "napalm". Some nutrients provide the immune cells with more "napalm" or "bullets" in the form of granulocytes and nitric oxide.

Many nutrition factors affect the ability of the immune system to recognize and destroy cancer cells and invading bacteria.

ALTER GENETIC EXPRESSION OF CANCER

Cancer involves DNA that has "gone mad" or lost its ability to properly replicate and then die at the appropriate time. There are numerous checks and balances in the control of abnormal DNA.

Nutrients, like folate and B-12, help to provide correct duplication of DNA. Nutrients, like vitamin D, help to squelch the growth of abnormal genetic fragments, or episomes. Nutrients, like vitamin A, actually have a receptor site on the DNA, without which cancer is likely to happen. Nutrition factors, like genistein from soy and oligomeric proanthocyanidins from bioflavonoids, can actually help a cancer cell to revert back to a normal healthy cell in the process of cell differentiation.

Your 60 trillion cells possess a thread of material that holds all the "blue print" information to make another you. This thread, called DNA, is truly the essence of life itself. DNA looks like a spiral staircase that is so long and flexible, it begins to wind around and wrap into "X" shapes. Stored on 23 pairs of chromosomes are 50,000 to 100,000 genes, collectively called the human genome. If you could unravel and place end to end the DNA in one adult body, it would reach to the moon and back--8,000 times!![1]

This long spiral staircase is constantly under attack. Dr. Bruce Ames and his colleagues at the University of California at Berkeley have shown that each cell in the human body takes an average of 1,000 to 10,000 "hits" or DNA breaks each day. Imagine sitting on your roof in the middle of a hurricane while shingles are constantly being ripped off and you have to continuously repair this damage. Make a mistake, and cancer could be the consequence. Geneticists have estimated that each DNA molecule contains about the same amount of information as would be typed on 500,000 pages of manuscript. Imagine if trillions of times daily, you had to type a half million pages error-free. A mistake can lead to cancer.

Fortunately, the body is well prepared to keep the inevitable DNA errors from turning into cancer. DNA polymerase is a repair enzyme system that moves along this spiral staircase, like a railcar on railroad tracks, finding and fixing broken rail ties, or base pairs. This crucial repair system is fueled by folacin, zinc and other nutrients. A low intake of folacin increases the likelihood that cancer will become metastatic. One of the earlier drugs used against cancer, methotrexate, is a folacin inhibitor that limits access new cell growth. Giving folacin to a patient on methotrexate does not inhibit the effectiveness of the drug, since it is folinic acid, a more metabolically active form of folacin, that is required to rescue a patient from methotrexate therapy.

Mechanical injury, especially when repeated, means that the repair process has accelerated beyond the normal hurricane into something much wilder. During these vulnerable phases, the body needs to be free of contaminants and have an adequate supply of growth nutrients--lest cancer surface.

I worked with a young patient who developed a cancerous growth in the exact same area where he had experienced a mechanical injury. This 32 year old male had been in a snow skiing accident, in which he fell and accidentally stabbed himself in his thigh muscle with his ski pole. He was a smoker and ate a typical American diet, which is low in zinc and folacin. His wound seemed to heal well within the expected few months; then one year later he developed a massive metastatic sarcoma exactly where he had injured himself and died soon thereafter. The injury created the stress, the tobacco provided generous amounts of a carcinogen to interrupt the repair process and his typical American diet lacked the growth nutrients required for accurate DNA synthesis. Another patient that I worked with was a typical 20 year old college male, who had crowded dentition and his wisdom teeth constantly gnashing at the insides of his cheeks. Which is where he developed cancer. He started a wise nutrition program and used restrained medical therapies and survived his brush with cancer.

This continuous repair process of DNA is like a high speed bullet train that is easily derailed. Cancer is the resulting train wreck. We need to get these DNA repair mechanisms working properly in the cancer patient.

CELL MEMBRANE DYNAMICS

Most of the 60 trillion cells in an adult body are like "water balloons" floating in an ocean of extracellular fluid, in the sense that they are full of fluid and have a barrier that keeps them intact. This barrier, or cell membrane, has a 3 layered look with water soluble molecules on the outside and fatty tails toward the inside. This lipid bilayer gives rise to the ability of the cell to accept the proper nutrients along with oxygen, eliminate the hazardous toxins produced within the cell, and reject the circulating toxins and cancer cells that try to penetrate the cell membrane barrier. A healthy cell membrane is built from the essential fatty acids from fish oil (eicosapentaenoic acid), flax oil (alpha linolenic acid), evening primrose oil (gamma linolenic acid), lecithin (phosphatidylcholine), cholesterol and other nutrients. A defective cell membrane is built from hydrogenated fats (trans fatty acids), too much saturated fats, has been "tanned" by exposure to excess sugar floating through the bloodstream and various nutritional deficiencies. A healthy cell membrane allows the cell to "breathe" aerobically and expel waste products. Otherwise, cancer can be the result.

The ratio of minerals in the "electrolyte soup" that drives cell membrane potential also influences cell membrane dynamics. The ratio of sodium to potassium to calcium to magnesium is crucial. We also probably have a need for the ultra-trace minerals that are found in the ocean at about 1% concentration, need to be in our diet, but are missing in standard commercial salt.

K/Na Ratio Probably Affects Tumor Growth

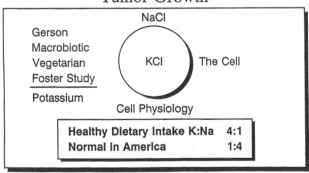

Source: Thompson S, American Institute Cancer Research, unpublished, Fine B, IBID

Potassium is found primarily in unprocessed plant food, like vegetables, fruit, whole grains and legumes. There is some sodium in all foods, with higher concentrations in animal foods, and much more of it in processed foods. Americans eat 10 times the sodium that our ancestors consumed. An ideal ratio of sodium to potassium would be 1 to 4, but ours is 4 to 1. By drastically changing this ratio, we have changed the "electrolyte soup" that bathes all cells and creates the electrical battery of life. This electrical charge influences the gatekeeper. High sodium diets increase both cancer incidence and metastasis.

DETOXIFICATION

America's increasing incidence of cancer has closely paralleled our increasing exposure to cancer-causing substances in our environment. We consume toxins:

⇒ voluntarily through alcohol, drugs, and tobacco
⇒ involuntarily through industrial and agricultural pollutants that end up in the food, air and water supply
⇒ internally (endogenously) produced toxins from energy metabolism in the cell and bacterial fermentation in the gut.

We detoxify by eliminating waste products through urine, feces, sweat and liver detoxification. Nutrients assist each of these processes. The liver is a chemical detoxification "factory" in its ability to bind toxins (conjugate), split toxins (hydrolyze), and neutralize toxins through Phase I and Phase II enzyme pathways. These pathways are augmented with nutrients, like garlic, calcium D-glucarate, selenium, vitamin E, and glutathione.

In many people, cancer cannot be cured without the assistance of an aggressive detoxification program.

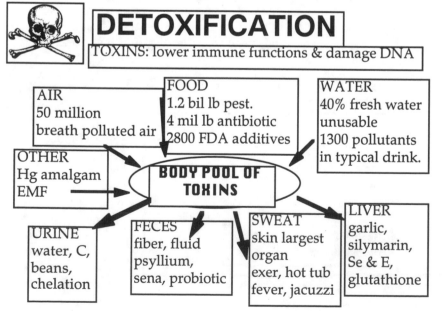

DETOXIFICATION
TOXINS: lower immune functions & damage DNA

| AIR 50 million breath polluted air | FOOD 1.2 bil lb pest. 4 mil lb antibiotic 2800 FDA additives | WATER 40% fresh water unusable 1300 pollutants in typical drink. |

OTHER
Hg amalgam
EMF

BODY POOL OF TOXINS

| URINE water, C, beans, chelation | FECES fiber, fluid psyllium, sena, probiotic | SWEAT skin largest organ exer, hot tub fever, jacuzzi | LIVER garlic, silymarin, Se & E, glutathione |

ACID & BASE BALANCE

Humans have a very specific need to maintain a proper pH balance. pH refers to "potential hydrogens" and is measured on a scale from 1 (very acidic) to 7 (neutral) to 14 (very alkaline, base). Foods that encourage a healthy pH are vegetables and other plant foods. Foods that encourage an unhealthy pH include beef, dairy and sugar. Proper breathing, exercise, and adequate water intake further improve pH to discourage cancer growth. Cancer cells give off lactic acid in anaerobic fermentation of foodstuffs. This Cori cycle generates a lower pH which then further compromises the cells ability to fight off the cancer. Acid foods (like tomatoes, citrus, and vinegar) help to create an "alkaline tide" which helps to discourage cancer and fungus growth.

You can tell if you have an abnormal pH by some of the following characteristics: your jewelry, rings and metal watch bands turn color (oxidize) quickly; insects like mosquitos are not attracted to you; you frequently develop yeast infections like toenail fungus. Acid/base is best tested by having your blood checked for pH in the veins. A quicker and cheaper method of testing your pH is using pH litmus paper (such as Baxter Diagnostics pH Indicator Strips) from your pharmacy store. If your saliva is much lower than the comparison color charts, then you may need to heed this section closely. If your pH is significantly below (which is common) or above normal pH values, then your "host defense mechanisms are compromised and cannot fight off the cancer.

A diet rich in beef, milk and sugar plus poor breathing habits and no exercise will create a disease-prone pH. Proper deep diaphragm breathing, exercise, lots of clean water and a diet including more vegetables and legumes will help to rectify most pH problems. Some people who are supposed to be omnivores (including meat) will become ardent vegetarians and end up with abnormally high pH. These people may need meat; like lean chicken, fish and turkey; to bring their pH value down to normal healthy levels.

CELLULAR COMMUNICATION

Cells communicate between each other, a.k.a. intercellular or "gap junction" communication, through ions that float in and out of pores in the cell membranes. Vitamin A and beta-carotene are among the crucial nutrients that encourage this "telegraph" system that keeps cells healthy and non-cancerous. There is also evidence that communication exists within a cell (intracellular communication) through such nutrients as the glycoproteins in aloe vera.

MOST ALKALINE → NEUTRAL → MOST ACIDIC

Category	MOST ALKALINE				NEUTRAL			MOST ACIDIC
THERAPEUTICS	salt	mineral water	sake	algae	aspartame	vanilla	psychotropics	cocoa
SWEETENERS		molasses	rice syrup	sucanat	honey	tapioca	saccharin	sugar
OTHERS		sea salt	green tea		maple syrup	black tea	antibiotics	fried foods
VINEGAR		soy sauce	apple cider	umeboshi	rice	balsamic	white	
DAIRY				human milk	cream/yogurt	milk/aged chez	casein, soymilk	ice cream, chez
MEAT, EGGS					eggs, organs	lamb	pork, veal	beef
FOWL, GAME					duck, venison	goose, turkey	chicken	pheasant
FISH, & SHELL					fish, crab	shell f., mollusk	eel, crustacea	lobster, oyster
NUTS, OILS	pumpkin, lotus	poppy, chestnut	primrose, sprout, sesame	avocado, flax, coconut	grape, sunflower, pine	almond, cashew	pistachio, chestnut, lard	cottonseed, hazel, walnut
GRAINS				oats, quinoa, wild rice	millet, kasha, amaranth	buckwheat, wheat, spelt	maize, corn, rye	barley
BEANS, VEGETABLES	lentil, yam, sea vegetables, onion	parsnip, garlic, kale, endive	potato, bell pepper, mushroom, cauliflower, egg plant	beet, brussel sprout, chive, okra, turnip gr.	spinach, fava, kidney, string bean	tofu, pinto, white, navy beans	green pea, peanut, carrot, garbanzo	soybean, carob
FRUIT	nectarine, watermelon, raspberry, tangerine	citrus, cantaloupe, honeydew, mango	pear, pineapple, apple, blackberry, cherry, peach, papaya	apricot, banana, blueberry, grape, strawberry	guava, pineapple, figs, persimmon, date	plum, prune, tomato	cranberry, pomegranate	

PROSTAGLANDIN SYNTHESIS

Prostaglandins are hormone-like substances that are produced regionally within most cells and have an incredible influence on the functions that help us to beat cancer. Essentially, when our intake of simple carbohydrates (like sugar and easily digested starches) is high and our intake of fish oil and primrose oil is low, then emergency prostaglandins (PGE-2) are generated to augment cancer growth.

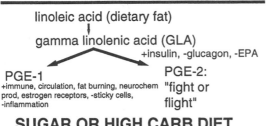

PROSTAGLANDINS
the "Napoleans" of the body

linoleic acid (dietary fat)

gamma linolenic acid (GLA)

+insulin, -glucagon, -EPA

PGE-1
+immune, circulation, fat burning, neurochem
prod, estrogen receptors, -sticky cells,
-inflammation

PGE-2:
"fight or
flight"

SUGAR OR HIGH CARB DIET
COUNTERPRODUCTIVE

When our blood sugar levels are kept low (around 60 to 90 milligrams per deciliter) through a proper diet low in sweets, and when we eat enough fish oil and evening primrose oil, then the favorable prostaglandin of PGE-1 will:
⇒ stimulate immune activity
⇒ improve circulation through vasodilation
⇒ reduce the stickiness of cells which inhibits metastasis through platelet aggregation
⇒ help to produce estrogen receptors to dull the potential damage from circulating estrogen
⇒ and much more.

Only a concerted effort of dietary regulation and proper supplements can produce healthy prostaglandins to suppress cancer.

STEROID HORMONE ACTIVITY

Certain cancers that are very dependent on testosterone (prostate cancer) or estrogen (for breast, ovarian and cervical cancer). These hormones are not only produced by the gonads (testosterone) and ovaries (estrogen), but also produced by fat cells. Meaning that, the more body fat a person has, the higher the likelihood of generating more tumor-enhancing hormones. A calculated program to gradually reduce excess body fat is crucial in the treatment of hormone dependent tumors.

Also, a number of nutrition factors help to reduce the tumor-enhancing capacity of hormones, including fish oil, evening primrose oil, cruciferous sulforphane, calcium D-glucarate, and others.

BIOENERGETICS: AEROBIC VS ANAEROBIC

Cancer cells are anaerobic sugar feeders, while healthy cells are aerobic (oxygen-requiring) cells that can burn sugar, protein or fats. Professor Otto Warburg was awarded the Nobel prize in medicine in 1931 for his work in cell respiration and received a second Nobel prize in 1944 for his work in electron transfer. This brilliant researcher spent considerable time investigating the differences between healthy cells and cancer cells: "...the prime cause of cancer is the replacement of the respiration of oxygen in normal body cells by a fermentation of sugar."[2]

The more dense and anaerobic the mass of cancer, the more resistant it is to treatment, medical or otherwise. In order to beat cancer, one must make the body a well oxygenated aerobic organism. Proper breathing and exercise are crucial to generate an aerobic environment.

Also, there are nutrients, including Coenzyme Q-10, chromium GTF (glucose tolerance factor), thiamin, niacin, riboflavin, lipoic acid and others that enhance aerobic metabolism.

BACTERIA IN THE GUT

According to Nobel prize winner, Eli Metchnikoff, PhD, "death begins in the colon". There are more bacteria in our lower intestines than cells in our body. The bacteria in our gut either enhance or detract from immune functions and general health. Healthy bacteria (probiotics) help to:

◊ produce essential vitamins (like K and biotin)
◊ generate a critical immune factor IgA
◊ protect the gut mucosa against translocation of bacteria into the bloodstream
◊ improve the pH in the colon
◊ aid in digestion and absorption of essential nutrients
◊ reduce the carcinogenic by-products that are produced in the colon from putrefaction of fecal matter.

Healthy bacteria are encouraged by a diet low in sugar and meat and high in vegetables, whole grains, and active-cultured foods (like yogurt or soy tempeh). High fiber and fluid intake help this crucial balance of friendly bacteria. Fructo-oligosaccharides are special starches found in whole grains and onions (and ImmunoPower) that help to nourish the friendly bacteria.

PRO-OXIDANTS VS ANTIOXIDANTS

Our greatest enemy is oxygen, since it generates free radicals (a.k.a. pro-oxidants, reactive oxygen species) which can damage the delicate DNA, immune factors, and cell membranes. Yet our greatest ally is a well-oxygenated system. How, then, to balance this seeming paradox? A well-oxygenated (aerobic) system along with optimal protection from free radicals via antioxidants is the ideal combination for good health. Free radicals are an inherent aspect of generating energy (ATP) from foodstuff in the mitochondria. Free radicals are the weapons used by immune cells to kill cancer cells. So free radicals cannot be eliminated in the human body, but must be controlled or they turn into "forest fires" that devastate the cells.

A strategic blend of antioxidants can provide broad spectrum protection against damage from chemotherapy, radiation therapy, protecting the immune cells from their own poisons, and improving vigor in the cancer patient undergoing treatment. Vitamins C, E, beta-carotene, selenium, lipoic acid, lycopene, glutathione, tocotrienols, quercetin, Coenzyme Q, oligomeric proanthocyanidins from grape seed, curcumin, Ginkgo biloba, and green tea are in the ImmunoPower to provide complete protection from an entire hierarchy of antioxidants.

ANTI-PROLIFERATIVE AGENTS

While most nutritionists agree on the importance of growth (proliferative) nutrients, few nutritionists respect the importance for anti-proliferative nutrients. For every force in the body, there must be an opposing force to regulate that mechanism. There are agents that cause fluid loss from the kidneys (diuresis) and other agents that stem this fluid loss when it is excessive (anti-diuretic hormone). Just as there is a need for nutrients to augment growth, there is a need for nutrients to control excessive growth and shut down the process.

Selenium, fish oil, garlic, Cat's claw, Maitake D-fraction, vitamin E succinate, vitamin K, quercetin, genistein, and bovine cartilage all may assist the cancer patient in this manner.

ALTER TUMOR PROTECTIVE MECHANISMS

The tumor is a well-adapted parasite, which hides from the body's immune system by generating a "stealth" coating of human chorionic gonadotropin (HCG) which provides regional immune suppression. The cancer pretends to be a fetus, which then stops the attack by the immune system. High doses of niacin (B-3) as inositol hexanicotinate work to dissolve this "stealth" coating of the tumor. Additionally, digestive enzymes of protease can be beneficial in augmenting this dissolving of the tumor's protective coating.

THE POWER OF NUTRITIONAL SYNERGISM

Synergism: the action of two or more substances to achieve an effect of which each is individually incapable

There are two primary lessons to be learned in nutritional synergism:

1) Enhanced effects.

⇒ **Nutrient & nutrient combinations** augment each other to achieve greater healing capacity. Either vitamin C or essential fatty acids were able to inhibit the growth of melanoma in culture, yet when combined their anti-cancer activity was much stronger.[3]

⇒ **Nutrient & medicine combinations** help to protect the patient while selectively destroying the cancer cells. Maitake D-fraction inhibited tumor growth by 80% while the drug Mitomycin C inhibited tumor growth by 45%. Yet when both were given together, but at half the dosage for each, tumor inhibition was 98%.

2) Lower doses are required when nutrients are used synergistically. In animals with implanted tumors, vitamin C and B-12 together provided for significant tumor regression and 50% survival of the treated group, while all of the animals not receiving C and B-12 died by the 19th day.[4]   C and B-12 seemed to form a cobalt-ascorbate compound that selectively shut down tumor growth. When vitamin C and K were added to cancer cells in culture, the dosage required to kill cancer cells dropped by 98% compared to the dosage required by either of these vitamins alone.[5] Combining vitamins C and K-3 against cultured human breast cancer cells allowed for inhibition of the cancer growth at doses 90-98% less than what was required if only one of these vitamins was used against the cancer.[6]

"No [nutrient] is an island, entire of itself; every [nutrient] is a piece of the continent, a part of the main." paraphrasing John Donne

Listening to the rapture of a symphonic orchestra, I was impressed with the complex synergistic nature of most aspects of our lives. No one and nothing operates in isolation. Both 20th century research and our multi-billion dollar pharmaceutical-based medical system are rooted in the concept of using a single agent to treat a single symptom. Unfortunately, life is much more complicated than that.

NEGATIVE SYNERGISM OF TOXINS

We know that barbiturates have a certain toxicity on the liver, which is synergistically enhanced when alcohol is consumed at the same time. We know that tobacco brings a major risk for lung cancer, as does asbestos exposure, yet when a person is exposed to both there is a 500% greater risk for lung cancer than what would have been expected by adding the two risks (1+1=2). Scientists recently found that pesticides amplify one another's toxicity by 500-1000 fold.[7] Thus, 1+1=500. This discovery of synergistic toxicity presents the chilling possibility that the 1.2 billion pounds of pesticides sprayed on our domestic food supply may not be as safe as we once thought.

In 1976, a study examined animals that were fed 2% of their diet as either red dye, sodium cyclamate or an emulsifier--all approved at the time by the Food and Drug Administration. Animals fed one food additive showed no harmful effects. Animals fed two of the food additives exhibited balding scruffy fur, diarrhea, and retarded weight gain. Animals fed all three additives all died within 2 weeks.[8] The take-home lesson is that poisons probably amplify each other's toxicity in logarithmic fashion. Given the cavalier spirit with which Americans have nonchalantly discarded and intentionally added toxins to our air, food and water supply; synergistic toxicity gives me an uneasy feeling about the future health of our nation.

POSITIVE SYNERGISM OF NUTRIENTS

While the prospects of synergistic toxicity are daunting, the prospects of synergistic nutritional healing may be the key to solving many of our health problems. Perusing any biochemistry textbook we find an abundance of synergistic nutritional relationships: calcium with magnesium with potassium with sodium; vitamin E with selenium; polyunsaturated fats with vitamin E; protein with B-6; and so on.

Antioxidants have surfaced as the "fire extinguishers" that minimize the cellular damage from reactive oxygen species, or free radicals. Yet, these antioxidants work in a hierarchy, not unlike a game of "hot potato", trying to pass along the unpaired electron until the energy dissipates. In this hierarchy, vitamin C recharges vitamin E. Biologists find this complex hierarchy of antioxidants consists of 20,000 bioflavonoids; 800 carotenoids; known essential vitamins, like C and E; conditionally essential vitamins, like lipoic acid and coenzyme Q; and endogenously synthesized antioxidants like superoxide dismutase (SOD) and glutathione peroxidase (GSH-Px). The possible combinations and permutations of antioxidants in the human body makes the combinations in the Rubik's cube look like mere child's play. When these antioxidants are all in their proper place in optimal amounts, we have a relatively impenetrable barrier against oxidative damage. Researching any one of these nutrients in isolation is overly simplistic and doomed to misleading results.

```
┌────────────────────────────────────────────────┐
│         BETA-CAROTENE CAUSES                     │
│            LUNG CANCER?                           │
│  YES                 NO                           │
│  1994 Finnish study  Over 200 epidemiology       │
│  29,000 smokers      studies show                │
│  beta 5-8 yrs        fruits & veg lower risk      │
│  1996 CARET study    11 studies show beta         │
│  18,000 smoker/      protective                   │
│    asbestos          against lung ca              │
│  30 mg beta 25,000 A 8+ studies show beta reverses│
│  NO BENEFIT          premalignant lesions         │
│  1995 Phys Health    3 studies show beta improves │
│    Study             human cancer outcome         │
│  22,000 MDs          4 animal studies show        │
│  50 mg beta 12 yr    beta cures ca                │
│                      As sole nutrient, AOX        │
│                      can be PROX                   │
│                                                   │
│  RECOMMENDATIONS: Eat a diet rich in green &      │
│  orange fruits & veg.                             │
│  Take beta, mixed carot, other AOX. Don't smoke.  │
└────────────────────────────────────────────────┘
```

The National Cancer Institute reported in 1994 that beta-carotene supplements provided a slightly elevated risk for lung cancer in heavy smokers.[9] Yet other prominent researchers in nutrition and cancer have published papers showing that antioxidants, like beta-carotene, can become pro-oxidants in the wrong biochemical environment, such as the combat zone of free radicals generated by heavy tobacco use.[10] At the International Conference on Nutrition and Cancer, sponsored by the University of California at Irvine, held in July 1997, there were several watershed presentations showing that one nutrient alone may be ineffective or counterproductive while a host of compatible nutrients in the proper ratio can be extremely effective at slowing or reversing cancer.

NUTRITIONAL SYNERGISM AGAINST CANCER

While vitamin C or K alone had mild anti-neoplastic activity against cancer cells in culture, when combined together these nutrients showed improved tumor cell destruction at 10 to 50 times lower dosages.[11] Other scientists found that vitamins C and B-12 have a synergistic action at slowing cancer growth in animal studies.[12] Apparently, the cobalt from the B-12 attaches to the ascorbic acid to form cobalt ascorbate, a selective toxin against cancer cells.

In another animal study, researchers found that all DMBA-exposed animals died. When provided a single chemopreventive nutrient (either selenium, magnesium, vitamin C, or vitamin A), cancer incidence after DMBA exposure was cut in half. When two nutrients were combined, the cancer incidence was cut by 70%; with 3 chemopreventive nutrients the cancer incidence was 80%, and with 4 nutrients the cancer incidence was cut by 88%.[13]

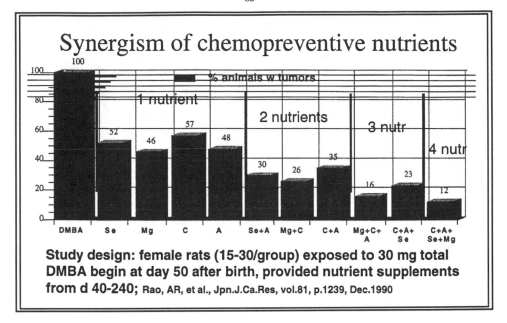

Study design: female rats (15-30/group) exposed to 30 mg total DMBA begin at day 50 after birth, provided nutrient supplements from d 40-240; Rao, AR, et al., Jpn.J.Ca.Res, vol.81, p.1239, Dec.1990

Lamm and colleagues found that a multi-nutrient packet of vitamins A, E, C, B-6 and the mineral zinc cut cancer recurrence more than half in bladder cancer patients treated with BCG.[14] A group of Finnish oncologists treated 18 non-randomized lung cancer patients with chemotherapy, radiation and a collection of nutrition factors. The anticipated outcome in this group of poor prognostic patients is 1% survival at 30 months after diagnosis. In these nutritionally supported lung cancer patients, 44% were still alive 6 years (72 months) after diagnosis with half of these surviving patients in remission.[15] Something in multi-nutrient synergism had provided a major boost over the anticipated outcome in these patients.

One of the brightest nutritional physicians of the 20th century, Abram Hoffer, MD, PhD and his colleague, twice Nobel laureate, Linus Pauling, PhD, tracked 129 human cancer patients for over 11 years. Of the 31 patients who received only medical intervention for their cancer, the average lifespan was about 6 months. Of the remaining 98 patients who received a combination of medical and nutritional therapies, the average lifespan was about 6 years, a 1200% increase in lifespan, with poor responders (20%) somewhat offsetting exceptional responders (33%).[16]

EASY SCIENCE OR REALISTIC SCIENCE?

Our bodies are composed of around 60 trillion cells, working in synergistic unison. While our textbooks speak of around 50 essential nutrients for the human body, the number is probably much higher if the endpoint were "thriving" versus the Recommended Dietary Allowance goal of "surviving". Those nutrients work in synergism, not isolation. While mono-nutrient studies are easier to get funded, easier to statistically interpret, and more likely to lead to some drug patent application; these projects fail miserably at appreciating the grandiose complexities of the human body. Nutritional synergism is a biological law that we can either ignore, or capitalize on to improve outcome in a variety of disease states.

PATIENT PROFILE: SLOWS PROSTATE CANCER

H.E. is a 74 year old male diagnosed in February of 1996 with advanced prostate cancer, with Gleason's scale of 8 (10 is worst). Upon exploratory surgery, 1 lymph node was removed. Other lymph involvement was significant and non-resectable. His physician expected a rapid spread of malignancy with no therapy available to slow tumor growth. His PSA was 25 at that time. He began nutrition therapy in July of 1996 along with hormone ablation injections. His PSA dropped to 0.9. He quit hormone shots October 1996 due to drastic side effects. His PSA rose to 6.0. After orchiectomy on April 1997, his PSA dropped to 0.4. He works full time, up to 14 hours per day and hikes 15 miles per weekend because he runs a retreat in the Rocky Mountains. His PSA has been below 1.0 for 6 months. He has no pain and good energy. He is very pleased with the value of nutrition therapy.

ENDNOTES

[1]. Naisbitt, J., et al., MEGATRENDS 2000, p.257, Morrow, NY, 1990
[2]. Levine, SA, et al., ANTIOXIDANT ADAPTATION, p.209, Biocurrents, San Leandro, CA 1986
[3]. Gardiner, N, et al., Pros.Leuk., vol.34, p.119, 1988
[4]. Poydock, ME, Am.J.Clin.Nutr., vol.54, p.1261S, 1991
[5]. Noto, V., et al., Cancer, vol.63, p.901, 1989
[6]. Noto, V., et al., Cancer, vol.63, p.901, 1989
[7]. Arnold. SF, et al., Science, vol.272, p.1489, 1996
[8]. Ershoff, BH, Journal of Food Science, vol.41, p.949, 1976
[9]. Alpha tocopherol beta-carotene cancer prevention study group, New England Journal of Medicine, vol.330, p.1029, 1994
[10]. Schwartz, JL, Journal of Nutrition, vol.126, 4 suppl, p.1221S, 1996
[11]. Noto, V., et al., Cancer, vol.63, p.901, 1989
[12]. Poydock, ME, American Journal of Clinical Nutrition, vol.54, p.12661S, 1991
[13]. Rao, AR, et al., Japanese Journal Cancer Research, vol.81, p.1239, Dec.1990
[14]. Lamm, DL, et al., Journal of Urology, vol.151, p.21, Jan.1994
[15]. Jaakkola, K., et al., Anticancer Research, vol.12, p.599, 1992
[16]. Hoffer, A., et al., Journal Orthomolecular Medicine, vol.5, no.3, p.143, 1990

Chapter 8
by Noreen Quillin & Patrick Quillin
FOOD: NUTRITIOUS & DELICIOUS

"Let thy food be your medicine and your medicine be your food." Hippocrates, father of modern medicine, 400 B.C.

Nutrition and health. It makes so much sense: "you are what you eat." Veterinarians know the irreplacable link between nutrient intake and health. Actually, most of our pets eat better than most Americans. Your dog or cat probably gets a balanced formula of protein, carbohydrate, fat, fiber, vitamins and minerals. Yet, most of us eat for taste, cost, and convenience. The most commonly eaten food in America is heavily refined and nutritionally

bankrupt white flour. Meanwhile, our livestock eat the more nutritious wheat germ and bran that we discard. When our crops are not doing well, we examine the soil for nutrients, fluid and pH content. Our gardens prosper when we water, fertilize, and add a little broad spectrum mineral supplement, such as Miracle Gro.

A sign posted near the junk food vending machines in a major city zoo warns: "Do not feed this food to the animals or they may get sick and die." Think about it. The food that might kill a 400 pound ape is okay for a 40 pound child who is biologically very similar? If our gardens, field crops, pets, exotic zoo creatures and every other form of life on earth are all heavily dependent on their diet for health, then what makes us think that humans have transcended this dependence?

FOOD

Food is a rich tapestry of various chemicals. For some advanced cancer patients, TPN is often the only route which can provide adequate nutrient intake. However, for other patients, food can be an integral part of their recovery. Food contains anti-cancer agents that we are only beginning to understand. One third of all prescription drugs in America originated as plant products. It is food that provides macronutrients, like carbohydrate, fat and protein, that drive extremely influential hormones and prostaglandins in your body. It is food that establishes your pH balance and electrolyte "soup" that bathes every cell in your body. While supplements are valuable, they cannot replace the fundamental importance of a wholesome diet.

This chapter can make or break your cancer-fighting program. The food discussed in this chapter has been fine tuned over the years to be tasty, nutritious, inexpensive and easy to prepare. Our eating habits are all acquired. We base our current diet on what mother cooked when we were younger; what our society, ethnic and religious groups prefer; what is advertised in print and electronic media, and what is available in the local grocery store. People in the Phillipines or the Amazon are born with structurally identical taste buds to Americans, yet they eat entirely different foods.

It takes about 3 weeks to acquire new eating habits. Try this program for 3 weeks, at which time it will become easier to stay with and you may just find that the nutrient-depleted junk food of yesterday really doesn't satisfy your taste buds like the following whole foods outlined by Noreen Quillin.

TRUE CONFESSIONS

Patrick Quillin has not always eaten as he does now. I now talk the talk and walk the walk. But I was raised in middle America, with roast beef, potatoes and gravy every Sunday afternoon; Captain Crunch for breakfast and a soda pop if you were good. White bread and bologna were the standard fare at home. My parents provided what they felt were lavish and well balanced meals to the best of their knowledge, as millions of other American families.

I remember one semester in college while taking 19 units, 3 labs and working part time, I had no spare time to cook or even eat, so I kept a large box of Twinkies in the back of my van to provide "sustenance" when needed. For many months those Twinkies baked in the hot southern California sun and were always as fresh as the day they were bought. I began to question the shelf life of this food: "If bacteria is not interested in this food, then what makes me think that my body cells are interested in it!!"

At that turning point in my life, my lovely and talented wife Noreen began exploring alternative cooking styles. For the past 8 years, Noreen has taught cooking classes to cancer patients. What you have in this chapter is a condensed and extremely practical approach to making your anti-cancer diet practical and tasty. Bon appetit!

RATING YOUR FOODS

Based on "risk versus benefit" and "nutrient density" (i.e. vitamins, minerals, fiber, & protein per 100 calories) the following foods have been judged from "best" to "worst" for the average healthy adult. Eat foods high on the chart.

BEST

oranges	beet greens	brussel sprouts	parsley	garlic	barley	bass
limes	cauliflower	dandelion	greens	cabbage	green peppers	wheat
halibut	tangerine	tomato	chard	endive	carrots	oats
sole	banana	asparagus	pumpkin	sprouts	black eyed	whole grain
cod	strawberries	low fat yogurt	winter squash	kale	peas	bread
haddock	cantaloupe	nonfat milk	sweet potatoes	pinto beans	wheat germ	millet
octopus	guava	buttermilk	turnip greens	soybeans	brewer's yeast	amaranth
apricot	spinach	garbanzo	brown rice	spirulina	papaya	onions
beans	rye	navy beans				

GOOD

cherries	low fat milk	lettuce	low fat beef,	trout	ginger	blueberries
low fat	peas	tuna	pork, veal,	chicory	grapes	parmesan
cheese	lima beans	swordfish	lamb	cinnamon	honeydew	potatoes
corn	clams	turkey	melon	radishes	popcorn	oysters
chicken	watermelon	zucchini	grits	abalone	kidney	pineapple
celery	tortilla	lobster	heart	apple	beets	green tea
shrimp	eggs	pear	hot peppers	salmon	liver	vinegar

FAIR

prunes	walnuts	homemade pizza &	raisins	vegetable juice
whole milk	peanuts	whole wheat crust	dates	sesame seeds
high fat beef,	homemade low	most cheeses	duck	almonds
pork, veal	fat granola	plums	rhubarb	
whole wheat &	pumpkin seeds	sunflower seeds	fruit juice	
fresh fruit pie	peanut butter	dried fruit		

POOR

molasses	ice cream	white rice	honey	soy, corn, olive,
commercial pizza	sweetened	commercial granola	crackers	safflower, sunflower,
canned fruit	condensed milk	pancakes	avocado	cottonseed oils
waffles	white flour	creamed vegetables	white noodles	

BAD

sausage	sugar	commercial pies	cake	sugared breakfast
hotdog	wine	corn chips	syrup	cereals
bacon	beer	gelatin desserts	butter	salami
tea	mayonnaise	coconut	coffee	ketchup
vinegar &	diet soft	spices	bologna	
oil salad	drinks			
dressings				

WORST

pastries	distilled spirits	lard	doughnuts	soft drinks
mayonnaise &	salt	olives	pretzels	monosodium
blue cheese	potato chips	hydrogenated fat	pickles	glutamate
salad dressings	stick margarine	soup mixes		

SYNERGISTIC FORCES IN FOODS

Although 1000 mg daily of vitamin C has been shown to reduce the risk for stomach cancer, a small glass of orange juice containing only 37 mg of vitamin C is twice as likely to lower the chances for stomach cancer. <u>Something</u> in oranges is even more chemo-protective than vitamin C. Although most people only absorb 20-50% of their ingested calcium, the remaining calcium binds up potentially damaging fats in the intestines to provide protection against colon cancer.

In 1963, a major "player" in the American drug business, Merck, tried to patent a single antibiotic substance that was originally isolated from yogurt. But this substance did not work alone. Since then, researchers have found no less than 7 natural antibiotics that all contribute to yogurt's unique ability to protect the body from infections. There are many anti-cancer agents in plant food, including beta-carotene, chlorophyll, over 500 mixed carotenoids, over 600 various bioflavonoids, lutein, lycopenes and canthaxanthin. The point is: we can isolate and concentrate certain factors in foods for use as therapeutic supplements in cancer therapy, but we must always rely heavily on the mysterious and elegant symphony of ingredients found in wholesome food.

USING GUIDELINES THAT ARE UNIVERSAL

There have been a number of diets developed for the cancer patient: Drs. Moerman[1], Livingston[2], Gerson[3], and the macrobiotic[4] diets to mention a few. Each of these visionaries was a physician who spent at least several decades ministering to cancer patients. While there are some differences in these diets, there is also some common ground. Peculariarities about each program include:

-Dr. Moerman recommends supplements of iron for cancer patients, yet other data shows that elemental iron may accelerate cancer growth. He allows the yolk of the egg, but not the white part.

-Macrobiotics allow liberal amounts of soy sauce and pickles, yet restrict intake of fruit and fish.

-Dr. Gerson used to encourage raw pureed calf's liver, which can contain a number of dangerous bacteria.

-Dr. Livingston prohibits any chicken intake, since a cancer-causing organism thrives in chicken.

The points just mentioned are the oddities about each program which lack a good explanation. Yet, we don't want to throw out the "baby with the bath water". Each of these programs embraces a common thread, which includes a number of explanable nutrition principles. They all provide a diet that:

-uses only unprocessed foods, nothing in a package with a label

-uses high amounts of fresh vegetables

-employs a low fat diet

-emphasizes the importance of regularity

-uses little or no dairy products, with yogurt as the preferred dairy selection

-stabilizes blood sugar levels with no sweets and never eat something sweet by itself

-increases potassium and reduces sodium intake

SUPERFOODS

Though there are many nourishing foods, there are only a few superfoods that contain such a potent collection of protective factors that they deserve regular inclusion in most diets.

-Garlic. This stinky little vegetable has been used for 5000 years in various healing formulas. Pasteur noted that garlic killed all of the bacteria in his petri dishes. More importantly, garlic has been found to stimulate natural protection against tumor cells. Tarig Abdullah, MD of Florida found that white blood cells from garlic-fed people were able to kill 139% more tumor cells than white cells from non-garlic eaters.[5] Garlic and onions fed to lab animals helped to decrease the number of skin tumors.[6] Researchers found that onions provided major protection against expected tumors from DMBA in test animals.[7] Mice with a genetic weakness toward cancer were fed raw garlic with a lower-than-expected tumor incidence.[8]

The most common form of cancer worldwide is stomach cancer. Chinese researchers find that a high intake of garlic and onions cuts the risk for stomach cancer in half.[9] Garlic provides the liver with a certain amount of protection against carcinogenic chemicals. Scientists find that garlic is deadly to invading pathogens or tumor cells, but is harmless to normal healthy body cells; thus offering the hope of the truly selective toxin against cancer that is being sought worldwide.

-Carotenoids. Green plants create sugars by capturing the sun's energy in a process called photosynthesis. The electrons that must be corralled in this process can be highly destructive. Hence, nature has evolved an impressive system of free radical protectors, including carotenoids and bioflavonoids, that act like the lead lining in a nuclear reactor to absorb dangerous unpaired electrons. Both of these substances have potential in stimulating the immune system while there is preliminary evidence that carotenoids may be directly toxic to tumor cells.

Carotenoids are found in green and orange fruits and vegetables. Bioflavonoids are found in citrus, whole grains, honey, and other plant foods.

-*Cruciferous vegetables*. Broccoli, brussel sprouts, cabbage, and cauliflower were involved in the "ground floor" discovery that nutrition is linked to cancer. Lee Wattenberg, PhD of the University of Minnesota

found in the 1970s that animals fed cruciferous vegetables had markedly lower cancer rates than matched controls. Since then, the active ingredient "indoles" have been isolated from cruciferous vegetables and found to be very protective against cancer. Scientists at Johns Hopkins University found that lab animals fed cruciferous vegetables and then exposed to the deadly carcinogen aflatoxin had a 90 percent reduction in their cancer rate.[10]

Cruciferous vegetables are able to increase the body's production of glutathione peroxidase, which is one of the more important protective enzyme systems in the body.

-*Mushrooms*. Gourmet chefs have long prized various mushrooms for their subtle and exotic flavors. Now there is an abundance of scientific evidence showing that Rei-shi, Shiitake, and Maitake mushrooms are potent anti-cancer foods.[11] Actually, Maitake literally means "dancing mushroom" since people would dance with joy when finding these delicate mushrooms on a country hillside. Oral extract of Maitake provided complete elimination of tumors in 40% of animals tested, while the remaining 60% of animals had a 90% elimination of tumors. Maitake contains a polysaccharide, called beta-glucan, which stimulates the immune system and even lowers blood pressure.

-*Legumes*. Seed foods (like soybeans) have a substance that can partially protect the seed from digestion, called protease inhibitors (PI). For many years, these substances were thought to be harmful. New evidence finds that PIs may squelch tumor growth.[12] Researchers at the National Cancer Institute find a collection of substances in soybeans, including isoflavones and phytoestrogens, appear to have potent anti-cancer properties.[13] Dr. Ann Kennedy has spent 20 years researching a compound in soybeans that:

-prevents cancer in most animals exposed to a variety of carcinogens

-retards cancer in some studies

-lowers the toxic side effects of chemo and radiation therapy

-reverts a cancer cell back to a normal healthy cell.[14]

-Others. There are numerous foods that show an ability to slow tumor growth in some way. Apples, apricots, barley, citrus fruit, cranberries, fiber, figs, fish oil, fish, ginger, green tea, spinach, seaweed and other foods are among the reasons that I heavily favor the use of a mixed highly nutritious diet as the foundation for nutrition in cancer therapy.

Food treats malnutrition. Food contains known essential nutrients that stimulate the immune system and provide valuable protection against carcinogens. Foods also contain poorly understood factors that may add measurably to the recovery of the cancer patient. Many foods have tremendous therapeutic value in helping the patient to internally fight cancer.

HOW TO USE THIS SECTION

This cookbook chapter was written with the cancer patient in mind and can also be helpful to people who want to eat properly but have little time to spend in the kitchen. Remember: the more wellness you have, the less illness you can have. The recipes are just a guide to show you the possibilities in creative cooking.

There is a section of tips to stimulate the appetite or lose weight rationally. Also included is the concept of bulk cooking, which is a great way to have a freezer full of ready-made meals at 1/4 the cost. "Fast food" at our house usually means microwaving some frozen beans, adding leftover chicken or fish, and rolling this tasty collection into whole wheat tortillas with fresh salsa. The seasonings of Spike and Gayelords powdered vegetable broth may be purchased at your local health food store.

Realize that there is no one perfect diet. Laying out a weekly menu of "nutritious" food is frought with peril, since other nutritionists could have their own valid criticisms of this program. Life is not perfect, nor are our eating habits. The most nourishing meal in the world is useless unless eaten. This chapter demonstrates healthy eating habits within the context of practical and tasty recipes. There are some noteworthy spartan cancer diets that only an extremely dedicated cancer patient can follow.

Given the choice between an unpalatable and labor-intensive eating program or returning to their old destructive eating habits, many cancer patients chose the later. Gleaning from dozens of good cookbooks and years of experience, the menu provided in this chapter makes precious few compromises in nutritional quality while emphasizing taste, cost and practical preparation.

TO GAIN WEIGHT

* -Don't drink fluids or have soup or salad before the meal. It will fill you up on foods that are low in calorie density.
* -Eat on a large plate, thus avoiding food portions that appear overwhelming. Have small portions, knowing you can always have more.
* -People eat more when dining in groups than by themselves. Go to buffets. Eat with friends or other patients if possible. At our hospital, we were constantly battling the problem of patients not wanting to eat, no matter how appetizing the food looked and smelled. One Fourth of July, we set up a family picnic, with broiled chicken, baked beans, watermelon, corn on the cob and more. People who had not eaten well all week suddenly developed a ferocious appetite. We have been serving buffet family style meals ever since.
* -Distract your mind. Rent a good video and have your meal in front of the TV. Have you ever sat down with a bowl of popcorn and realized you had eaten the whole batch and didn't even realize it?

TO LOSE WEIGHT

* -Eat 6 times a day. That doesn't mean 6 Big Macs. It means a light breakfast upon rising; a piece of fruit later in the midmorning; a salad and half a sandwich at lunch; and the other 1/2 of the sandwich at mid-afternoon. Even if you over-indulge at one meal, make sure you eat on schedule. This concept, called periodicity, trains the mind and body that food is constantly coming into the system and there is no need to overindulge or become exceedingly efficient at storing calories.
* -Have warm fluids, like tea or soup, about 20 minutes before mealtime.
* -Use a smaller plate. It gives the illusion that you're eating more.
* -Drink plenty of purified water. It's good for both weight loss, constipation and wrinkles.
* -Adjust your bathroom scale to the exact weight you want to be. As you lose weight, you can readjust it closer to the zero, but always see your weight as you want it to be. This way when you think about having that huge piece of cake, you will think to yourself, "A person of my weight won't eat that.
* -Exercise within your ability. Make sure you enjoy it.
* -Eat more high-fiber foods, such as fruits, vegetables, beans and whole-grain cereals.
* -Plan your meals and snacks instead of waiting until you are hungry.

EATING OUT

-Iceberg lettuce is the most common salad bar offering, but is "junk food" relative to most other vegetables. Skip the iceberg lettuce and enjoy the healthier fruits, vegetables and whole-grain foods from the salad bar. A good rule of thumb: the deeper the color of the vegetable, the more nourishing it is. Dark greens are better than pale greens, dark orange squash is better than pale squash, and so on. In nature, cauliflower is a dark green vegetable, until human intervention ties the leaves around the developing flower to deprive it of sunlight.

-Many restaurants offer low-calorie or light meals with gourmet versions.

-Instead of accepting that "fried" meal from a restaurant menu, most places will steam or broil your food.

-Airlines can be very accommodating in having a special meal ready for you. Give them at least 1 week advance notice.

-Ask for the salad dressing to be served on the side.

-Have the rich sauces or gravies left out.

-Avoid sauteed and deep-fried food.

FOODS TO HIGHLIGHT

-sprouts
-onions
-garlic
-ginger
-cabbage, broccoli, Brussel sprouts, cauliflower
-carrots
-soybeans, garbanzo beans and other legumes
-rice, barley and other whole grains
-sea vegetables, a.k.a. seaweed
-dark green and dark orange fruits & vegetables
-apples, berries
-eggs
-figs
-fish
-honey
-yogurt**, if no dairy allergy

BEVERAGES

-Purified water
-Cafix
-Roma
-Herb tea
-Vitamin C powder & honey in hot water
-Ginger tea
-Hot natural apple juice with vitamin C
-Fresh orange juice
-Postum
-Chickory
-Japanese Green tea
-Roasted rice or barley tea
-Vinegar, honey & water

DRAGON-SLAYER SHAKE

I hate taking pills, even when I know the value of using supplements to improve my health. That's why I developed this "shake". While most of us are familiar with milkshakes, there are many variations on that theme which can provide nutrient-dense foods in a convenient format. I have found that many cancer patients would avoid taking their supplements of vitamins, minerals and botanicals because they didn't like swallowing pills. To solve that problem, I have developed this shake, which can incorporate many nutrients in powder form, thus eliminating taking pills at all, and the remaining pills are easier to swallow with the lubricating ability of this smooth shake.

Shakes can be a quick and easy breakfast. Depending on your calorie requirements, use this shake in addition to or instead of the breakfast suggestions listed later. My typical breakfast consists of this Dragon-Slayer shake, whole grain rolls, bagles, muffins or Pita bread, along with a large serving of fresh fruit in season.

Take up to half of your pills with the "Dragon-Slayer shake" and save the remaining pills for later in the day. Taking supplements in small divided dosages helps to maintain sustained levels of nutrients in the bloodstream.

Ingredients:

4-8 ounces of rice milk (see recipe in this chapter) or dilute fruit juice, including apple, cranberry, orange, fresh squeezed, juice extracted, etc. I add twice the specified water to a can of frozen unsweetened concentrated apple juice from your grocery store.

10-15 grams of powdered protein from (listed in order of preference): ImmunoPower, whey, rice, soy, alfalfa, egg white, non-fat yogurt solids, spirulina. Do not use powdered proteins that are based upon non-fat milk solids. Too many people are allergic to this product. Your health food store should have a dozen different products to select from. ProMod is a name brand pure whey protein product.

1/2 tablespoon of Perfect 7. This is an excellent product to maintain regularity and encourage proper detoxification. It includes fiber, an herbal laxative, proper bacteria for colonizing the intestines and botanicals for detoxification. You may be surprised at the fecal matter eliminated in the first few weeks on this program.

One sliced ripe banana or less, depending on how thick you like your shakes. Banana adds texture via pectin to make this shake have true milk shake viscosity. If the banana is frozen, it will give a thick "milkshake-like" texture to your drink.

2-4 grams of buffered vitamin C powder from Emergen-C or Seraphim. Both products have an effervescent action that brings a "soda pop" like flavor to this drink, along with high doses vitamin C that won't upset even the most delicate stomach.

1 tablespoon of flaxseed oil or Essential Balance oil from your health food store or mail order (Staywell 888-333-5346)

For those who need to slow down weight loss or gain weight, add 2 tablespoons of MCT (medium chain triglyceride) oil from Twin Labs (800-645-5626)

Directions:

Use a large blender or a small hand held blender, like the ones originally developed to mix diet drinks. First add the oils to coat the bottom of the container for easy mixing and cleaning. Add the powdered ingredients and cut up fruit next. Blend until smooth, or about 15 seconds.

BULK COOKING

Growing Your Sprouts

You will need a glass jar (quart size or larger), a soft plastic screen for the top, and a rubber band to hold the screen in place. There are also commercial sprouting kits available in most health food stores. Place about one heaping tablespoon of seeds in your glass container with the screen doubled on the top. The seeds will expand about tenfold as they sprout, so allow enough room for their expansion. Fill the container half full of purified water and let stand overnight. Next morning drain and rinse the seeds. Let stand inverted over the sink for proper drainage. Rinse and drain twice each day for the next 6-7 days. Keep the jar in a dimly lit area.

Larger seeds, like peas, beans, and lentils take a shorter time to grow and should not be allowed to grow more than a half inch long, since they will develop a bitter flavor. Mung bean sprouts can get up to two inches in length without bitter flavor. Wheat, barley, oats, and other grass plants make terrific sprouts. Smaller seeds, like alfalfa, can grow to an inch in length without any bitter flavor. For some extra vitamin A, let the alfalfa sprouts sit in a sunny window for the last day before eating. The green color indicates the welcome addition of chlorophyll, folacin and beta-carotene.

In excess quantities, sprouts can blunt the immune system in humans. Do not eat more than two cups of sprouts daily.

SPICEY BEANS
3 cups of pinto beans
1 large onion cup up
3-4 garlic cloves minced
2-3 dry red peppers cut up fine
1 tablespoon chili powder

1 tsp cumin powder
1/3 cup olive oil
Lite salt

Sort and wash beans in a colander. Soak the beans overnight in about 8 cups of water in a heavy saucepan. Drain, then fill with another 8 cups of clean water. Add rest of the ingredients. Cover and simmer for 90-120 minutes or until beans are tender. Blend with an egg beater. Add a bit of salt to taste.

If you need the beans sooner:

Rinse beans. Then fill pot with beans and 8 cups of water. Allow to boil for 2 minutes. Let sit in a covered pot for 1 hour. Proceed to next step.
If you have a pressure cooker:

Place the soaked and rinsed beans in 5 cups of water in pot. Add ingredients. Bring lid weight to a gentle rocking motion, then pressure cook for 25 minutes. Let cool down. Beat with a mixer to desired consistency.

BARLEY

Rinse barley and cook for 35-45 minutes in a large volume of boiling water. Barley increases its bulk by four fold when cooked. Drain excess water. Store extra barley in baggies and place in freezer for later use. Season the barley with spices that go with the entree. Spike, Mrs. Dash and other herbal seasonings go with anything.

If using a pressure cooker, use twice the amount of barley measurement for the water. Bring to a rock, then immediately remove from stove burner. Follow rest of the directions .

Whole Wheat Piecrust

1 cup whole wheat pastry flour
1/2 teaspoon salt
3 tablespoons canola oil
1/4 cup water

Stir dry ingredients together. Mix in oil. Add enough of the water to make the dough form a ball. Roll flat between sheets of waxed paper and lift into pan. Make edge.

Roasted Brown Rice or Barley Tea
Dry roast uncooked grain over medium flame for 10 minutes or until a
fragrant aroma develops. Stir and shake pan occasionally. Add 2 to 3
tablespoons of the grain to 1 1/2 quarts of purified water. Bring to a boil,
simmer 10 to 15 minutes.

The following recipes are not carved in stone. If you do not
like a certain spice or seasoning, leave it out. These menus were based
more on giving variety with different foods.

Also, it is a good idea to have leftovers to freeze in serving sizes
so you can just pull out easy-to-serve dinners on days you want to relax.

Make a meal appetizing. Think color. Instead of bland colors
with the same look (i.e. turkey, mashed potatoes and cauliflower), dress
up the plate. You might even try your yard for some creative ideas for
the meal.

Flowers
Marigold petals (subtle but peppery flavor)
Nasturtiums (stronger peppery flavor)
Rose (sweet, gentle flavor)
Lavender (very strong)
Violets (sweet, but slightly spicey)
Borage flowers (cucumber-like taste)
Woodruff flower sprigs (give off vanilla-like scent)
Pansies (valued for their velvet like texture)

Some Kitchen Tips

⇒ Better Butter. Make Better Butter by whipping together: 1/2 cup olive oil and 1/2 cup butter. Refrigerate.

⇒ Make food ahead. You might have more energy on certain days than others.

⇒ A pressure cooker is a must. Cook in bulk. Good items to have on hand are: beans, rice, refried beans, etc. Freeze in your average size meal servings. This way you can make your own TV dinners.

⇒ Crock pots are very handy to have in the kitchen. You just place the ingredients into to pot in the morning and by evening, the meal is ready.

⇒ Using liquid lecithin. Measure it by your eye. It's hard to get off a measuring spoon. If you do want to measure with a utensil, put a bit of oil on the utensil first. You can use liquid lecithin for a thickening agent if you are substituting. Too much will make dough gummy.

⇒ Look for lecithin in spray vegetable oil. There are some that have olive oil also.

⇒ Measuring honey. Measure the oil first. The honey will just slide out of the measuring cup.

⇒ The garlic recipe is one to have as often as possible. You might find that if you have it with dinner, you are energized and might not be able to fall asleep easily. Switch the time to lunch.

⇒ Soak produce that will not be peeled in a gallon of tepid water and 1-2 Tbs. cheap vinegar. Leave for about 5 minutes, then rinse off.

⇒ Leave peeled baby carrots in purified water in the refrigerator. This will make them sweeter.

⇒ Sweeten desserts by adding extra cinnamon and vanilla.

⇒ Grow alfalfa sprouts. It's fun to watch them grow and you know they are organic. It only takes about a week.

⇒ Buy baking powder without alum in it.

⇒ You can add flax meal to salads and vegetables. Just sprinkle a bit on the top for a nice change of flavor.

⇒ Use leftovers for breakfast meals.

⇒ Grow a pot of parsley in the kitchen. It's great to have on hand when you serve onions or garlic.

⇒ You can use unsweetened applesauce to replace 1/2 amount of oil in dessert recipes and add 1/4 to 1/2 tsp. lecithin.

⇒ Become a Label Reader! Check and see if that whole wheat bread lists "enriched flour" as first ingredient. Beware of "fat free". See if sugar was added. Limit saturated fat and sugar. Sugar can be listed as: maltos, dextrose, fructose, sucrose, corn syrup, date sugar, etc.

Substitutes for 1 Cup White Sugar   Reduce Liquids in Recipe

Honey	2/3 cup	1/8 cup
Fructose	1/2 - 2/3 cup	
Molasses	1/2 cup	
Unsweetened Applesauce	3/4 cup	1/3 to 1/2 cup
Sucanat	1 cup	

Stevia (herbal concentrate) follow label directions for dilution in water

Desserts are given at the end of each dinner. This doesn't mean you have to always have a dessert! Try and keep sweets to a minimum.

**ROYAL SALAD DRESSING

1/2 cup raw-unfiltered organic apple cider vinegar (i.e. Bragg)
3-4 Tbs. purified water
1 package dry Italian Salad Dressing Mix (i.e. Good Seasons)
1/2 cup certified organic flax seed oil or Essential Balance, which is a blend of organic oils from flax, sunflower, sesame, pumpkin, and borage by Omega Nutrition (Staywell 888-333-5346)
1-2 tsp. liquid lecithin
      Add the first 3 ingredients together in a jar with a lid. Then add the oil and lecithin. Shake vigorously. Keep refrigerated.

WHICH DIETARY PROGRAM SHOULD YOU FOLLOW?
NO WORK, VEGETARIAN, OR OMNIVORE?

      This is an important question with no easy answer. There has been no shortage of attempts to category people into groups in order to make individualized recommendations on the type of diet to follow. While all of these theories have some merit, none of them have been exposed to the bright light of scientific scrutiny, and, more importantly, you cannot designate 6 billion people into only 3 or 4 dietary patterns. One of those theories, from Elliott Abravanel, MD, seems to have widespread applications. See the chart on Metabolic Type. My recommendation?

      Eat your ancestral diet. There has been an endless parade of diets that were hailed as "the perfect diet". But there is no one perfect diet. Behold the fascinating spectrum of 6 billion people on the planet earth. We are all different. While macrobiotics may be helpful for some, it is counterproductive for a few. In order to have a decent grasp on the core diet for humans, we need to take a ride in our time machine back to our hunter and gatherer ancestors who roamed the earth before the dawn of agriculture. By examining the diet of primitive hunter gatherer societies plus archeological findings, a trio of modern day "Indiana Jones" researchers turned up some of the most important nutrition data of the 20th century.[15]

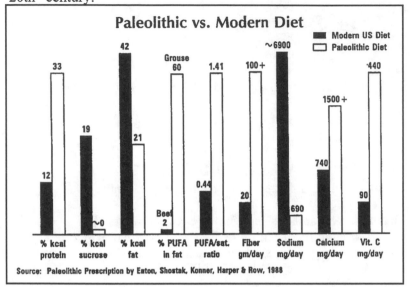

Paleolithic vs. Modern Diet

Source: Paleolithic Prescription by Eaton, Shostak, Konner, Harper & Row, 1988

Most of our hunter-gatherer ancestors ate a diet consisting of about 1/3 lean animal tissue with the remaining 2/3 of the diet unprocessed plant food; mostly vegetables, some grains, some fruit, nuts, seeds and legumes. If the creature runs, flies, or swims, then it may be about 4% body fat, with obvious exceptions including duck and salmon. Cows, the staple meat of America, do none of the above and are about 30-40% body fat. While there are certainly variations on this theme, this is the basic diet of our ancestors and a good starting point for our cancer-fighting diet. Both studies and my clinical experience show that a low fat diet with lots of fresh vegetables will improve cancer outcome. Take a look at the graphic illustration of the contrast between the modern American diet and our "factory specification" ancestral diet. Notice how far we have strayed from our ancestral diet.

Keep in mind that you may have to "fine tune" this diet to suit your ethnic background. The macrobiotic diet was developed by a Japanese physician who cured himself of cancer in the 19th century. The macrobiotic diet tends to encourage anything Oriental (even soy sauce and pickles) and discourage anything Western, including chicken, turkey, fish and fruit. Macrobiotics may be ideally suited for many Orientals, and has helped some Caucasians because it is such a vast improvement over the nutritional quality of the typical American diet. I encourage people to determine the diet of their ancestors 5000 years ago and use that food pattern as a starting point.

METABOLIC TYPE

	Shape	Exercise	Eat	Don't eat	Characteristics	Vulnerabilities
Gonadal	smaller above waist, lbs on rear	dance, gymnastics, jog w. heavy hands, tai-chi, nautilus	Pituitary stim: low fat, fr & veg, wh grains, yogurt, poultry, fish, light dairy	creamy & spicy foods; red meat, sour cr, ice cr., butter, rich desserts	mothering instincts can smother, frustration is stress, good at advertising	lumpy breasts, competition, interruptions, disorder, change in routine, assertiveness, risks
Thyroid	tall, long limbs, fine bones, fat on midriff, i.e. Victoria Principle, Jeremy Jones	swim, row, packback, nautilus, aerobic, no biking	Adrenal stim: eggs, poultry, veg & fr, fish, cheese, yogurt, wh grain, decaf, butter, veg oil	starches & sweets, refined carb, pasta, coffee, tea	solve all w bursts of flighty ideas, nervous, irritable, good at communication, the arts, entrepreneur	colds, flu, colitis, allergies, repetition, continuing demands, details, rejection, pain, lack of stim.
Adrenal	solid, muscular, beer belly, fat across back & neck, i.e. Mr. T, Nick Nolte, Linda Evans, Carroll O'Connor	handball, squash, tennis, b-ball, ping pong, Nordic track, no weight	Pituitary stim: lowfat dairy, fish, fr & veg, wh grain, poultry, coffee, tea, desserts	meat & potatoes, salty food, hi fat cheese, red meat, butter	stubborn, inflexible, impatient, good at business, sports, sales	CAD, DB, needs control, emotional, vacations stressful, children, creativity
Pituitary	child's body, slightly big head, baby fat all over, only 10% of US	aerobic dancing, karate, tai chi, martial arts, no wt lift, long distance running	Adrenal stim: beef, lamb, pork, organ meat, fr & veg, poultry, fish, skim milk, eggs, decaf, tea	regular dairy, coffee	try to use more intellect when emotions needed, good at computer design, architect	allergies (milk esp), emotions, sex, food, unresolved conflicts, animals, sickness

Imagine the following experiment. Dr. Rabbit, Dr. Cat and Dr. Squirrel are conducting a study of the nutrient needs of their patients, consisting of 100 subjects of 33 cats, 33 rabbits and 34 squirrels. Dr. Rabbit puts everyone on a vegetarian diet, because Dr. Rabbit is a vegan. Some of the 100 "patients" get much better, some get worse and some stay the same. Dr. Cat steps up to the plate and takes the same "monomania" approach of putting everyone on a carnivorous diet, just like Dr. Cat. Same results: 1/3 get better, 1/3 get worse and the rest stay the same. Dr. Squirrel has the same luck with the mixed grain and nuts diet of squirrels. Moral of the story: there is no one perfect diet. In spite of various noble efforts to categorize people based upon their blood type, their build, their nervous system type, their Ayurvedic status or whatever...you need to ask the question: "What did my ancestors eat for most of the past thousands of years?" When I asked this question in one group of cancer patients, a person responded, "Then I guess I should be eating hog fat, like my grandpappy who was a farmer in Arkansas." I replied that, in order to give adequate credit to the adaptive forces of Nature, we need to go back further than 50 or 100 years.

MERITS OF FOLLOWING YOUR ETHNIC DIET

- Nutrition & Physical Degeneration, Price, 1945
- Pottenger's Cats, Pottenger, 1983
- Paleolithic Prescription, Eaton, 1988
- Native Nutrition, Schmid, 1994
- Coronary Heart Disease, Mann, 1993
- The Zone, Sears, 1995
- 10 adult male aborigine diabetics, return to wild, diet high in meat, 7 wk: 18 lb loss, TG 75% drop, BG 50% drop, "cured", O'Dea, Diabetes, vol.33, p.596, 1984

Basically, if you are very weak and have no one to cook for you, then use the "No Work" cooking section, until you can regain enough strength to begin cooking. If your ancestors came from a warm and sunny climate, then they probably ate more plant food, which is available year round in the warmer climates. Therefore, you should follow the Vegetarian Week, or some variation of that theme. If your ancestors came from a colder climate, then you probably need some lean and clean animal food. How many people from Scandinavia and Great Britain were vegetarians 5000 years ago? Not many. Follow the Omnivore Week.

NO COOKING WEEK

The foods listed in this weeks menu are meant to be easy to find in most grocery stores. The ideas are showing some simple, fast, and balanced meals that are made with store bought prepared foods. They are not meant to be the norm! But there might be a day you just don't feel like being in the kitchen. Many companies are trying to market healthy products. You might have different brand names in your area that are similar to the ones listed below. Be vigilant in reading labels. Make sure you check the sugar content! Remember, sugar feeds cancer so you want to minimize desserts to a treat once a week. Many grocery stores have a deli with selections of salads and meats already prepared. Making Royal TV dinners is a great way to avoid this expensive alternative. For example, if you cook beans and rice and freeze leftovers in individual baggies, you have the makings of a meal. Just add leftover poultry and wrap in whole wheat tortillas and add a salad. This way, you will have so much more control of what goes into the meal.

Make sure you remember to soak your produce that won't be peeled in a solution of one to two tablespoons of vinegar to one gallon of water. An easy way to do this is to fill the sink half full of water and splash in some vinegar . Add the produce and let soak for five minutes. Rinse and store dried, such as apples patted dry or spinach wrapped in a paper towel.

MONDAY
Breakfast
Ready to eat healthy cereal (i.e. Shredded Wheat, Grapenuts, Grapenut flakes, Cheerios).
Serve with skim milk or apple juice.
Country Farms stone ground whole wheat toast with:
Simply fruit spread jam or Smuckers Natural Style reduced fat peanut butter.
Louis Rich Turkey-ham slices
Fresh cherry tomatoes.

Lunch
Fantastic Foods Hummus Mix
International Mr. Pita 100% whole wheat pita bread
Janet Lee California pitted ripe olives
Sliced fresh red onion or spring onion
Bunny-Lur ready to eat carrots, soaked in purified water

Dinner
Healthy Choice Country Glazed Chicken (or one of their entrees you prefer)
Rainbo Grants Farm whole wheat bread with:
Sue Bee spun honey
Great Value frozen peas (microwaved)
Old Fashioned Ginger Snaps (1-2 cookies)

TUESDAY
Breakfast
Earth Grains 100% whole wheat English muffin with:
Healthy Choice cream cheese or Smuckers reduced fat peanut butter broccoli microwaved for 4-5 minutes
*Royal Dressing
Soy milk, skim milk or apple juice

Lunch
Taste Adventure Lentil Chili,
Roman Meal rice cakes
Healthy Choice low fat bologna
Birds Eye Farm frozen fresh mixtures
Musselman's Natural applesauce

Dinner
Fantastic Foods Instant Refried
Beans or
Old El Paso fat free refried beans
Old El Paso salsa
Land O Lakes no-fat sour cream
Tyson whole wheat tortillas
Healthy Choice grated cheese
Minute Brand or Uncle Ben's
Instant whole grain brown rice
Tomatoes, avocado and sprout
salad
*Royal Dressing
Baked Tostitos low fat corn chips

WEDNESDAY
Breakfast
Celestial Seasonings green tea
Quaker Oatmeal (instant)
Natures Best Wheat Fields oat
bran bagels
Louis Rich turkey slices
Smuckers Simple fruit jam

Lunch
Healthy Choice Country Vegetable
Soup
Ezekiel bread
Kraft fat free cheese slices
Fresh Express fresh spinach
*Royal Dressing

Dinner
Near East Tabouli with:
Homeland Pride chickpeas,
drained and added to tabouli
International Mr. Pita 100%
whole wheat pita bread
Green Giant frozen broccoli
Blue Bunny non-fat frozen yogurt
(small scoop)

THURSDAY
Breakfast
Caffix, or favorite beverage
Earthgrains Bagels-hearty wheat
Healthy choice fat free cream
cheese or
Boiled egg or egg fried in Pam
onion slices fried in Pam

Lunch
Campbell's chunky old fashion
chicken soup
Health Valley rice bran crackers
Kraft no-fat cheese slice or
Healthy Choice lunch meat
Fresh tomato wedges
grocery package cabbage
*Royal Dressing

Dinner
Healthy Choice hot dogs
Roman Meal whole wheat buns
Birds Eye frozen farm fresh
mixture
*Royal Dressing
Nabisco whole wheat fig cookies

FRIDAY
Breakfast
Bigelow No Caffeine herb tea or
favorite beverage
Food for Life sprouted wheat
bread
Boiled egg
Grapefruit

Lunch
Campbells Chunky Soup Hearty
Bean 'n Ham
Oroweat 100% stoneground
whole wheat bread
Del Monte lite pear half with
frozen raspberries (thawed) and
placed in center of pear
Good Sense raw sunflower seeds

Dinner
Fantastic Foods Nature's Burger
Roman Meal whole wheat bun
Slice red onion, hamburger
condiments
Baked Tostitos reduced fat tortilla
chips
Fresh spinach salad with tomatoes
and mushroom slices with:
*Royal Dressing
Dannon low fat vanilla yogurt
with some of the raspberries left
from lunch

SATURDAY
Breakfast
Seneca frozen concentrated apple
juice, diluted; power vitamin C
added
Louise Rich turkey bacon, cooked
Natures Best Wheat Fields whole
wheat bagel
Fresh Express celery sticks

Lunch
Scrambled eggs
Rosarita's no fat refried beans
Litehouse medium salsa
Mission Soft Wheat Fajita tortillas
Baked Tostitos low fat corn chips
Package fresh spinach leaves
*Royal Dressing

Dinner
Tyson Honey Roasted Chicken
dinner
Thin sliced onions and tomatoes
with:
*Royal Dressing
Quaker Oats rice cakes spread
with:
Y.S. Royal organic unprocessed
honey

SUNDAY
Breakfast
Nabisco shredded wheat with:
Seneca frozen concentrated apple
juice diluted and poured over
cereal
banana
Oroweat 100% Whole wheat
bagels
Alpine low fat plain yogurt with
Simply fruit jam added

Lunch
Starkist tuna (packed in water)
made into a sandwich served on:
Roman Meal whole wheat bun or:
Smuckers reduced fat peanut butter
and Simply fruit sandwith
Knudsen non-fat cottage cheese
served with fruit in season

Dinner
Hormell's Turkey Chili
Uncle Ben's Brown & Wild Rice
Fresh vegetable platter
*Royal Dressing

VEGETARIAN WEEK

Monday
Breakfast:
Ginger tea
1/2 to 1 tsp. grated ginger
1/4 tsp. vitamin C
1/2 to 1 tsp. honey
1 cup hot water
Mix all ingredients together.

Alpine Barley
2 cups cooked barley
1 tsp. sesame oil
1/4 tsp. ground cumin
1/4 tsp. ground coriander
1/2 tsp. ground cinnamon
1/4 cup golden raisins
1/4 cup dried apricots, chopped
1/2 cup chopped, roasted almond, walnuts or sunseeds (opt.)
Cook barley according to directions or use leftovers. Heat oil in pot. Quickly saute spices to bring out their flavors. Add dried fruit and 1 cup water. Cover and simmer 5 minutes. Add cooked barley; heat thoroughly. More water may be needed to reach desired consistency. Serve with chopped nuts.

Lunch:
Soy Pilaf
2 Tbs. canola oil or olive oil
1/8 tsp. black pepper
1 bay leaves, crumbled
1 pinch cloves
1/4 tsp. cinnamon
1 Tbs. minced fresh onion
1 clove minced garlic
1/2 tsp. grated fresh ginger
1/8 tsp. cayenne

1 cup diced celery
1/2 cup cooked brown rice
1 cup cooked soybeans
Toast first 10 ingredients. Add grain and beans and heat. Add vegetable salt or soy sauce to taste.

Bright Broccoli
1 head broccoli
sunflower seeds (opt.)
*Royal Dressing
Cut off outside part of stock. Dice stock and cut top into bit size pieces. Cut top into small "flowerettes". Put into a covered glass bowl and microwave for about 5 minutes on high. Sprinkle with seeds and dressing.

Dinner:
Lentil Soup
4 cups vegetable stock
2 cups dried lentils
1 onion, sliced
1 large carrot, sliced
1 large celery stalk, sliced
2 cloves, crushed
1/4 cup chopped celery
1 bay leaf
1/2 tsp. dried oregano
3 Tbs. tomato paste
2 Tbs. white wine vinegar or herbal vinegar
1 tsp. Spike unsalted (opt.)
2 tsp. sea salt
1 can (28 ounces) whole tomatoes
1/2 tsp. pepper
1/4 tsp. summer savory or oregano or thyme (opt.)
Saute in a large sauce pan, the onion, carrot, celery and garlic until tender, about 10 minutes. Bring the stock to a boil in the pan. Rinse the lentils and add to

boiling stock. Add all the remaining ingredients except the vinegar. Reduce the heat, cover and simmer, until the lentils are very soft, about 1 hour. Remove the soup from heat and add the vinegar. Discard bay leaf. (If you want a creamer soup, puree half the soup. Return the puree back to the saucepan and reheat.) Or you can place all ingredients in a crock, (minus 1 cup fluid) in the morning and set on low for 9 to 10 hours.

**Variation: Lentil Chili, Mildly Spicy; Quick Cooking, ready in 10 minutes. (Company is called: Taste Adventure-Fine Foods)

Miso Rice
2 cups cooked brown rice
2 - 3 tsp. miso
1 tsp. vegetable broth
1 tsp. Spike
1 tsp. finely chopped parsley
celery leaves chopped (opt.)
1 tsp. minced spring onion
　　　Mix all ingredients together. Heat in the microwave.

100% Whole wheat pita bread

Peeled baby carrots that have been soaked and chilled in purified water.

Baked Apples
4 large flavorful apples
1/4 cup toasted wheat germ
1/4 cup raisins
1/4 cup chopped walnuts
juice of 1/4 of a lemon
1/8 tsp. cinnamon
1 Tbs. brown sugar

pinch salt
1 Tbs. whole wheat flour
3/4 cup apple juice
　　　Preheat oven to 350 degrees. Core apples and place in a greased baking dish with a cover. It's good if the apples are a snug fit. If not, cut up a fifth apple in quarters and pack it in. Mix the wheat germ, raisins, nuts, lemon juice, cinnamon, sugar, and salt and press lightly into the apple cores. Mix the flour and apple juice and pour over the apples. Bake 40 minutes, or until the apples are very soft. Let cool slightly before serving for best flavor.

Tuesday
Breakfast:
Dragon Slayer Drink (found in the beginning of this chapter)
Whole wheat bagel
tomatoes, sliced

Lunch:
Healthy Wheat Balls
3 cups water
1 1/2 cups cracked wheat
1/2 cup dry oatmeal
1/4 cup chopped parsley
1 Tbs. miso
1/4 tsp. each, nutmeg, thyme, basil
1/2 tsp. sage
1/2 cup sunflower seeds
1/4 cup sesame seeds
1 tsp. oil
　　　Bring 3 cups water to a boil; stir in the wheat and oats. Lower the heat and simmer for 10 to 12 minutes until water is absorbed. Mix the rest of the ingredients, except the sesame

seeds, into the hot mixture. Spoon into a bowl and allow to cool enough to handle. Moisten hands with water and form into walnut-sized balls; roll in sesame seeds. Place in oiled (or Pam sprayed) baking dish. Warm in 350 degree oven for 10 to 15 minutes. Serve with 100% whole wheat bread or pita bread.

Three Bean Salad
1 cup frozen green beans, cooked in microwave for 1 to 2 minutes
1 cup cooked kidney beans
1/2 cup cooked garbanzo beans
1/2 cup cooked pinto beans
4 spring onions, chopped
2 cloves garlic, crushed
1/4 cup snipped parsley (opt.)
1/3 cup *Royal Dressing
soy bacon bits or Turkey bacon (cooked and crumbled)(opt.)
        Mix all ingredients in a bowl. Cover and refrigerate, stirring before serving.

Dinner:
Teriyaki Ginger Tofu
1/4 cup soy sauce
1/4 cup honey
1/4 tsp. garlic
1/4 tsp. onion powder
1" to 1 1/2" chunk of fresh ginger grated
6 cups tofu, chunks or sliced
        Blend first 4 ingredients together. Pour over slices or pieces of tofu that have been placed on a large pam sprayed baking dish. Cover with foil and bake at 375 degree for about 20 minutes. Lift up corner of foil to make sure tofu is boiling and swollen. Remove foil and flip tofu

over with a spatula. Bake 25-35 minutes or until sauce dries out and tofu is brown. Stir a few times in between.

Honey Baked Onions
2 large mild onions
2 Tbs. honey
1/6 cup water
1 Tbs. olive oil
1/2 tsp. paprika
1/2 tsp. ground coriander
1/8 tsp. lite salt
1/8 tsp. cayenne pepper
        Peel and cut onions in half crosswise. Place cut side down in a baking dish just large enough to hold all the onions in one layer. Sprinkle with water. Cover with foil and bake at 375 degrees for about 20 minutes. Turn onions cut side up. Combine remaining ingredients and spoon half of the mixture over the onions. Return to oven and bake uncovered 15 minutes. Baste with remaining honey mixture and bake 10 more minutes.

Rice Porridge
1 cup cooked brown rice, cold
1/2 cup apple juice
1/2 cup water
2 tbs. raisins or other dried fruit
1/2 tsp. cinnamon (opt.)
2 Tbs. chopped nuts (opt.)
        Place all ingredients in a saucepan. Bring to a boil, then reduce heat and simmer, covered, 15 minutes stirring frequently. Most of the liquid should be absorbed. Serve warm. If creamier porridge is desired, puree half.

Wednesday
Breakfast:
Rice Milk
1/4 cup brown rice
1 1/4 quarts of purified water
1/8 tsp. sea salt
1 1/2 Tbs. honey
1/2 Tbs. canola oil
      Bring rice and water to a boil; then simmer for 45 minutes. Strain the rice, saving the liquid, and add back 1/4 cup of the liquid. Add the salt, honey and oil. Whip in a blender on high. Add back to fluid. Chill. Shake before using.

**Variation: For a dynamite glass of unchocolate milk, mix 8 ounces of rice milk with 2 Tbs. of carob powder (chocolate flavor) and 1/2 Tbs. of Roma (coffee substitute). Use electric blender for 10 seconds. Serve chilled.

Breakfast Muffins
2 cups whole wheat flour
1 cup cornmeal
1 Tbs. baking powder
1 tsp. cinnamon
1/8 tsp. sea salt
1/4 cup Sucanat or fructose
1/3 cup canola oil
1/4 - 1/2 tsp. liquid lecithin
1/2 cup natural unsweetened applesauce
3/4 cup water
4 oz. tofu
      Preheat oven to 375 degrees. Sift dry ingredients in large bowl. Puree tofu with the liquids in a blender until creamy smooth. Add wet ingredients to the dry ones; mix gently. (If batter is dry, add up to 1/4 cup extra water. Some flours absorb more liquid than others.) Don't over-mix. Spray Pam in muffin pan or use paper muffin cups. Fill 2/3 full. Bake for 20 minutes or until done.

**Variations:
-add 1 cup washed blueberries
-add 1 cup cranberries and 1/2 cup chopped nuts
-1/4 cup bran, 1 cup raisins soaked in 3/4 cups orange juice. Omit water.
-Substitute whole wheat flour for cornmeal for a lighter muffin

Celery sticks
      Served with a small amount of natural peanut butter.

Lunch:
Tofu With Swiss Chard
1/2 lb. firm tofu
1 Tbs. sesame or olive oil
pinch of sea salt or soy sauce to taste
1 small bunch Swiss or red chard, washed and chopped
1 Tbs. fresh basil or dill (optional)
      Press the fluid out of the tofu with a paper towel. Slice lengthwise. Heat oil and pan-fry tofu on one side until golden. Gently turn tofu with spatula. Sprinkle with sea salt or soy sauce. Place chopped chard and herbs on top of tofu. Cover and reduce heat. The greens will cook down in 5 minutes. Add 1/4 cup water if needed to steam greens. Serve the tofu with greens on the side.

Couscous with Nuts
1 cup boiling water
1 tsp. olive or sesame oil (opt.)

1 cup couscous
1/3 cup chopped nuts or seeds
chopped parsley.

Bring water to a boil. Add oil; pour couscous in gently. Cover and remove from heat. Allow grains to absorb water another 3 to 5 minutes. Add the nuts or seeds and parsley. Fluff with a fork.

Dinner:
Soyburgers
4 cups cooked soybeans
1/2 cup water or tomato sauce
1/4 tsp. onion powder
1/4 tsp. garlic powder
2 Tbs. nutritional yeast
1/4 cup soy sauce
1/4 tsp. liquid smoke (opt.)
1 tsp. Spike
1/2 to 1 cup bran and/or rolled oats

Blend first 8 ingredients in a blender until smooth, using only 2 cups of soybeans. Pour into a bowl. Grind remaining 2 cups of soybeans in blender without any liquid so they are coarsely chopped. Add to mixture in the bowl and add grains. Mix well and let sit 10 to 15 minutes so grains can absorb moisture. Shape 1/2 cup of the mixture at a time into patties and fry in a pan wiped with olive oil. Cook until brown then flip and cook until brown on the other side. Serve with whole grain buns.

Oven Baked French Fries
4 potatoes
Lite salt or sea salt to taste
vegetable oil pray (i.e. Pam)

Cut potatoes into strips. Arrange on oven paper or a teflon baking sheet. Spray with the oil. You can try other seasonings such as garlic powder, onion powder, or chili powder. Bake at 425 degrees for 15-20 minutes or until golden brown. Turn. Bake 15-20 more minutes or until tender. Note: To shorten baking time, microwave sliced potatoes for 3 minutes before placing in oven.

Carrots with Bean Sprouts
2 large carrots, shredded
2 cups alfalfa sprouts
1 cup bean sprouts
1/2 cup walnuts or pecans
1/4 cup sliced almonds
2 Tbs. white-wine vinegar
2 tsp. Dijon-style mustard (opt.)
1 Tbs. sesame oil
1 Tbs. olive oil
salt and pepper
2 tsp. chopped fresh coriander, parsley, or dill

Mix the carrots, sprouts, and nuts together and place in a serving dish. Blend the rest of ingredients together. Pour over the salad. Or you can use *Royal Dressing.

Maple-Baked Pears
2 pears
1 Tbs. maple syrup
1/4 tsp. vanilla extract
2 tsp. wheat germ
2 tsp. butter

Preheat oven to 350 degrees. Spray a nonstick baking dish with vegetable oil spray. Cut pears in half and core. Place in baking dish. Mix syrup and vanilla extract. Drizzle over pears.

Sprinkle with wheat germ. Divide butter among pears. Bake 10 minutes or until tender.

Thursday
Breakfast
Roma Beverage
Hot Grain Cereal
1/3 cup bulgur
1/2 cup cornmeal
3 oz. dried fruit bits or raisins
1/4 cup toasted almond slivers
1/2 tsp. maple extract
cinnamon to taste
2 cups boiling water
　　　Combine all the ingredients with the boiling water in an uncovered pot; stir slowly. Return to a boil and lower to simmer for 10 to 15 minutes, or until ingredients reach desired consistency.

Squash
Cook frozen squash in the microwave per directions. Sprinkle with cinnamon and nutmeg. Drizzle a tiny bit of honey over the top.

Lunch
BBQ Tempeh
1 lb. tempeh
2 Tbs. mustard
2 Tbs. miso
water to cover
　　　Cut tempeh in "burger-size" portions. Place in a pot and cover with water. Dissolve miso and mustard in 1/4 cup water; add to tempeh and bring to a boil. Lower heat and simmer for 20 minutes. Remove from liquid. Place in frying pan with sauce (recipe below) and use the sauce to baste. Cook 5 to 10 minutes on each side. Serve on whole wheat bun or roll, with sliced onion, lettuce and sprouts.

Sauce:
1/2 cup apple juice
1 Tbs. soy sauce
1/2 Tbs. lemon juice
1/2 Tbs. rice syrup (opt.)
1 small piece ginger root, grated
1 tsp. arrowroot dissolved in a little water
　　　Place apple juice, soy sauce and syrup in a small saucepan. Simmer gently on a low heat to reduce volume slightly. Thicken with arrowroot. Add ginger. Adjust flavor.

Spanish Tomato Salad
4 fresh tomatoes, cut into sixths
1/4 cup fresh cilantro, chopped
4 green onions, chopped
1 red bell pepper, finely chopped
3 Tbs. fresh lemon juice
1 Tbs. soy sauce
　　　Mix ingredients together. Allow flavors to blend.

Dinner
Mock Turkey
2 cups chickpeas, cooked and mashed
2 cups brown rice (or instant brown rice)
1/2 cup vegetable bouillon liquid
1 cup finely diced bread crumbs
1/2 cup whole wheat flour
1/3 cup chopped walnuts
2 Tbs. butter
1/4 tsp. lecithin
1/2 tsp. celery seed
1/2 tsp. vegetable salt
1/2 tsp. black pepper
1/2 tsp. sage

1/2 tsp. thyme
1/2 tsp. garlic powder
1/2 tsp. onion powder
paprika

Cook (or use canned) chickpeas, then mash. Cook and cool rice. Dissolve bouillon in hot water. Toast spices in butter. Combine all ingredients, mix and mash together well. Shape into slices or patties. Place on oiled baking sheet, sprinkle with paprika and bake at 375 degrees for 45 minutes or until browned.

Sweet Potatoes
Bake some sweet potatoes when cooking the Mock Turkey. If they are thick, microwave for 4-5 minutes before placing in oven.

Glazed Carrots
2 cups fresh carrots
2 tsp. honey
1/2 tsp. salt
1/2 tsp. grated orange peel
1 tsp. butter

Cut carrots into lengthwise strips. Cook in the microwave until tender, 4 to 5 minutes. Cook and stir honey, salt, orange peel in the butter in a skillet until bubbly. Add carrots; cook over low heat, stirring occasionally, until carrots are glazed and heated through, about 4 minutes.

Banana Dessert
1 banana
Natural unsweetened applesauce

Slice banana and place in a bowl. Pour a bit of applesauce over the slices. Can sprinkle with cinnamon. Serves one.

FRIDAY
Breakfast
Granola
4 cups old-fashioned oats, uncooked
3/4 cup unprocessed wheat bran
1/2 cup whole wheat pastry flour
2 cups wheat germ
1/2 cup oat bran
1/4 cup canola oil
2 Tbs. honey
1/2 to 1 cup sunflower seeds
1 cup raisins
2 tsp. vanilla

Heat oven to 300 degrees. Mix together oats, wheat bran, flour, wheat germ, oat bran, oil and honey. Spread into a large, shallow pan. Bake for 45 minutes, stirring every 15 minutes. Add the sunflower seeds during the last 10 minutes of baking. Add the raisins and vanilla at the end of the baking time. Let cool. Can serve with soy milk or apple juice as the liquid instead of milk.

Vegetable protein drink: Using powdered protein from soy, sprouted grains with legumes, or rice, blend with fruit juice or rice milk.

Lunch
Soy Spread
2 cups cooked, mashed soybeans
1 or 2 small red chili peppers
1 small chunk ginger
1/2 tsp. onion powder
1/4 tsp. garlic powder
1 Tbs. soy sauce
1/4 cup olive oil
1/2 cup lemon juice
1 cup water

Blend all ingredients in a blender. Use on top of pita bread or whole wheat crackers.

Crisp Chop Suey
1/2 cup Chinese peas, sliced
1/4 cup each: green and red bell pepper (slice lengthwise thinly, then in half)
1/2 cup celery, diced
1/2 cup carrots, slivered
2 cups cabbage, bite-sized pieces
1 cup bean sprouts, cut
1 Tbs. sesame seeds
1/4 cup almonds, slivered
1 tsp. toasted sesame oil
Sweet 'n Sour Ginger Dressing
Cut vegetables Chinese style cutting diagonally across the vegetable-in the sizes suggested. Add seeds and nuts. Then toss with last 2 ingredients.
Sweet 'n Sour Ginger Dressing
1 Tbs. soy sauce
1 Tbs. honey
3 Tbs. water
1 Tbs. grated fresh ginger
1/2 tsp. arrowroot
Mix ingredients for sauce in a small pot until arrowroot dissolves. Cook over medium heat, stirring constantly until thickened like a gravy. Pour over salad and toss.

Dinner
Spicy Mexican Beans
2 cups pinto beans
1 large onion, diced
4 cloves garlic, minced
2-3 dry red peppers, minced (can cut with scissors)
1 Tbs. chili powder
1 tsp. cumin powder
1/4 cup olive oil or canola oil
2 tsp. sea salt
purified water
Sort and wash beans in a colander. Place beans in a pressure cooker and add enough water to cover the beans and then 4 cups more. Bring to a boil and boil for 2 minutes. Cover and leave for 1 hour. Drain and rinse beans. Place beans back into the pressure cooker and add water to just cover the beans. Add the rest of ingredients and close lid. Heat on high until the weight starts rocking. Turn down the heat but keep the weight moving for 25 minutes. Turn off heat. Let the pressure cooker sit until the indicator shows that all pressure has been released. Remove lid and mash the beans with an egg beater until about 1/2 of the beans are mashed.

If you don't want to use a pressure cooker, follow the steps except when placing the beans with the rest of the ingredients, place the beans and ingredients in a large pot and let boil for about 90-120 minutes or until beans are tender. More water will be needed.

To give you a few ideas, these beans can be used to make: burritos, tacos, a bean sandwich with a slice of onion on top,or a hot dip with baked corn chips.

Spanish Rice
Cooked brown rice
Salsa to desired amount
Spring onions sliced
chopped fresh parsley
Mix all ingredients together and heat in the microwave.

Whole wheat tortillas

Microwave garlic
1 bulb of garlic
1 tsp. Teriyaki sauce (opt.)
olive oil
Spike
     Cut garlic bulb in half
through the equator. Break up
bulb into pieces and place in a
glass cup. Drizzle olive oil and
teriyaki on top and sprinkle with
spike. Place a piece of plastic
wrap over the top of the cup and
microwave for 1 minute. The
skins of the garlic just fall off.

Fruit & Sprout Salad
1 ripe banana
1/2 Tbs. honey
3 apples, grated
2-3 Tbs. lemon juice
1 cup germinated sunflower seeds
1 cup wheat sprouts or alfalfa
sprouts
1/2 cup wheat germ
Chopped almonds
     In a large bowl, mash
banana with honey. Add next 2
ingredients and mix well. Fold in
next 3 ingredients. Serve in
individual bowls and top with
chopped almond. (Makes 4
generous servings.)

SATURDAY
Breakfast
Scrambled Corn-Tofu
1 tsp. sesame oil
3 or 4 scallions, finely sliced
1 red pepper, cut into 1/4 -inch,
diced
2 ears corn, cooked and cut off
cob or frozen corn defrosted

1/2 lb. tofu
pinch sea salt
1 Tbs. chopped fresh dill or basil
     Heat oil in pan; saute
vegetables, starting with the
pepper and corn, the scallions are
next: saute until pepper begins to
get soft, a pinch of sea salt will
help. Crumble tofu over
vegetables. Continue to cook for
5 minutes over low heat. Fresh
herbs can be added a few minutes
before done.

Sweet Essene Bread (found in
health food stores) or 100% whole
wheat bread

Lunch
Potato Celery Soup
4 cups water
4 medium-sized potatoes, diced
1 medium stalk of celery, chopped
1/4 cup butter
1/4 cup nutritional yeast
2 Tbs. soy sauce
2 Tbs. nut or seed butter (sesame,
almond, etc.)
Spike seasoning added to taste
     Combine first 4
ingredients in a saucepan. Bring
to a boil and simmer for 10 to 12
minutes or until tender. With
slotted spoon, take out 2 cups of
vegetables. Then combine
remaining vegetables and soup
stock in a blender with the last 3
ingredients and blend until
smooth. Combine all ingredients
and serve.

Bean Dip
1 (16 oz.) can kidney beans or
black beans, drained
1/2 small jalapeno pepper, sliced

2 garlic cloves
1 dozen corn tortillas
Spike or seasoned salt

Blend 1st 3 ingredients in a blender or food processor until smooth. Cut tortillas into 8 triangles. Place on a vegetable-sprayed or oven paper covered baking sheet and bake at 375 degrees about 5 minutes, or until crispy. Sprinkle with Spike. Serve with the dip.

Dinner
Baked Lentil Surprise
2 cups lentils, cooked
1 cup bulgar, cooked
1/2 cup sunflower seed meal
1/2 cup wheat germ
3 Tbs. nutritional yeast
1 Tbs. soy sauce
1 Tbs. oil
1/4 tsp. basil

Thoroughly blend all ingredients. Turn into oiled muffin pans. Bake at 300 degrees for 30 to 40 minutes. Yields 6 servings.

Banana Salad
3 bananas
1 Tbs. sesame tahini
1/2 Tbs. honey
1 Tbs. protein powder
Raisins, seeds, nuts, etc.
Sprouts

Mix tahini, honey and protein powder together. Chop bananas and mix with desired seeds into sauce. Serve over sprouts.

Broccoli

Cut fresh broccoli into bit size pieces. Microwave in a covered glass dish for about 5 minutes until soft but not overdone. Squeeze lemon juice over broccoli and serve.

Raspberry Couscous Cake
1 cup couscous
pinch sea salt
2 cups unsweetened apple juice
1/2 lemon juice
1/2 pt. raspberries
1-2 tsp. almond slivers
1 tsp. vanilla or almond extract

Bring apple juice and sea salt to a boil in a saucepan; then add lemon juice, couscous and nuts. Lower heat and stir until almost thick. Remove from stove; stir in washed berries. Pour cake into glass baking dish that has been lightly sprayed with vegetable oil. Allow to cool and cut into squares. Can serve as is or garnish with roasted nuts or own granola.

SUNDAY
Breakfast:
Tofu Scrambled Eggs
1 to 2 Tbs. oil
1/2 tsp. turmeric
1 Tbs. soy sauce
1/2 tsp. sea salt (opt.)
Dash black pepper
1/4 tsp. onion powder
1/4 tsp. garlic powder
parsley, or 1/4 tsp. Spike (opt.)
2 cups tofu, well-drained and mashed

Combine first all of the ingredients except the tofu in a skillet and lightly cook. Add tofu and scramble for about 5 to 10 minutes. Serve like scrambled eggs.

Button Mushrooms
Saute with a squirt of lemon in a pan sprayed with vegetable oil.
100% Whole wheat toast.

Lunch
(can prepare in the morning)
Tabouli
1 cup bulgur wheat
2 cups boiling water
1/4 cup sunflower seeds
1 cup chopped tomato
1/2 cup minced fresh parsley
1/4 cup chopped green onions
1 Tbs. minced fresh mint leaves
1/4 cup lemon juice
1 Tbs. olive oil
1/4 tsp. salt
1/4 tsp. pepper
Pour boiling water over bulgur and let stand for 2 hours. Drain bulgur. Add tomato, parsley, onion, sunflower seeds and mint. In a separate bowl, combine remaining ingredients. Pour over bulgur and stir to combine. Chill before serving.
Sprout salad
Top a dish of alfalfa sprouts with tomatoes and sliced avocados. Sprinkle with *Royal Dressing.

Dinner
Vegetable Burgers
1 cup garbanzo flour (chickpea)
1 tsp. salt or 1 tsp. kelp
1/8 tsp. black pepper
1 tsp. parsley flakes
1 tsp. thyme powder
1 tsp. oregano
1 tsp. basil
1 tsp. Spike (or veg. seasoning)
dash of tabasco (opt.)

3/4 cup water
1/2 cup grated carrot
1/2 cup slivered green beans or 1/2 cup chopped celery
1/4 cup finely chopped spring onions
Combine first 10 ingredients and mix until free from lumps to make a thick batter. Add next 3 ingredients and mix well. Shape into patties. Place in a skillet that has been brushed with olive oil and cook on both sides until crisp. Serve on a whole wheat bun.

Spice Beets
2 cups cooked beets, grated
1/4 cup water
1/3 cup vinegar
1 Tbs. fructose
1/2 tsp. cinnamon
1/4 tsp. cloves
1/4 tsp. salt
Mix all ingredients together and simmer 7-10 minutes.

Apple Walnut Gelatin
2 cups unsweetened apple juice
1 1/2 sticks agar-agar (3/4 cup flakes)
1 Tbs. lemon juice
2 Tbs. honey
2 apples, grated
1/4 cup finely chopped walnuts
Pour apple juice into saucepan. Tear agar-agar apart and let soak in apple juice for 1 hour. Bring juice to a boil and then let simmer until all the agar-agar has dissolved. Add remaining ingredients, mixing well. Pour into square pan (8" or less). Set in refrigerator and chill until firm.

OMNIVORE WEEK

MONDAY
Breakfast
100% whole wheat bagel
egg fried in better butter (recipe in beginning of chapter)
baby carrots soaked in purified water

Lunch
Tuna Stuffed Potatoes
2 large, hot baked potatoes (can be cooked in the microwave)
1/4 cup hot skim milk or rice milk
1 green onion, minced
1 egg
2 tsp. butter or canola oil
1/4 tsp. salt
1/2 tsp. black pepper
1/2 cup diced tomato
7 ounce can water packed tuna, drained
2 tsp. Parmesan cheese, grated (opt.)

Cut a thin slice off the top of each baked potato, scoop out potato and combine with hot milk, green onion, beaten egg and butter. Whip well. Add salt, pepper and gently stir in tomato and tuna. Fill potato skins with this mixture by mounding it high. Sprinkle with Parmesan cheese. Place on baking sheet and cook at 400 degrees for 10-15 minutes.

Colorful Salad
Spinach leaves
alfalfa sprouts
carrots, grated
pickled beets, grated
edible flower (i.e. pansy)

On a bed of spinach leaves, place some sprouts, carrots and pickled beets. Sprinkle with *Royal Dressing and place a flower on the top.

Dinner
Sesame Chicken
4 split chicken breasts, skinned and boned
1/2 Tbs. lemon pepper
1 tsp. basil
1/2 tsp. garlic, chopped
2 eggs lightly beaten
1/4 cup barley flour or whole wheat flour
1/8 cup sesame seeds

Wash chicken and remove all visible fat. Place chicken in a zip lock bag with lemon pepper, basil and garlic and eggs and coat the chicken. Mix barley flour and sesame seeds together. Dip each piece of marinated chicken in the flour mixture and place meat side up in a baking dish that has been sprayed with vegetable oil (i.e. Pam) or you can use oven paper. Spray the chicken with the vegetable oil. Bake at 350 degrees for 45-50 minutes spraying spraying the chicken 25 minutes into the cooking time.

Raw Cauliflower Salad
1 cup raw cauliflower, grated
1 cup raw tender garden peas
1/2 cup avocado, diced
green pepper
couple of black olives (opt.)

Toss with *Royal Salad Dressing. Serve on spinach leaves. Garnish with green pepper strips and olives for color contrast.

Chewy Carrot Brownies
3/4 cup barley flour or whole wheat flour
1 tsp. baking powder
1 cup rolled oats
1/4 cup raisins
1 cup shredded carrots
1/4 cup honey
1/3 cup canola oil
1/2 tsp. liquid lecithin
1/4 cup unsweetened applesauce
1 tsp. maple extract (opt.)

Preheat oven to 375 degrees. In bowl mix dry ingredients together. In separate bowl, stir together liquid ingredients, carrots and raisins. Stir into dry ingredients until well moistened. Place in a greased 8x8 square pan. Bake for about 25 minutes until slightly browned. Can also make the dough into cookies and bake for 10-12 minutes or until golden brown on top. May add nuts or sunflower seeds when adding the raisins.

TUESDAY
Breakfast
Dragon slayer drink (found in beginning of this chapter)
Grapenuts or favorite non-sweetened cereal with non-fat milk or unsweetened apple juice

Lunch
This can make a simple dinner by adding the ingredients, minus 1/2 cup of water, into a crock pot with some leftover meat (that has been chopped). Cook on low for 10 hours.
Lentil Chili
1 1/2 cups lentils
4 cups water

1 cup ground turkey, fried
1/2 onion, diced
1 stalk celery, diced
3/4 Tbs. chili powder
1/2 Tbs. cumin
1/2 Tbs. garlic crushed
1/4 cup onion, diced
1/2 Tbs. fresh basil, diced
1 cup tomato
1/2 cup tomato paste
1 can green chilies
1 Tbs. parsley chopped fine
1/4 cup bell pepper, diced (opt)
Lite salt and pepper (opt.)

Cook lentils in water until done, approximately 1 hour. Add rest of ingredients. Simmer 30 minutes. May add a spoonful of no-fat sour cream to center of dish. Serve with whole wheat crackers.

Vegetable Platter
bell pepper, sliced
cherry tomatoes
baby carrots
radish, sliced
broccoli, cut in bite size pieces

Arrange on a plate and serve with *Royal Dressing.

Grapefruit Salad
Peel and secton gratefruit and arrange on top of spinach leaves or alfalfa sprouts. Can garnish with almond slices.

Dinner
Spicy Turkey Loaf
1 cup onion (large) diced
1/2 cup green pepper, diced
2 cloves garlic, minced
1/2 tsp. black pepper
1 piece whole wheat bread, cubed
1 egg

1 tsp. liquid lecithin
1 tsp. Worcestershire sauce
1/4 tsp. Tabasco
1 tsp. Spike, or dry poultry
seasoning
1 tsp. dry oregano
1 Tbs. chopped parsley
12 ounces tomato sauce
1 pound raw ground turkey
　　　　Preheat oven to 425
degrees. Mix all ingredients
reserving 1/2 cup tomato sauce.
Spray a 4x8 loaf pan with
vegetable coating spray and place
mixture in pan. Pat down until
firm and top with remaining sauce.
Bake at 425 degrees for 1 hour
until lightly browned around edges.

Baked Sweet Potatoes
　　　　Wash and bake sweet
potatos with the Turkey Loaf for
45 minutes or until done. If they
are large potatoes, you can
microwave them for 4-5 minutes.
Can use no-fat sour cream or
natural unsweetened applesauce,
chives, sea salt and pepper.

Marinated Vegetables
zucchini
broccoli
cauliflower
fresh mushrooms
carrots
*Royal Dressing
a few whole black olives for color
(opt.)
Parmesan cheese, grated (opt.)
　　　　Cut vegetables into bite-
size pieces. Marinate in salad
dressing for at least an hour.
Drain. May sprinkle with
Parmesan cheese before serving.

Highlight Cake
1/3 cup fructose
1/4 cup canola oil
1 egg
2/3 cup unsweetened applesauce
2 tsp. vanilla
1/4 to1/2 tsp. liquid lecithin
1 cup whole wheat flour
2 tsp. baking powder
1/4 tsp. salt
　　　　Beat together the first 6
ingredients. Add the remaining
ingredients, stirring until smooth.
Pour batter into a greased glass
baking dish. Cook in microwave
on medium or power level 7 for
about 10 minutes. Then cover
until cool. Don't overcook.
　　　　A frosting can be:
mashed banana with peanut butter
or a bit of honey; or pouring off
all of the oil on top of natural
peanut butter and using some of
the peanut butter with honey
mixed together; or frozen berries
mashed and poured on top of the
slices of cake.

WEDNESDAY
Breakfast
100% whole wheat bagel or toast
Turkey bacon cooked
Tomato slices

Lunch
Pita Bread Sandwich
　　　　Fill a pita pocket with
some of the following and sprinkle
with *Royal Dressing if
appropriate:
tomato slices
grated carrot
natural peanut or almond butter
raisins
mashed banana

low-fat cheese
sprouts
avocado slices
spinach leaves
sliced mushrooms

Deviled Eggs
4 hard-boiled eggs, peeled and cut
in half lengthwise
1-2 tsp. mayonnaise or ranch
salad dressing
1/2 tsp. prepared mustard
1 tsp. pickle relish
dash of onion powder
salt and pepper to taste
Remove yolks from eggs
and mash. Set aside egg white
halves. Mix yolks with remaining
ingredients. Spoon mixture into
egg whites. Garnish tops with a
dash of paprika.

Dinner
Easy Salmon Dinner
1-2 pound salmon filet or steak
Teriyaki sauce
Turn on broiler. Place
salmon on broiler pan sprayed
with vegetable oil where you will
be placing the salmon. Broil on
one side for about 8 minutes. Flip.
Spread the teriyaki sauce on the
top of salmon. Bake another 8
minutes or until done. You might
have to move the fish to a lower
shelf so the top doesn't burn. If
you are broiling halibut or a less
oily fish, you can put foil on the
broiling pan to save on clean up
time.
*If you don't have access to
fresh fish:*
Salmon Cakes
1 can (14.75 oz) salmon
1 cup dry oatmeal cereal

2 eggs
1/2 Tbs. lemon juice
2 tsp. minced parsley
1 tsp. onion powder
Drain salmon. Skim off
skin and bones. Mix all
ingredients. Make into patties.
Fry in 2 tsp. olive oil or canola
oil. When brown, flip and brown
other side.

Tomato & Red Onion Salad
Sliced tomatoes
Thinly sliced red onion, seperate
rings
Alternate sliced tomatoes
and onions. Can top with:
-grated parmesan cheese
-basil
-fresh herbs
-Grapenuts (if you like crunchy
food)
-sunflower seeds
-*Royal Dressing

Whole wheat dinner rolls

Gingersnap-baked Apples
2 apples, halved and cored
4 gingersnaps, finely crushed
1 tsp. sucanat
1 tsp. butter (opt.)
Put gingersnaps in running
blender to make crumbs. Place
crumbs in small bowl and add
sucanat and butter. Mix until
combined. Divide into fourths and
place in middle of apple. Bake at
350 degrees for about 15 minutes.

THURSDAY
Breakfast
Oat Raisin Scones
1 cup oats
1 cup whole wheat flour

1 Tbs. Sucanat
1 1/2 tsp. baking powder
1/4 tsp. soda
1/8 tsp. salt (opt.)
1/4 cup raisins
1/4 cup canola oil
1/2 cup unsweetened applesauce
1/4 to 1/2 tsp. liquid lecithin
1 Tbs lemon juice
1/4 tsp. cinnamon (opt.)
1 egg

Blend together the dry ingredients. Add the raisins. Combine the rest of the ingredients. Mix. Turn dough out onto a lightly floured surface. Flour your hands. Dough might be a bit sticky. Don't add too much flour or it will toughen the scones. You can use a spatula to help in the kneading. Knead until about 8-10 turns. Divide dough into two equal parts. Pat each part into a circle 1/2 inch thick. Cut into quarters. Transfered onto a baking sheet sprayed with vegetable oil or lined with oven paper. Bake until golden, about 20-25 minutes in 400 degree preheated oven. The scones can make a great dessert by serving warm and adding honey to the top.

1 egg - poached or boiled

Lunch
Pita Pizzas
1 whole wheat pita bread
fresh tomato slices
thinly sliced onion rings
green pepper, diced
sliced mushrooms (opt.)
oregano

light olive oil, sprinkled over vegetables
grated low fat cheese

You can use oven paper on a cookie sheet. Top bread with items listed. Baked in preheated 375 degree oven for about 8 to 10 minutes or until cheese is bubbly.

Cabbage Pecan Salad
1 1/2 cups finely shredded green cabbage
1/4 cup red seedless grapes, halved (opt.)
1/4 cup red apple, diced
1/4 cup pineapple, diced (opt.)
1 Tbs. chopped pecans

Place the cabbage in a serving bowl. Add the rest of the ingredients. Toss. Serve with *Royal Dressing.

Dinner
Turkey Feast
18 -20 pound turkey
canola oil

(Depending on the size, we thaw our turkey in a chest cooler for 1 1/2 to 2 days). Take out the parts inside of the turkey. Take out any wad of fat if there is one. Rinse. Pat dry. Tie the bird with cotton string so the wings and legs don't move. Place in roasting pan. Spread a little canola oil over the top of the bird. Cover with lid or foil. (You might need to take two pieces of foil and fold the two edges together lengthwise about 1/4 inch. Repeat. When placing foil over turkey, go around the edge of pan and push gently on the foil so it fits below the rim on the inside of pan. (This will keep the juices from escaping and soiling the oven.) No basting is needed. Bake at 350 degrees for about 5 1/2 to 6 hours (less time if you like turkey very moist). Clean meat off turkey while it's still warm. (The meat falls off easily). Divide in serving size portions and place in freezer baggies. Cool in refrigerator, then freeze what you will not eat in a few days.

Many people don't know what to do with the dark meat. A good sandwich paste can be made by using dark meat with your mayonnaise (recipe in chapter), mustard, onion powder, salt and pepper. Blend in a food processor. Or use the meat in burritos, tacos, soups and casseroles.

Brown Rice Delight
2 cups cooked instant brown rice or cooked brown rice
1 apple, diced
1-2 Tbs. walnuts or pecans, chopped
1-2 Tbs. raisins
2 Tbs celery leaves,chopped
1 tsp. poultry seasoning
Mix all ingredients together. Add a few teaspoons of water if too dry. Microwave for 1 minute.

Red Pepper & Zucchini Saute
1 lb. sweet red peppers
1 lb. zucchini
1 Tbs. olive oil
1/2 tsp. minced garlic
salt & pepper to taste
Cut peppers into 1-inch pieces. Wash and trim the zucchini. Quarter lengthwise and then cut into 1-inch pieces. Salt and drain. Pat dry. Heat the oil and saute zucchini for 3-4 minutes, until lightly browned and barely softened. Stir in the garlic, cook 30 seconds, then add the peppers. Heat together for about 2 minutes. Season with salt and pepper to taste. Serve hot.

Spinach and Mandarin Orange Salad
spinach leaves
canned mandarin oranges
coconut (opt.)
nuts, chopped
Place cleaned spinach in individual serving bowls. Ladle out a few of the mandarin oranges with some of the juice on the top of the spinach. Can sprinkle a bit of coconut, chopped nuts or seeds on the top.

Spicy Ginger Snaps
1/3 cup molasses
1/4 cup canola oil
2 Tbs sucanat
1 1/4 cup whole wheat flour
1/2 tsp. salt
1/4 tsp. baking soda
1/4 tsp. baking powder
1/2 tsp. cinnamon
1/2 tsp. ginger
1/4 tsp. ground cloves
Dash of nutmeg
Dash of allspice
Measure out the oil first and then the molasses. (The molasses will slide out of cup). Mix the first 3 ingredients together. Mix in remaining ingredients. Cover and refrigerate at least 4 hours. Heat oven to 375 degrees. Shape dough into a

log and roll dough into about a 3 inch log on wax paper or oven paper. Cut into 1/8 inch sections. Place on an ungreased cookie sheet and flatten out cookies with palm of hand. Bake until light brown, about 8 minutes. Thinner ones are about 5 minutes.

FRIDAY
Breakfast
Brown Rice Muffins
1 cup cooked brown rice, cold
1 cup unsweetened applesauce
3 eggs
2 Tbs. sucanat
2 tsp. vanilla
1/4 -1/2 tsp. liquid lecithin
1/4 cup canola oil
1 tsp. cinnamon
1 1/4 cups whole wheat flour
1 Tbs. baking powder
Combine rice, milk, eggs, sucanat and vanilla. Add dry ingredients and stir just enough to moisten. Pour batter into muffin tins that have been sprayed with oil. Bake at 400 degrees for 30 minutes or until golden brown on top. Makes 12 muffins.

Plain yogurt
may add 1/2 cup fresh fruit, diced or mashed, mixed into the yogurt

Lunch
Bacon, Tomato, Spinach Sandwich
Turkey bacon, cooked
tomato slices
spinach leaves, cleaned
100% whole wheat bread, toasted
On toast, layer the bacon, tomato, and spinach leaves. Can spread toast with *Royal Dressing or mayonnaise.

Own Mayonnaise
1 block soft tofu
3 Tbs. flax oil
3 Tbs. apple cider vinegar
salt to taste
your favorite seasoning (opt.)
Place the ingredients in a blender and puree until smooth.

Sweet Potato Delight
2 medium sweet potatoes, grated
1 medium onion, grated
1/3 tsp sea salt
1-2 Tbs. olive oil
Place the oil in frying pan and spread around. Add the rest of the ingredients and cook, covered, on medium heat. When brown on bottom, flip and cook with lid off until golden brown.

Dinner
Tuna Cakes
6 ounces water-packed tuna, drained
6 whole grain crackers, finely crushed
1/4 cup oats
1/4 cup minced red bell pepper
2 Tbs. fresh, minced parsley
2 Tbs. minced onions
1 egg
2 tsp. yogurt or water
1 1/2 tsp. lemon juice
1 tsp. Worcestershire
1/8 tsp. ground red pepper or 1/4 tsp. chili powder
1-2 tsp. minced fresh basil
1/2 tsp. marjoram
1 clove garlic, minced
No stick cooking spray
Spray a frying pan with the oil. In large bowl, gently mix all ingredients. Using scant 1/4

cup mixture for each, make 6 cakes. Shape mixture into circle, pressing flat. (If they are too dry to hold a shape, add a bit more water.) Place in frying pan and fry on both sides until golden brown.
Serves two.

Cold Tomato Sauce with Hot Pasta
1 1/2 cups diced tomato pulp
1/4 cup finely chopped sweet onions
1 tsp. minced garlic
1/6 cup chopped fresh basil
2 Tbs. chopped parsley
Wine vinegar or apple cider vinegar
Lite salt and freshly ground pepper
1/2 lb. whole wheat spaghetti
1/8 cup olive oil
Freshly grated Parmesan cheese (opt.)
Mix tomato pulp with onions, garlic, and herbs. Toss with a teaspoon of vinegar and season with salt and pepper. Cook spaghetti until cooked through but still slightly chewy. Drain. Combine tomatoes and oil and toss with the pasta. Serve with cheese.

Apple Bread Pudding
3 slices whole wheat bread, cubed
1 1/2 Tbs. chopped walnuts or pecans (opt.)
3 small apples, peeled and chopped
1/4 cup unsweetened apple juice
3 eggs
3/4 cup non fat plain yogurt or unsweetened applesauce

1/4 to1/2 tsp. lecithin
1/4 tsp. ground cinnamon
1 tsp. vanilla
Preheat oven to 350 degrees. Sprinkle bread cubes and walnuts into a square pan coated with non-stick cooking spray. Sprinkle with chopped apples; set aside. Beat together apple juice, eggs, yogurt, lecithin, cinnamon and vanilla until smooth; pour over bread and fruit in pan. Bake for 30 minutes. Press apples down into custard with spatula and bake an additional 20 minutes until custard is set. Serve warm or cold.

SATURDAY
Breakfast
Oatmeal
oatmeal
dried fruit (raisins, apricots, dates)
1 tsp.maple extract.
cinnamon
Cook oatmeal according to package directions adding any of the ingredients you choose. Serve with:
Turkey sausage, cooked
Whole wheat toast

Lunch
Three Bean Salad
2 cups cooked kidney beans (canned is okay)
2 cups cooked black-eyed peas (canned is okay)
2 cups fresh or frozen green beans, cooked but still firm
1 small red onion, cut into rings
2 Tbs. parsley, chopped
Marinate with:
*Royal Salad Dressing, or:
1/4 cup honey
1/3 cup vinegar

1/4 cup canola or flax oil
1 tsp. tarragon
1/2 tsp. basil
1/2 tsp. dry mustard.
        Mix marinate well and pour over the other ingredients. Refrigerate.

Low-fat Cottage Cheese Tomatoes
Large tomatoes
Cottage cheese
cinnamon to taste
        Cut tomatoes into quarters. Put a scoop of cottage cheese in the center and sprinkle with cinnamon.

Dinner
Easy Chicken & Sweet Potato Dinner
2-4 chicken breasts, washed
Onion powder
Spike seasoning or:
Lowery's seasoning without MSG
2-4 medium sweet potatoes or yams
        Place sweet potatoes that have been pierced with a knife in a foil-lined pan. In a 375 degrees preheated oven, cook the sweet potatoes for fifteen minutes. Then add the chicken that has been placed in a foil lined baking dish and sprinkled with the seasonings. Bake for 45 to 50 minutes more. If the sweet potatoes are large, you can microwave them for 4 or 5 minutes before placing in oven.

Delicious Garlic
1 bulb/head of garlic
Spike, or your favorite seasonings
1 tsp. olive oil

teriyaki sauce
        Cut the garlic head through the center. Break up the pieces. Place in a glass cup and sprinkle with olive oil, teriyaki sauce and seasonings. Microwave for 1 minute.

Stir-Fried Spinach with Ginger
1 lb. fresh spinach
1 small onion
1 Tbs. olive oil
1 clove garlic, minced fine
1/2 Tbs. ginger, finely minced
1 Tbs. soy sauce
1 tsp. honey
        Wash and trim spinach and cut leaves into wide strips. Chop onion. Heat oil and add onion, garlic, and ginger. Stir-fry on high heat for 1 minute. Add spinach and stir for just a few minutes. Add soy sauce and honey; turn down heat and cook about 1-2 minutes longer.

Pumpkin Cake
1/2 cup dry 1-minute oat cereal
1/2 cup wheat germ
1/2 cup whole wheat flour
1/3 cup sucanat
1 tsp. maple extract
2 tsp. cinnamon
1 tsp. pumpkin spice
1 tsp. baking powder
1 tsp. baking soda
1/2 tsp. sea salt
1/2 cup raisins
1 cup mashed cooked pumpkin (or canned)
2 eggs (unbeaten)
1/4 - 1/2 tsp. liquid lecithin
1/4 cup canola oil
2/3 cup low-fat yogurt or unsweetened applesauce

Sucanat

In bowl, combine bran, flour, oats, sucanat, spices, baking powder, baking soda, salt, and raisins and mix. Add rest of the ingredients and stir just until combined. Spoon batter into oil sprayed baking dish. Can sprinkle a little sucanant over the top of the batter and bake in 400 degree oven for 35-40 minutes or until firm to the touch and a toothpick stuck into the cake comes out dry.

SUNDAY
Brunch
Scrambled Eggs with Rice
4 eggs
1 cup cooked brown rice or wild rice, (not hot)
2 Tbs. skim milk or water
1 tsp. Worcestershire
1 Tbs. Parmesan cheese (opt.)
1/4 tsp. oregano
1 tsp. parsley
2 tsp. salsa

Combine all ingredients in a bowl. Beat ingredients until well blended. Lightly coat a nonstick skillet with better butter; place over medium heat. Pour in egg mixture. Scramble the eggs until they are cooked. The mixture will still be moist. Serve with extra salsa.

Serve with:
Turkey bacon, cooked
Whole wheat tortillas
Tomato slices

Dinner
Pressure Cooked Beef
3-4 pounds of lean roast (i.e. London Broiler)
1/3 pkg. of dry onion soup mix
1 cup water, wine, or vegetable stock

Place the beef on the rack in the pressure cooker. Add the soup mix and fluid. Bring the pressure cooker to a rock. Rock for 25 minutes. Turn off the heat. Let the steam valve go down on it's own.

Carrot and Cabbage Salad
2 cups grated carrots
2 cups grated cabbage
1 spring onion chopped (opt.)

Mix together and cover with *Royal Salad Dressing.

Basil Pesto
1 cup fresh basil leaves
1 1/2 cup spinach leaves
2 garlic cloves
1 Tbs. pine nuts or walnuts
2 Tbs. Parmesan cheese
1/2 Tbs. olive oil
2 Tbs. water

Add all ingredients together in a blender container. Process until a smooth paste. Use spatula and off/on motions to help processing. If you don't want to add the cheese, cut the water to 1 Tbs.

100% whole wheat rolls

Oatmeal Raisin Cookies
3 cups uncooked oatmeal
1 cup whole wheat flour
1 tsp. cinnamon
1/2 tsp. nutmeg
1/2 tsp. baking soda
1/2 cup unsweetened applesauce
1/2 cup canola

1/4 to 1/2 tsp. liquid lecithin (opt.)

2 tsp. vanilla

1 egg

1/2 cup chopped nuts (opt.)

1/2 cup raisins

Heat oven to 375 degrees. Lightly spray cookie sheet with no stick cooking spray or use oven paper. Combine dry ingredients, mixing well. Mix the rest of the ingredients stirring until well mixed. Place rounded spoonfuls of mixture on the cookie sheet. Bake approximately 10 to 12 minutes until golden brown.

PATIENT PROFILE: SLOWING PROSTATE CANCER

R.J. is a 69 year old male diagnosed August 1990 with prostate cancer, followed by prostatectomy. In January 1997, his PSA levels rose to 1.4 and his home town physician wanted to begin radiation therapy. In January 1997, a surgical biopsy of his lymph nodes in upper chest region showed enlargement and atypia (possible spreading of prostate cancer). He began nutrition therapy in January 1997 and lupron injections once each 90 days in March 1997. As of June 1997, his PSA levels were down to 0.6 and lymph nodes have returned to normal size. He is feeling good & working full time. He is very pleased with the results from his nutrition therapy.

ENDNOTES

[1]. Jochems, R., DR. MOERMAN'S ANTI-CANCER DIET, Avery, Garden City, NY, 1990
[2]. Livingston-Wheeler, V., et al., THE CONQUEST OF CANCER, Waterside, San Diego, 1984
[3]. Gerson, M., A CANCER THERAPY, Gerson Institute, Bonita, CA 1958
[4]. Aihara, H., ACID & ALKALINE, George Ohsawa Foundation, Oroville, CA, 1986; see also Kushi, M., THE CANCER PREVENTION DIET, St. Martin Press, NY, 1983
[5]. Abdullah, TH, et al., Journal of the National Medical Association, vol.80, no.4, p.439, Apr.1988
[6]. Belman, S., Carcinogenesis, vol.4, no.8, p.1063, 1983
[7]. Kiukian, K., et al., Nutrition and Cancer, vol.9, p.171, 1987
[8]. Kroning, F., Acta Unio Intern. Contra. Cancrum, vol.20, no.3, p.855, 1964
[9]. You, WC, et al., Journal of the National Cancer Institute, vol.81, p.162, Jan.18, 1989
[10]. Ansher, SS, Federation of Chemistry and Toxicology, vol.24, p.405, 1986
[11]. Chihara, G., et al., Cancer Detection and Prevention, vol.1, p.423, 1987 suppl.
[12]. Kennedy, A., and Little, JB, Cancer Research, vol.41, p.2103, 1981
[13]. Messina, M., et al., Journal National Cancer Institute, vol.83, no.8, p.541, Apr.1991
[14]. Oreffo, VI, et al., Toxicology, vol.69, no.2, p.165, 1991; see also von Hofe, E, et al., Carcinogenesis, vol.12, no.11, p.2147, Nov.1991; see also Su, LN, et al., Biochemical & Biophysical Research Communications, vol.176, no.1, p.18, Apr.1991
[15]. Eaton, SB, et al., New England Journal of Medicine, vol.312, no.5, p.283, Jan.1985

SUPPLEMENTS AGAINST CANCER

★

"We live in a world in a world of problems which can no longer be solved by the level of thinking which created them." Albert Einstein, PhD

The risk to benefit to cost ratio of nutrition supplements is heavily in favor of using them WHERE APPROPRIATE. Meaning, you need some professional guidance. Our health care system is so dominated by allopathic drugs, most of which have many harmful side effects, that the question is often asked: "If these nutrients are so helpful, then what is the risk of using them, especially at the higher doses recommended for cancer patients?" Here's your answer.

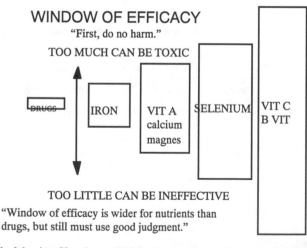

All substances consumed, from chemotherapy, to allopathic drugs, to vitamins, minerals, herbs and even food--all have a "window of efficacy". Above that level is too much and may cause damage. Below that level is probably ineffective. With drugs, the window of efficacy is much narrower, and hence great caution must be used in administering prescription medication. All nutrients have a wider window of efficacy than all drugs. Yet some nutrients are more likely to harm than others. Iron, copper, selenium, vitamin A, and D are the nutrients that must be used with discretion. Most other nutrients are unlikely to harm.

RISKS OF NUTRITION THERAPY

In an extensive review of the literature found in the New York Academy of Sciences textbook BEYOND DEFICIENCIES (vol.669, p.300, 1992), Dr. Adrienne Bendich found the following data on nutrient toxicity

>B-6 can be used at up to 500 mg (250 times RDA) for up to 6 years with safety.

>Niacin (as nicotinic acid) has been recommended by the National Institute of Health for lowering cholesterol at doses of 3000-6000 mg/day (150-300 times RDA). Time release niacin is more suspect of causing toxicity as liver damage.

>Vitamin C was tested in eight published studies using double blind placebo controlled design. At 10,000 mg/day for years, vitamin C produced no side effects.

>High doses of vitamin A (500,000 iu daily) can have acute reversible effects. Teratogenecity is the most likely complication of high dose vitamin A intake.

>Vitamin E intake at up to 3000 mg/day for prolonged periods has been shown safe.

>Beta-carotene has been administered for extended periods in humans at doses up to 180 mg (300,000 iu) with no side effects or elevated serum vitamin A levels.

In a separate review of the literature on nutrient toxicity found in the New York Academy of Sciences textbook MICRONUTRIENTS AND IMMUNE FUNCTION (vol.587, p.257, 1990) by John Hathcock, PhD, a Food and Drug Administration toxicologist, the following data was reported:

>Vitamin A toxicity may start as low as 25,000 iu/day (5 times RDA) in people with impaired liver function via drugs, hepatitis, or protein malnutrition. Otherwise, toxicity for A begins at several hundred thousand iu/day.

>Beta-carotene given at 180 mg/day (300,000 iu or 60 times RDA) for extended periods produced no toxicity, but mild carotenemia (orange pigmentation of skin).

>Vitamin E at 300 iu/day (10 times RDA) can trigger nausea, fatigue, and headaches in sensitive individuals. Otherwise, few side effects are seen at up to 3,200 iu/day.

>B-6 may induce a reversible sensory neuropathy at doses of as low as 300 mg/day in some sensitive individuals. Toxic threshold usually begins at 2000 mg for most individuals.

>Vitamin C may induce mild and transient gastro-intestinal distress in some sensitive individuals at doses of 1000 mg (16 times

RDA). Otherwise, toxicity is very rare at even high doses of vitamin C intake.

>Zinc supplements at 300 mg (20 times RDA) have been found to impair immune functions and serum lipid profile.

>Iron intake at 100 mg/day (6 times RDA) will cause iron storage disease in 80% of population. The "window of efficacy" on iron is probably more narrow than with other nutrients.

>Copper can be toxic, though dose is probably related to the ratio with other trace minerals.

>Selenium can be toxic at 1-5 mg/kg body weight intake. This would equate to 65 mg/day for the average adult, which is 812 times the RDA of 80 mcg. Some sensitive individuals may develop toxicity at 1000 mcg/day.

>Manganese can be toxic, though little specific information can be provided for humans.

There are many vitamins, minerals, botanicals (herbs), fatty acids, food extracts, glandulars and other nutrient compounds that can be of benefit to the cancer patient. You may take all of these "a la carte" at a cost of $1500-$2000 per month and 200+ pills per day, or you may consider using the ImmunoPower supplement. ImmunoPower (web site: www.immunopower.com; toll free order 1-888-741-LIFE) is a mixture of 65 nutrition factors, mostly in powder form that is much more convenient, complete and cost-effective than the usual "life and death scavenger hunt" that cancer patients have embarked upon. Dosages listed in the following 3 chapters of supplements are suggested per meal. Double or triple these dosages per day for maximal therapeutic effects. Choose the supplement regimen that best suits your ability to tolerate vitamins and ability to pay for them.

IMMUNOPOWER INGREDIENTS

One scoop of powder contains:
Vitamins

A (palmitate)	8,000 iu
betacarotene (betatene)	15 mg (=25,000 iu)
D-3 (cholecalciferol)	200 iu
E (2/3 succinate, 1/3 natural)	400 iu
K (menadione)	100 mcg
C total	2500 mg
ascorbic acid 1000 mg	
sodium ascorbate 1500 mg	
B-1 (thiamine mononitrate)	10 mg
B-2 (riboflavin)	10 mg
B-3 (hexanicotinate)	500 mg
B-5 (D-calcium pantothenate)	20 mg
B-6 total	50 mg
Pyridoxal 5 pyrophosphate 3.3 mg	
pyridoxine HCl 46.6 mg	
B-12 (cyanocobalamin)	1 mg
Folic acid	200 mcg
Biotin	50 mcg

Minerals

Calcium (aspartate)	150 mg
Magnesium (aspartate)	150 mg
Potassium (aspartate)	333 mg
Zinc (chelate)	10 mg
Iron (chelate)	3.3 mg
Copper (chelate)	1 mg
Iodine (potassium iodide)	50 mcg
Manganese (chelate)	1.67 mg
Chromium (GTF niacinate)	200 mcg
Selenium (selenomethionine)	200 mcg
Molybdenum (chelate)	167 mcg
Vanadium (vanadyl sulfate)	33 mcg
Nickel (sulfate)	3.3 mcg
Tin (chloride)	3.3 mcg

Accessory Factors

Lipoic acid	33 mg
Lycopene	3 mg
Aloe powder	mg
Dimethylglycine	16.7 mg
L-carnitine	100 mg

Bovine cartilage (VitaCarte)	3 gm
Nucleic acid (DNA)	500 mg
Nucleic acid (RNA)	500 mg
FOS, fructo-oligosaccharides	1 gm
Tocotrienols	20 mg
Quercetin	167 mg
Medium chain triglycerides	1 gm
Lecithin, phosphatidylcholine	1500 mg
Genistein (soy)	6 mg
L-glycine	1 gm
Glucaric acid (cal D glucarate)	500 mg
vanilla flavoring	

DIRECTIONS: 1 scoop taken 1 to 3 times daily (maximum 3 scoops per day) with meals, or as directed by your health care professional.

EACH PACKET CONTAINS 10 pills consisting of:
1 capsule of:

Garlic, (Kyolic)	600 mg

2 capsules of:

Coenzyme Q-10	100 mg
Thymic concentrate	500 mg
Spleen concentrate	500 mg

2 capsules of:

Oligomeric proanthocyanidins	50 mg
Silymarin (milk thistle)	140 mg
Echinecea (purpurea)	80 mg
Curcumin (curcuma longa)	50 mg
Ginkgo biloba (24% heteroside)	40 mg
Astragalus (membranaceus)	167 mg
Panax ginseng (8%)	167 mg
Green tea polyphenols	67 mg
Cruciferous 400, sulforaphane 80 mg	
Cat's claw, 3:1	200 mg
Maitake D-fraction	20 mg
L-glutathione	100 mg

Lipids

Marine lipids (2 caps)	2 grams
Evening primrose oil (2 caps)	1 gram
Shark oil (1 capsule)	1 gram

DIRECTIONS: 1 packet taken 1 to 3 times daily (maximum of 3 packets per day) with meals, or as directed by your health care professional.

CHAPTER 9

SUPPLEMENTS AGAINST CANCER
★
BOTANICALS, GLANDULARS, LIPIDS, MINERALS, ENZYMES

"Behold, I have given you every green plant, and it shall be food for you." Genesis 1:29

HERBAL MEDICINE

AS SUPPLEMENTS:	AS FOODS:	AS SEASONINGS:
echinecea	soy	garlic
astragalus	green & orange	onion
Cat's claw	dandelion greens	hot peppers
Pau D'arco	citrus	cinnamon
ginseng	tomato	ginger
grape seed extract	green tea	real licorice
aloe vera	broccoli/cabbage	tumeric (curry)
red clover	beets	parsley
milk thistle	sprouts	sage
Essiac	flaxseed meal	chicory
Hoxsey	sesame seeds	thyme
Floressence	Maitake mushrm	basil

Our ancestors used to practice botanical medicine all day everyday--in the kitchen. While we have a tendency to think of herbs as mysterious plant concoction blended up for a very sick person by some eccentric older woman (the quintessential herbalist), in fact our ancestors ate potent anti-cancer herbs in their diet and as seasonings each day.

Columbus set sail in a mad suicidal adventure over the edge of the earth in the unlikely event that he might find the Spice Islands, near India. Spices (a.k.a. seasonings, herbs, botanicals) have been used throughout history to cover the rotting stench of unrefrigerated food. As an unintentional by-product of using these seasoning agents, like cinnamon, garlic, hot pepper, ginger, and curry, our ancestors were able to keep the cancer incidence well below what we currently have. While this section pays homage to the scientific data using botanical extracts as anti-cancer medicines, I would strongly encourage you to use the herbs listed as foods and seasonings on a regular basis.

The list of scientific references presented here is only representative of the peer-reviewed data on the use of nutrition supplements as part of comprehensive cancer treatment.

Oligomeric proanthocyanidins (OPC)   50 mg
Potent antioxidant, supports vitamin C functions, penetrates the blood brain barrier, reduces capillary fragility, enhances peripheral circulation, protects DNA from damage by radiation and chemotherapy.

Scurvy (deficiency of vitamin C) has played a huge role in human history. Humans roamed the oceans of the world throughout the 15th through the 19th centuries, often losing up to half of the people on board ship due to scurvy. The English physician, James Lind, discovered that limes cured scurvy in 1747 and began to wind down the death toll from scurvy, while also labeling the English sailors as "limeys". In 1930, Nobel prize winner, Albert Szent-Gyorgy, MD, PhD, isolated pure vitamin C. Ironically, the pure white crystalline vitamin C that Dr. Szent-Gyorgy isolated would not cure bleeding gums, whereas the crude brown mixture of citrus extract would. The difference between these two mixtures was "bioflavonoids", which include over 20,000 different chemical compounds that generally assist chlorophyll in photosynthesis and protect the plant from the harmful effects of the sun's radiation. The rainbow colors of fall foliage are Nature's art exhibit of bioflavonoids and carotenoids.

Some of the main categories of bioflavonoids include:
◊ anthocyanins; deep purple compounds found in black grapes, beets, red onions, and berries
◊ catechins and epigallocatechin, which are polyphenols found in apples and green tea
◊ ellagic acid, a true anti-cancer compound found in cranberries, raspberries, and other berries.
◊ flavones, found in citrus fruit, red grapes and green beans
◊ flavanols, such as quercetin, myricetin, found in kale, spinach, onions, apples, and black tea

◊ flavanones, such as hesperidin and naringen found in citrus fruits of grapefruit, oranges and lemons.

Some of the better known bioflavonoids include rutin, which is defined in the DORLAND'S MEDICAL DICTIONARY as capable of "preventing capillary fragility." Hesperidin, quercetin (also in and discussed later), pycnogenol from pine bark, and proanthocyanidins are other popular bioflavonoids. While bioflavonoids are known to be essential in the diet of insects, bioflavonoids are not yet considered essential in the human diet.

Proanthocyanidins can exist in a variety of forms, including dimers, trimers, etc.. A collective group of these proanthocyanidins are known as OPC. As the science of nutrition matures, we are finding that some of the "star" nutrients of the past may be just "supporting actors" for the real star nutrients. For instance, tocotrienols and Coenzyme Q may be more important than vitamin E in human health. Eicosapentaenoic acid (EPA from fish oil), though not considered essential, may be more important than alpha-linolenic acid (ALA from flax oil), which is considered essential. And bioflavonoids may be more important than vitamin C. OPC bound to phosphatidylcholine (lecithin) has been shown to improve absorption and cell access to OPC, which is one of the reasons why there are 4.5 grams of lecithin in a full day's supply of .

Animals with implanted tumors lived longer when given anthocyanin from grape rinds.[1] Flavonoids administered in the diet of rats helped to reduce DNA damage from benzopyrene carcinogens.[2] Bioflavonoids are potent chelators, helping to eliminate toxic minerals from the system.[3] Bioflavonoids in general help to reduce allergic reactions, which create an imbalanced immune attack against cancer and infections. OPC traps lipid peroxides, hydroxyl radicals, delays the onset of lipid peroxidation, prevents iron-induced lipid peroxidation, inhibits the enzymes that can degrade connective tissue (hyaluronidase, elastase, collagenase) which then helps to prevent cancer cells from "knocking down the walls" of surrounding tissue for metastasis. Bioflavonoids may inhibit tumor promotion.[4] Bioflavonoids enhance the activity of T-lymphocytes.[5] Various flavonoids have produced striking reductions in cancer incidences in animals, sometimes up to almost total inhibition of tumorogenesis.[6]

Silymarin (milk thistle) 140 mg
Stimulates liver detoxification and tissue regeneration, may also augment immune functions.

Silybum marianum, or milk thistle, is a stout annual plant that grows in dry rocky soils in parts of Europe and North America. Its seeds, fruit and leaves are widely prescribed medication in Europe for most diseases affecting the liver. Silymarin has been shown to help regenerate liver tissue, protect the liver against toxic chemicals, increase the production of glutathione (GSH) which is fundamental in the cell protecting itself against hydrogen peroxide produced.[7]

Since the liver is the primary detoxifying organ of the body and automatically becomes involved in the internal cancer battle, metastasis to the liver complicates cancer treatment. Among other functions, the liver also stores many vitamins and minerals, produces bile salts for fat digestion and absorption, and is generally one of the more versatile and essential organs in the body. For recovery from cancer to be possible, the liver must be healthy.

Echinecea (purpurea)   80 mg
> Immune stimulant.

Echinacea species consist primarily of E. angustifolia, E. purpurea, and E. pallida. Native American herbalists used echinacea more than any other plant for medicinal purposes. There are over 350 scientific articles worldwide on the immune enhancing effects of echinacea, including the:
◊ activation of complement, which promotes chemotaxis of neutrophils, monocytes, and eosinophils; "gearing up" the immune cells
◊ solubilization of immune complexes
◊ neutralization of viruses.[8]

One of the components of echinacea, arabinogalactan, has shown promise as an anti-cancer agent in vitro.[9]

In patients with inoperable metastatic esophageal and colorectal cancers, supplements of echinacea (as Echinacin) provided modest improvements in immune functions, slowed the growth of some tumors, and increased survival time.[10] Outpatients with advanced colorectal cancers were given echinacea as part of therapy with some patients experiencing stable disease, reduction in tumor markers, increases in survival time and no toxicity reported.[11]

Curcumin (curcuma longa)   50 mg
> Potent antioxidant, protector of DNA.

Curry is an Indian spice that includes tumeric as one of the flavoring agents. The active component in tumeric appears to be a bright yellow pigment, curcumin (a.k.a.curcuma longa) which helps to enhance the immune system by protecting immune cells from their own poisons (pro-oxidants) used to kill cancer cells. Mustard is a good source of curcumin.

Curcumin appears to be a potent inhibitor of cancer.[12] In animal experiments, curcumin was shown to be directly toxic to tumor cells.[13] In a study with smokers, tumeric tablets were able to dramatically reduce the excretion of urinary mutagen levels (indicators of the possibility of cancer). [14] In patients with skin cancers (squamous cell carcinomas) who had failed therapy with chemo, radiation and surgery, supplements or ointment of tumeric were able to provide significant reduction in the smell, size, itching, pain, and exudate of the lesions.[15]

Ginkgo biloba (24% heteroside)   40 mg
Improves circulation, augments the production of healthy prostaglandin PGE-1, immune stimulant, and adaptogen (helps to regulate many cellular functions).

The ginkgo tree is one of the oldest living species on earth, having been around for over 200 million years. The ginkgo tree is an incredibly adaptable and tenacious plant. One ginkgo tree survived the near-ground zero nuclear blast in Hiroshima, Japan. Millions of these cone-shaped evergreen trees survive amidst air pollution, drought and poor soil throughout the world. A ginkgo tree may live as long as 1000 years. The leaves and berries contain a wide assortment of phytochemicals (collectively called "ginkgoflavonglycosides") that have been a pivotal medicine in China for 5000 years. There are now over 1,000 scientific studies published over the past 40 years demonstrating the medicinal value of ginkgo, with ginkgo extract becoming one of the more widely prescribed medications in Europe today. In 1989, over 100,000 physicians worldwide wrote over 10 million prescriptions for ginkgo.

There are several ways in which ginkgo may help the cancer patient:

◊ Vasodilator, expands the tiny capillaries that nourish 90% of the body's tissues, thus bringing oxygen and nutrients to the cells. In doing so, ginkgo improves depression[16] and general circulation to the organs.[17]

◊ Inhibits platelet aggregation, or the stickiness of cells. Stroke, heart attacks, and cancer metastasis are fueled by sticky cells which are generated by Platelet Activating Factor (PAF). Ginkgo inhibits PAF.[18] By modifying PAF, ginkgo helps to reduce inflammation and allergic responses.[19]

◊ Antioxidant of exceptional efficiency.[20] Slows down free radical destruction of healthy tissue, therefore protects immune cells in their semi-suicidal quest to kill cancer cells and also protects the favorable prostaglandin, PGE-1. This antioxidant activity also helps to stabilize membranes, where the lipid bi-layer is vulnerable to lipid peroxidation. This protection extends to the DNA, which is why Chernobyl workers were given ginkgo to protect them from further damage via radioactivity.

Astragalus (membranaceus)   167 mg
      Adaptogen and immune stimulant.

Adaptogens are a small and elite group of herbal compounds, including garlic and ginseng, which coordinate and regulate a broad spectrum of biochemical processes, including prostaglandins, cell membranes, blood sugar levels, etc..   "Adaptogen" is the term coined in 1957 by the Russian pharmacologist I. Brekhman. Criteria for an adaptogen is that it must be:[21]
⇒ innocuous, cause minimal harm in reasonable quantities
⇒ non-specific in activity, that is, able to influence a wide range of physical, chemical and biochemical pathways in the body
⇒ a normalizer of functions; meaning that it will lower or raise a bodily measurement, depending on what needs to happen for improvement in overall health to occur, such as raising blood pressure in hypotensive individuals and lowering blood pressure in hypertensive individuals.[22]

Astragalus has also demonstrated anti-viral activity as it was able to shorten the duration and severity of the common cold in humans.[23] Researchers at M.D. Anderson Hospital in Houston found that astragalus was able to enhance the immune capacity using the cultured blood of 14 cancer patients[24] as well as augment the anti-tumor ability of Interferon-2.[25] In a study of 176 patients undergoing chemotherapy for cancers of the gastro-intestinal tract, astragalus and ginseng were able to prevent the normal immune depression and weight loss that occurs.[26] In a variety of human studies, astragalus has been shown to stimulate various parameters of the immune system, has anti-tumor activity, and inhibits the spreading (metastasis) of cancer.[27]

Panax ginseng (8%)   167 mg
      Adaptogen, immune stimulant, anti-tumor activity, inhibits metastasis.[28]

Ginseng is one of the oldest, most widely used and scientifically studied of all the world's herbs. The original proponents of ginseng were Chinese physicians several thousand years ago, using it to treat nearly every conceivable ailment. Given the known "adaptogenic" qualities of ginseng, the enthusiasm of these ancient Chinese doctors may have been well placed. Ginseng is a plant species term (Panax) which is further subdivided into Panax quinquefolium (American ginseng), Panax japonicum (Japanese ginseng), Panax pseudoginseng (Himalayan ginseng) and Panax trifolium.[29] Eleutherococcus senticosus is a relative newcomer to this category, contains some ginseng-like compounds (triterpenoid saponins), but is not considered true ginseng. Panax ginseng C.A. Meyer is the best studied in the scientific literature and referred to in the followed studies.

The wide disparity in outcome of clinical studies using ginseng probably stems from the lack of active ingredients in many substandard ginseng products sold today. Ginseng's therapeutic value comes from the 13 different triterpenoid saponins, collectively known as ginsenosides, which are found in various concentrations in various types of ginseng grown on various soils and experiencing various drying and storage techniques. While most ginseng is about 1-3% ginsenosides, better products will offer 8% concentration. In one study published in 1979, of the 54 ginseng products analyzed, 60% were worthless and 25% had no ginseng at all![30] It is the regularly formed root from wild Panax ginseng that is the most highly prized. Nearly 60,000 people are employed in Korea for the raising and processing of ginseng.

Ginseng may help cancer patients for the following reasons:

◊ **Adaptogenic qualities**. Ginseng is nearly unsurpassed in the plant kingdom for its ability to bring about biochemical adjustments in whatever direction is necessary.

◊ **Central nervous system stimulant**.[31] In various animal and human studies, ginseng provides both calming and stimulating effects simultaneously. It allows people to better adapt to stressful situations, including cancer. It also provides for energizing effects and improvement of moods and alertness.

◊ **Blood glucose regulator**. While ginseng will lower blood glucose levels in the diabetic individual or the one fed a high sugar diet, it will not lower blood glucose in the healthy individual fed a normal diet.[32] Since cancer is a sugar feeder, keeping blood glucose levels in check is a crucial job of ginseng.

◊ **Immune-stimulating effects**. Ginseng has been shown to stimulate the reticuloendothelial system, which means getting more macrophages ("big eaters") to gobble up (phagocytosis) cancer cells and cell debris.[33] In animals, ginseng was shown to prevent viral infections.[34] Ginseng can dramatically bolster host defense mechanisms in animals and humans.

◊ **Liver cleansing, protection and stimulation**. Ginseng activates the macrophages in the liver, known as Kupffer cells, which are responsible for removing cellular debris from the body's most important detoxifying organ, the liver. Macrophages in the liver help to "take out the trash". Ginseng also helps to improve protein synthesis in the liver[35], reverse diet-induced fatty liver and protect the liver from chemically-induced damage.[36]

◊ **Anti-clotting and metastatic**. Cancer spreads by adhering to blood vessel walls. Hence reducing the stickiness, or platelet aggregation, of cells is a major plus. Ginseng reduces platelet aggregation.[37]

◊ **Anti-cancer properties**. Ginseng is a potent inhibitor of cancer in animals[38] and humans.[39] Ginseng has the unique, paradoxical and nearly miraculous ability to control cell growth, or hyperplasia. In healthy cells with adequate nourishment, ginseng encourages cell division. Yet under adverse conditions, ginseng helps to suppress abnormal cell division.[40] Ginseng helps to repair damaged DNA.[41]

In tumor bearing mice, 8 days of ginseng administration brought about a 75% reduction in average tumor size.[42] Oral administration of ginseng in tumor bearing mice inhibited the growth of liver cancer (solid ascites hepatoma), while inhibiting metastasis to the lungs.[43] Panax ginseng was able to enhance the uptake of mitomycin (an antibiotic and anti-cancer drug) into the cancer cells for increased tumor kill.[44] Ginseng was able to slow tumor growth and improve survival time in rats with chemically-induced liver cancer.[45]

SAFETY ISSUES
Ginseng and estrogen.

Of the many supplements that may be useful for cancer patients, 2 of them contain estrogen-like compounds: soy and ginseng, which merit a special discussion. There is some controversy in the scientific community regarding the use of estrogen-like compounds in the treatment of breast or ovarian cancer patients.

First, it is critical to set the records straight regarding the importance of estrogen. Estrogen is an essential hormone produced by women throughout their menstruating years as part of fertility. Estrogen has 260 different functions in the human body, including antioxidant, maintenance of bone structure, and protection against cardiovascular diseases. Estrogen does not cause breast or ovarian cancer, but it is a growth hormone and can accelerate the growth of anything, including hormone-dependent cancers.

There are 4 primary categories of estrogen-like compounds:

⇒ **Estrogen,** which actually refers to a family of hormones, including estradiol, estriol and estrone, manufactured in the female body for specific bodily functions.[46]

⇒ **Phytoestrogens**, which are estrogen-like compounds in plants, which have about 0.05% (1/2000) the strength of estrogen and have demonstrated beneficial effects both pre and post cancer diagnosis. These compounds compete with estrogen for binding to estrogen receptor sites.[47]

⇒ **Xenoestrogens**, which are estrogen-like compounds in herbicides, pesticides and other commercial chlorinated hydrocarbons. These have been shown to have disastrous consequences of antagonizing all of the negative aspects of estrogen.[48] Women with breast cancer have been found to have more chlorinated hydrocarbons, or xeno-estrogens, in their bloodstream. These xeno-estrogens are creating havoc in the wild, where male animals end up with dramatically deformed genitals and females have reduced fertility and increases in birth defects.

⇒ **Estrogen-receptors**, which are compounds that escort estrogen from the body, hopefully after it has performed its essential functions. The human body makes estrogen-receptors through the PGE-1 prostaglandin pathways when blood sugar levels are kept low and essential fatty acids (EPA, ALA, GLA, LA) are sufficient. Other compounds in , sulforaphane and calcium D-glucarate, are included for the purposes of escorting estrogen from the body in a non-toxic manner.

Tamoxifen is an estrogen binder that can be of value in short term use to slow down breast cancer, but in long term use elevates the risk for heart attack [49] eye[50] and liver damage[51] and INCREASING the risk of endometrial cancer.[52]

Researchers, like Stephen Barnes, PhD at the University of Alabama, find that soy is able to inhibit the growth of hormone-dependent tumors, including breast and prostate. Soy and ginseng are Nature's "kinder, gentler" forms of Tamoxifen.

Adding all of this complex biochemistry together and trying to make the recommendations simple, there are several reasons why the 4 above-mentioned categories of estrogen-like compounds are not equal. Soy products and ginseng have been used both to prevent and reverse cancer. The macrobiotic diet, which uses soy as a pivotal source of protein, has not been shown to accelerate the course of breast or ovarian cancer. There are several soy-based products, including Haelan 851 and Dr. Ann Kennedy's Bowman Birk Inhibitor that help to slow various cancers, including breast and ovarian. While soy and ginseng products can reduce the symptoms of menopause by working as phytoestrogens, they do not increase the risk for breast or ovarian cancer nor do they accelerate the disease once present.

Green tea polyphenols   67 mg
Antioxidant, protector of DNA, immune stimulant.

America was founded upon a tea revolt. The American colonists decided that, rather than pay the English King's taxes on tea without representation in the British Parliament, the colonist would rather go into caffeine "cold turkey" by throwing the tea into Boston harbor. While the British have brought "high tea time" into its revered limelight, tea was first introduced to England in the 17th century via trade with China where it had been a favorite beverage for over 3,000 years. Of the 2.5 million tons of dried tea produced each year worldwide, most is grown and consumed in the Orient.

Tea comes from the plant Camellia sinensis, an evergreen shrub in which the young leaves can be either:
◊   lightly steamed to produce **green tea** or
◊   air dried and oxidized to produce **black tea**.

The potent polyphenols are maintained in green tea, since steaming denatures the enzymes that would normally convert the polyphenols to less beneficial ingredients. Green tea is healthier than black tea. While both forms of tea have caffeine, only 20% of tea produced annually comes as green tea.

One of the first scientific references to tea and cancer came from the watershed report from the World Health Organization in 1964, "Prevention of Cancer" in which these experts found a higher incidence of esophageal cancer among people in the Middle East who drink extremely hot tea on a regular basis.[53] This boiling tea burns the esophagus and creates a state of lifelong hyperproliferation, which invites cancer if nutrition intake is less than ideal. There is still some question as to whether black tea at normal drinking temperature constitutes a risk or a protection against cancer.[54] Green tea has such an extensive scientific foundation as a non-toxic and inexpensive anti-cancer agent, that the National Cancer Institutes of China and Japan are researching green tea with the same fervor that the American NCI researches chemotherapy drugs.

Green tea contains a variety of polyphenolic compounds, including catechin, epicatechin, and the reputed chief active ingredient, epigallocatechin gallate. One cup of green tea contains 300 to 400 mg of polyphenols and 50 to 100 mg of caffeine. Green tea works as an antioxidant, perhaps even more potent than vitamins C or E.[55] In animals, green tea was able to induce major improvements in antioxidant and detoxifying enzymes in the body.[56] In human studies, green tea users have about half the cancer incidence of non-tea drinkers.[57] In test tube studies, green tea shut down the tumor promoters involved in breast cancer.[58]   Green tea inhibits the formation of cancer-causing agents in the stomach, including nitrosamines.[59]

The anti-cancer properties of green tea include:[60]

◊ Immune stimulant.
◊ Inhibits platelet adhesion, and possibly metastasis.
◊ Antioxidant which protects immune cells for a higher tumor kill rate while protecting the valuable prostaglandin PGE-1.
◊ Inhibits metastasis.
◊ Inhibits the breakdown of connective tissue via collagenase, which is the primary mechanism for the spreading of cancer cells.[61]

Cruciferous 400, sulforaphane   80 mg
Detoxifying agent, helps to neutralize the damaging effects of estrogen, may selectively slow the cancer process.

It was the cabbage family that was first highlighted in this new and exciting field of phytochemicals. Although the father of modern medicine, Hippocrates, taught us 2400 years ago "Let food be your medicine and medicine be your food", modern medicine has only recently begun to accept the importance of this ancient truth. For instance, researchers in the Cold War era of 1950 fed two different groups of animals either beets or cabbage and then exposed them to radiation. The animals fed cabbage had much less hemorrhaging and death from radiation. But since no one in those days could conceive of a radio-protective effect of a food, the scientists concluded that "something in beets makes radioactive exposure more lethal."[62] Actually, "something" in cabbage makes radiation much less damaging to healthy tissue.

Cruciferous vegetables include cabbage, broccoli, brussel sprouts, cauliflower and others. Among the phytochemicals in cruciferous vegetables that have been researched, sulforaphane is one of the more promising as a cancer fighter. It was Professor Lee Wattenburg of Minnesota who found that cabbage extract has the ability to prevent the initiation and promotion of cancer cells.[63] Of the various fractions in cruciferous plants, including indole-3-carbinol, isothiocyanates, glucosinolates, dithiolethiones and phenols; they are able to:[64]

◊ Prevent chemicals from being converted into cancer-causing compounds
◊ Induce liver detoxification systems, such as glutathione S-transferase and P-450, to help rid the body of poisons.
◊ Scavenge free radicals, thus working as an antioxidant.
◊ Prevent tumor promoters from reaching their cell targets, such as blocking the binding of estrogen to estrogen-dependent tumors.

Cat's claw, 3:1 concentrate   200 mg
Immune stimulant, anti-inflammatory, DNA protector, antioxidant.

Cat's claw, or Uncaria tomentosa, is a relative newcomer to Western botanical medicine. It has been used therapeutically for centuries by Native South Americans in the higher elevations of the Peruvian Amazon rain forest. Cat's claw is a woody vine that grows to 100 feet by wrapping around nearby trees. The root and inner bark are used to prepare herbal concoctions that have demonstrated some effectiveness at cleansing the gastro-intestinal tract of parasites and re-establishing a favorable environment for healthy microflora bacteria.
Cat's claw may be able to:
◊   Inhibit free radicals.[65]
◊   Stimulate the immune system.[66]
◊   Cleanse and strengthen the intestinal tract.
◊   Inhibit auto-immune diseases, such as Crohn's and rheumatoid arthritis.
◊   Protect the DNA from damage.[67]
◊   Slow down cancer growth.[68]

Maitake D-fraction (20 mg)
Adaptogen, immune stimulant.

Mushrooms, or fungi, have long been valued for their contributions as foods and medicines for humans. Penicillin was first discovered as bread mold, or fungi, and found to inhibit bacterial growth. Mushrooms usually grow as mold on rotten tree stumps or in manure. Of the various mushrooms that have been tested for their medicinal value, including lentinan, Shiitake, and PSK; Maitake (Grifola frondosa) has shown the most consistent anti-cancer effects from oral intake. The other mushrooms may have active ingredients that are effective when injected, but not when orally consumed.
Maitake literally means "dancing mushroom" since Japanese people who discovered these basketball-sized mushrooms growing on tree stumps would "dance with joy" at the prospects of the taste and health-giving properties. In the 1980s, Japanese firms began cultivating Maitake mushrooms on sawdust and intensely investigating the therapeutic value of this mushroom. An isolated fraction, D-fraction with active constituents of 1,6 and 1,3 beta-glucans, has been found to be the most potent and best absorbed from the diet.
Maitake may help cancer patients via:
◊   Immune stimulation, capable of doubling the activity of Natural Killer cells in animals. D-fraction was able to increase interleukin-1

production from macrophages and potentiate delayed type hypersensitivity response, which is indicative of tumor growth suppression.[69]

◊ Adaptogen that lowers hypertension[70], lowers excess blood sugar levels, protects the liver, and has anti-viral activity.[71]

◊ Inhibition of metastasis of cancer by 81% in one animal study.[72]

◊ Augmenting the anti-cancer activity of drugs like Mitomycin. In a comparison study between Maitake D-fraction and Mitomycin C, Maitake provided superior tumor growth inhibition of 80% vs. 45% for the drug. Yet when both were given together, but at half the dosage for each, tumor inhibition was 98%.

◊ Reducing toxic side effects from chemotherapy while augmenting tumor kill of the drug. There was a 90% drop in the incidence of appetite loss, vomiting, nausea, hair loss and leukopenia (deficiency of immune cells) in human cancer patients treated with Maitake D-fraction while undergoing chemotherapy.

OTHER BOTANICALS: There are literally thousands of botanical agents that hold promise in cancer treatment. The above list offers some of the better studied and more widely available herbal agents to help the cancer patients. Herbal combinations worthy of consideration include the Hoxsey formula (available as Herbal Veil Tonic from Lenox Labs 800-256-2253), Essiac formula available in raw herb form (Herbal Healing Academy 501-269-4177) or in finished form at a higher price from Essiac Intl. (613-820-0503). Individual herbs that merit consideration for cancer patients include: goldenseal, licorice, Pau D'Arco. While I am not mentioning the thousands of herbs commonly used in the Orient that are not widely available in the U.S., these herbs can be very helpful when recommended by a qualified herbalist. Among the more promising Oriental herbs for cancer patients are Codonopsis available from China Herb Co. (800-221-4372) or Frontier Herbs (800-669-3275).

SKIN CANCER. A special note about basal cell and squamous cell carcinoma. These cancers are extremely common, with about 800,000 medical office procedures done annually to remove minor skin cancers. Surgical excision is about 90% effective as a long term cure. Melanoma is a much more lethal and rare form of skin cancer that requires professional attention. For those people interested in treatment options for routine non-malignant skin cancer, you may consider the herbal escharotics (selectively burn away cancerous tissue when applied topically) of Cansema from Applied Botanical Research (800-256-2253) or Curaderm available from Masters Marketing Company, No.1 Marlborough Hill, Harrow, Middlesex HA1 1 TW, ENGLAND, phone 011-44-181-424-9400, fax -427-1994).

Garlic, (Kyolic, 1 capsule) 600 mg
Immune stimulant[73], detoxifying agent, antioxidant[74], powerful anti-fungal compound[75], protects[76] and rebuilds the liver[77], controls blood sugar levels, reduces the toxic effect of chemotherapy and radiation[78] on healthy cells, increases energy.

First mentioned as a medicine about 6000 years ago, garlic has been a major player in human medicines throughout the world. In the tomb of the Egyptian king, Tutankhamen, were found gold ornaments and garlic bulbs. Slaves who built the Great Pyramids relied heavily on the energizing power of garlic for their work. Hippocrates, father of modern medicine, used garlic to heal infections and reduce pain. Although garlic has been a medical staple of many societies for over 4000 years, only in the past few decades when over 2000 scientific studies have proven its healing value, has garlic received the respect and attention that it deserves.

Garlic grown on selenium-rich soil, such as found in Kyolic, may be directly toxic to tumor cells.[79] Garlic may be able to impact the cancer process[80] by inhibiting:

◊ carcinogen formation in the body (i.e. nitrosamines)
◊ the transformation of normal cells to pre-cancerous cells[81]
◊ the promotion of pre-cancerous cells to cancer[82]
◊ spreading (metastasis) of cancer cells to the surface of blood vessels
◊ formation of blood vessels in tumor mass, i.e. anti-angiogenesis

The debate continues regarding the active ingredients in garlic, but they may include amino acids (like the branched chain amino acids of leucine and isoleucine), S-allyl cysteine, allicin, and organically-bound selenium. In a double blind trial in humans with high serum cholesterol, aged deodorized garlic with no allicin content was able to lower serum cholesterol by 7%.[83] While garlic, in general as either aged, fresh, cooked or in supplement form, is a healthy addition to anyone's nutrition program; aged garlic extracts were effective at protecting animals from liver damage.[84] An extensive review of the literature on garlic and its influence on the cancer process shows the impressive and multiple ways that garlic can help the cancer patient.[85] In a Chinese study, people who ate more garlic had a 60% reduction in the risk for stomach cancer.[86]

Aged garlic was effective at preventing the initiation and promotion phase of esophageal cancer in animals.[87] In one animal study, garlic was more effective against bladder cancer than the drug of choice in human bladder cancer, BCG (bacillus Calmette-Guerin).[88] Garlic grown on selenium-rich soil was more effective than selenium supplements at inhibiting carcinogen-induced tumors in animals.[89] A study published in the Journal of the National Medical Association referred to garlic as "...a potent, non-specific biologic response modifier."[90] Garlic protects against the DNA-damaging potential of DMBA[91] and the liver carcinogen, aflatoxin.[92] Stimulates immune functions by activating macrophages and spleen cells.[93] Enhances Natural Killer cell activity.[94]

Coenzyme Q-10, 100 mg
    Improves aerobic metabolism, immune stimulant, membrane stabilizer, improves prostaglandin metabolism.

        CoQ is found in the energy transport system of mammals, specifically the mitochondrial membrane. Dr. Peter Mitchell was awarded the Nobel prize for his work in 1975 on CoQ. CoQ is nearly a wonder drug in reversing cardiomyopathy.[95] CoQ is either manufactured in the human body from the amino acid tyrosine and mevalonate or consumed in the diet, with heart and liver tissue being particularly rich in CoQ-10 for humans. Hence, CoQ, along with carnitine, EPA and other nutrition factors are considered "conditionally essential nutrients", since we may not be able to manufacture enough of these nutrients at certain phases of the life cycle. Niacin is an essential vitamin that also is produced within the body (endogenous source) and consumed in the diet (exogenous sources). CoQ is also called ubiquinone, since various forms of this molecule are found everywhere, as in ubiquitous. CoQ may help cancer patients by:
◊   correcting CoQ deficiency states[96], since we don't eat liver or heart and lose the capacity to make CoQ within as we age
◊   radical scavenger (antioxidant) that works with vitamin E in the fat soluble portions of the body and cells[97]
◊   stabilizes cell membranes through interaction with phospholipids[98]
◊   correction of mitochondrial "leak" of electrons during oxidative respiration, which improves aerobic production of ATP[99]
◊   improving prostaglandin metabolism[100]
◊   stabilizing calcium dependent channels on cell membrane receptor sites[101]
        CoQ may enhance immune functions.[102] CoQ reduces the damage to the heart (probably by sparing mitochondrial membranes) from the chemotherapy drug adriamycin.[103] Long term users of adriamycin risk cardiac arrest, unless given adequate CoQ, vitamin E, niacin and other nutrients to reduce the damage to the heart. Using 300 mg daily of CoQ as sole therapy, 6 of 32 breast cancer patients (19%) experienced partial tumor regression, while one woman took 390 mg daily and gained complete remission.[104] Given the fact that CoQ probably becomes an essential nutrient as we age and become ill, there is good reasons to include CoQ in your nutrition supplement program. Best absorbed in the presence of fats in your digestive tract, especially lecithin, fish, shark, and borage oils.

Glandulars

Glandular therapy has been practiced, at least inadvertently, since the dawn of mankind. In the seminal book, NUTRITION AND PHYSICAL DEGENERATION by Weston Price, DDS, he found that Native Americans in the cold regions of northern Canada avoided scurvy in the winter by first eating the raw adrenal gland from any animal captured. Adrenal glands provide the most concentrated depot of vitamin C in the body. Our hunter-gatherer ancestors would offer the liver and heart of the captured animal to the slayer. Liver and heart are among the organs that are rich in CoQ, carnitine, lipoic acid, trace minerals and a variety of nutrients that are missing in our diets.

Today, there are millions of people taking prescription supplements of thyroid gland from animals to bolster a failing thyroid gland. This is glandular therapy. We now use gelatin extracts (which are from connective tissue of hooves and hides) of glucosamine sulfate and chondroitan sulfate to improve connective tissue diseases, like osteo and rheumatoid arthritis. There are peptides in each gland that are specific to that gland, such as thymus and spleen, which will be targeted to that gland once consumed.

As we mature, many of our glandular functions deteriorate.[105] Although our biochemistry textbooks would have us believe that polypeptides, such as found in glandular extracts, are all hydrolyzed in the digestive processes of the gut, in fact many peptides survive this chemical gauntlet. How else do we explain the passage of Immunoglobulin A from mother's milk to bolster the newborn infant's immune system or the food proteins which pass directly into the bloodstream and trigger allergic responses. Glandular replacement therapy, such as thymus and spleen, may be essential for many people who are struggling with life threatening diseases.

Thymic concentrate   500 mg
Bolsters functions of thymus gland, which is crucial to the maturation of immune cells into T-cells.

The thymus gland in humans usually atrophies with aging. Anyone over 30 years of age probably has a thymus gland that is well below optimal in size and functional capacity. There are thymus-derived factors with hormone-like activity, called thymosins, that have long been recognized for their potential at stimulating immune functions.[106] An extract of thymus, thymosin 5, was able to stimulate immune functions in mice with induced tumors.[107] Other researchers found that thymus extract is more of an immune regulator than an immune stimulant. In human lung cancer patients receiving chemotherapy, thymus supplements provided for longer survival time.[108]   Other researchers found that thymus extract (TP-1) was able to increase lymphocyte counts in incurable gastro-intestinal cancer patients treated with chemotherapy.[109] Other researchers followed over 1000 patients who had been treated with thymus extract (TFX) over the course of 15 years and found the thymus to be extremely helpful in normalizing immune panels and improving outcome in a wide variety of immune suppressive disorders.[110] Researchers at the University of California isolated a fraction of thymus (thymic protein A) which improved immune parameters in mice.[111] Probably a wide variety of subsets of peptides and glycoproteins in thymus work to improve differentiation of bone marrow (B-cells) lymphocytes into active T-cells that can recognize and destroy cancer cells.

Spleen   concentrate   500 mg
        Bolsters functions of the spleen gland, a storage and filtering organ for the blood and immune system.

        The spleen oftentimes atrophies with aging in humans. Supplements of spleen extract have been used in conjunction with ginseng (also in) as a clinically tested immune stimulant for cancer and AIDS patients in Europe.

Digestive enzymes (especially protease) 50,000 USP units taken 1-6 times daily
        Break up circulating immune complexes to improve efficiency of immune system, erode protective coating on tumor, break down toxic by-products of tumor metabolism that create weight loss and depression in cancer patients.

        Enzymes are organic catalysts that speed up the rate of a biochemical reaction. Enzymes either put things together, called conjugases, or take things apart, called hydrolases. There are literally millions of enzymes produced by your body each second. Without hydrolase enzymes in your gut, the digestion of food could not occur. Our body makes digestive enzymes to break down large food particles into usable molecules:
        -proteins are digested into amino acids by the action of proteases, including trypsin and chymotrypsin
        -starches are digested into simple sugars by the action of amylase
        -fats are digested into fatty acids and glycerol by the action of lipase.
        Our ancestors ate a diet high in uncooked foods. Cooking food denatures enzymes, like changing the white on an egg from waxey to

white when it is cooked. All living tissue contains an abundance of hydrolase enzymes as part of the lysosomes, or "suicide bags", which are there to mop up cellular debris and destroy invading organisms. When our ancestors ate this diet high in uncooked food, they were receiving a regular infusion of "enzyme therapy" as a lucky by-product. These hydrolytic enzymes would help to digest the food, and about 10% of the unused enzymes would end up crossing through the intestinal wall into the blood stream.

It is clear that people who are undernourished without being malnourished live a longer and healthier life. Why this occurs is less obvious. Many good European studies support the use of digestive enzymes as a critical component of cancer treatment. Your mouth, stomach and intestines will make a certain amount of enzymes to digest your food into smaller molecules for absorption through the intestinal wall into the bloodstream. Enzymes absorbed into the bloodstream help to break up immune complexes, expose tumors to immune attack and assist in cell differentiation. People who eat less food may live longer because they are able to absorb a certain percentage of their unused digestive enzymes, which then have many therapeutic benefits. Indeed, as far back as 1934, an Austrian researcher, Dr. E. Freund found that cancer patients do not have the "solubilizing" tumor-destroying enzymes in their blood that normal healthy people have.

One of the founders of alternative cancer treatment, Donald Kelley, DDS, felt that cancer was caused by a deficiency of digestive enzyme production, just as diabetes is caused by a deficiency of insulin production. Both the diabetic and cancer patient have some genetic predisposition that makes he or she vulnerable to the disease. The symptoms of diabetes and cancer may be controlled with proper lifestyle, but the underlying genetic vulnerability will never go away. This enzyme theory may help to explain why the vast majority of cancer patients are older people, who have demonstrated a reduced output of digestive enzymes; and also explains why raw foods, which are high in hydrolytic enzymes, may sometimes help cancer patients.

There is twenty years of good research from Europe showing that enzyme therapy helps many types of cancer patients. Digestive enzymes can:

* reduce tumor growth and metastasis in experimental animals.[112]
* prevent radon-induced lung cancer in miners.[113]
* improve 5 year survival in breast cancer patients. Stage I at 91%, stage II at 75% and stage III at 50%.[114]
* bromelain (enzyme from pineapple) inhibited leukemic cell growth and induced human leukemia cells in culture to revert back to normal (cytodifferentiation). [115]
* reduce the complications of cancer, such as cachexia (weight loss), pain in joints, and depression.

* reduced the secondary infections that result from certain chemo and radiation methods, especially bleomycin-induced pneumotoxicity.[116]

Wobenzym (800-899-4499) is a unique clinically-tested product from Germany with a proprietary blend of various plant and animal-derived digestive enzymes, coupled with rutin (a bioflavonoid) all packaged in an enterically coated pill to survive the acid bath of the stomach and move into the intestines for absorption.

Enzymes are measured in USP (United States Pharmacopeia) comparison to pancreatic extract. One of the functions of the pancreas is to make digestive enzymes. A 4x label on your enzymes means "4 times the potency of pancreatin USP". Therefore, 500 mg of 4X pancreatin is equal in digestive capacity to 2000 mg of pancreatin USP. 50,000 USP units is a good target for any given meal or in between meal dosage.

Enzymes taken with a meal will help to digest the food, but will not be absorbed into the bloodstream to help fight the cancer. About 10% of enzymes taken on an empty stomach will be absorbed into the bloodstream to help fight the cancer. Good digestive enzymes that are not enterically coated should have a raunchy "vomit" smell to them, or they are not active. Enzymes are one of the more fragile molecules in Nature, easily denatured by temperatures above 108 F. Therefore, much of the enzyme products sold in health food stores are either minimally active or completely useless. Among the good products, Super Enzyme Caps from TwinLabs (800-645-5626).

PATIENT PROFILE: SAILED THROUGH 2 BONE MARROWS
J.W. is a 52 year old male diagnosed July of 1984 with plasma cytoma, which was later diagnosed in October 1995 as multiple myeloma. He received radiation to arm and rib cage in October 1995. He was admitted to a cancer hospital January 1997 as a medical emergency. He was placed on Total Parenteral Nutrition, began harvesting stem cells (for bone marrow transplant), followed by 3 weeks of radiation therapy. He began bone marrow transplant April of 1997, then began nutrition therapy in May of 1997. He completed his second BMT July 11, 1997. He felt good throughout both BMT procedures, suffered no infections, no colds, had good energy, and circulated in public--all of which is very unusual for anyone in a BMT unit. All of his blood values have returned to normal, except mildly low platelet count.

ENDNOTES

[1] . Koide, T., et al., Cancer Biotherapy & Radiopharmaceuticals, vol.11, p.273, Aug.1996
[2] . LeBon, AM, et al., Chem.Biol.Interactions, vol.83, p.65, 1992
[3] . Havsteen, B, Biochem Pharmacol., vol.32, p.1141, 1983
[4] . Fujiki, H., et al., in Plant Flavonoids in Biology and Medicine, vol.1, p.429, Liss Publ., NY, 1986

[5] . Berg, P., et al., in Plant Flavonoids in Biology and Medicine, vol.2, p.157, Liss Publ., NY, 1988
[6] . Wattenberg, L., et al., Cancer Research, vol.30, p.1922, 1970
[7] . Werbach, M., et al., BOTANICAL INFLUENCES ON ILLNESS, p.30, Third Line Press, Tarzana, CA, 1994
[8] . Werbach, M., IBID, p.189
[9] . Luettig, B., et al., J. Natl.Cancer Inst., vol.81, p.669, 1989
[10] . Lersch, C., et al., Tumordiagen Ther., vol.13, p.115, 1992
[11] . Lersch, C., et al., Cancer Invest., vol.10, p.343, 1992
[12] . Nagabhushan, M., et al., J. Am.Coll. Nutr., vol.11, p.192, 1992
[13] . Kuttan, R., et al., Cancer Lett., vol.29, p.197, 1985
[14] . Polasa, K., Mutagen, vol.7, p.107, 1992
[15] . Kuttan, R., et al., Tumori, vol.73, p.29, 1987
[16] . Schubert, H., et al., Geriatr Forsch, vol.3, p.45, 1993
[17] . Kleijnen, J., et al., Br. J. Clin.Pharmacol. vol.34, p.352, 1992
[18] . Kleijnen, J., et al., Lancet, vol.340, p.1136, 1992
[19] . Koltai, M., et al., Drugs, vol.42, p.9, 1991
[20] . Pincemail, J., et al., Experientia, vol.45, p.708, 1989
[21] . Shibata, S., et al., Econ.Med.Plant Res., vol.1, p.217, 1985
[22] . Siegel, RK, JAMA, vol.243, p.32, 1980
[23] . Chang, HM, et al., Pharmacology and Applications of Chinese Materia Medica, vol. 2, World Scientific Publ., Teaneck, NJ, p.1041, 1987
[24] . Sun, Y, J. Biol Response Modifiers, vol.2, p.227, 1983
[25] . Chu, DT, et al., J. Clin.Lab.Immunol., vol.26, p.183, 1988
[26] . Li, NQ, et al., Chung Kuo Chung Hsi I Chieh Ho Tsa Chih, vol.12, p.588, 1992
[27] . Boik, J., CANCER AND NATURAL MEDICINE, p.177, Oregon Medical Press, Princeton, MN, 1995
[28] . Boik, J. CANCER AND NATURAL MEDICINE, p.180 Oregon Medical Press, Princeton, MN, 1995
[29] . Murray, MT, HEALING POWER OF HERBS, p.265, Prima Publ., Rocklin, CA 1995
[30] . Ziglar, W., Whole Foods, vol.2, p.48, 1979
[31] . Samira, MMH, et al., J.Int.Med.Res., vol.13, p.342, 1985
[32] . Ng, TB, et al., Gen.Pharmacol., vol.6, p.549, 1985; see also Yamato, M., et al., Proceedings of the 3rd Intl Ginseng Symp, p.115, 1980
[33] . Jie, YH, et al., Agents Actions, vol.15, p.386, 1984; see also Gupta, S., et al., Clin.Res., vol.28, p.504A, 1980
[34] . Singh, VK, et al., Planta Medica, vol.51, p.462, 1984
[35] . Oura, H., et al., Chem.Pharm.Bull., vol.20, p.980, 1972
[36] . Hikino, H., et al., Planta Medica, vol.52, p.62, 1985; see also Oh, JS, et al., Korean J.Pharmacol., vol.4, p.27, 1968
[37] . Yamamoto, M., et al., Am.J.Chin.Med., vol.11, p.84, 1983
[38] . Yun, TK, et al., Cancer Detect.Prev., vol.6, p.515, 1983
[39] . Yun, TK, et al., Int.J.Epidemiol., vol.19, p.871, 1990
[40] . Lee, KD, et al., Jpn.J.Pharmacol., vol.21, p.299, 1971; see also Fulder, SJ, Exp.Gerontol., vol.12, p.125, 1977
[41] . Rhee, YH, et al., Planta Medica, vol.57, p.125, 1991
[42] . Hau, DM, et al., Int. J. of Oriental Med., vol.15, p.10, 1990
[43] . Yang, G., et al., J. of Trad. Chin. Med., vol.8, p.135, 1988
[44] . Kubo, M., et al., Planta Med, vol.58, p.424, 1992
[45] . Li, X., et al., J. Tongji Med Univ., vol.11, p.73, 1991
[46] . Murray, RK, et al., HARPER'S BIOCHEMISTRY, 24th edition, p.550, Lange, Stamford, CT 1996
[47] . Boik, J., CANCER AND NATURAL MEDICINE, p.44, Oregon Medical Press, Princeton, MN 1995
[48] . Davis, DL, et al., Environmental Health Perspectives, vol.101, p.372, Oct.1993
[49] . Nakagawa, T., et al., Angiology, vol.45, p.333, May 1994
[50] . Pavlidis, NA, et al., Cancer, vol.69, p.2961, 1992
[51] . Catherino, WH, et al., Drug Safety, vol.8, p.381, 1993
[52] . Seoud, MAF, et al., Obstetrics & Gynecology, vol.82, p.165, Aug.1993
[53] . World Health Organization, PREVENTION OF CANCER, technical report 276, WHO, Geneva, 1964
[54] . LaVecchia, CL, et al., Nutr.Cancer, vol.17, p.27, 1992
[55] . Ho, C., et al., Prev.Med., vol.21, p.520, 1992
[56] . Khan, SG, et al., Cancer Res., vol.52, p.4050, 1992
[57] . Yang, CS, et al., J. Natl., Cancer Inst., vol.85, p.1038, 1993
[58] . Komori, A., et al., Jpn.J.Clin.Oncol., vol.23, p.186, 1993
[59] . Stich, HF, Prev.Med., vol.21, p.377, 1992

[60]. Boik, J., CANCER AND NATURAL MEDICINE, p.178, Oregon Medical Press, Princeton, MN 1995
[61]. Beretz, A, et al., Plant Flavonoids in Biology and Medicine II, p.187, Liss Publ., 1988
[62]. Lourau, G., et al., Experientia, vol.6, p.25, 1950
[63]. Wattenburg, LW, Cancer Res. (suppl), vol.52, p. 2085S, 1992
[64]. Kensler, TW, et al., p.154-196, in FOOD CHEMICALS AND CANCER PREVENTION, vol.1, American Chemical Society, Wash DC, 1994
[65]. McBrien, DC, et al., LIPID PEROXIDATION AND CANCER, Academy Press, NY 1982
[66]. Wagner, H., et al., Planta Medica, vol.12, p.34, 1985
[67]. Rizzi, R., et al., J. Ethnopharmacol., vol.38, p.63, 1993
[68]. DeOlivera, MM, et al., Anals Acad.Brasil Ciencias, vol.44, p.41, 1972
[69]. Hishida, I., et al., Chem.Pharm.Bull., vol.36, p.1819, 1988
[70]. Adachi, K., et al., Chem.Pharm.Bull., vol.36, p.1000, 1988
[71]. Nanba, H., J. Orthomolecular Med., vol.12, p.43, 1997
[72]. Nanba, H., Cancer Prevention, NYAS, p.243, Sept.1995
[73]. Lau, BHS, et al., Molecular Biotherapeutics, vol.3, p.103, June 1991
[74]. Imai, J., et al., Planta Medica, p.417, 1994
[75]. Tadi, PP, et al., International Clinical Nutrition Reviews, vol.10, p.423, 1990
[76]. Nakagawa, S., et al., Phytotherapy, Research, vol.1,p.1, 1988
[77]. Horie, T., et al., Planta Medica, vol.55, p.506, 1989
[78]. Lau, BHS, International Clinical Nutrition Reviews, vol.9, p.27, 1989
[79]. Ip, C., et al., Nutr.Cancer, vol.17, p.279, 1992
[80]. Dausch, JG, et al., Preventive Medicine, vol.19, p.346, 1990
[81]. Wargovich, MJ, et al., Cancer Letters, vol.64, p.39, 1992
[82]. Belman, S, Carcinogenesis, vol.4, p.1063, 1983
[83]. Steiner, M., et al., Amer.J.Clin.Nutr., vol.64, p.866, 1996
[84]. Nakagawa, S., et al., Phytotherapy Res., vol.1, p.1, 1988
[85]. Dausch, JG, et al., Preventive Med., vol.19, p.346, 1990
[86]. You, WC, et al., J. Nat.Cancer Inst., vol.81, p.162, 1989
[87]. Wargovich, MJ, et al., Cancer Letters, vol.64, p.39, 1992
[88]. Marsh, CL, et al., J. Urology, vol.137, p.359, Feb.1987
[89]. Ip, C., et al., Nutrition and Cancer, vol.17, no.3, p.279, 1992
[90]. Abdullah, TH, et al., J.Nat.Med.Assoc., vol.80, p.439, 1988
[91]. Amagase, H., et al., Carcinogenesis, vol.14, p.1627, 1993
[92]. Yamasaki, T., et al., Cancer Letters, vol.59, p.89, 1991
[93]. Hirao, Y., et al., Phytotherapy Research, vol.1, p.161, 1987
[94]. Abdullah, TH et al., Onkologie, vol.21, p.53, 1989
[95]. Langsjoen, PH, et al., Int. J. Tiss Reac, vol.12, p.163, 1990
[96]. Folkers, K, et al., International Journal of Vitamin and Nutrition Research, vol.40,p.380, 1970
[97]. Sugiyama, S, Experientia, vol.36, p.1002, 1980
[98]. Gwak, S. et al., Biochem et Biophys Acta, vol.809, p.187, 1985
[99]. Turrens, JF, Biochem J., vol.191, p.421, 1980
[100]. Ham, EA, et al., J. Biol Chem, vol.254, p.2191, 1979
[101]. Nakamura, Y, et al., Cardiovasc Res, vol.16, p.132, 1982
[102]. Folkers, K., Med Chem Res, vol.2, p.48, 1992
[103]. Folkers, K., Biomedical and Clinical Aspects of Coenzyme Q, vol.3,p.399, Elsevier Press, 1981
[104]. Lockwood, K., et al., Biochem and Biophys Res Comm, vol.199, p.1504, Mar.1994
[105]. Klatz, R., et al., STOPPING THE CLOCK, Keats, New Canaan, CT, 1996
[106]. Oats, KK, et al., TIPS, p.347, Elsevier Press, Aug.1984
[107]. Wada, A., et al., J.Nat.Cancer Institute, vol.74, no.3, p.659, Mar.1985
[108]. Chretien, PB, et al., NY Acad Sci, vol.332, p.135, 1979
[109]. Shoham, J., et al., Cancer Immunol. Immunother., vol.9, p.173, 1980
[110]. Skotnicki, AB, Med. Oncol. & Tumor Pharmacother., Vol.6, no.1, p.31, 1989
[111]. Hays, EF, et al., Clin Immun. & Immunopath., vol.33, p.381, 1984
[112]. Ransberger, K, et al., Medizinische Enzymforschungsgesellschaft, International Cancer Congress, Houston 1970
[113]. Miraslav, H., et al., Advances in Antimicrobial and Antineoplastic Chemotherapy, proceedings from 7th international congress of chemotherapy, Urban & Schwarzenberg, Munchen, 1972
[114]. Rokitansky, O., Dr. Med., no.1, vol.16ff, Austria
[115]. Maurer, HR, et al., Planta Medica, vol.54, no.5, p.377, 1988
[116]. Schedler, M., et al., 15th International Cancer Congress, Hamburg, Germany, Aug.1990

Chapter 10

VITAMINS

"Nature alone cures and what nursing has to do is put the patient in the best condition for Nature to act upon him." Florence Nightingale, founder of modern nursing, circa 1900

> **A (palmitate) 8,000 iu**
>   Down regulates cancer at genetic level, immune stimulant, improves cell differentiation process, helps with cell to cell communication.

Along with iron, vitamin A is one of the most common micronutrient deficiencies in the world. Around the world, an estimated 500,000 people each year go permanently blind because of clinical vitamin A deficiency. Vitamin A was the first micronutrient to be recognized for its role in preventing cancer. Vitamin A is one of the most multi-talented of all substances in human nutrition and plays a key role in preventing and reversing cancer. While vitamin A and beta-carotene are considered interchangeable, more recent evidence shows that these two nutrients have some overlapping functions and some distinctly different functions. A drug analog of vitamin A (all trans retinoic acid) has become a near cure all for acute promyelocytic leukemia, with one study showing a 96% cure rate.[1] Some companies use an emulsified vitamin A so that it stays in the blood stream longer, which may be important for extremely high doses of A (>100,000 iu/day) in cancer patients.

        All of the known functions of vitamin A relate either directly or indirectly to the cancer patient:

◊ **Cell division**. Billions of times each day, cells divide in the precarious process of cell division, a.k.a. proliferation or hyperplasia. Without vitamin A, this fragile process can easily turn into cancer, or neoplasia. Vitamin A is crucial for cancer prevention.[2] Vitamin A deficiency may be one of the primary insults leading to lung cancer.[3] There are probably binding sites on the human DNA for vitamin A. Researchers found that one of the most common cancers in Third World countries, cervical cancer, was linked to Human Papilloma Virus, which was then linked to shutting off the cancer-protective gene, called p53, which was then linked to a low intake of vitamin A. Essentially, vitamin A keeps the p53 active and protecting our DNA against cancer, even from viral attack.

◊ **Cell to cell communication**, a.k.a. gap junction. Cells communicate via a "telegraph" system of ions floating in and out of cell membrane pores. This intercellular communication helps to maintain cooperation and coordination of cell functions. Without vitamin A, the "telegraph" system becomes distorted and cancer can arise.

◊ **Maintenance of epithelial tissue**, or skin. The vast majority of cancers, including lung, breast, colon, and prostate, all arise from the epithelial tissue and are called carcinomas. Other categories of cancers include: leukemia (cancer of the bone marrow that produces red & white cells), lymphoma (cancer of the lymph cells and glands), and sarcomas (cancers of the structural tissue).[4] When the body is deprived of vitamin A, skin (epithelial) cancer is more likely to result. Giving therapeutic doses of vitamin A has been shown to slow down and reverse some forms of cancer.

◊ **Immune stimulant**. Vitamin A deficiency brings changes in the mucosal membranes, changes in lymphocyte sub-populations, and altered T- and B-cell functions.[5] There are many studies linking vitamin A supplements to the curing of measles.[6] Vitamin A supplements brought a 19% reduction in respiratory infections in children.[7] Pregnant women with the lowest quartile of serum vitamin A had a 400% increase in the risk of transmitting their HIV virus to their unborn infant.[8]

◊ **Anti-cancer activity**. Vitamin A supplements as sole therapy in patients with unresectable (cannot be surgically removed) lung cancer measurably improved immune functions and tumor response.[9] Vitamin A, and not beta-carotene, improved lymphocyte levels and reduced complications after surgery in lung cancer patients.[10] In patients treated for bladder cancer, the incidence of recurrence was 180% higher in patients who consumed the lowest quartile of vitamin A in the diet.[11] High doses of vitamin A (200,000 iu/week) were able to reduce damaged and potentially cancerous mouth cells by 96%.[12] Vitamin A and its synthetic analogues have been shown to improve cancer treatment in oral leukoplakia, laryngeal papillomatosis, superficial bladder carcinoma, cervical dysplasia, bronchial metaplasia, and preleukemia.[13] Vitamin A supplements of 300,000 iu per day were provided in a placebo-controlled trial with 307 patients with stage I non-small-cell lung cancer. 37% of the treated group experienced a recurrence, while 48% of the non-treated group had a recurrence, thus bringing a 25% reduction in tumor recurrence when used as sole therapy.[14]

SAFETY ISSUES. While vitamins, in general, are much safer than drugs, it is important to discuss vitamin A toxicity, which is by far the most common cause of vitamin toxicity. Up to 1 million iu of vitamin A per day has been given for 5 years without side effects in European cancer clinics.[15] One study found that women taking as little as 10,000 iu/day during pregnancy had a slightly elevated risk for having a child with birth defects (teratogenicity).[16] Another study from the National Institutes of Health found no increase in birth defects in women taking 25,000 iu/day of vitamin A. An FDA biochemist, John Hathcock, PhD, states that toxicity with vitamin A at these low levels mainly involves people with confounding medical conditions, including compromised liver function.[17] Cancer clinics in Europe often administer up to 2.5 million iu/day of vitamin A in emulsified form for several months under medical supervision. While these doses are not recommended without medical supervision, it shows the relative safety of vitamin A in the general population. Giving at least 300,000 iu per day of retinol palmitate in 138 lung cancer patients for at least 12 months created self-terminating unremarkable symptoms in less than 10% of these patients and only caused interruption of treatment in 3% due to symptoms that were potentially related to vitamin A excess. Upset stomach (dyspepsia), headache, nosebleeds and mild hair loss were the most common and self-limiting symptoms.

Since meat eating populations would usually eat the liver of the animal first, which is the most concentrated source of pre-formed vitamin A, descendents of carnivorous people probably have a much greater tolerance and need for higher doses of A. By increasing the intake of vitamin E, many people will be able to avoid toxicity from high doses of vitamin A, since it is the lipid peroxide products from A that can cause damage to the liver. Vitamin E prevents lipid peroxidation. **PREGNANT WOMEN SHOULD NOT USE HIGH DOSES OF VITAMIN A.**

Betacarotene   15 mg (=25,000 iu)
    Immune stimulant, helps with cell to cell communication.

It is easy to appreciate the beauty of carotenoids on a crisp fall day with the autumn foliage at its peak. Carotenoids are usually pigmented substances produced by plants to assist in photosynthesis and protect the plant from the damaging effects of the sun's radiation. Of the 800 or so carotenoids that have been isolated, the most famous are beta-carotene, alpha-carotene, lutein, zeaxanthin, lycopene, and beta-cryptoxanthin. Most carotenoids are pigmented molecules that are red, yellow or orange in color. A few carotenoids, such as phytoene and phytofluene, are colorless.

Over 200 epidemiological studies[18] show that a diet rich in fruit and vegetables will lower the risk for a variety of cancers. Of the 15% of annual lung cancer patients who are not smokers, which totals over 22,000 deaths per year, fruits and vegetables can provide major protection against lung cancer.[19]

Beta-carotene and other carotenoids have been thoroughly reviewed regarding their role in cancer and found: "...carotenoids exert an important influence in modulating the actions of carcinogens."[20] Beta-carotene has been shown to play a major role in the "telegraph" communication between cells that prevents or reverses abnormal growths. This "gap junction communication" is one of many reasons why beta-carotene protects us from cancer.[21] Beta-carotene selectively inhibited the growth of human squamous cancer cells in culture.[22] Beta-carotene and canthaxanthin provided significant protection in animals against the cancer-causing effects of radiation.[23]

Carotenoids may partially compensate for the "sins" of our unhealthy lifestyles. In one study, researchers from the National Cancer Institute and Harvard tracked over 47,000 healthy individuals and found that lycopenes, even from pizza sauce, were protective against prostate cancer.[24] Other studies have found that beta-carotene supplements can reverse the pre-cancerous condition (oral leukoplakia) brought about by chewing betel nut,[25] which is a Third World version of chewing tobacco.

Beta-carotene affects the cancer process in a variety of ways:
◊ alters the adenylate cyclase activity in melanoma cells in culture, which affects cell differentiation, and thus whether a cell will turn cancerous or not[26]
◊ potent anti-oxidant,[27] which spares immune cells in the microscopic "war on cancer" and protects the healthy prostaglandins
◊ provides a certain level of tumor immunity in mice innoculated with cancer cells[28]
◊ protects the DNA against the damaging effects of carcinogens[29]
◊ according to studies by Food and Drug Administration researchers, beta-carotene protects against the cancer causing effects of a choline deficient diet in animals
◊ once cancer has been initiated, either chemically or physically, beta-carotene inhibits the next step in the cancer process of neoplastic transformation [30]
◊ there is a synergistic benefit of using vitamin A with carotenoids in patients who have been first treated with chemo, radiation and surgery for common malignancies[31]

◊ beta-carotene and vitamin A together provided a significant improvement in outcome in animals treated with radiation for induced cancers[32]

◊ carotenoids (from Spirulina and Dunaliella algae) plus vitamin E and canthaxanthin were injected in animal tumors, with the result being complete regression as mediated by an increase in Tumor Necrosis Factor (TNF) in macrophages in the tumor region[33]

◊ in 20 patients with mouth cancer who were given high doses of radiation and chemo, beta-carotene provided significant protection against mouth sores (oral mucositis) induced by medical therapy, although there was no significant difference in survival rates[34]

◊ in animals, beta-carotene provided cancer protection against a carcinogenic virus, which would normally damage the DNA[35]

Betatene is a special mixed carotenoid extract from Dunaliella algae which has been shown in scientific studies to potently inhibit the development of breast tumors in animals.[36] Betatene consists of a rich mixture of various carotenoids, primarily naturally occurring betacarotene, along with smaller amounts of lycopene, alpha-carotene, zeaxanthin, cryptoxanthin and lutein.

BETACAROTENE CAUSES LUNG CANCER?

SAFETY ISSUES. There is virtually no toxicity to beta-carotene at any dosage, other than the mild pigmentation (carotenemia) that occurs in the skin region.[37] With our primitive analytical tools, scientists isolated the most likely champion of the carotenoids, beta-carotene, and conducted several human intervention trials funded by the National Cancer Institute to examine if beta-carotene would reduce the incidence of lung cancer in heavy smokers. It didn't.[38] And in two studies, the beta-carotene supplemented groups had slightly elevated incidences of lung cancer. The press loved this huge controversy and made sure that everyone knew about it. Unfortunately, only a small portion of the story was told.

Issues not covered by the press included:

-Those individuals who had the highest SERUM beta-carotene at the start of these two studies had a lower incidence of lung cancer. Beta-carotene ABSORBED does indeed reduce the risk of suicidal lifestyles, like smoking.

- Prominent researchers in nutrition and cancer have published papers showing that antioxidants, like beta-carotene, can become pro-oxidants in the wrong biochemical environment, such as the combat zone of free radicals generated by heavy tobacco use.[39] Nowhere in Nature do we find a food with just beta-carotene. All foods contain a rich and dazzling array of anti-oxidants.

-After 35 years of heavy smoking, the damage is done. The damaging effects of tobacco cannot be neutralized by one "magic bullet" pill of synthetic beta-carotene with coal tar based food dyes added to insure a homogenous color in the beta-carotene capsules.

-It is the synergism of multiple carotenoids that protects people. If beta-carotene truly provoked lung cancer then what about the 200 studies showing that a diet rich in fruit and vegetables (best sources of beta-carotene) significantly lowers the incidence of cancer.

-At the International Conference on Nutrition and Cancer, sponsored by the University of California at Irvine, held in July of 1997, there were several watershed presentations showing that one nutrient alone may be ineffective or counterproductive for cancer patients while a host of compatible nutrients in the proper ratio can be extremely effective at slowing or reversing cancer.

D-3 (cholecalciferol)   200 iu
   Helps to squelch cancer at genetic level, reducing the production of gene fragments (episomes) by working with calcium receptors.

As the fledgling science of nutrition grows in knowledge and analytical tools, we keep discovering more nutrients and more functions of the nutrients that we thought we already understood. Such is true for vitamin D, which actually is not a real vitamin in the sense of needing it in the diet.[40] We can manufacture vitamin D in the body by the action of sunlight on the skin converting cholesterol to D.

As a simple metaphor, think of most human cells containing a "switch" that can activate cancer, called the oncogene. Vitamin D puts a protective plate over that oncogene "switch" to prevent cancer from starting or spreading.

Nature always seems to provide. In areas of the world where sunshine is unpredictable at best, these people had traditional diets that were rich in fish liver, which is the most concentrated food source of vitamin D. Cloudy regions of the world have had notoriously higher rates of tuberculosis; cancers of the breast[41], ovaries[42], colon[43] and prostate; hypertension and osteoporosis[44]; multiple sclerosis, and other health problems.

If sunshine is the "medicine" in these diseases, then vitamin D and melatonin are the most likely by-products of sunlight exposure. Vitamin D has demonstrated the ability to enhance the immune system to fight off tuberculosis.[45] Our primitive ancestors consumed or produced about 5 times more vitamin D than we get because they ate whole foods, lots of fish and lived outside in the sun. Most Americans, and nearly all women receive far below the RDA (200-400 iu) for vitamin D.[46] One international unit (1 iu) of vitamin D-3 (a measurement of biological activity) is equal to 0.025 micrograms in weight.

Ergosterol is a plant steroid which is converted commercially to vitamin D-2 and used to fortify milk, a move that has virtually eliminated the deficiency syndrome of rickets in cloudy regions of the world. Vitamin D-3, cholecalciferol, is the natural vitamin produced in the skin by the action of sunlight. Once activated in the kidneys and liver, the steroid version of vitamin D-3 is: 1 alpha 25 dihydroxy cholecalciferol (1,25 D-3), which works with the hormones of parathyroid and calcitonin to regulate calcium metabolism, absorption, transport and more.

So, how does all of this information relate to the cancer process? Probably by regulating calcium transport into and out of the cell, which has been shown to be crucial in the cell differentiation process.[47]

◊ In animals fed a high fat diet, which normally would produce a higher incidence of colon cancer, supplements of calcium and vitamin D blocked this carcinogenic effect of the diet.[48]

◊ Vitamin D inhibits the growth of breast cancer in culture, and also seems to subdue human breast cancer.[49]

◊ Cells from human prostate cancer were put into a "...permanent nonproliferative state.", or shut down the cancer process, by the addition of vitamin D.[50]

◊ Human cancer cells have been shown to have receptor sites, or stereo specific "parking spaces" for vitamin D.[51]

Vitamin D prevents the formation of gene fragments, episomes, that may be the beginning of the cancer process. Bone cells that generate new blood and immune cells (hematopoietic cells) have receptors for 1,25 D-3 and activated macrophages from the immune system can synthesize 1,25 D-3.[52] Vitamin D induces differentiation to suppress cell growth in numerous tumor lines tested.[53] In tumor-bearing mice, vitamin D-3 supplements inhibited the immune suppression from the tumor secretion (granulocyte/macrophage colony stimulating factor, GM-CSF), while also reducing tumor growth and metastasis.[54] Due to the success of vitamin D at down-regulating various forms of cancer, many drug companies are researching patentable vitamin D analogs to treat cancer. But nothing works like Mother Nature's original.

SAFETY ISSUES. Nature has checkpoints in place to control the possibility of vitamin D toxicity in the body. People who are native to sunny climates have darker skin which is full of melanin to reduce the production of vitamin D in the skin while also protecting against the damaging effects of ultraviolet light. Dark skinned people are also more vulnerable to rickets (vitamin D deficiency) when moving to cloudy climates. Also, African-American men have a much higher incidence of prostate cancer, perhaps due to variations in vitamin D metabolism.

In order for dietary intake of vitamin D to become toxic, there needs to be activation of vitamin D in the kidney and liver, which are other safeguards in the body. Nonetheless, young children are potentially vulnerable to vitamin D toxicity, which may begin as low as 1800 iu/day for extended periods of time.[55] Symptoms of toxicity include hypercalcemia, hypercalciuria, anorexia, nausea, vomiting, thirst, polyuria, muscular weakness, joint pains, and disorientation.[56] At full dosage, 600 iu/day is well within the safety range, even for the few people who consume large amounts of vitamin D in the diet.

> **E (2/3 succinate, 1/3 natural) 400 iu**
>   Natural E (mixed tocopherols) stimulates immune functions and works as an antioxidant. E succinate may be selectively toxic to tumor cells.

More than a few physicians have assumed that, since vitamin E is an antioxidant and chemo and radiation work by generating prooxidants to kills cancer cells, therefore vitamin E will reduce the efficacy of medical therapy in cancer patients. Nothing could be further from the truth. Vitamin E is a valuable ally for both the cancer patient and the oncologist.

My college professors in the 1970s would facetiously chuckle at

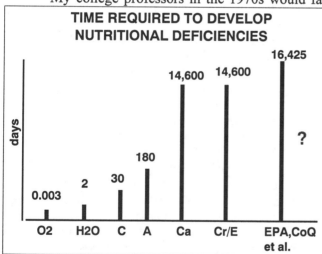

the "health nuts" who popped vitamin E capsules, claiming that "vitamin E was in search of a disease." In one study, healthy students were deprived of vitamin E in the diet for up to 2 years with no blatant vitamin deficiency syndrome, such as is found with vitamin C and scurvy, or vitamin D and rickets. Deficiencies of vitamin E cause an increase in lipid peroxidation (prooxidants) that decrease energy production (due to mitochondrial membrane damage), increase mutation of DNA, alter the normal transport mechanisms in the cell membrane.[57] Hemolytic anemia (premature bursting of red blood cells) has been found in infants who are fed a diet high in polyunsaturated fats (which generate lipid peroxides) and iron (which is a prooxidant). Malabsorption syndromes, such as biliary cirrhosis (blockage of the liver duct to the gallbladder), can generate blatant vitamin E deficiency in humans.[58]

Actually, clinical deficiencies of vitamin E probably take decades to turn into full blown cataracts, Alzheimer's, heart disease, arthritis or cancer. While 1 milligram of vitamin E (alpha tocopheryl acetate) equals 1 international unit, other versions (racemates) of E are not as potent, and hence have less iu per mg.

Most substances in life are either fat soluble (can be dissolved in alcohol) or water soluble, with a few magical substances, like lecithin, able to work in either universe. Vitamin E is the most critical of all fat soluble antioxidants. Imagine that little "fires", or prooxidants, break out all over the human body all of the time. The primary "fire extinguisher" that can put out fires in the fat soluble portion of the body, including the vulnerable cell membrane--is vitamin E.[59] Because of this fundamental role in cell biology, vitamin E helps to:

◊ protect the beneficial prostaglandins
◊ stimulates immune function
◊ protects healthy cells against toxins and radiation while making cancer cells more vulnerable to medical therapy
◊ a special form of vitamin E (succinate) is selectively toxic to cancer cells.

Vitamin E actually refers to a family of 8 related compounds, the tocopherols and tocotrienols. Tocopherols got their name from "pherein", meaning to carry, and "tocos", meaning birth, because vitamin E from wheat germ was found to be essential for fertility. True natural vitamin E is a mixture of alpha, beta, delta and gamma tocopherols plus some tocotrienols, which are more concentrated in rice bran and palm oil. Vitamin E may help the cancer patient in numerous ways:

NUTRITIONAL SYNERGISM. Zinc deficiency in animals further compounds a vitamin E deficiency, meaning that zinc must be present to properly utilize vitamin E.[60] Also, vitamin E protects the body against the potentially damaging effects of iron and fish oil. Human volunteers given high doses of fish oil experienced an immune abnormality (mitogenic responsiveness of peripheral blood mononuclear cells to concanavalin A) which was reversed with supplements of vitamin E.[61]

IMMUNE REGULATOR. Vitamin E plays a powerful role as an immune regulator.[62] When 32 healthy elderly adults were given supplements of 800 iu daily of vitamin E there were measurable improvements in immune functions.[63] Following 28 days of supplements of vitamins E, C and A; researchers found that 30 elderly institutionalized patients had substantial improvements in immune functions (absolute T-cells, T4 subsets, T4:T8 ratio and lymphocyte proliferation).[64] E seems to work by protecting immune factors from immediate destruction in their suicidal plunge at cancer cells. E also works by bolstering the activity of the thymus and spleen organs to stimulate lymphocyte proliferation. In burned animals, vitamin E supplements offered substantial protection in the intestinal mucosa to prevent bacterial translocation (gut bacteria migrating into the blood to cause septicemia).[65]

PROTECTION FROM TOXINS. Vitamin E protected animals from the cancer-causing effects of alcohol on the esophagus[66] and a carcinogen on the colon.[67] Vitamin E and selenium protected animals against the potent carcinogenic effects of DMBA from tobacco.[68] Vitamin E protected the damaged liver of rats from developing fatty liver and collagen content.[69] Vitamin E protects us against the greatest toxin and essential nutrient of them all--oxygen, as shown in exercised animals.[70] By sparing fats in the blood from becoming lipid peroxides, vitamin E supplements were very effective at preventing heart disease.[71] Vitamin E prevents the formation of one of the more common carcinogenic agents in humans; nitrosamines, which are formed by the combination of nitrates in the diet and amino acids in the stomach. Vitamin E prevents the damage to the skin from ultraviolet radiation.[72] According to researchers from Bulgaria, vitamin E protects us against the harmful effects of too much iron-generating free radicals and damage to our detoxification system, cytochrome P-450. Much of the damage caused by iron in the human body is due to: 1) wrong form of iron, we need chelated iron, not iron salts as we get in fortified white flour, 2) not enough antioxidants to prevent this oxidizing metal from "rusting" in the cell and creating harm.

REVERSE PRE-CANCEROUS CONDITION. Vitamin E supplements (200-400 mg/d for 3 months) reversed fibrocystic breast disease (a major risk for breast cancer) in 22 out of 26 women.[73] Other women have found reversal of fibrocystic breast disease through elimination of caffeine, chocolate, and colas which contain methylxanthines.

PROSTAGLANDINS. We can generate very healthy prostaglandins if we have the right dietary precursors in our blood, which comes from:
⇒ enough fish oil (EPA) or flax oil (ALA) and borage oil (GLA)
⇒ healthy levels of blood sugar (60-100 mg%)
⇒ optimal amounts of vitamin E.[74]

Because of this beneficial impact on prostaglandins, vitamin E helps to inhibit platelet adhesion[75], which helps to slow down the spreading of cancer. And yet, as shown below, vitamin E does not influence blood clotting, or prothrombin time, which is good news for people worried about proper clotting during and after surgery.

SLOWS AND REVERSES CANCER. In human studies, low intake of vitamin E increases the risk for cancer of various body sites.[76] Patients with head and neck cancers are more likely to have a recurrence if they have low blood levels of vitamins E, A and betacarotene.[77] Vitamin E injected into animal mouth tumors was able to significantly reduce or completely eliminate tumors.[78] In patients with colorectal cancer, vitamin E, C, and A supplements were able to reduce the growth of abnormal cells in the colon, indicating a possible slowing of the cancer process.[79] In human epidemiology studies, people with the highest intake of E (still very low compared to ideal intake) had a 40% reduction in the risk for colon cancer.[80] In animals, vitamin E supplements prevent lung tumors from developing.[81]

VITAMIN E SUCCINATE AND CANCER. When vitamin E is esterified (combined) with succinic acid, a new molecule is formed with surprising ability to selectively shut down cancer growth, but not harm healthy tissue, [82] slowing the growth of brain (glioma and neuroblastoma) and melanoma cells in culture.[83] E succinate is able to reduce the genetic expression of c-myc oncogenes in cultured cancer cells.[84] E succinate inhibits virally-induced tumors in culture.[85] E succinate has been studied as a potent regulator of cell proliferation.[86]

IMPROVES MEDICAL THERAPY OF CANCER. Vitamin E helps generally toxic medical therapies to distinguish between healthy and cancerous cells. The best proposed mechanism for this action is the anaerobic state of many tumors. Vitamin E apparently is not well absorbed, or needed, by tumors, since they are anaerobic (without oxygen). An antioxidant is of little interest to an oxygen independent cell. Because of this function of vitamin E, chemotherapy and radiation can be made much more selectively toxic to the cancer cells, while protecting the patient from host damage.

It has long been known that a vitamin E deficiency, common in cancer patients, will accentuate the cardiotoxic effects of adriamycin.[87] The worse the vitamin E deficiency in animals, the greater the heart damage from adriamycin.[88] Patients undergoing chemo, radiation and bone marrow transplant for cancer treatment had markedly depressed levels of serum antioxidants, including vitamin E.[89] Given the fact that both chemo and radiation can induce cancer, which reduces the chances for survival, it is noteworthy that vitamin E protects animals against a potent carcinogen, DMBA.[90] Vitamin E supplements prevented the glucose-raising effects of a chemo drug, doxorubicin.[91] Since cancer is a sugar-feeder, preventing this glucose-raising effect may be another valuable contribution from vitamin E in patients receiving chemo. Meanwhile, vitamin E improves the tumor kill rate of doxorubicin.[92] Vitamin E modifies the carcinogenic effect of daunomycin (chemo drug) in animals.[93]

Human prostate cancer cells were killed at a higher rate when adriamycin (chemo drug) was combined with vitamin E at concentrations that can easily be obtained from supplementation.[94] Vitamin E supplements (1600 iu/day) taken one week prior to adriamycin therapy protected 69% of patients from hair loss, which is nearly universal in adriamycin-treated patients.[95] Vitamin E helped to repair kidney damage caused by adriamycin in animals.[96] Vitamin E and selenium supplements in animals helped to reduce the heart toxicity from adriamycin.[97] Selenium and vitamin E supplements were given to 41 women undergoing cytotoxic therapy for ovarian and cervical cancers, with a resulting drop in the toxicity-related rise in creatine kinase.[98] Vitamin E, A and prenylamine reduced the toxicity of adriamycin on the heart of animals studied.[99]

In animals with implanted tumors, those pretreated with vitamin E had a much greater tumor kill from radiation therapy.[100] Radiation therapists know that the ability to kill cancer with radiation diminishes as the tumor becomes more anaerobic or hypoxic. Vitamin E seems to sensitize tumors, making them more vulnerable to radiation therapy. In cultured human cancer cells, vitamin E increased the damaging effects of radiation on tumor cells.[101] Brain cancer cells were easier to kill once pretreated with vitamin E succinate.[102] Tumor kill in animals receiving radiation therapy was greatly increased by pretreatment with vitamin E.[103] Vitamin E supplements reduced the breakage of red blood cells in animals given radiation therapy.[104] Vitamin E supplements improved the wound recovery in animals given preoperative radiation.[105]

Vitamin E combined with vitamin K, leucovorin (anti-metabolite cancer drug) and 5FU (fluorouracil) significantly enhanced the cell growth inhibition curves for 5FU.[106] One of the more troublesome side effects of chemotherapy is peripheral neuropathy, or a tingling numbness in the extremities. Low vitamin E status is likely to blame for peripheral neuropathy. [107]

Mouth sores (oral mucositis) are a common problem arising from the use of many chemotherapy drugs. These mouth sores are so painful that cancer patients stop eating, which creates malnutrition, which really deteriorates the general health picture. Vitamin E topically applied healed 67% of cancer patients in a double blind trial at M.D. Anderson Hospital in Houston.[108] To use this therapy, puncture the end of a soft gelatin vitamin E capsule and spread the vitamin E oil over the mouth sore. Do this several times each day.

Can't get enough in food

Vitamin E supplements have even been endorsed by the National Cancer Institute [109], American Heart Association and the United States Department of Agriculture, because in order to consume 400 international units of vitamin E, you would have to eat either:

-2 quarts of corn oil, or
-5 pounds of wheat germ, or
-8 cups of almonds, or
-28 cups of peanuts

SAFETY ISSUES. Taking many times the RDA of vitamin E had some researchers worried about toxicity, so they fed 900 iu (90 times the RDA) daily to healthy college students for 12 weeks with no changes in liver, kidney, thyroid, **blood clotting** or immunoglobulin levels.[110] These results are valuable because vitamin E inhibits the platelet aggregation that can cause stroke, heart disease or cancer metastasis; yet does not alter blood clotting activity. Therefore, pre-surgical patients do not need to reduce vitamin E intake for fear of not clotting during and after surgery. According to a review of the world's literature on vitamin E toxicity, there are virtually no side effects at dosages under 3200 iu/day.[111]

K (menadione)   100 mcg
        Selectively toxic to tumor cells. In combination with vitamin C forms anti-cancer compound.

When vitamin K was first researched in 1929, it was labelled the "Klotting" factor by the Dutch scientist Henrik Dam. Since then, much has been learned about this fascinating molecule. There are three primary variations of vitamin K, all with certain levels of activity in the body.

⇒ K-1, or phylloquinone, is produced in higher plants such as spinach, broccoli, brussel sprouts and kale.

⇒ K-2, or menaquinone, is produced by bacterial fermentation, which means that we manufacture varying amounts of vitamin K in a healthy human gut; also fermented foods like cheeses and soy foods carry some K.

⇒ K-3, or menadione, is the synthetically derived version of vitamin K, called Synkavite in drug form.

        Although mother's milk will quickly begin generating vitamin K in the infant's gut, physicians have developed a standard hospital protocol of giving injections of Synkavite to all newborns. About 1/3 of all patients with chronic gastrointestinal problems have clinical vitamin K deficiency.[112]

        There are several handsome lessons to be learned as we review vitamin K in :

◊ **Metavitamin functions**. Many nutrients develop unique functions when given at anything beyond survival doses. Niacin, vitamin A, vitamin C, fish oil and others all reflect the fact that low dose of a nutrient will give you basic survival functions, while higher doses give us "above-vitamin" or meta-vitamin functions. In this case, vitamin K is basically a clotting factor that helps to activate prothrombin so that we do not bleed to death when cutting open the skin envelope.[113] In higher doses, vitamin K becomes a potent anti-cancer agent which is non-toxic to healthy cells.[114]

◊ **Synergism yields two main benefits**: 1) significant increase in healing capacity; 2) the need for lower doses. Researchers found that combining vitamins C and K-3 against cultured human breast cancer cells allowed for inhibition of the cancer growth at doses 90-98% less than what was required if only one of these vitamins was used against the cancer.[115]

◊ **Look beyond the obvious**. Coumarin (a.k.a. dicumarol, warfarin) is an anti-coagulant drug that holds promise in cancer treatment by shuting down cancer cell metabolism and helping to slow metastasis. Vitamin K has a primary function of inducing coagulation. The obvious deduction is that vitamin K (a coagulant) would neutralize the benefits of coumarin (anti-coagulant). In real life, Vitamin K-3 does not neutralize the effects of coumarin[116] but actually improves the anti-cancer effects of coumarin.[117] The reason that K-1 reverses the effects of coumarin and K-3 does not lies in the slight difference in chemical structure in which K-3 cannot participate in the gamma carboxylation of prothrombin.

◊ **Similar is not the same as identical in chemical structures**. Oftentimes, drug companies find a substance that has therapeutic action, such as vitamin A or indole-3-carbinol from broccoli, and will try to create a slightly different molecule so that it can be patented. These slight differences nearly always translate into high toxicity from these newly-formed molecules. For instance, the difference between a man and woman rests primarily on the difference between the hormones testosterone and estrogen, which are nearly identical molecules except for one OH group. Over 40 years ago, Professor J.S. Mitchell of England showed that patients receiving K-3 had measurable shrinkage of tumors. Later, the drug doxorubicin was introduced as an anti-cancer drug. K-3, doxorubicin and coumarin all share related chemical structures as "naphthoquinone" molecules. Yet, of all these compounds, K-3 has been shown by Chlebowski and colleagues at the University of California Los Angeles to have 70 times (7000%!!!) more anti-cancer activity than coumarin and 25 times more cancer killing capacity than vitamin K-1.

Vitamin K-3 works against cancer both by directly antagonizing cell replication in cancer cells[118] and by inhibiting metastasis. K-3 also works as a potentiator of radiation therapy. In one study, patients with mouth cancer who were pre-treated with injections of K-3 prior to radiation therapy doubled their odds (20% vs. 39%) for 5 year survival and disease free status.[119] Animals with implanted tumors had greatly improved anti-cancer effects from all chemotherapy drugs tested when vitamins K and C were given in combination.[120] In cultured leukemia cells, vitamins K and E added to the chemotherapy drugs of 5FU (fluorouracil) and leucovorin provided a 300% improvement in growth inhibition when compared to 5FU by itself.[121] Animals given methotrexate and K-3 had improvements in cancer reversal with no increase in toxicity to the host tissue.[122] In one case study, a patient with recurrent and drug refractory bone cancer metastasized to the lungs, was put on a regimen of hydrazine sulfate and vitamin K-3 injections, with a resulting weight gain and complete regression of her cancer.[123] In 13 cancer patients, some with demonstrated drug resistant tumors, menadiol (vitamin K analog, a.k.a. K-4) was given at up to 3200 mg per meter squared per week along with various chemo drugs with no increase in host toxicity but some improvements in tumor responses.[124]

SAFETY ISSUES. There is no known toxicity associated with the plant-derived version, K-1.[125] The toxicity of menadione (K-3) is very low, with animals having no adverse side effects after being fed 1000 times the daily requirement.[126] The typical dietary intake of K-1 in America is somewhere between 100-500 micrograms daily, with little understanding of the role played by the production of K-2 in the healthy human gut.

A special note on coumarin. Many cancer patients on coumarin are directed by their physician to avoid foods high in vitamin K-1, including kale, spinach, broccoli and other anti-cancer greens. Actually, much more important is to have a PREDICTABLE intake of vitamin K-1. The doctor will take blood samples and conduct a Pro test (prothrombin test, time required for the blood to clot) and prescribe coumarin based on this test. It is much more essential to have a PREDICTABLE amount of vitamin K-1 in the diet than to avoid it, which will allow for the safest and most effective use of anti-coagulant drugs.

C 2500 mg (1000 mg from ascorbic acid & 1500 mg from sodium ascorbate)
    Immune stimulant, antioxidant, helps envelop cancer, shuts down cancer growth.

If vitamin A was the mother of all anti-cancer vitamins, then vitamin C is the grandmother of all. The problem started millions of years ago when primates lost the liver enzyme necessary to convert sugar into vitamin C.[127] Of the millions of animals, reptiles, amphibians, insects and other things that walk, crawl, fly and swim--humans are among the few creatures on earth that do not make our own vitamin C. Our primitive ancestors were able to consume 300-500 milligrams daily of vitamin C, which definitely prevents scurvy. Throughout the golden ages of world exploration by ship, thousands of people died--sometimes up to half of the crew--due to scurvy. Highly perishable fresh fruits and vegetables are the richest sources of vitamin C and were unavailable on ship voyages longer than a few weeks. Around 1750, the English physician, James Lind, found that limes could prevent and reverse scurvy (does that make limes a prescription drug?).

"Time lags" are a known phenomenon that separate a discovery from the actual implementation of a breakthrough. It was another 50 years after Dr. Lind's research before limes were required to be carried aboard ships, thus costing the world thousands of unnecessary deaths in this delay. Are we doing the same thing by delaying aggressive nutrition support for millions of cancer patients?

Vitamin C is one of the more versatile vitamins in human nutrition. Its functions include:
⇒ potent protector against free radicals
⇒ maintenance of tough connective tissue (collagen and elastin) which is the "glue" that keeps our body together
⇒ production of adrenaline for energy
⇒ production of serotonin for thought and calmness
⇒ stimulates various immune components to protect against infections and cancer
⇒ converts cholesterol into bile for its elimination in the bowels
⇒ maintains fat stores in the adipose tissue to prevent heart disease
⇒ important for bone formation
⇒ critical in many detoxification pathways to better tolerate pollutants
⇒ reduces allergic reactions by preventing histamine release
⇒ helps insulin to better control blood sugar levels.

And remember, these are just the normal everyday functions in healthy people. In sick people, vitamin C develops additional therapeutic roles. Is it any wonder that Dr. Linus Pauling was so enthusiastic about using above-RDA levels of vitamin C to improve outcome in cancer?

HOW MUCH???

Part of the controversy surrounding vitamin C is the extreme range of dosages that can be consumed in humans or produced in animals:

⇒ 10 milligrams daily will prevent blatant scurvy in most healthy adults
⇒ 60 mg is the Recommended Dietary Allowance
⇒ 200-300 mg would be consumed by people who are following the NCI suggestion of 5 servings of fruit and vegetables daily
⇒ 300 mg of supplemental vitamin C was shown to increase quantity of life by 6 years in men
⇒ 1000 mg is required in many hospitalized patients just to maintain adequate serum ascorbate levels
⇒ 10,000 to 20,000 mg is often taken by many people using C to curtail some illness, like cancer, AIDS, viral infections, and injury recovery
⇒ 100,000 mg/day has been given IV, or intravenously with no side effects
⇒ 20,000 mg is produced daily by many animals, like goats and dogs, on a per weight basis using a 154 pound reference man; internal production goes up further when the animal is exposed to stress, infections, or toxins

Although Linus Pauling, PhD was not the first scientist to suggest that vitamin C might help cancer patients, he was definitely the most vocal and decorated of the lot. With 2 unshared Nobel prizes and 3 Presidential citations, you would think that the scientific community would be more open to Dr. Pauling's comments. Though Pauling was considered to be one of the 2 greatest scientists of the 20th century, along with Albert Einstein, the 1970s found Pauling to be an academic nomad for his innovative views on vitamin C.

However, as time marched on, data continued to gather to support Pauling's viewpoint. By 1982, the National Academy of Sciences was willing to admit that vitamin C might prevent cancer.[128] And by 1990, the National Institutes of Health hosted a conference on "Vitamin C and Cancer", which showed that Pauling was truly on to something.[129] While Pauling's strident critics claimed that he was trying to cure cancer with vitamin C, in fact Pauling only suggested high doses of C in concert with medical therapies would augment cancer outcome, as he wrote:

"The optimum treatment of the cancer patient requires a concerted multi-disciplinary approach employing the full resources of surgery, radiotherapy, chemotherapy, immunotherapy and supportive care. The last named has received the least attention, although it might well possess great potential for therapeutic advance."[130]
Linus Pauling, PhD,1974

Pauling later went on to explain the reasons that vitamin C may improve outcome in cancer treatment, including the increased need for C in cancer patients, ability of C to prevent cancer breaking down connective tissue for metastasis, ability of C to help "wall off" or encapsulate the tumor, role of C in immune attack on cancer, and the role of C in hormonal balance.[131] One of the highlights of my career has been having Dr. Pauling eat supper at my house in 1992 while he was spry and alert at 91 years of age.

Vitamin C can help cancer patients in several critical categories:

1) Prevention. Cancer patients have already demonstrated a genetic vulnerability to cancer and toxins. Cancer patients will likely be exposed to even more potent carcinogens in medical therapy. Therefore, the need to prevent secondary and iatrogenic tumors is great. In a study encompassing 16 groups in 7 countries covering 25 years, higher vitamin C intake was strongly related to lowering cancer incidence.[132] Another study examined the cancer protective effect of vitamin C and found that 33 of 46 epidemiological studies showed it helped, while none showed any increase in cancer with higher vitamin C intake.[133] Vitamin C protects humans against a whole assortment of toxic chemicals[134] while accelerating wound recovery[135] and stabilizing iron compounds (ferritin) in the blood.[136] Vitamin C reduced the incidence and severity of kidney tumors in animals exposed to the hormones estradiol or diethylstilbestrol. [137] Through a wide variety of mechanisms, vitamin C is a potent inhibitor of cancer.[138]

2) Augmenting medical therapy. C may be able to enhance the toxicity of chemo and radiation against the cancer cells while protecting the patient from possible harm. C was able to enhance the effectiveness of a drug (misonidazole) that improves outcome in radiation treatment of cancer.[139] C improved the tumor-stopping abilities of a wide range of medical therapies against brain cancer (neuroblastoma) cells in culture.[140] Animals given the chemo drugs vincristine (from the periwinkle plant) and vinblastine were given supplements of vitamin C with an increase in the excretion of these very toxic drugs.[141] Animals given adriamycin (a common chemotherapy drug) along with vitamin C had a significant prolongation of life and reduction in the expected heart damage (cardiotoxicity) from this drug.[142] Given the widespread use of adriamycin and its known lethal toxicity on the heart[143], it should be standard procedure to give high doses of antioxidants prior to administration of adriamycin.

Animals with implanted tumors were injected with high doses of C one hour prior to whole body radiation therapy, all scaled to mimic the effects in a human cancer patient. Vitamin C did not affect the tumor killing capacity of the radiation, but did provide substantial protection to the animals.[144] 50 previously untreated cancer patients were randomly divided into 2 groups, with #1 receiving radiation therapy only and #2 receiving radiation plus 5 grams daily of C. After 1 month, 87% of the vitamin C group had achieved a complete response (disappearance of all tumors) compared to 55% in the control group.[145]

   3) Slowing or reversing cancer. High doses of C are preferentially toxic to tumor cells while not harming healthy tissue. One of the explanations why C kills cancer but not healthy cells lies in the fact that C generates large amounts of hydrogen peroxide, H_2O_2, a potent free radical, which is neutralized in healthy cells by catalase.[146] Cancer cells do not have catalase to protect them. Animals exposed to a carcinogen and then vitamin C had their basal cell cancers examined under electron microscope. The cancer cells exposed to C showed a disintegration of cell structure, cell membrane disruption, increased collagen synthesis and general reduction in the number and size of tumors.[147] The researcher concluded: "...vitamin C exerts its antineoplastic effects by increasing cytolytic and autophagic activity, cell membrane disruption, and increased collagen synthesis, and thus, inhibits cancer cell metabolism and proliferation."

   C may be the ultimate selective toxin against cancer that researchers have been searching for.[148] Vitamin C was toxic to melanoma cells but not healthy cells in culture.[149]   When researchers took leukemia cells from 28 patients and cultured them with vitamin C, 25% of the cultures were inhibited by at least 79%.[150]   In animals with implanted tumors, vitamin C and B-12 together provided for significant tumor regression and 50% survival of the treated group, while all of the animals not receiving C and B-12 died by the 19th day.[151] C and B-12 seemed to form a cobalt-ascorbate compound that selectively shut down tumor growth. When vitamin C and K were combined to cancer cells in culture, the dosage required to slow and kill cancer cells dropped to only 2% compared to the dosage required by either of these vitamins alone.[152] Vitamin C or essential fatty acids were able to inhibit the growth of melanoma in culture, yet when combined their anti-cancer activity was much stronger.[153]

   In both case studies and clinical trials in the scientific literature, C helps many cancer patients and hurts no one. Show me a drug that has the same risk to benefit to cost ratio. In one case report, a 70 year old man had been treated for kidney cancer, and then experienced a metastatic recurrence. He refused further medical therapy and started on 30 grams daily of intravenous vitamin C. Six weeks later, his chest X-rays showed that he was disease free.[154] A 42 year old man with reticulum cell sarcoma was treated on two different occasions with high dose intravenous vitamin C as sole therapy and each time resulted in a complete remission with 17 years of followup.[155]

Pauling and Cameron found that 10,000 mg (10 grams) daily of vitamin C brought a 22% survival rate in end-stage untreatable cancer patients after 1 year on C, compared to a 0.4% survival in patients without C.[156] Charles Moertel, MD of the Mayo Clinic allegedly followed the Pauling protocol and found no benefit with vitamin C.[157] Actually, even though Moertel did not follow Pauling's protocol, none of the untreatable, drug refractory colon cancer patients in Moertel's study died while on vitamin C for 3 months.

Finnish oncologists used high doses of nutrients (including 2-5 grams of C) along with chemo and radiation for lung cancer patients. Normally, lung cancer is a "poor prognostic" malignancy with a 1% expected survival at 30 months under normal treatment. In this study, however, 8 of 18 patients (44%) who were given vitamin C and other nutrients were still alive 6 years after diagnosis.[158]

Oncologists at West Virginia Medical School randomized 65 patients with transitional cell carcinoma of the bladder into either the "one-per-day" vitamin supplement providing the RDA, or into a group which received the RDA supplement plus 40,000 iu of vitamin A, 100 mg of B-6, 2000 mg of vitamin C, 400 iu of vitamin E, and 90 mg of zinc. After 10 months, tumor recurrence was 80% in the control group (RDA supplement) and 40% in the experimental "megavitamin" group. Five year projected tumor recurrence was 91% for controls and 41% for "megavitamin" patients. Essentially, high dose nutrients, including vitamin C, cut tumor recurrence in half.[159]

In a non-randomized clinical trial, Drs. Hoffer and Pauling instructed patients to follow a reasonable cancer diet (unprocessed food low in fat, dairy, and sugar), coupled with therapeutic doses of vitamins (including 12 grams of C) and minerals.[160] All 129 patients in this study received concomitant oncology care. The control group of 31 patients who did not receive nutrition support lived an average of less than 6 months. The group of 98 cancer patients who received the diet and supplement program were categorized into 3 groups:

-Poor responders (n=19) or 20% of treated group. Average lifespan of 10 months, or a 75% improvement over the control group.

-Good responders (n=47), who had various cancers, including leukemia, lung, liver, and pancreas; had an average lifespan of 72 months (6 years).

-Good female responders (n=32), with involvement of reproductive areas (breast, cervix, ovary, uterus); had an average lifespan of over 10 years, which is a 2100% improvement in lifespan over untreated patients!! Many were still alive at the end of the study.

4) Higher need. There is an elevated need for this nutrient during disease recovery. In one study, 15 patients with melanoma and colon cancer who were receiving immunotherapy (interleukin 2 and lymphokine-activated killer cells) showed blood levels of vitamin C indicative of scurvy.[161] In 20 adult hospitalized patients on Total Parenteral Nutrition (TPN), the mean daily vitamin C needs were 975 mg, which is over 16 times the RDA, with the range being 350-2250 mg.[162] Of the 139 lung cancer patients studied, most tested deficient or scorbutic (clinical vitamin C deficiency).[163] Another study of cancer patients found that 46% tested scorbutic while 76% were below acceptable levels for serum ascorbate.[164]

SAFETY ISSUES. Vitamin C is extremely safe, even in high doses. In one review of the literature regarding safety of vitamin C, 8 different double blind placebo controlled trials giving up to 10,000 mg daily of C for years produced no side effects.[165] In some sensitive individuals, doses of as little as 1000 mg produce gastro-intestinal upset, including diarrhea. Allegations that vitamin C mega-doses would produce oxalate kidney stones or cause B-12 deficiency have never been seen in millions of humans taking mega-doses of C for years. Up to 100,000 mg of C has been safely administered IV. As doses of oral C increase, the percentage that is absorbed goes down. Some experts claim that 10-20 grams of C per day is the upper threshold of what humans can tolerate and efficiently absorb. There is some evidence that ascorbic acid is quickly absorbed, more likely to cause GI upset and quickly excreted; all of which has certain value. Meanwhile, mineral bound ascorbate (such as sodium ascorbate found in) provides a more prolonged and sustained blood level of serum ascorbate.

B-1 (thiamine mononitrate)   10 mg
     Improves aerobic metabolism.

Every time humans process our food into something less than whole we learn a valuable, if not painful, lesson. When the British first learned to mill wheat and remove the outer bran and inner germ, they called the remaining cadaver of a food substance "the Queen's white flour". Bringing this technology around the world, the Dutch showed the South Pacific people of Java how to refine their rice, leaving only white rice behind and disposing of the bran and germ. Many of these people developed a condition of weakness and inability to function, called beri-beri, or literally translated: "I cannot. I cannot." Thiamin was one of the first vitamins to be studied and isolated in the early 20th century.

The importance of thiamin lies in its critical role in energy metabolism and the need for energy in every cell of the body. Thiamin becomes incorporated into a critical enzyme (thiamin pyrophosphate) for production of ATP energy. Low intake of thiamin was associated with an increase in the risk for prostate cancer.[166] Although thiamin is added back to enriched white flour, it is not added back to pastry flour (as in doughnuts) and is often deficient in the elderly[167] and those who regularly consume alcohol.[168] Best food sources of thiamin include brewers yeast, peas, wheat germ, peanuts, whole grains, beans, liver.

B-2 (riboflavin)   10 mg
   Improves aerobic metabolism.

Again, like thiamin above, riboflavin is mainly concerned with generating ATP energy from foodstuffs through the enzyme FAD (flavin adenine dinucleotide). However, riboflavin is also essential for the generation of a critical protective enzyme, glutathione peroxidase, which mops up free radicals. With optimal amounts of riboflavin in the body, there is less damage to cell membranes, DNA and immune factors. Low intake of riboflavin is associated with an increased risk for cancer of prostate and esophagus. Although riboflavin is added back to enriched white flour, many elderly[169] and poor people are low in riboflavin intake.[170] Alcohol interferes with the absorption and metabolism of riboflavin. Best food sources of riboflavin include brewer's yeast, kidney, liver, broccoli, wheat germ, milk and almonds.

B-3 (hexanicotinate)   500 mg
   Improves aerobic metabolism & tumor killing capacity of medical therapy, also may work like an enzyme to dissolve protective coating surrounding tumor.

Like the energy vitamins mentioned above, niacin generates ATP energy via the enzyme NAD (nicotinamide adenine dinucleotide) and also has other duties that impact the cancer patient. Niacin supplements in animals were able to reduce the cardiotoxicity of adriamycin while not interfering with its tumor killing capacity.[171] Niacin combined with aspirin in 106 bladder cancer patients receiving surgery and radiation therapy provided for a substantial improvement in 5 year survival (72% vs. 27%) over the control group.[172]

Tumors can hide from radiation therapy as hypoxic (low oxygen) lumps. Niacin seems to make radiation therapy more effective at killing these hypoxic cancer cells.[173] Loading radiation patients with 500 mg to 6000 mg of niacin has been shown to be safe and one of the most effective agents known to eliminate acute hypoxia in solid malignancies.[174] There is also intriguing evidence that high doses of niacin can act like enzymes, which means:

⇒ changing the coating of the tumor to make it more vulnerable to the immune system and medical intervention.

⇒ breaking up inefficient clumps of immune cells, or circulating immune complexes

⇒ altering Tumor Necrosis Factor (TNF) that can lead to depression, weight loss and pain.

B-5 (D-calcium pantothenate)   20 mg
    Improves stress response.

Pantothenic acid is named for "pantos", which is Greek for "found everywhere".   Indeed, all plants and animals require or make pantothenic acid as part of a crucial energy enzyme, acetyl Coenzyme A, which is vital for generating ATP energy and a chemical for stress response. Injections of pantothenic acid improved wound healing in rabbits.[175] Based on the fact that the average American diet provides about 6 mg of pantothenic acid daily, the recommended intake (no formal RDA) is 4-7 mg. Deficiencies of pantothenic acid will generate symptoms of paresthesia (burning, prickling, tingling of extremities), headache, fatigue, insomnia, and GI distress. Pantothenic acid works closely with carnitine and CoQ (both in) to maximize the efficiency of burning dietary fats. Supplements of pantothenic acid can help in the stress response, proper balancing of adrenal hormones, energy production and manufacturing of red blood cells. Best food sources of pantothenic acid are royal bee jelly, liver, kidney, egg yolk, and broccoli.

B-6 total of 50 mg
3.3 mg from Pyridoxal 5 pyrophosphate, and 46.6 mg from
pyridoxine   HCl
    Improves immune functions and may reduce toxicity from
radiation therapy.

B-6 occurs in 3 natural forms: pyridoxine, pyridoxal, and pyridoxamine. B-6 works chiefly in an enzyme, pyridoxal-5-phosphate, which shifts amine groups from molecule to molecule. At least 100 different enzyme systems in humans involving protein metabolism, catabolism, anabolism or enzyme production all require B-6. B-6 is essential for:

⇒ regulating proper blood glucose levels
⇒ production of niacin from tryptophan
⇒ lipid metabolism and carnitine synthesis
⇒ making nucleic acids (RNA and DNA)
⇒ immune cell production
⇒ regulation of hormones.

Among its many functions, B-6 is required for producing thymidine, without which cells are more likely to develop cancerous mutations. [176] In a group of 12 non-medicated newly diagnosed cancer patients who had been smokers, all showed indications (based on coenzyme stimulation) of B-6 deficiency.[177] A low intake of B-6 increases tumor susceptibility and tumor size.[178]

In huge surveys conducted by the United States Department of Agriculture, 80% of Americans did not consume the RDA of 2 mg daily of B-6. There are many aspects of the typical American lifestyle that will exacerbate a marginal deficiency of B-6: many drugs, common food dyes, alcohol, and a high protein intake. Deficiency symptoms will reflect the functions of B-6, which means that almost anything can go wrong.

In one study, 25 mg (1250% of RDA) provided measurable improvements in immune functions in healthy adults. B-6 supplements (50-500 mg) have been shown to cure up to 97% of Carpal Tunnel Syndrome, a painful condition of the wrist and hands. B-6 is very helpful in: ⇒preventing and reversing neuropathy, or a tingling numbness in the hands and feet, which is common in chemo patients.
⇒preventing the "tanning" of blood proteins, a.k.a. glycosylation or glycation, that occurs when too much sugar is regularly found in the bloodstream. [179] Above-normal intake of B-6 offers many possible benefits to the cancer patient, including:
◊   Immune stimulation.[180]
◊   Blood sugar control
◊   Protection from radiation damage.
◊   Inhibits growth in melanoma.

Early studies in animals indicated that depriving them of B-6 might slow down tumor growth and increase survival time.[181] More recent studies find the opposite to be true. Animals supplemented with B-6 and then injected with a deadly strain of cancer, melanoma, showed an enhanced resistance to the disease.[182] B-6 inhibits melanoma in vivo.[183] B-6 supplements of 25 mg/day in 33 bladder cancer patients provided for marked reduction in tumor recurrence compared to the control group.[184] More recently, oncologists randomized 65 patients with transitional cell carcinoma of the bladder into either the "one-per-day" vitamin supplement providing the RDA, or into a group which received the RDA supplement plus 40,000 iu of vitamin A, 100 mg of B-6, 2000 mg of vitamin C, 400 iu of vitamin E, and 90 mg of zinc. High dose nutrients, including B-6, cut tumor recurrence in half.[185] B-6 supplements of 300 mg/day throughout 8 weeks of radiation therapy in patients with endometrial cancer provided a 15% improvement in survival at 5 years. [186]

SAFETY ISSUES. Less than 500 mg/day appears to be safe for most adults.[187] P-5-P appears to be the more readily available and active form of B-6, yet most people can convert pyridoxine into active P-5-P.

B-12 (cyanocobalamin) 1 mg
　　Assists in proper cell growth, i.e. making of new immune factors and proper division of other cells. Combines with vitamin C to create selective anti-cancer compound.

In 1926, Minot and Murphy were awarded the Nobel prize for showing that feeding large quantities of liver could cure the dreaded disease, pernicious anemia, or B-12 deficiency. As people mature beyond age 40, the likelihood of developing pernicious anemia goes up substantially as the gut loses its efficiency at binding with this gigantic molecule and escorting it across the intestinal mucosa. The RDA of 2 micrograms (mcg) can easily be obtained in a typical "meat and potatoes" diet in America, since the best sources are liver, meat, fish, chicken, clams and egg yolk. However, absorbing the nutrient is another challenge. When this "intrinsic factor" in the gut is missing, large amounts in the diet can somewhat overwhelm the mucosal barrier in the gut and allow some absorption into the bloodstream, which is what happened when liver was used to cure pernicious anemia.

Since B-12 is a methyl donor, it is involved in all new cell growth, which makes it rather important in processes like red blood cell and immune cell formation, energy metabolism, and nerve function. There is a huge body of data now pointing to B-12 and folacin as primary nutrients that can interrupt the production of homocysteine, which is a major risk factor in heart disease.

For the cancer patient, B-12 supplements may bolster host defense mechanisms, plus it can combine with vitamin C to form a unique cobalt ascorbate complex that is selectively toxic to tumor cells.[188]

Folic acid 200 mcg
　　Assists in proper cell growth, immune stimulant, helps to check abnormal DNA production.

Folic acid (a.k.a. folate, folacin) presents a unique challenge in cancer treatment. On one side of the fence stand the oncologists who use have used the chemotherapy drug methotrexate for decades as an antagonist to the B vitamin, folic acid, to slow cancer growth, with leucovorin (folinic acid) as the rescue agent to summon the patient back from near death, or "the vital frontier". On the other side stand nutritionists who understand the pivotal role that folic acid plays in

HEALTHY cell growth. The efficacy of methotrexate, now being used to treat some cases of rheumatoid arthritis, is not affected by patients taking supplements of folic acid.[189]

Without optimal amounts of folic acid in the cell, growth is erratic and prone to errors, such as birth defects and cancer. Low folate status during pregnancy will generate common birth defects, including spinal bifida. Humans with low B-12 and folate status present a clinical picture that looks like leukemia.[190] The importance of folate in new cell growth is highlighted in the fact that it is the only nutrient whose requirement doubles during pregnancy.

Folic acid may be the most common vitamin deficiency in the world, since more people are chosing animal foods (poor source of folic acid) over plant foods.[191] The name, folic acid, comes from the Latin term "folium", meaning foliage, since dark green leafy vegetables are a rich source of folic acid. Other good sources of folic acid include brewer's yeast, legumes, asparagus, oranges, cabbage, root vegetables and whole grains. Since folic acid is essential for all new cell growth, disturbances in folic acid metabolism are far reaching, including heart disease (due to more homocysteine in the blood), birth defects, immune suppression, cancer, premature senility and a long list of other conditions. Without adequate folate in the diet, cell growth is like a drunk driver heading down the highway--more likely to do some harm than not.

Since folic acid and B-12 work together in methyl donor reactions, a deficiency of one can be masked by an excess of the other. Hence, the FDA has stipulated that non-prescription supplements cannot contain more than 800 micrograms of folic acid. Experts have estimated that up to 20% of all senility in older adults is merely a long term deficiency of folic acid and vitamin B-12. The RDA of folate is 200 mcg for adults and 400 mcg for pregnant women, although the Center for Disease Control has recommended that 800 mcg of folic acid would prevent most cases of spinal bifida. Without adequate folic acid in the body, there is a buildup of homocysteine in the blood, which probably generates 10% or more of the 1 million cases of heart disease each year in the U.S..

Cancer is not an "on-off" switch. There are varying shades of gray in between the black and white of normal cells and full blown metastatic malignancies. In cervical cancer, there is a rating system where a stage I dysplasia shows abnormal cell growth, while stage IV is life-threatening cancer. In one study, 40% of women with stage I and II cervical dysplasia showed clear signs of folic acid deficiency.[192] In a double blind placebo controlled trial, 10 milligrams daily of folate (50 times the RDA) reversed cervical dysplasia in the majority of women tested.[193] Low folate intake increases the risk for colorectal cancer.[194] Human cells in a culture of low folate show immune suppression (impaired delayed hypersensitivity).[195] Folate deficiency is common throughout the world and America, especially among the elderly and adolescent females.[196] Alcohol and many drugs interfere with the absorption and metabolism of folate. Average intake of folate in the U.S. is about 240 mcg, which is one half to one fourth of what a good diet will contribute.

Biotin   50 mcg
   Improves energy metabolism for glucose and fats, involved in pH maintenance through carbon dioxide binding, and helps regulate cell growth.

   Biotin is a B vitamin that is incorporated into 4 different carboxylase enzymes, which makes it essential for processing fats, sugar and various amino acids. Biotin is also involved in the production of glucokinase, an enzyme in the liver that is essential for burning glucose. Biotin supplements have been helpful at improving glucose tolerance in insulin-dependent diabetics (Type 1, using 16 milligrams/day) and non-insulin dependent diabetics (Type 2, using 9 mg/day).[197] Biotin supplements have been able to improve peripheral neuropathy (tingling numbness) in diabetics. Peripheral neuropathy is common in patients after extensive chemotherapy.

   Richest food sources of biotin are brewer's yeast, liver, soy, rice, peanut butter and oats. Biotin is also produced in the intestines through bacterial fermentation, which complicates the understanding of what an optimal intake might be. A healthy gut environment of adequate fiber, fluid and probiotics probably improves the production of biotin in the gut. Recommended intake of biotin is 30-300 mcg per day.

PATIENT PROFILE: CONQUERED BREAST CANCER
   D.S. is a 61 year old female diagnosed in November of 1995 with Stage III breast cancer. Underwent radical mastectomy (1 breast) with 4 of 22 nodes found to have cancer. Two subsequent rounds of chemotherapy produced severe side effects--patient passed out within 5 minutes of beginning chemo. Told by oncologist that without chemo, D.S. had a 5% chance of survival. Discontinued therapy. February of 1997 went to different physician who detected possible disease in the remaining breast. Surgeon performed lumpectomy and there was no cancer in this tissue, as per the pathologist report. March 1997, she began nutrition therapy as sole therapy. In June of 1997, she was found to have enlarged lymph nodes with possible disease. August 1997 checkup found these nodes to have disappeared. As of January 1998, no recurrence of disease. She is very pleased with the healing power of nutrition.

ENDNOTES

[1] . Huang, ME, Am.J.Hematol., vol.28, p.124, 1988

[2] . Watson, R., et al., Nutr.Res., vol.5, p.663, 1985

[3] . Zhang, XM, et al., Virchows Archiv.B Cell.Pathol., vol.61, p.375, 1992

[4] . Friedberg, EC, CANCER QUESTIONS, p.32, Freeman & Co, NY, 1992

[5] . Semba, RD, Clin. Infect.Dis., vol.19, p.489, 1994

[6] . Rumore, MM, Clin.Pharm., vol.12, p.506, 1993

[7] . Pinnock, CB, et al., Aust.Paediatr.J., vol.22, p.95, 1986

[8] . Nutrition Reviews, vol.52, p.281, 1994

[9] . Micksche, M., et al., Onkologie, vol.1, p.57, 1978

[10] . Vagner, VP, et al., Klin.Med., vol.69, p.55, 1991

[11] . Michalek, AM, et al., Nutrition and Cancer, vol.9, p.143, 1987

[12] . Stich, HF, Am.J.Clin.Nutr., vol.53, p.298S, 1991

[13] . Lippman, SM, et al., J.Am.Coll.Nutr., vol.7, p.269, 1988

[14] . Pastorino, U., et al., J. Clin.Oncol., vol.11, p.1216, 1993

[15] . Hruban, Z, Am.J.Pathol., vol.76, p.451, 1974

[16] . Rothman, KJ, et al., N.Engl.J.Med., vol.333, p.1369, 1995

[17] . Hathcock, JN, et al., Am.J.Clin.Nutr., vol.52, p.183, 1990

[18] . Block, G., et al., Nutr.Cancer, vol.18, p.1, 1992

[19] . Mayne, ST, et al., J. Nat.Cancer Inst., vol.86, p.33, 1994

[20] . Krinsky, NI, Amer.J.Clin.Nutr., vol.53, p.238S, 1991

[21] . Zhang, L., et al., Carcinogenesis, vol.12, p.2109, 1991

[22] . Schwartz, JL, Biochem.Biophys Res.Comm., vol.169, p.941, 1990

[23] . Mathews-Roth, MM, et al., Photochem Photobiol., vol.42, p.35, 1985

[24] . Giovannucci, E., et al., J.Nat.Cancer Inst., vol.87, p.1767, 1995

[25] . Garewal, HS, et al., Archives Otolaryngol Head Neck Surg., vol.121, p.141, Feb.1995

[26] . Hazuka, MB, et al., J. Amer.Coll.Nutrition, vol.9, p.143, 1990

[27] . Burton, GW, J.Nutrition, vol.119, p.109, 1989

[28] . Tomita, Y., et al., J.Nat.Cancer Inst., vol.78, p.679, 1987

[29] . Santamaria, L., et al., Modulation and Mediation of Cancer by Vitamins, p.81, Karger, Basel, 1983

[30] . Bertram, JS, et al., Nutrients and Cancer Prevention, Prasad, KN (eds), p.99, Humana Press, 1990

[31] . Santamaria, L., et al., Nutrients and Cancer Prevention, p.299, Prasad, KN (eds), Humana Press, 1990

[32] . Seifter, E., et al., J.Nat.Cancer Inst., vol.71, p.409, 1983

[33] . Shklar, G., et al., Eur.J.Cancer Clin.Oncol., vol.24, p.839, 1988

[34] . Mills, EED, British J.Cancer, vol.57, p.416, 1988

[35] . Seifter, E., et al., J.Nat.Cancer Inst., vol.68, p.835, 1982

[36] . Nagasawa, H., et al., Anticancer Res., vol.9, p.71, 1989

[37] . Meyers, DG, et al., Archives Internal Med., vol.156, p.925, 1996

[38] . Alpha tocopherol beta-carotene cancer prevention study group, New England Journal of Medicine, vol.330, p.1029, 1994

[39] . Schwartz, JL, Journal of Nutrition, vol.126, 4 suppl, p.1221S, 1996

[40] . Norman, AW, in PRESENT KNOWLEDGE IN NUTRITION, p.120, Ziegler, EE (eds), ILSI, Washington 1996

[41] . Gorham, ED, et al., Intern.J.Epidemiol. vol.20, p.1145, Dec.1991

[42] . Lefkowitz, ES, et al., Intern.J.Epidemiol., vol.23, p.1133, Dec.1994

[43] . Garland, CF, et al., Lancet, p.1176, Nov.18, 1989

[44] . Barger-Lux, MJ, J. Nutr., vol.124, p.1406S, Aug.1994

[45] . Crowle, AJ, et al., Infection and Immunity, vol.55, p.2945, Dec.1987

[46] . Newmark, HL, Adv.Exp.Med.Biol., vol.364, p.109, 1994

[47] . Lancet, p.1122, May 16, 1987

[48] . Pence, B., et al., Proc Amer.Assoc. Cancer, vol.28, p.154, 1987

[49] . Colston, KW, et al., Lancet, p.188, Jan.28, 1989

[50] . Peehl, DM, et al., J. Endocrinol. Invest., vol.17, p.3,, 1994

[51] . Eisman, JA, et al., Modulation and Mediation of Cancer by Vitamins, p.282, Karger, Basel, 1983

[52] . Kizaki, M., et al., Vitamins and Cancer Prevention, p.91, Wiley-Liss, NY, 1991

[53] . DeLuca, HF, Nutrients and Cancer Prevention, p.271, Humana Press, NY, 1990

[54] . Rita, M., et al., Cancer Immunol. Immunother., vol.41, p.37, 1995

[55] . Food and Nutrition Board, National Research Council, Recommended Dietary Allowances, National Academy Press, p.97, Washington, DC, 1989

[56] . Buist, RA, Intern.Clin.Nutr.Rev., vol.4, p.159, 1984

[57] . Sokol, RJ, in PRESENT KNOWLEDGE IN NUTRITION, p, 132, Ziegler, EE (eds), ILSI, Wash DC, 1996

[58]. Munoz, SJ, et al., Hepatology, vol.9, p.525, 1989
[59]. Niki, E. et al., Amer.J.Clin.Nutr., vol.53, p.201S, 1991
[60]. Bunk, MJ, et al., Proc.Soc.Exp.Biol.Med., voo.190, p.379, 1989
[61]. Kramer, TR, et al., Am.J.Clin.Nutr., vol.54, p.896, 1991
[62]. Nutrition Reviews, vol.45, p.27, Jan.1987
[63]. Meydani, SN, et al., Am.J.Clin.Nutr., vol.52, p.557, 1990
[64]. Penn, ND, et al., Age Ageing, vol.20, p.169, 1991
[65]. Kuroiwa, K, et al., J.Parenteral Enteral Nutr., vol.15, p.22, 1991
[66]. Odeleye, OE, et al., Nutr.Cancer, vol.17, p.223, 1992
[67]. Cook, MG, et al., Cancer Research, vol.40, p.1329, 1980
[68]. Horvath, PM, et al., Anticancer Research, vol.43, p.5335, Nov.1983
[69]. Sclafani, L, et al., J.Parenteral Enteral Nutr., vol.10, p.184, 1986
[70]. Packer, L., Med.Biol., vol.62, p.105, 1984
[71]. Rimm, EB, et al., New Engl J.Med., vol.328, p.1450, 1993
[72]. Record, IR, et al., Nutr.Cancer, vol.16, p.219, 1991
[73]. J.Amer Med.Assoc, vol.244, p.1077, 1980
[74]. Panganamala, RV, et al., Annals NY Acad Sci, vol.393, p.376, 1982
[75]. Jandak, J., et al., Blood, vol.73, p.141, Jan.1989
[76]. Knekt, P., et al., Am.J.Clin.Nutr., vol.53, p.283S, 1991
[77]. deVries, N., et al., Eur.Arch.Otorhinolaryngol, vol.247, p.368, 1990
[78]. Shklar, G., et al., J.Nat.Cancer Inst., vol.78, p.987, 1987
[79]. Paganelli, GM, et al., J.Nat.Cancer Inst., vol.84, p.47, 1992
[80]. Longnecker, MP, et al., J.Nat.Cancer Inst., vol.84, p.430, 1992
[81]. Yano., T., et al., Cancer Letters, vol.87, p.205, 1994
[82]. Prasad, KN, et al., J. Amer.Coll.Nutr., vol.11, p.487, 1992
[83]. Rama, BN, et al., Proc.Soc.Exper.Biol. Med., vol.174, p.302, 1983
[84]. Cohrs, RJ, et al., Int.J.Devl.Neuroscience., vol.9, p.187, 1991
[85]. Kline, K., et al., Nutr.Cancer, vol.14, p.27, 1990
[86]. Prasad, KN, et al., NUTRIENTS AND CANCER PREVENTION, Prasad, KN (eds), p.39,
Humana Press, 1990
[87]. Singal, PK, et al., Mol.Cell.Biochem., vol.84, p.163, 1988
[88]. Singal, PK, et al., Molecular Cellular Biochem., vol.84, p.163, 1988
[89]. Clemens, MR, et al., Am.J.Clin.Nutr., vol.51, p.216, 1990
[90]. Shklar, G., et al., J.Oral Pathol.Med., vol.19, p.60, 1990
[91]. Geetha, A., et al., J.Biosci., vol.14, p.243, 1989
[92]. Geetha, A., et al., Current Science, vol.64, p.318, Mar.1993
[93]. Wang, YM, et al., Molecular Inter Nutr.Cancer, p.369, , Arnott, MS, (eds), Raven Press, NY, 1982
[94]. Ripoll, EAP, et al., J.Urol., vol.136, p.529, 1986
[95]. Wood, L, N.Engl.J.Med., vol.312, p.1060, 1985
[96]. Washio, M., et al., Nephron, vol.68, p.347, 1994
[97]. VanVleet, JF, et al., Cancer Treat.Rep., vol.64, p.315, 1980
[98]. Sundstrom, H., et al., Carcinogenesis, vol.10, p.273, 1989
[99]. Milei, J., et al., Am.Heart J., vol.111, p.95, 1986
[100]. Kagerud, A., et al., vol.20, p.1, 1981
[101]. Prasad, KN, et al., Proc.Soc.Exper.Biol.Med., vol.161, p.570, 1979
[102]. Sarria, A., et al., Proc.Soc.Exper.Biol.Med., vol.175, p.88, 1984
[103]. Kagerud, A., et al., Anticancer Research, vol.1, p.35, 1981
[104]. Hoffer, A., et al., Radiation Research, vol.61, p.439, 1975
[105]. Taren, DL, et al., J.Vit.Nutr.Res., vol.57, p.133, 1987
[106]. Waxman, S., et al., Eur.J.Cancer Clin.Oncol., vol.18, p.685, 1982
[107]. Traber, MG, et al., N.Engl.J.Med., vol.317, p.262, 1987
[108]. Wadleigh, RG, et al., Amer.J.Med,vol.92, p.481, May 1992
[109]. J.Nat.Cancer Inst., vol.84, p.997, July 1992
[110]. Kitagawa, M., et al., J. Nutr.Sci. Vitaminology, vol.35, p.133, 1989
[111]. Hathcock, JN, NY Acad Sciences, vol.587, p.257, 1990
[112]. Nutrition Reviews, vol.44, p.10, Jan.1986
[113]. Suttie, JW, in PRESENT KNOWLEDGE IN NUTRITION, p.137, Ziegler, EE (eds), ILSI,
Washington, 1996
[114]. Chlebowski, RT, et al., Cancer Treatment Reviews, vol.12, p.49, 1985
[115]. Noto, V., et al., Cancer, vol.63, p.901, 1989
[116]. Dam,H., et al., in Harris, RS (eds), VITAMINS AND HORMONES, p.329, vol.18, Academic
Press, NY, 1960
[117]. Chlebowski, RT, et al., Proc.Am.Assoc.Cancer Res., vol.24, p.653, 1983
[118]. Nutter, LM, et al., Biochem.Pharmacol., vol.41, p.1283, 1991
[119]. Krishanamurthi, S., et al., Radiology, vol.99, p.409, 1971

[120] . Taper, HS, et al., Int.J.Cancer, vol.40, p.575, 1987
[121] . Waxman, S., et al., Eur.J.Cancer Clin.Oncol., vol.18, p.685, 1982
[122] . Gold, J., Cancer Treatment Reports, vol.70, p.1433, Dec.1986
[123] . Gold, J., Proc.Amer Assoc Cancer Researchers, vol.28, p.230, Mar.1987
[124] . Nagourney, R., et al., Proc.Amer.Assoc.Clin.Oncol., vol.6, p.35, Mar.1987
[125] . National Research Council, VITAMIN TOLERANCE OF ANIMALS, National Academy Press, Washington, DC 1987
[126] . Suttie, IBID
[127] . Levine, M., et al., in PRESENT KNOWLEDGE IN NUTRITION, p.146, ILSI, Washington, 1996
[128] . National Academy of Sciences, DIET NUTRITION AND CANCER, National Academy Press, Washington, 1982
[129] . Block, G., Annals Intern.Med., vol.114, p.909, 1991
[130] . Cameron, E, and Pauling, L., Chem.Biol.Interactions, vol.9, p.272, 1974
[131] . Cameron, E., Pauling, L., Cancer Research, vol. 39, p.663, Mar.1979
[132] . Ocke, MC, et al., Int.J.Cancer, vol.61, p.480, 1995
[133] . Block, G., Am.J.Clin.Nutr., vol.53, p.270S, 1991
[134] . Tannenbaum, SR, et al., Am.J.Clin.Nutr., vol.53, p.247S, 1991
[135] . Ringsdorf, WM, et al., Oral Surg, p.231, Mar.1982
[136] . Nutrition Reviews, vol.45, p.217, July 1987
[137] . Liehr, JG, Am.J.Clin.Nutr., vol.54, p.1256S, 1991
[138] . Bright-See, E., et al., Modulation and Meditation of Cancer by Vitamins, p.95, Karger, Basel., 1983
[139] . Josephy, PD, et al., Nature, vol.271, p.370, Jan.1978
[140] . Prasad, KN, et al., Proc.Natl.Acad.Sci., vol.76, p.829, Feb.1979
[141] . Sethi, VS, et al., in Modulation and Mediation of Cancer by Vitamins, p.270, Karger, Basel, 1983
[142] . Fujita, K., et al., Cancer Research, vol.42, p.309, Jan.1982
[143] . Minow, RA, et al., Cancer Chemother.Rep., vol.3, p.195, 1975
[144] . Okunieff, P., Am.J.Clin.Nutr., vol.54, p.1281S, 1991
[145] . Hanck, AB, Prog.Clin.Biol.Res., vol.259, p.307, 1988
[146] . Koch, CJ, et al., J.Cell.Physiol., vol.94, p.299, 1978
[147] . Lupulescu, A., Exp.Toxic.Pathol. vol.44, p.3, 1992
[148] . Riordan, NH, et al., Medical Hypotheses, vol.44, p.207, 1995
[149] . Bram, S., et al., Nature, vol.284, p.629, Apr.1980
[150] . Park, CH, et al., Cancer Research, vol.40, p.1062, Apr.1980
[151] . Poydock, ME, Am.J.Clin.Nutr., vol.54, p.1261S, 1991
[152] . Noto, V., et al., Cancer, vol.63, p.901, 1989
[153] . Gardiner, N, et al., Pros.Leuk., vol.34, p.119, 1988
[154] . Riordan, HD, et al., J. Orthomolecular Med., vol.5, p.5, 1990
[155] . Campbell, Al, Oncology, vol.48, p.495, 1991
[156] . Cameron, E., Pauling, L., Proc.Natl.Acad.Sci., vol.75, p.4538, Sept.1978
[157] . Moertel, CG, et al., N.Engl.J.Med., vol.312, p.137, 1985
[158] . Jaakkola, K., et al., Treatment with antioxidant and other nutrients in combination with chemotherapy and irradiation in patients with small-cell lung cancer, Anticancer Res 12,599-606, 1992
[159] . Lamm, DL, et al., Megadose vitamin in bladder cancer: a double-blind clinical trial, J Urol, 151:21-26, 1994
[160] . Hoffer, A, Pauling, L, Hardin Jones biostatistical analysis of mortality data of cancer patients, J Orthomolecular Med, 5:3:143-154, 1990
[161] . Marcus, SL, et al., Am.J.Clin.Nutr., vol.54, p.1292S., 1991
[162] . Abrahamian, V., et al., Ascorbic acid requirements in hospital patients, JPEN, 7, 5, 465-8, 1983
[163] . Anthony, HM, et al., Vitamin C status of lung cancer patients, Brit J Ca, 46, 354-9, 1982
[164] . Cheraskin, E., Scurvy in cancer patients?, J Altern Med, 18-23, Feb.1986
[165] . Bendich, A., in BEYOND DEFICIENCIES, NY Acad.Sci., vol.669, p.300, 1992
[166] . Kaul, L., et al., Nutr.Cancer, vol.9, p.123, 1987
[167] . Bowman, BB, et al., Am.J.Clin.Nutr., vol.35, p.1142, 1982
[168] . Rindi, G., in PRESENT KNOWLEDGE IN NUTRITION, p.163, ILSI, Washington, 1996
[169] . Elsborg, L., Int.J.Vitamin Res., vol.53, p.321, 1983
[170] . Lopez, R., et al., Am.J.Clin.Nutr., vol.33, p.1283, 1980
[171] . Schmitt-Graff, A., et al, Pathol.Res.Pract., vol.181, p.168, 1986
[172] . Popov, Al, Med.Radiol. Mosk., vol.32, p.42, 1987
[173] . Kjellen, E., et al., Radiother.Oncol., vol.22, p.81, 1991
[174] . Horsman, MR, Radiotherapy Oncology, vol.22, p.79, 1991
[175] . Aprahamian, M., et al., Am.J.Clin.Nutr., vol.41, p.578, 1985
[176] . Prior, F., Med.Hypotheses, vol.16, p.421, 1985
[177] . Chrisley, BM, et al., Nutr.Res., vol.6, p.1023, 1986
[178] . Ha, C., et al., J.Nutr., vol.114, p.938, 1984

[179] . Solomon, LR, et al., Diabetes, vol.38, p.881, 1989

[180] . Gridley, DS, et al., Nutrition Research, vol.8, p.201, 1988

[181] . Tryfiates, GP, et al., Anticancer Research, vol.1, p.263, 1981

[182] . DiSorbo, DM, et al., Nutrition and Cancer, vol.5, p.10, 1983

[183] . DiSorbo, DM, et al., Nutrition and Cancer, vol.7, p.43, 1985

[184] . Byar, D., et al., Urolog7, vol.10, p.556, Dec.1977

[185] . Lamm, DL, et al., Megadose vitamin in bladder cancer: a double-blind clinical trial, J Urol, 151:21-26, 1994

[186] . Ladner, HA, et al., Nutrition, Growth, & Cancer, p.273, Alan Liss, Inc., 1988

[187] . Cohen, M., et al., Toxicology Letters, vol.34, p.129, 1986

[188] . Poydock, ME, Am.J.Clin.Nutr., vol.54, p.1261S, 1991

[189] . Leeb, BF, et al., Clin.Exper.Rheumat., vol.13, p.459, 1995

[190] . Dokal, IS, et all, Br.Med.J., vol.300, p.1263, 1990

[191] . Bailey, LB, FOLATE IN HEALTH AND DISEASE, Marcel Dekker, NY 1995

[192] . Fekete, PS, et al., Acta. Cytologica, vol.31, p.697, 1987

[193] . Butterworth, CE, et al., Am.J.Clin.Nutr., vol.35, p.73, 1982

[194] . Freudenheim, J., Int.J.Epidemiol., vol.20, p.368, 1991

[195] . Levy, JA, BASIC AND CLINICAL IMMUNOLOGY, p.297, Lange, Los Altos, 1982

[196] . Werbach, M., NUTRITIONAL INFLUENCES ON ILLNESS, p.625, Third Line Press, Tarzana, 1996

[197] . Koutsikos, D., et al., Biomed.Pharmacother., vol.44, p.511, 1990

Chapter 11

✯

ACCESSORY FACTORS

"If we worked on the assumption that what is accepted as true really is true, then there would be little hope for advance."
Orville Wright, first pilot in history

WHAT ARE "ACCESSORY FACTORS"?

While there are around 50 nutrients that are considered essential in the diet of humans, there are literally thousands of other "accessory factors" found in various foods. There is increasing evidence that we may need these substances in our diet in order to maintain optimal health. These accessory factors may someday be considered "conditionally essential" nutrients, which means that during some phases of life (i.e. very young, older, sick), these nutrients would become essential in the diet. Cancer patients often have a compromised system which is unable to manufacture optimal amounts of these nutrients in the body. A poorly chosen diet, which is common in cancer patients, further compounds the possibility that these accessory factors will be deficient in the cancer patient. The difference between "surviving" and "thriving to beat cancer" may rest in the intake of these accessory factors.

Lipoic acid 33 mg
Alpha lipoic acid (a.k.a. thioctic acid) is involved in energy metabolism, but also works as a potent antioxidant, regulator of blood sugar metabolism, chelator (remover) of heavy metals, improves memory, discourages the growth of cancer, prevents glycation (sugar binding to cell membranes) that can change the flexibility of cell membranes and blood vessels.

Lipoic acid works with pyruvate and acetyl CoA in a critical point in energy metabolism.[1] Partly because of this pivotal job in generating ATP, lipoic acid becomes an incredibly multi-talented nutrient. Though lipoic acid is not considered an essential nutrient yet, as humans age we produce less and less of lipoic acid internally.[2] Because of its unique size and chemical structure, lipoic acid works as an antioxidant that can penetrate both fat soluble (like vitamin E) and water soluble (like vitamin C) portions of the body.[3] This gives lipoic acid access to virtually the entire body, whereas most antioxidants only protect isolated areas of the body.

Lipoic acid prevents "glycation" or glycosylation, which means the binding of sugar molecules to important proteins in the bloodstream, cell membrane, nerve tissue, etc. Glycation is a disastrous "tanning" that occurs, not unlike turning soft cow skin into hard leather in the tanning process. These new proteins that are bound to sugars do not have the same abilities as before the glycation process. Supplements of lipoic acid have been found to reverse the peripheral neuropathy from diabetes in as little as 3 weeks.[4] Lipoic acid improves blood flow to the nerves, which then improves nerve conduction.[5] Many cancer patients suffer peripheral neuropathy as a by-product of the damaging effects of chemotherapy. Lipoic acid may prevent and reverse this destruction of nerve tissue. Because of its role in aerobic metabolism, lipoic acid supplements in animals provided an increase in the amount of oxygen reaching the heart by 72% and the liver by 128%. Since cancer is an anaerobic growth, enhancing aerobic metabolism in a cancer patient is like shining daylight on a vampire.

Lipoic acid increases the available levels of other antioxidants in the body, like vitamin E[6] and glutathione.[7] While there are many antioxidants found in a healthy diet and produced in the body (like uric acid), lipoic acid is the only antioxidant that meets the "wish list" of Dr. Lester Packer of the University of California at Berkeley. That "perfect" antioxidant should:
⇒ neutralize free radicals
⇒ be rapidly absorbed and quickly utilized by the body cells
⇒ be able to enhance the action of other antioxidants
⇒ be concentrated both inside and outside cells and cell membranes
⇒ promote normal gene expression
⇒ chelate metal ions, or drag toxic minerals out of the body.[8]

Because of its role as an antixoxidant and the critical need for immune cells to be protected from their own cellular poisons, lipoic acid has been shown to improve antibody response in immunosuppressed animals.[9]

Lipoic acid also works to improve the efficiency of insulin by allowing blood glucose into the cells. Animal studies showed that supplements of lipoic acid increased insulin sensitivity by 30-50% and reduced plasma insulin and free fatty acids by 15-17%.[10]

SAFETY ISSUES. In over 30 years of extensive use and testing in European clinical trials there have been no serious side effects reported from the use of lipoic acid.

> **Lycopene   3 mg**
>   Potent antioxidant and immune stimulant.

Lycopenes are one of the most potent antioxidants yet tested, having double the protective capacity of betacarotene.[11] Lycopenes are reddish pigments from the carotenoid family. Most fruits and vegetables contain little to no lycopenes. Tomatoes are the richest source of lycopenes, with watermelon, and red grapefruit containing appreciable amounts of lycopenes.[12]   100 grams of raw tomatoes, or about 1 cup, contains about 3 milligrams of lycopenes. Lycopenes made headlines around the world, and cheers in many college dorms, in December of 1995 when a scientific study published in the Journal of the National Cancer Institute found that men who ate more PIZZA experienced less prostate cancer.[13]   Pizza is obviously not a "nutrient dense" healthy food with all the fat, difficult-to-digest cheese and white flour. Yet lycopenes from tomatoes are such potent antioxidants, immune stimulants and regulators of cancer gene expression; that a little tomato sauce on the pizza could neutralize the otherwise unhealthy meal of pizza and offer significant protection against the second most common cancer in American men.

As little as one serving per week of tomatoes could reduce esophageal cancer risk by 40% and other sites by 50%.[14]. In another study, blood samples from 25,000 people were frozen for 15 years. Of the people in this study who developed cancer, those with the highest levels of lycopenes had the lowest incidence of pancreatic cancer.[15]

> **L-glutathione (GSH)   100 mg**
>   Stimulator of immune system, detoxification, regulator of cell
> division and prostaglandin metabolism.

Glutathione is one of the most widely distributed and important antioxidants in all of nature, yet there has been some confusion regarding its use in cancer patients and its absorption. So keep your thinking cap on as we review this nutrient.

Glutathione is a tripeptide, meaning a molecule formed from three amino acids: glutamine, cysteine and glycine. Some clinicians have chosen to use N-acetyl-cysteine, as a means of augmenting the production of glutathione in the body. Glutathione, also abbreviated GSH, is one of the most widely distributed antioxidants in plants and animals, and is the chief thiol (sulfur bearing) molecule in most cells. Glutathione plays a central role in the enzyme system glutathione peroxidase which is crucial for cell metabolism, cell regulation, detoxification, DNA synthesis and repair, immune function, prostaglandin metabolism and regulating cell proliferation through apoptosis (programmed cell death).[16] GSH is particularly helpful in protecting the liver from damage upon exposure to toxins.[17] GSH levels are decreased in most disease states, infertility, aging, toxic burden and other unfavorable health conditions.[18] Lower levels of blood GSH are associated with more illness, higher blood pressure, higher percent body fat, and reduced general health status.[19] Cancer patients have less GSH in their blood than healthy people.[20] So far, no controversy.

glutamine+cysteine+glycine=glutathione

Help cancer patients? Some oncologists have reasoned that GSH provides one of the main protective mechanisms for cancer cells to develop resistance to chemotherapy.[21] Thus, efforts have been made to develop drugs which deplete the cancer patient of GSH. However, supplements of glutathione in patients being treated for ovarian cancer with the drug cisplatin had an improvement in outcome and reduced kidney toxicity from the cisplatin.[22] In another study of 55 patients with stomach cancer, GSH prevented the neurotoxicity usually associated with cisplatin and did not reduce the anti-neoplastic activity of the drug.[23] In animals exposed to a potent carcinogen (DMBA), GSH provided significant reduction in the size and incidence of tumors.[24] Animals exposed to DMBA and given GSH, vitamin C, E, and betacarotene had substantial reduction in the number and size of cancers.[25]

In animals with chemically-induced (aflatoxin) liver cancer (an extremely poor prognostic cancer) 100% died within 20 months, while 81% of the animals with liver cancer who were treated with GSH were disease-free 4 months later.[26] Eight patients with advanced refractory (resistant to medical therapy) liver cancer were given 5 grams daily of oral GSH with most surviving longer than expected and one being cured.[27] Glutathione in the diet has been shown to protect the intestinal wall of animals from the insult of chemical carcinogens.[28] In cultured cancer cells, GSH was able to induce apoptosis (programmed cell death), which may be one of the ways that GSH can assist cancer patients.[29]

Can you absorb GSH in the gut? In one study, 7 healthy human subjects were given increasingly higher oral supplements of GSH up to 3 grams daily with blood levels showing no significant increase in glutathione, cysteine or glutamate.[30] However, many other studies with humans and animals[31] have found GSH well absorbed into the bloodstream. GSH may be converted into a different molecule for transport through the bloodstream. Best sources of GSH are dark green leafy vegetables, fresh fruit and lightly cooked fish, poultry and beef. Processing inevitably reduces the GSH levels of foods. On a logical basis, would Nature waste one of the more effective and pervasive antioxidants in plants and animals by making GSH unavailable for absorption? I don't think so.

Aloe powder   167 mg
   Immune stimulant, aids in cellular communication.

For 5000 years, many cultures and herbalists around the world have been using aloe vera as a primary medicinal plant. King Solomon used it as his favorite laxative. Hippocrates, the father of modern medicine 2400 years ago, used at least 14 different medicine formulas containing aloe. Alexander the Great conquered an island in order to have aloe for his soldiers. As I write this section, I am looking at one of many aloe plants that we keep in our house. Aloe thrives on neglect. All the plant needs is decent soil and a little water and sun, then you get to harvest one of Nature's most versatile and impressive healers. Fresh aloe gel applied topically may be the greatest skin cream on the planet earth. The yellow bitter part of the plant leaf is a proven laxative that has brought relief to many of my patients.   And whole leaf extracts have the ability to gear up the immune system, reduce swelling, improve healing, kill bacteria and viruses, and improve communication between cells (intercellular) and within the cell (intracellular).

Of the 300 species of aloe, it is aloe vera that has received the most attention. Aloe certainly typifies the complexity of understanding the healing properties of plants. There are over 200 biologically active ingredients in aloe vera, including prostaglandins, essential fatty acids (including GLA), vitamins, minerals, anthraquinones, and polysaccharides (longer chains of sugar-like molecules).[32]

In the movie, MEDICINE MAN, a doctor (Sean Connery) discovered a cure for cancer from a plant in the Amazon forest, which was rapidly being levelled by bulldozers and fire. But now he cannot reproduce his original concoction from the same plant. To ruin the suspense and tell you the ending, the active ingredient in his original cancer cure was from the spider feces that was found in the sugar used to dilute the herbal concoction. Moral of the story: We are still neophytes when it comes to understanding just what is the active ingredient (s) in medicinal plants. Which is why using low heat processing of the whole leaf aloe is crucial for preserving the active ingredient.

While once discussing the merits of aloe with a noted researcher on the subject, I commented: "It seems like aloe cures almost everything [33], as if it were an essential nutrient that we are not getting in our diet!!" He grinned and commented: "You may be right. For most of the millions of years of human history, our ancestors ate food that was not refrigerated, hence our food supply had all sorts of mold (yeast) growing on it. I think that we have an essential need for the unique collection of sugar-like molecules (mannans) that come from the cell wall of yeast and the aloe plant."

Indeed, there are receptor sites on immune cells (macrophages) for D-mannose (one of the sugars in aloe) just like a key fitting a keyhole. [34] Aloe seems to act like a mild vaccination in the human body, by bringing a substance that appears to be a bacterial cell wall into the bloodstream, which then whips the immune system into a state of red alert preparedness.

Aloe may help the cancer patient in many ways.

◊ **Antibacterial & antifungal**. Aloe vera applied topically to burn regions of animals was superior to the common antibacterial medication used, silver sulfadiazine. [35]

◊ **Antiviral activity**. Feline leukemia is a form of cancer contracted by cats and caused by a virus. This disease is invariably fatal, with 70% of cats dying within 8 weeks of early symptoms. Most cats are euthanized as soon as the diagnosis is made. In one study, acemannan from aloe was injected weekly for 6 weeks into the cats, with a followup 6 week waiting period. After this 12 week study, 71% of the cats were alive and in good health. [36] Acemannan has also demonstrated a potent ability to fight the flu virus, measles and the HIV virus while also reducing the dosage required of the drug AZT. [37]

◊ **Anti-inflammatory**. Drugs, like cortisone, that are effective at reducing inflammation also shut down wound recovery. Aloe has the ability to reduce swelling while also enhancing wound recovery.

◊ **Immune stimulant**. Aloe has been shown to increase the activity of the immune system. [38] Aloe seems to provide neutrophils with more "bullets", or toxic substances to kill cancer and invading organisms. [39] Aloe (acemannan) increases the production of nitric oxide, a potent anti-cancer "napalm" used by immune cells. [40]

◊ **Anti-cancer activity**. Various fractions of aloe (mannans and glucans) have been found to have potent anti-neoplastic activity. [41]

◊ **Radio-protective**. Some forms of mannan are bone marrow stimulants and can protect mice against cobalt-60 radiation. [42] In my experience with cancer patients, those who took aloe before and during radiation therapy had minimal damage of healthy tissue while still getting an impressive anti-cancer effect from the radiation. Generalized radiation to the pelvic region for prostate or colon cancer can be particularly nasty in harming the bladder and gastro-intestinal tract. I remember one cancer patient who used aloe throughout 40 rounds of pelvic radiation and suffered no burns and only mild GI distress.

◊ **Cell communication**. Many forms of carbohydrates, called glycoproteins, may play a key role in promoting healthy communication within the cell and between cells. Aloe may contribute an important carbohydrate (mannan) which becomes part of this crucial "telegraph system" which prevents or slows down cancer.[43] Given the 8 monosaccharides used in the body and the 18 configurations used to arrange these molecules, the possible "words" in this complex "telegraph" system works out to 18 to the 8th power, or over 11 billion "messages". No doubt, more important breakthroughs will come out of this new and exciting field of cell communication.

SAFETY ISSUES. While aloe can be a valuable laxative, too much aloe can cause diarrhea. In 1983, the Food and Drug Administration Advisory Panel for over-the-counter drugs reviewed over a hundred reports on aloe and found that no adverse events had been reported, concluding "clearly, the substance is safe."

Dimethylglycine   16.7 mg
    Once called "vitamin" B-15. Immune stimulant and energizer.

Dimethylglycine, or DMG, has a relatively short but colorful track record in nutrition science. Ernst Krebs, MD discovered pangamic acid (also called "vitamin" B-15) in the pits of apricots along with laetrile ("vitamin" B-17) in 1951. Neither DMG nor pangamic acid are considered essential vitamins, though whole grains, brewer's yeast, pumpkin seeds and beef blood are rich sources of pangamic acid. DMG combines with gluconic acid in the body to form pangamic acid[44], which was the subject of considerable attention and research in Russia and Europe, thus initially branding pangamic acid as a non-essential substance with only foreign research documentation to support it. Pangamic acid has been used to enhance athletic performance and to reverse the aging process in European clinics. DMG may work by:
⇒ becoming part of pangamic acid in the body
⇒ being broken down into glycine, which may help to generate more glutathione peroxidase (see glutathione above).

DMG has been shown to increase immune functions (antibody titer) by 300-500% in vaccinated animals.[45] In a double blind study with healthy human subjects, 120 mg daily of DMG along with 180 mg of calcium gluconate provided a 400% increase in antibody response to pneumococcal vaccine.[46] The 10 subjects with illness showed similar improvements in immune response, adding that mitogen response to lymphocytes in the patients with diabetes and sickle cell anemia was increased by 300%. DMG may improve aerobic energy metabolism, detoxify the body and liver, inhibit allergic responses, reduce blood pressure, and stimulate the nervous and endocrine systems.

L-carnitine   100 mg
    Involved in energy metabolism of fats, thus preventing fatty buildup in heart and liver and encouraging the complete combustion of fats for energy. Cancer cells cannot use fat for energy.

Think of carnitine as the "shoveller throwing fresh coals into the furnace" of the cell's mitochondria. Carnitine was first isolated from meat extracts in 1905, hence the "carnitine", refers to animal sources. Indeed, there is virtually no carnitine in plant foods, with red meats having the highest carnitine content.[47] The typical American diet provides from 5-100 mg/day of carnitine. Humans can manufacture carnitine in the liver and kidney from the precursors (raw materials to make) of lysine and methionine, and the cofactors of vitamin C, niacin, B-6 and iron. A deficiency of any of these precursors may lead to a carnitine deficiency, which involves buildup of fats in the blood, liver and muscles and may lead to symptoms of weakness. Since infants require carnitine in their diet and other individuals have been found to have clinical carnitine deficiencies, some nutritionists have lobbied to have carnitine included as an essential nutrient, not unlike niacin.[48]
    Carnitine may help the cancer patient by:
◊   protecting the liver from fatty buildup[49]
◊   improving energy and endurance[50]
◊   protecting the heart against the damaging effects of adriamycin.[51]
◊   In cultured cells, carnitine supplements provided for bolstering of immune functions (polymorphonuclear chemotaxis) and reduced the ability of fats to lower immune functions.[52]
    Carnitine is probably essential in the diet for people who are very young, or sick, stressed, older, burdened with toxins, etc.

Bovine cartilage   2.5 gm
    Immune stimulant, anti-mitotic agent (shuts down cell division in abnormal cells), anti-angiogenesis (shuts down production of blood vessels from tumors), adaptogen.

Bovine tracheal cartilage (BTC) is one of the more crucial and expensive ($180/month alone) of all nutrition factors to help the cancer patient, so we will spend more than a little time discussing this ingredient. Imagine these headlines: "Major drug company finds new treatment for cancer, arthritis, shingles, and many other infectious disorders". The story would be featured on TV and newspapers around the world. The stock value of that company would skyrocket. But what if that same substance was a humble little unpatentable food extract? Would the enthusiasm be as great? Bovine cartilage may be in that category.

Good luck never hurt anyone's career. In 1954 John Prudden, MD (Harvard), PhD (Columbia) noticed an article from the reknowned Columbia-Presbyterian researchers, Drs. Meyer, Regan, and Lattes, on how topical cartilage could neutralize the disastrous effect that cortisone had on inhibiting wound recovery. This tip on the therapeutic value of cartilage had come from a mysterious "Dr. Martin" from Montreal, who has never since been located.

The next lucky event for Prudden came when a 70 year old woman came to him with advanced breast cancer that was literally eating away her chest cavity, stage IV fungating breast cancer. Prudden tried the topical bovine cartilage along with injecting bovine cartilage solutions into obvious tumor areas with the hopes that it might help to heal these awful ulcerated wounds. Surprisingly, the woman returned to Dr. Prudden with the wounds healed AND the cancer gone. It has been said that "chance favors the prepared mind".

Over the course of 40 years, Prudden has been involved in $7 million of research to better understand BTC. Prudden received a patent on cartilage in 1962 for its anti-inflammatory properties when topically applied to arthritic regions of the body. Prudden is an affable man and dog lover who saved one of his dogs from mastocytoma (a terminal cancer) using BTC.

Prudden found that the "wind pipe" of cows was considered offal or waste products of the butchering process. Given the world's hunger for beef, this seemed to be a bountiful supply of inexpensive raw material. Prudden developed the complex process for removing the fat from the cartilage, then drying and powdering. He named his original product Catrix, short for Cicatrix, which means "healed wound".

While some people might think that eating shark cartilage is just rewards for a predatory animal, actually many environmental groups are concerned about endangering the shark population, which sits atop the ocean's precarious food chain. Sharks have a pivotal role in population control and "pruning" the sick and unfit creatures of the oceans. You are much more likely to be struck by lightning than bitten by a shark while swimming in the ocean.

Cartilage resembles fetal mesenchyme, which is the source for developing muscle, bones, tendons, ligaments, skin, fat, and bone marrow. It probably is this unique origin which gives rise to the many therapeutic benefits of cartilage. Initially, there was some interest in using only young (less than 6 month old) cows for BTC. Prudden feels that this is an unnecessary effort and an unproven theory.

SHARK VERSUS BOVINE. In the 1970s, I. William Lane, PhD, served as a consultant to the Shah of Iran on harvesting sharks from the

Persian Gulf. In the 1980s, Dr. Lane was taught how to process cartilage by Prudden. In December of 1991, Lane received a use patent on anti-angiogenesis therapy using shark cartilage. In 1993, the "60 Minutes" TV show popularized Lane's book, SHARKS DON'T GET CANCER[53], and made shark cartilage a leading contender among alternative cancer therapies. Although the National Cancer Institute initially showed interest in helping Lane, they backed out on endorsing or researching shark cartilage.

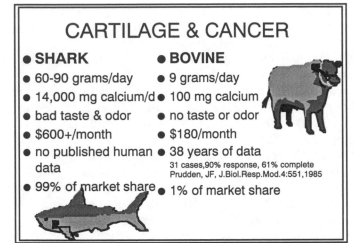

CARTILAGE & CANCER

● SHARK	● BOVINE
● 60-90 grams/day	● 9 grams/day
● 14,000 mg calcium/d	● 100 mg calcium
● bad taste & odor	● no taste or odor
● $600+/month	● $180/month
● no published human data	● 38 years of data
	31 cases,90% response, 61% complete Prudden, JF, J.Biol.Resp.Mod.4:551,1985
● 99% of market share	● 1% of market share

Advantages of bovine cartilage over shark cartilage:

◊   Efficacy.   The original research involving cartilage in human intervention trials all used bovine.   In published peer reviewed literature, and after 22 years clinical use by Prudden, and 40 years of safety studies costing over $7 million, bovine cartilage is by far the safest and most effective of the cartilage products:

◊   More potent.   Ten times more shark cartilage (1000% more) in weight must be used in order to get a clinical response in cancer patients.

◊   No taste or odor.   Compared to shark cartilage, which induces nausea & diarrhea in many users, bovine cartilage is relatively free from taste and odor.

◊   More economical.   Bovine cartilage saves 75% in cost over shark cartilage.

◊   Calcium content.   Hypercalcemia is common in cancer patients. 22% of shark cartilage is calcium, which provides 14 grams of calcium (14,000 mg, or 14 times the RDA) compared to 1% calcium concentration in bovine cartilage.   The 7.5 gram/day of bovine cartilage in * contains 75 mg of calcium.

◊   Additional components.   Among the other substances in cartilage that may have therapeutic benefit, including chondroitan sulfate and glycosaminoglycans, shark cartilage contains less than 10% while bovine cartilage contains greater than 20% by weight.

◊ Reduce toxic side effects in chemo & radiation. Bovine may improve outcome in herpes zoster (shingles) and AIDS.

Active ingredient(s)?? Finding the active ingredient may not be easy with cartilage, which is a complex collection of protein, carbohydrate, fats, minerals, and accessory factors. Some companies boast that their cartilage product is higher in the protein factors that inhibit the making of blood vessels (anti-angiogenesis) from tumors.

Prudden thinks that some mucopolysaccharide, or starch-like molecule, is responsible for all the therapeutic magic of BTC. This theory makes sense, given the therapeutic mucopolysaccharides that have been isolated from Maitake mushroom and aloe vera gel.

Anti-angiogenesis? Lane's theory that shark cartilage may shut down the making of blood vessels from tumors (anti-angiogenesis) has some foundation. In 1976 Dr. Robert Langer of MIT and Dr. Judah Folkman of Harvard published work showing that something in cartilage can shut down angiogenesis in cultured tumors.[54] Later studies by this same group showed that rabbits with corneal cancers had measurable benefits from cartilage topically applied in slowing the growth of tumors.[55] In 1983, Langer and colleague Anne Lee found that something in shark cartilage could slow the growth of tumors through anti-angiogenesis.[56]

Langer pursued this line of research, finding that tumors could not grow larger than 1-2 centimeters (1/2 to 1 inch) without vascularization to support further growth.[57] Dr. Patricia D'Amore of Harvard endorsed the concept that if you shut down angiogenesis then you shut down tumor growth.[58] Folkman's team then found that when a cell switches from normal growth (hyperplasia) to rapid and uncontrolled tumor growth (neoplasia), then the angiogenesis process gears up dramatically.[59] Other Harvard researchers found that something in cartilage definitely shuts down angiogenesis, which is essential for tumor growth.[60] Japanese researchers reported on this anti-angiogenic agent found in shark cartilage.[61] More Harvard researchers reported on the strong link between angiogenesis and tumor progression.[62] Folkman further explained the importance of anti-angiogenesis in cancer, yet added that perhaps genetic regulation is more important than some dietary protein.[63]

In discussions with pathologists and Dr. Prudden, there seems to be a difference between the blood vessels that extend "cork screw-like" from a tumor and the blood vessels that extend "tree root-like" from healthy tissue. If there is an anti-angiogenesis factor in cartilage, then it cannot inhibit the making of normal healthy blood vessels. How does a baby shark grow into a large adult shark if shark cartilage shuts down the making of ALL blood vessels?

"Sharks don't get cancer" while cows do get cancer. Yet, the shark's skeleton is entirely cartilage, or roughly 20% of its weight; while cartilage is found in much smaller quantities in a cow's body.

Alan Gaby, MD, President of the American Holistic Medical Association stated in the April 1994 Townsend Letter: "I have not met any physicians who are excited about their results with shark cartilage."

Prudden believes that BTC is effective because it is a biodirector, or "normalizer". There are parallels of these "homeostatic regulators" in the botanical medicine field called adaptogens, like ginseng or astragalus, which will raise your blood pressure if it is too low or lower it if it is too high. Think about the enigma of cartilage:

⇒ topically applied, it **accelerates** healthy growth for wounds but **slows** abnormal cancer growth

⇒ taken internally, it **increases** various immune factors, including B-cells (from the bone), macrophages (literally: "big eaters"), and cytotoxic T-cells (important in the "war on cancer"); YET it also **slows** down auto-immune attacks involved in allergies, arthritis, and lupus

⇒ taken internally, it slows the wasting disease, cachexia, caused by cancer and AIDS

⇒ taken internally, it **slows** the division in abnormal cells (anti-mitotic), but **allows** healthy cells to divide

⇒ taken internally, it **reduces** inflammation, such as in arthritis

Prudden pioneered the use of BTC for its

•wound healing properties, which culminated in textbook acceptance [64]

•anti-inflammatory agent in arthritis[65]

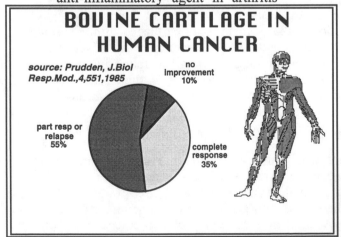

BOVINE CARTILAGE IN HUMAN CANCER

source: Prudden, J.Biol Resp.Mod.,4,551,1985

no improvement 10%

part resp or relapse 55%

complete response 35%

•anti-cancer activity.[66]

Prudden's peer-reviewed article showed a 90% response rate in 31 human cancer patients followed for 15 years. Of the 31 total patients, 35%, or 11 of these terminal patients were **cured** using 9 grams daily of oral bovine tracheal cartilage as sole therapy, while 55% or 17 showed some benefit then relapsed, and 10% or 3 showed no improvement. Prudden has used BTC in over 1000 cancer patients, with good followup on 100 patients. His latest research paper has been submitted for peer review before being published in a journal.

Dr. Brian Durie has found equally impressive results using BTC to halt cancer growth in vitro.[67] Prudden's other research shows that BTC probably works by turbo-charging the immune system.[68] For his noteworthy persistence and brilliance in spearheading BTC research, Prudden received the coveted "Linus Pauling Scientist of the Year" award at the Third International Symposium on Adjuvant Nutrition in Cancer Treatment in Tampa in September of 1995.

Of all the impressive healing agents in Nature's "pharmacy", none is more safe, cost-effective, versatile, and promising than BTC.

Nucleic acids (nucleotides from brewer's yeast): DNA   500 mg and RNA 500 mg
Immune stimulants, help to regulate genetic expression and discourage the excessive production of Tumor Necrosis Factor, which can lead to tissue wasting.

At the very core of our cells are the "blueprints" of DNA that allow that cell to make another exact copy. RNA has various forms that basically are the "servants" of DNA, clamping on the DNA to read the base pair sequence, then going out into the cell to construct proteins, enzymes or whatever the cell needs based on the DNA blueprints. Obviously, this is a very crucial pathway for human health. When DNA goes awry, cancer can result. Somehow the DNA in the healthy host tissue can become corrupted and start creating cells that lack normal regulation properties, have no plan and reproduce without any restraint.

We make our own DNA and RNA (also called nucleic acids) in our cells from amino acids in the purine and pyrimidine pathways. We also eat some DNA/RNA in metabolically active foods including brewer's yeast, liver, seeds (especially the germ), organ meats, and bee pollen. The debate has never been over the value of DNA/RNA, but rather "can we absorb these nutrients into the bloodstream intact?" To answer that question, we need to step back and look at other examples of:

* fatty acids that are dissected with bile salts and enzymes in the GI tract and then reassembled in the bloodstream
* the known passage of large proteins through the intestinal wall to cause food allergies in the bloodstream
* the use of glandular therapy (such as natural dessicated thyroid) to treat the target gland with a large protein molecule that should be destroyed in the acid bath of the gut.
* how infants receive their immunity from the immunoglobulins in mother's millk.

Either these molecules have special "windows" in the gut or these molecules are torn apart in the gut and then reassembled on the other side of the intestinal mucosa in the bloodstream. Supplements of RNA/DNA have shown benefits in both immunity and wound recovery when taken orally in both human and animal studies.

Animals fed a nucleotide-deficient diet had impaired immune functions which were corrected when fed uracil (a DNA precursor).[69] In protein depletion, RNA supplements may be essential in order to return immune functions to normal.[70] Several human trials have studied an enteral formula, Impact, which uses RNA, arginine and fish oil to provide substantial improvement in immune factors.[71] RNA seems to improve wound recovery after surgery.[72] RNA supplements provide a boost to memory in the elderly.[73] RNA supplements were able to help regenerate the damaged livers of rats.[74] Early indications were that RNA may be able to help cancer patients.[75] Of course, a patentable drug (Poly A/Poly U) was developed to continue these studies, with very encouraging results.[76] RNA supplements seem to encourage Natural Killer cells to attack cancer and bacteria.[77]

In personal discussions with Arsinur Bircaglu, MD, an oncologist from Turkey, she showed very intriguing human clinical data that large amounts of RNA and DNA taken orally could shut down the tissue wasting process (cachexia) that is so common in cancer and AIDS. Precursors to make more nucleic acids seems to dampen down the cytokines (Tumor Necrosis Factor) that trigger the downward spiral of cancer cachexia.

FOS, fructo-oligosaccharides 1 gm
Stimulates growth of probiotic organisms in gut, with the far-reaching effects of favorable bacterial growth, reduced production of carcinogens in the gut, maintenance of gut integrity and immune functions.

It was the Nobel laureate from Russia, Dr. Eli Metchnikoff, who told us at the turn of the century: "Death begins in the colon." Metchnikoff isolated the bacteria in yogurt, Lactobacillus, that ferments milk sugar and spent much of his illustrious career shedding light on the function of bacteria in the gut.

In order to better appreciate the importance of FOS for cancer patients, we need to rewind the video cassette recorder to Louis Pasteur's deathbed confession in 1895: "I have been wrong. The germ is nothing. The terrain is everything." Pasteur was the famous French chemist who developed pasteurization, or the killing of bacteria with heat. Pasteur spent much of his life trying to figure out how to kill all the bacteria in the universe. Didn't work. By "terrain", Pasteur was referring to the land that bacteria grow on--your body. We now find that some bacteria are helpful, such as those which manufacture biotin and vitamin K in the gut. Many bacteria are relatively harmless, unless we have compromised immune functions. Many bacterial infections are called "opportunistic" because they only happen when the bacteria seizes the opportunity while the host is weakened. Many bacteria in the gut can produce carcinogens and estrogens, to further a cancer process.[78] To finally give long overdue respect to an important area of human nutrition, the classical textbook MODERN NUTRITION IN HEALTH AND DISEASE now contains a chapter on intestinal microflora.[79]

Oncologists have toiled for 3 decades trying to isolate cancer patients from all external bacteria, since death from infections is so common in cancer patients, especially those treated with chemotherapy. Oncologist working in bone marrow transplant (BMT) units will isolate cancer patients from family members and tell the patient to avoid fruits and vegetables, hoping to prevent an infection in the immune-compromised patient. Some BMT units would even autoclave the food to try to reduce exposure to bacteria. Meanwhile, we have more bacteria in our gut than all the cells in our body. There is an ongoing struggle in your gut between bifidobacteria (good guys) and putrefactive bacteria (bad guys). The typical American diet of too much fat, sugar, beef and not enough whole grains, fruits, and vegetables will often create a very lethal mixture of bacteria in the gut. One pound of fecal matter contains over 50 billion bacteria.

What happens in too many cancer patients is that the infection comes from the inside, called bacterial translocation, not from the outside.[80] Only one of three factors needs to be present for disease-causing bacteria from the intestines to slide through the intestinal wall and create a life-threatening infection in the blood (sepsis):
⇒ Disruption of the ecological balance of the normal intestinal microflora, resulting in overgrowth of certain harmful bacteria
⇒ Impairment of host immune functions
⇒ Physical disruption of the gut mucosal barrier.

Over 40% of our immune system is clustered around the gastro-intestinal tract. Lymph nodes sit on the intestinal wall like international border guards, keeping dangerous bacteria inside the gut from migrating into the bloodstream. Bacteria in the human gut can decompose undigestible plant matter into butyric acid, a potent anti-cancer agent.

Probiotics include a wide assortment of favorable bacteria, including Lactobacillus acidophilus from yogurt. When comparing the dietary habits of 1000 women with and 1000 women without breast cancer, yogurt was found to be the most protective of all foods analyzed.[81] Yogurt also helped to prevent the normal intestinal side effects caused by radiation therapy in women undergoing radiation for ovarian and cervical cancer.[82] There are soil-based organisms found in

Natur-Earth (Nature's Biotics 800-622-8986) that are equally intriguing as means of rectifying an imbalanced collection of bacteria in the human gut. Since dairy products are the most allergy-producing food in the world and can produce mucous in many individuals, it is unwise to recommend widespread use of yogurt for all cancer patients, though probiotic supplements can be of benefit.

Among carbohydrate molecules, there are:
⇒ short length molecules (mono and disaccharides)
⇒ medium length molecules (oligosaccharides)
⇒ long chain molecules (polysaccharides).

Oligosaccharides made from the monosaccharide fructose are the subject of this discussion, because they have been very potent at stimulating the growth of "friendly" bacteria. Oligosaccharides are poorly digested by human digestive juices, but easily digested by many forms of bacteria in the gut. Some oligosaccharides, such as stachyose and raffinose from beans and certain nuts, can feed bacteria that cause intestinal gas. FOS feeds the bacteria that fortify your gut wall and immune system, and should actually help to control gas. Best food sources of FOS are onions and whole grains.

In an extensive review of the scientific literature, FOS supplements have been shown to:
◊ encourage the growth of bifidobacteria
◊ reduce detrimental bacteria and their toxic metabolites
◊ prevent and reverse diarrhea or constipation caused by pathogenic bacteria
◊ protect liver functions
◊ reduce blood pressure
◊ induce the production of essential nutrients. [83]
◊ encourage the growth of "friendly" bacteria which have shown considerable anti-cancer activity in animal studies.[84]

Tocotrienols   20 mg
    Antioxidant, immune stimulant, regulates fatty acid metabolism.

I hiked up to the top of Mount San Gorgonio in southern California in 1984. The view was spectacular. However, when I pulled out my binoculars, I could see much more detail. And when I borrowed a pair of high powered binoculars from a friend, the details of the surrounding landscape became even more defined and clear. The same thing is happening in the field of nutrition. As our analytical equipment becomes more sophisticated, our ability to see subsets of molecules that work together becomes more impressive. The star nutrient of today may become a supporting actress tomorrow. Such may be the case for vitamin E (tocopherols) and its kissing cousin, tocotrienols.

While some nutritionists campaign against the use of palm oil, since it has a higher content of saturated fats than soy or corn oil, the data actually shows that palm oil may LOWER the risk for heart disease, since it is rich in tocotrienols which are potent antioxidants that protect the blood vessel walls.[85] Palm oil is the second largest volume of vegetable oil produced in the world.

Tocotrienols are very similar in structure to tocopherols, which is vitamin E. Palm oil and rice bran are the richest sources of tocotrienols. Tocotrienols have only 30% the vitamin E activity when compared to D-alpha-tocopherol, the "gold standard" of vitamin E.[86] Yet tocotrienols have demonstrated a greater anti-cancer activity than vitamin E.[87] Tocotrienols were able to delay onset of cancer in animals, while mixed carotenes from palm oil were able to regress these same cancers.[88] In vitro and in vivo, dietary palm oil (richest source of tocotrienols) was able to exhibit a "dose dependent" anti-tumor activity against several carcinogenic compounds.[89] Just as some researchers now feel that bioflavonoids are more important in human nutrition than the vitamin C that was discovered first, there are some very bright scientists who feel that the primary role of vitamin E is to help manufacture and protect tocotrienols, which may have the ultimate antioxidant and immune-stimulating activity in the human body.

Quercetin   167 mg
Bioflavonoid with unique immune stimulating and anti-neoplastic activity.

While a review paper from 1983 estimated that about 500 varieties of bioflavonoids existed in nature[90], more current estimates go as high as 20,000 different bioflavonoid compounds. Bioflavonoids are basically accessory factors used by plants to assist in photosynthesis and reduce the damaging effects from the sun. Best sources of bioflavonoids are citrus, berries, onions, parsley, legumes, green tea and bee pollen. The average Western diet contains somewhere between 150 mg/day[91] and 1000 mg/day[92] of bioflavonoids, with about 25 mg/day of quercetin. Best source of quercetin is the white rind in citrus fruits. Of all the nutrition factors discussed in this book, only a few, including quercetin, have shown the potential to revert a cancerous cell back to a normal healthy cell, called prodifferentiation.[93]

Quercetin has many talents that may help the cancer patient:[94]
◊   Induces apoptosis, or programmed cell death in otherwise "immortal" cancer cells
◊   Inhibits inflammation, by reducing histamine release
◊   Inhibits tumor cell proliferation

◊ Competes with estrogen for binding sites, thus defusing the damaging effects of estrogen
◊ Helps to inhibit drug resistance in tumor cells[95]
◊ Potent antioxidant
◊ May inhibit angiogenesis (making of blood vessels from the tumor)
◊ Inhibits capillary fragility which protects connective tissue against breakdown by tumors
◊ Has anti-viral activity
◊ Reduces the "stickiness" of cells, or aggregation, thus slowing cancer metastasis
◊ Reduces the toxicity and carcinogenic capacity of substances in the body[96] YET at the same time may enhance the tumor killing capacity of cisplatin[97]
◊ Helps to eliminate toxic metals through chelation[98]
◊ Increases the anti-neoplastic activity of hyperthermia (heat therapy) on cancer cells
◊ May revert cancer cells back to normal cells (prodifferentiation), possibly by repairing the defective energy mechanism in the cancer cells[99]

Quercetin has taught scientists a great lesson. "In vitro", literally "in glass", means doing an experiment on cells growing in a Petri dish or test tube. There are certain merits in doing in vitro studies, including ease and cost. Most chemotherapy drugs originated by "passing" the in vitro test for killing cancer cells in culture. The "gold standard" for the National Cancer Institute is the in vitro test. Since few nutrition factors kill cancer cells on contact and none of them are patentable, research on nutrition factors at the NCI has been disappointing. Quercetin was considered a possible carcinogen based upon the Ames in vitro test in 1977, since it caused mutagenic changes to cells. Yet, new studies show that quercetin is not a carcinogen, but may be one of the most potent anticarcinogens in nature.[100]

Another area of debate surrounding quercetin is bioavailability. One study gave a 4 gram oral dose once of quercetin to 6 healthy volunteers, then measured for quercetin in the blood. No quercetin could be found in the blood or urine and 53% of the dose ended up in the stools, giving suspicions that quercetin is not well absorbed from the diet.[101] However, since then many studies giving oral doses of quercetin to animals and humans have found major therapeutic benefits, indicating that it is somehow absorbed into the bloodstream, according to world reknowned experts in the field, Elliott Middleton, MD and Chithan Kandaswami, PhD. Quercetin may travel through the bloodstream as a similar structure molecule (called an analog), making it difficult to detect in bioavailability studies.

In animals fed 5% of their diet as quercetin, there was a 50% reduction in the incidence of tumors after exposure to carcinogens, while animals fed 2% quercetin had a 25% reduction in tumor incidence.[102] Quercetin has been shown to inhibit estrogen dependent tumors by occupying the critical estrogen receptor sites on the tumor cell membranes.[103] Quercetin, at relatively low concentration, has been shown to inhibit the proliferation of squamous cancer cells.[104] Quercetin and other bioflavonoids have shown the ability to inhibit metastasis in cultured cells.[105] Quercetin significantly increased the tumor kill rate of hyperthermia (heat therapy) in cultured cancer cells.[106] Head and neck squamous cancers in humans are resistant to most medical therapies and have a high rate of tumor recurrence. Quercetin was selectively toxic in both in vitro and in vivo head and neck cancers in a dose dependent fashion.[107]

One problem for cancer patients can be inflammation, or swelling of tissue. This is a crucial "tightrope walk", in which you want a certain amount of alarm in the immune system, which creates dumping of free radicals and swelling; yet you don't want too much of this or it creates weakness, pain, discomfort, and tissue wasting. Rigdon Lentz, MD is a pioneering oncologist who has developed and patented a device for filtering the factors in the blood of cancer patients (Tumor Necrosis Factor inhibitors) that prevent the immune system from attacking the tumor. Dr. Lentz finds that he must provide a gradual attack on the tumor, or else swelling and tumor lysis (bursting of cancer cells) can actually kill the cancer patient with toxic by-products. Quercetin can help reduce swelling by helping to produce anti-inflammatory prostaglandins.[108] Quercetin inhibits the release of histamine from mast cells, thus reducing allergic reactions.[109] Quercetin also helps to stabilize cell membranes, decrease lipid peroxidation and inhibit the breakdown of connective tissue (collagen) by hyaluronidase (one of the ways that cancer spreads).[110]

SAFETY ISSUES. There has been no demonstrated toxicity of quercetin in humans or animals.

Medium chain triglycerides (MCT) 1 gm
Slows down lean tissue wasting, enhances thermogenesis (making of heat) and augments burning of fat, a fuel source which cancer cells cannot use.

Fatty acids can have a length of anywhere from 2 carbons to 24 carbons. The long chain fats (or triglycerides, called LCT) include most dietary fats of soy oil and beef fat. LCT is difficult to absorb and requires special bile acids and absorption pathways in the lymphatic ducts.[111] Medium chain triglycerides (MCT) are much easier to absorb and are quickly burned in the human system. MCTs are primarily found in coconut oil and smaller amounts in other nuts. Almost like adding kindling (MCT) to a group of logs (LCT), medium chain triglycerides actually promote the burning of the body's fat stores, which helps to encourage thermogenesis (making of heat) in humans.[112] Cancer cells can be selectively destroyed by elevating the body temperature.

MCT has been shown to be a useful tool:

◊ in the control of obesity
◊ lowering serum cholesterol
◊ as a concentrated and readily available source of energy
◊ helps to prevent immune suppression in critically ill people[113]
◊ maintains body (visceral) protein stores during wound recovery.[114]

MCT is extremely safe, provides quick energy for the person, does not feed the cancer, protects protein reserves in the body and helps to slowly melt away unwanted fat stores in the adipose tissue.

Bee pollen   600 mg
Rich in amino acids, B-vitamins, and bioflavonoids; historically used as an energizer, blood builder and immune stimulant.

Bee pollen is a rich and well balanced collection of B-vitamins, vitamin C, RNA and DNA, amino acids, polyunsaturated fats, enzymes, trace minerals, bioflavonoids and an assortment of other unidentified nutrition factors.

Bee pollen has been used throughout history as a superfood to restore energy and recuperative powers to the ailing individual.[115] Bee pollen improves allergies in many individuals, and hence may have a regulating effect on the immune system by helping to dampen unnecessary autoimmune attacks which saves immune warriors for the real cancer battle. There is no toxicity to bee pollen. Other bee products with extraordinary healing properties include royal bee jelly and propolis, which is the antibiotic compound used by bees to disinfect their hives before occupation. Some people use propolis as a substitute for antibiotics in non-life threatening infections.

Lecithin, phosphatidylcholine   1500 mg
Helps to detoxify the liver, regulates cell growth, contributes choline for many other functions in the body, becomes part of healthy cell membranes for proper nutrient intake and toxin removal.

Lecithin is an incredible substance with great potential to help the cancer patient. Most substances in life are either fat soluble, such as butter, or water soluble, such as vitamin C. Lecithin is on a very short list of substances that can dissolve both fat and water soluble substances at the same time, also known as an emulsifier. Lecithin is used widely in the food industry to prevent separation of ingredients in cookies, etc.

Richest sources of lecithin are soybeans and egg yolks. For a little experiment, next time you finish with blending some eggs for scrambling, add water to the container and use an electric blender to see the "soap bubbles" rise from the leftover lecithin-rich egg yolks.

Lecithin is a molecule that is similar in structure to triglycerides found in soy oil and beef, except that one of the fatty acids has been replaced by phosphatidylcholine. This simple exchange gives lecithin unique properties, including the:

⇒ lowering of serum cholesterol and reduction of platelet aggregation in humans[116]
⇒ reversing the skin disease psoriasis[117]
⇒ improving the course of Alzheimer's disease[118]
⇒ reducing the tremors in tardive dyskinesia.[119]

Lecithin seems to work in the cell membrane to enhance "cell membrane dynamics", works in the nervous tissue (sphingomyelin), and contributes a key B-vitamin, choline. Choline works with folate, methione and B-12 as methyl donors, which are responsible for all new cell growth.

Choline is one of the few nutrients tested in which merely a deficiency (without any other compounding factor, like toxins or aging) is enough to spontaneously generate liver cancer in animals.[120] In animal and human studies, choline deficiency leads to fatty liver and compromised liver functions.[121] Lecithin is a major protective nutrient for the liver, helping to regenerate healthy liver tissue and excrete toxins. Protecting the liver, with substances like lecithin and milk thistle, is crucial for cancer patients.

Genistein (from soy)   6 mg
Helps to selectively slow down cancer growth.

When scientists reviewed the world's cancer incidences, they found some strange disparities. Japanese men had 1/5 the incidence of prostate cancer and Japanese women had 1/5 the incidence of breast cancer when compared to Americans. The reasons could be many, including a lower fat diet, more exercise, less beef, less obesity, more vegetables and seaweed. But researchers settled in on soybean products, including tofu and tempeh, as the primary protector against cancer. It has now been well established that regular consumption of soy products may lower the incidence of many forms of cancer.[122] While there are a rich collection of isoflavones, protease inhibitors and lectins in soybeans; researchers have focused on genistein as perhaps the principle cancer-protective bioflavonoid in soy.

Genistein may be able to:
◊   selectively kill cancer cells

◊ reduce the tumor growth capacity of sex hormones in both men and women
◊ induce programmed cell death (apoptosis) in cancer
◊ inhibit metastasis
◊ inhibit angiogenesis[123] (making of blood vessels from tumors)
◊ induce differentiation to help regulate proper cell growth.[124]

Genistein is one of the few agents on the planet earth that may be able to revert a cancer cell back to a normal healthy cell, called prodifferentiation. [125] Scientists have worked diligently to better understand the anti-cancer effects of protease inhibitors in soy.[126] Dr. Ann Kennedy spent 20 years at Harvard and now working at the University of Pennsylvania researching the extraordinary ability of the Bowman Birk Inhibitor (a protease inhibitor found in soy) to prevent and reverse cancer while also reducing the toxic effects of chemo and radiation on animals.[127]

Soy and breast cancer. Based on the fact that soy contains weak phytoestrogens that can induce infertility in zoo animals kept on a high soy diet, some experts have cautioned against the use of soy in estrogen/progesterone positive breast cancer. Tamoxifen is an estrogen binder drug that is given to women with estrogen positive breast cancer. Tamoxifen has a similar chemical structure to genistein, yet genistein does not have any of the toxic side effects of tamoxifen. Once again, Nature comes up with another brilliantly helpful molecule in genistein, which inhibits both breast and prostate cancer.[128] Genistein actually slows the growth of breast cancer cells in culture.[129] The macrobiotic diet uses large amounts of soy to help slow the growth of many cancers, including breast cancer. A fermented and concentrated soy product, Haelen 851, has been used successfully to reverse breast cancer. For more on this subject, refer to the explanation of ginseng, which also contains phytoestrogens.

L-glycine   1 gm
  Energizer, calmitive agent, detoxifier, controls fat levels in the blood, builds energy stores (glycogen) in the liver, helps in wound recovery and collagen synthesis.

Glycine's name reflects its sweet flavor. It is considered a non-essential amino acid, since it can be formed from the amino acids threonine and serine. Glycine may help the cancer patient in several ways:
◊ Acts as a preservative in foods
◊ Sweetening agent, since it tastes much like sugar, yet does not alter glycemic index

◊ May be converted into glutathione (see that section) for antioxidant and detoxification benefits

◊ May be converted in the body into Dimethylglycine (DMG, see that section)

◊ Works as a calming agent in the nervous system and also helps to improve spastic conditions[130] and muscular weakness.[131]

◊ Promotes collagen formation, thus possibly helping the body to encapsulate tumors

---

Glucaric acid (cal D glucarate)   500 mg
    Improves detoxification in the gut and liver, escorts estrogen out of the system, may have anti-proliferative activity.

Calcium D-glucarate, or CDG, is such a non-toxic and potentially helpful substance for cancer patients that it is undergoing Phase I trials sponsored by the National Cancer Institute and held at Memorial Sloan Kettering Hospital in New York. D-glucaric acid is a substance found in certain fruits (oranges) and vegetables (broccoli, potatoes). CDG has been shown to encourage critical phase II detoxification pathways in the gut by inhibiting the counterproductive enzyme produced by intestinal bacteria, beta-glucuronidase.[132] Oral administration of CDG provided a 50% drop in beta-glucuronidase for 5 hours.[133]   In animals fed CDG, serum estradiol levels were decreased (a good sign for breast cancer) by 23%.[134] Animals fed CDG experienced a 50-70% reduction in mammary cancers.[135] In cultured cancer cells, D-glucarate combined with retinoid (vitamin A analog) provided a synergistic inhibition of tumor growth.[136] When D-glucaric acid is bound to calcium, the resulting molecule, calcium D-glucarate, becomes a time-released version of glucaric acid in the gut, helping to detoxify poisons and hormones while dampening unregulated cell growth.

PATIENT PROFILE: REVERSING INCURABLE CYTOMA

S.M. is a 44 year old male diagnosed in April of 1997 with a rare form of cancer (hemangiopericytoma) that had caused pain, weakness and numbness in his back and legs. Began 13 rounds of radiation therapy to spinal region which produced considerable relief from pain and weakness. May of 1997, CAT scans and liver biopsy found metastatic disease throughout pancreas, liver, kidneys, lungs and pressing on spinal cord. Physicians agreed in medical staff meeting that this condition is "refractory to all medical therapy and invariably fatal." Patient began aggressive nutrition program of diet and supplements, along with detoxification (coffee enemas), 3 months chemotherapy (FUDR) and extensive prayer. As of November 1997, CAT scans showed 50% shrinkage in tumors on pancreas, lungs & kidneys with elimination of tumors on liver. Throughout this rigorous chemotherapy treatment protocol, S.M.'s bloodwork was constantly normal, whereas one would expect declines in white cell count (leukopenia) and red blood cell count (anemia). As of January 1998, patient has had excellent quality of life with no limitations, other than mild fatigue following chemotherapy injection.

ENDNOTES

[1] . Budavari, S. (eds), THE MERCK INDEX, p.1591, Merck & Co., Whitehouse Station, NJ 1996
[2] . Packer, L., et al., Free Radical Biol. Med., vol.19, p.227, 1995
[3] . Stoll, S., et al., Ann.NY Acad.Sci., vol.717, p.122, 1994
[4] . Passwater, R., LIPOIC ACID, Keats, New Canaan, CT, 1996
[5] . Nagamatsu, M., et al., Diabetes Care, vol.18, p.1160, Aug.1995
[6] . Podda, M., et al., Biochem.Biophys., Res.Commun., vol.204, p.98, 1994
[7] . Han, D., et al., Biochem.Biophys.,Res.Commun., vol.207, p.258, 1995
[8] . Ou, P., et al., Biochem.Pharmacol., vol.50, p.123, 1995
[9] . Ohmori, H., et al., Jpn.J.Pharmacol., vol.42, p.275, 1986
[10] . Jacob, S., et al., Diabetes, vol.45, p.1024, 1996
[11] . DiMascio, P., et al., Arch.Biochem.Biophysics, vol.274, p.532, 1989
[12] . Mangels, AR, et al., J.Am.Diet.Assoc., vol.93, p.284, 1993
[13] . Giovannucci, E., et al., J.Nat.Can.Inst., vol.87, p.1767, 1995
[14] . Franceschi, S., et al., Int.J.Cancer, vol.59, p.181, 1994
[15] . Comstock, GW, et al., Amer.J.Clin.Nutr., vol.53, p.260S, 1991
[16] . Bray, TM, et al., Biochem.Pharmacol., vol.47, p.2113, 1994; see also Shan, X, et al., Pharmacol.Ther., vol.47, p.61, 1990
[17] . DeLeve, LD, et al., Pharmac.Ther., vol.52, p.287, 1991
[18] . Bray, TM, et al., Biochem.Pharmacol., vol.47, p.2113, 1994
[19] . Julius, M., et al., J.Clin.Epidemiol., vol.47, p.1021, 1994
[20] . Beutler, E., et al., J.Lab.Clin.Ned., vol.105, p.581, 1985
[21] . Hercbergs, A., et al., Lancet, vol.339, p.1074, May 1992
[22] . DiRe, F., et al., Cancer Chemother.Pharmacol., vol.25, p.355, 1990
[23] . Cascinu, S., et al., J.Clin.Oncol., vol.13, p.26, 1995
[24] . Trickler, D., et al., Nutr.Cancer, vol.20, p.139, 1993
[25] . Shklar, G., et al., Nutr.Cancer, vol.20, p.145, 1993
[26] . Science, vol.212, p.541, May 1981
[27] . Ranek, DK, et al., Liver, vol.12, p.341, 1992
[28] . Lash, LH, et al., Proc.Natl.Acad.Sci., vol.83, p.4641, July 1986
[29] . Donnerstag, B., et al., Int.J.Oncol., vol.7, p.949, Oct.1995
[30] . Witschi, A., et al., Eur.J.Clin.Pharmacol., vol.43, p.667, 1992

[31]. Hagen, TM, et al., Am.J.Physiol., vol.259, p.G524, 1990

[32]. Haller, JS, Bull.NY Acad.Sci., vol.66, p.647, 1990

[33]. Danhof, IE, REMARKABLE ALOE, Omnimedicus Press, Grand Prairie, TX 1987

[34]. Lee, YC, Adv.Exp.Med.Biol., vol.228, p.103, 1984

[35]. Robson, MC, et al., J.Burn.Care Rehab., vol.3, p.157, 1982

[36]. Sheets, MA, et al., Mol.Biother., vol.3, p.41, 1991

[37]. Kahlon, JB, et al., Mol.Biother., vol.3, p.214, 1991

[38]. t'Hart, LA, et al., Planta.Med., vol.55, p.509, 1989

[39]. t'Hart, LA, et al., Int.J.Immunopharmacol., vol.12, p.427, 1990

[40]. Karaca, K., et al., Int.J.Immunopharmacol., vol.17, p.183, 1995

[41]. Kamasuka, T., et al., Gann, vol.59, p.443, 1968

[42]. Tizard, IR, et al., Mol.Biother., vol.1, p.290, 1989

[43]. Murray, RK, et al., HARPER'S BIOCHEMISTRY, p.648, Lange Medical, Stamford, CT 1996

[44]. Haas, EM, STAYING HEALTHY WITH NUTRITION, p.139, Celestial Arts, Berkeley, 1992

[45]. Reap, EA, et al., J.Lab.Clin.Med., vol.115, p.481, 1990

[46]. Graber, CD, et al., J.Infect.Dis., vol.143, p.101, 1982

[47]. Bremer, J., Physiol.Rev., vol.63, p.1420, 1983

[48]. Borum, PR, et al., J.Am.Coll.Nutr., vol.5, p.177, 1986

[49]. Sachan, DS, et al., Am.J.Clin.Nutr., vol.39, p.738, 1984

[50]. Dragan, GI, et al., Physiologie, vol.25, p.231, 1987

[51]. Furitano, G, et al., Drugs Exp.Clin.Res., vol.10, p.107, 1984

[52]. DeSimone, C., et al, Acta Vitaminol. Enzymol., vol.4, p.135, 1982

[53]. Lane, IW, and L. Comac, SHARKS DON'T GET CANCER, Avery, Garden City, 1992

[54]. Langer, R. et al., Science, p.70, July 1976

[55]. Langer, R. et al., Proceedings National Academy of Sciences, vol.77, no.7, p.4331, July 1980

[56]. Lee, A., et al., Science, vol.221, p.1185, Sept.1983

[57]. Folkman, J, et al., Science, vol.235, p.442, Jan.1987

[58]. D'Amore, PA, Seminars in Thrombosis & Hemostasis, vol.14, p.73, 1988

[59]. Folkman, J., et al., Nature, vol.339, p.58, May 1989

[60]. Moses, MA, et al., Science, vol.248, p.1408, June 1990

[61]. Oikawa, T., et al., Cancer Letters, vol.51, p.181, 1990

[62]. Weidner, N., et al., New England Journal of Medicine, vol.324, p.1, Jan.1991

[63]. Folkman, J., Journal Clinical Oncology, vol.12, p.441, Mar.1994

[64]. Madden, JW, in SABISTON'S TEXTBOOK OF SURGERY, p.268, WB Saunders, Philadelphia, 1972

[65]. Prudden, JF, et al., Seminars in Arthritis and Rheumatism, vol.3, p.287, Summer 1974

[66]. Prudden, JF, Journal of Biological Response Modifiers, vol.4, p.551, 1985

[67]. Durie, BGM, et al., Journal of Biological Response Modifiers, vol.4, p.590, 1985

[68]. Rosen, J, et al., Journal of Biological Response Modifiers, vol.7, p.498, 1988

[69]. Kinsella, J., et al., Crit.Care Med., vol.18, p.S94, 1990

[70]. Pizzini, RP, et al., Surgical Infection Society abstract, p.50, 1989

[71]. Cerra, FB, Am.J.Surg., vol.161, p.230, 1991; see also Cerra, FB, et al., Nutrition, vol.6, p.88, 1990; see also Lieberman, M., et al., Nutrition, vol.6, p.88, 1990

[72]. Aarons, S., et al., J.Surg.Onc., vol.23, p.21, 1983

[73]. Cameron, DE, et al., Am.J.Psychiatry, vol.120, p.320, 1963; see also Nodine, JH, et al., Am.J.Psychiatry, vol.123, p.1257, 1967

[74]. Newman, EA, et al., Amer.J.Physiol., vol.164, p.251, 1951

[75]. Pilch, YH, Am.J.Surg., vol.132, p.631, 1976

[76]. Michelson, AM, et al., Proc.Soc.Exper.Biol. Med., vol.179, p.1, 1985

[77]. Wiltrout, RH, et al., J.Biol.Resp.Mod., vol.4, p.512, 1985

[78]. Tomomatsu, H., Food Technology, p.61, Oct.1994

[79]. Goldin, BR, et al., MODERN NUTRITION IN HEALTH AND DISEASE, Shils, ME (eds), p.569, Lea & Febiger, Philadelphia, 1994

[80]. Deitch, EA, Archives Surgery, vol.125, p.403, Mar.1990

[81]. Le, MG, et al., J.Nat.Cancer Inst., vol.77, p.633, Sept.1986

[82]. Salminen, E., et al., Clin.Radiol., vol.39, p.435, 1988

[83]. Tomomatsu, H., Food Technology, p.61, Oct.1994

[84]. Fugiwara, S., et al., J.Japan Soc.Nutr.Food Science, vol.43, p.327, 1990

[85]. Qureshi, AA, et al., Am.J.Clin.Nutr., vol.53, p.1042S, 1991

[86]. Farrell, PM, et al., in MODERN NUTRITION IN HEALTH AND DISEASE, Shils, ME (eds), Lea & Febiger, Philadelphia, 1994

[87]. Komiyama, K., et al., Chem.Pharm.Bull., vol.37, p.1369, 1989

[88]. Tan, B., Nutrition Research, vol.12, p.S163, 1992

[89]. Azuine, MA, et al., Nutr. Cancer, vol.17, p.287, 1992

[90]. Havsteen, B., Biochem.Pharmacol., vo.32, p.1141, 1983

[91] . Murray, MT, ENCYCLOPEDIA OF NUTRITIONAL SUPPLEMENTS, p.321, Prima, Rocklin, CA 1996

[92] . Middleton, E., et al., in ADJUVANT NUTRITION IN CANCER TREATMENT, Quillin, P. (eds), p.319, Cancer Treatment Research Foundation, Arlington Heights, IL 1994

[93] . Middleton, E., et al., in ADJUVANT NUTRITION IN CANCER TREATMENT, Quillin, P. (eds), p.325, Cancer Treatment Research Foundation, Arlington Heights, IL 1994

[94] . Boik, J., CANCER & NATURAL MEDICINE, p.181, Oregon Medical Press, Princeton, MN 1995

[95] . Scambia, G., et al., Cancer Chemother. Pharmacol., vol.28, p.255, 1991

[96] . Wood, AW, et al., in PLANT FLAVONOIDS IN BIOLOGY AND MEDICINE, p.197, Cody, V. (eds), Liss, NY, 1986

[97] . Scambia, G., et al., Anticancer Drugs, vol.1, p.45, 1990

[98] . Afanasev, IB, et al., Biochem.Pharmacol., vol.38, p.1763, 1989

[99] . Suolinna, E., et al., J.Nat.Cancer Inst., vol.53, p.1515, 1974

[100] . Stavric, B., Clin.Biochem., vol.27, p.245, Aug.1994

[101] . Gugler, R., et al., Eur.J.Clin.Pharmacol., vol.9, p.229, 1975

[102] . Berma, AK, et al., Cancer Res., vol.48, p.5754, 1988

[103] . Ranelletti, FO, et al., Int.J.Cancer, vol.50, p.486, 1992

[104] . Kandaswami, C., et al., Anti-Cancer Drugs, vol.4, p.91, 1993

[105] . Bracke, ME, et al., in PLANET FLAVONOIDS IN BIOLOGY AND MEDICINE II, CELLULAR AND MEDICINAL PROPERTIES, p.219, Cody, E. (eds), Liss, NY, 1988

[106] . Kim, JH, et al., Cancer Research, vol.44, p.102, Jan.1984

[107] . Castillo, MH, et al., Amer.J.Surgery, vol.158, p.351, Oct.1989

[108] . Bauman, J., et al., Prostaglandins, vol.20, p.627, 1980

[109] . Middleton, E, et al., Arch.Allergy Appl.Immunol., vol.77, p.155, 1985

[110] . Busse, WW, et al., J.Allergy Clin.Immunol., vol.73, p.801, 1984

[111] . Bach, AC, et al., Am.J.Clin.Nutr., vol.36, p.950, 1982

[112] . Mascioli, EA, et al., J.Parenteral Enteral Nutr., vol.15, p.27, 1991

[113] . Jensen, GL, et al., J.Parenteral Enteral Nutr., vol.14, p.467, 1990

[114] . Maiz, A., et al., Metabolism, vol.33, p.901, Oct.1984

[115] . Page, LR, HEALTHY HEALING, p.76, Healthy Healing Publ, 1996

[116] . Brook, JG, et al., Biochem.Med.Metab.Biol.,vol. 35, p.31, 1986

[117] . Gross, P, et al., NY State J.Med., vol.50, p.2683, 1950

[118] . Little, A., et al., J.Neurology, Neurosurgery & Psychiatry, vol.48, p.736, 1985

[119] . Jackson, IV, et al., Am.J.Psychiatry, vol.136, p.11, Nov.1979

[120] . Yokoyama, S, et al., Cancer Res., vol.45, p.2834, 1985

[121] . Zeisel, SH, et al., Fed Amer Soc Exper Biol., vol.5, p.2093, 1991

[122] . Messina, M., et al., J.Nat.Cancer Inst., vol.83, p.541, 1991

[123] . Fostis, T., et al., Proc. Natl. Acad.Sci., vol.90, p.2690, 1993

[124] . Boik, J., CANCER & NATURAL MEDICINE, p.184, Oregon Medical Press, Princeton, MN 1995

[125] . Watanabe, T., et al., Exp.Cell Res., vol.183, p.335, 1989; see also Constantinou, A., et al., Cancer Res., vol.50, p.2618, 1990

[126] . Hocman, G., Int.J.Biochem., vol.24, p.1365, 1992

[127] . Kennedy, AR, in ADJUVANT NUTRITION IN CANCER TREATMENT, p.129, Quillin, P. (eds), Cancer Treatment Research Foundation, Arlington Heights, IL 1994

[128] . Adlercreutz, H., et al., Lancet, vol.342, p.1209, Nov.1993

[129] . Peterson, G., et al., Biochem.Biophy.Res.Commun., vol.179, p.661, 1991; see also Zava, DT, et al., Nutrition & Cancer, vol.27, p.31, 1997

[130] . Davidoff, RA, Annals Neurology, vol.17, p.107, 1985

[131] . Braverman, ER, et al., HEALING NUTRIENTS WITHIN, p.238, Keats, New Canaan, CT 1987

[132] . Dwivedi, C, et al, Biochem.Med. & Metabolic Biol., vol.43, p.83, 1990

[133] . Dwivedi, C., et al., Biochem.Med.Metabol.Biol., vol.43, p.83, 1990

[134] . Walaszek, Z, et al., Carcinogenesis, vol.7, p.1463, 1986

[135] . Walaszek, Z, Cancer Letters, vol.54, p.1, 1990

[136] . Curley, RW, et al., Life Sciences, vol.54, p.1299, 1994

Chapter 12

CHANGING THE UNDERLYING CAUSES OF CANCER

"Spread the good word that cancer is not as inevitable as death and taxes." National Academy of Sciences, 1982 book DIET, NUTRITION AND CANCER

> Help reverse disease by changing the underlying causes of the disease. These are listed in approximate order of importance. Find a professional who will help you detect and solve these problems.

B
ob J. was forced by his wife to go to the doctor. His "heartburn" had become so frequent and interrupted too many otherwise pleasant meals with the family. Bob's doctor put him on the drug, Tagamet, and his condition seemed to disappear. However, at his next physical, Bob showed up with high blood pressure at the tender age of 46. His doctor put him on beta-blockers and diuretics and the blood pressure came down. A year later, Bob started developing severe depression for the impotence that resulted from his diuretic medication. His doctor started him on Prozac for that symptom. This "shell game" of "hide the symptoms with drugs" continued for a few more years until Bob started passing blood in his stools and was diagnosed with colon cancer. No one had bothered to ask the simple but essential question: "What is causing these conditions?" In Bob's case, a very poor on-the-run diet, plus stress, no exercise and the side effects of excess medication came crashing down in a really serious life threatening condition.

No one with a headache is suffering from a deficiency of aspirin. And no one with elevated serum cholesterol is suffering from a deficiency of clofibrate. Arthritis sufferers are not suffering due to lack of cortisone, and cancer patients are not lacking chemotherapy. All of these therapies are short term, symptom-fixing drugs which provide immediate relief, but do nothing to change the underlying causes of a disease.

Studies have proven that patients who undergo coronary bypass surgery have no extension in lifespan, because no one has changed the cause of the disease by replacing 4 inches of plugged up "plumbing" or arteries near the heart. Same goes for other drugs and conditions. Beta-blockers and diuretics for the 60 million Americans with high blood pressure actually INCREASE the risk for a heart attack by causing a loss of the crucial cardio-protective minerals of potassium and magnesium.

The following listing is a very brief description of the underlying causes of disease, listed in order of importance (my professional opinion). These biological, psychological, chemical and electrical factors have been gleaned and synthesized from such classic works as THE TEXTBOOK OF NATURAL MEDICINE by Drs. Pizzorno and Murray, OPTIMAL WELLNESS by Dr. Ralph Golan, and the out-of-print 1957 copyright book CANCER: NATURE, CAUSE AND CURE by Alexander Berglas. The ideal combination therapy for any disease would include short term relief with minimal drugs, coupled with the long term goal of changing the underlying causes of the disease. For more information, consult with your health care professional. Naturopathic Doctors (ND) are usually well trained in these theories.

FIX WHAT'S BROKE

If you have a zinc deficiency, then a truckload of vitamin C will not be nearly as valuable as giving the body what it needs to end the zinc deficiency. If an accumulation of lead and mercury has crimped the immune system, then removing the toxic metals is more important than psychotherapy. If a low output of hydrochloric acid in the stomach creates poor digestion and malabsorption, then hydrochloric acid supplements are the answer. If a broken spirit brought on the cancer, then spiritual healing is necessary to eliminate the cancer.

The need to "fix what's broke" is a prime limiting factor in studies that examine cancer therapies. In a given group of 100 cancer patients, based upon my experience, 10 may need grievance counseling, 10 may need high dose supplements to stimulate the immune system, 5 may need serious detoxification, and the remaining 75 have a complex combination of problems. This issue complicates cancer treatment tremendously and makes "cookbook" cancer treatment an exercise in futility. Our progress against cancer has been crippled not only by the complexity of cancer, but also by the need for Western science to isolate one variable. While it is easier to conduct and interpret research with one or two variables, cancer and the human body are far more complex than that. We will eventually help most cancer patients by fixing whatever bodily function needs repair. This is easier said than done. Finding the underlying problem requires a physician trained in comprehensive medicine.

1) PSYCHO-SPIRITUAL.

Grief, loss of loved one, lack of purpose, depression, low self esteem, hypochondriasis as means of attention, need love for self and others, touching, be here now, sense of accomplishment, happiness, music, beauty, sexual satisfaction, forgiveness, etc..
>SOLUTION: Create a new way of thinking (crisis=opportunity or danger)

It was Hans Selye, MD who first scientifically showed that animals subjected to stress undergo thymic atrophy (immune suppression), elevations in blood pressure and serum lipids and erosion of the stomach lining (ulcers).[1] Since then literally thousands of human studies have demonstrated that an angry, stressed, or depressed mind can lead to a suppressed immune system, which allows cancer and infections to take over. Drs. Locke and Horning-Rohan have published a textbook consisting of over 1300 scientific articles written since 1976 that prove the link between the mind and the immune system.

We are finally beginning to accept what philosophers and spiritual leaders have been telling us for thousands of years: the mind has a major impact on the body and health. Proverbs 17:22 tells us "A joyful heart is good medicine, but a broken spirit dries up the bones." Over 100 years ago, observant physicians claimed that significant life events might increase the risk for developing cancer.[2] In the 1800s, emotional factors were related to breast cancer, and cervical cancer was related to sensitive and frustrated women. Loss of a loved one has long been known to increase the risk for breast and cervical cancer. When 2000 men were assessed and then followed for 17 years, it was found that depression doubled the risk for cancer.

Researchers at the National Institute of Health, spearheaded by Candice Pert, PhD, have investigated the link between catecholamines, endorphins and other chemicals from the brain as they influence cancer. A reknowned researcher, Jean Achterberg, PhD, has demonstrated a clear link between the attitude of the cancer patient and their quality and quantity of life.[3] In my years of experience, about 90% of the cancer patients I deal with have encountered a major traumatic event 1-2 years prior to the onset of cancer. This is especially true of breast cancer patients. There is even a medical textbook on the subject of "STRESS AND BREAST CANCER"[4]

Not only can mental depression lead to immune suppression and then cancer, but there may be a metaphorical significance to the location of the cancer. Divorced women who lose a breast as they feel a loss of their feminity. One of my patients developed cancer of the larynx a year after his wife left him. He tried to get her to talk about it, but she said there was "nothing left to say".

Your mind is probably the "lifeguard" that keeps cancer at bay, hence major stress is literally inviting cancer into the body. The good news is that the mind can be a powerful instrument at eliminating cancer. This is a frightening or empowering concept, depending on how you chose to perceive it. The cancer patient who knows that he or she can do something about getting well is more likely to beat the disease. Helplessness and hopelessness are just as lethal as cigarettes and bullets.

Norman Cousins cured himself of a painful collagen disease by using laughter and attitude adjustment, along with high doses of vitamin C. Bernie Siegel, MD, a Yale surgeon, noticed that certain mental characteristics in his cancer patients were indicators of someone who would beat the odds: live each moment, express yourself, value your dreams and maintain an assertive fighting spirit against the disease. Carl Simonton, MD, a radiation oncologist, found that mental imagery and other mind techniques vastly improved the results in his cancer patients. In a National Cancer Institute study conducted at the University of Texas, researchers were able to predict with 100% accuracy which cancer patients would die or deteriorate within a two month period--strictly based upon the patient's attitude.[5] While tobacco products contain carcinogenic substances, mentally handicapped people, many of whom smoke, experience a 4% death rate from cancer, compared to 22% for the population at large.[6] Indeed, there may be a certain amount of bliss in ignorance.

Enkephalins and endorphins, also called "the mind's rivers of pleasure", are brain chemicals that are secreted when the mind is happy. Endorphins improve the production of T cells, which improves the effectiveness of the immune system against cancer and infections. Enkephalins increase the vigor of T-cells attacking cancer cells as well as increasing the percentage of active T-cells. Essentially, your immune system is a well orchestrated army within to protect you against cancer and infections. And your mind is the four star general directing the battle. Depending on your attitude, your mind either encourages or discourages disease in your body.

The take-home lesson here is: you can take a soup bowl full of potent nutrients to fight cancer while you are being treated by the world's best oncologist; but if your mind is not happy and focused on the immune battle that must occur, then the following program of nutrition will not be nearly as effective as it should be.

We are all going to experience certain setbacks, losses and injustices in our lives. How we react to these life stresses will play a major role in our health and longevity. We all have to drive over the "bumps in the highway of life". Your "shock absorber system" is your coping ability that makes stressful events less damaging to your well being.

2) TOXIC BURDEN.
INTAKE from:
> **Voluntary pollutants of drugs, alcohol, tobacco**
> **Involuntary toxins of:**

⇒ Food (1.2 billion lbs/yr pesticides on fresh produce, 2800 FDA-approved food additives, 5 million lbs/yr of antibiotics to grow animals faster, herbicides, fungicides, wax on produce, parasites, veterinarian drug residue, hormones.

⇒ Water. EPA estimates that 40% of fresh water in US is unusable. 1300 different chemicals exist in the average "EPA-approved" city drinking water. Chlorine and lead are most common, with many industrial volatile organic chemicals ending up in the drinking water. 60,000 chemicals in regular use, according to American Chemical Society, half of these in contact with humans. Farm runoff of herbicides, pesticides, fertilizer (nitrates combine with amino acids in stomach to form carcinogenic nitrosamines).

⇒ Air. 50 million Americans breathe air that is dangerous for health. Smoking and second hand smoke are obvious. Millions of tons of known carcinogens are produced annually and legally from paper mills, petrochemical refineries, burning of medical waste (generate dioxin from PVC). Crop dusting, diesel fumes, leaded exhaust, etc.

⇒ Industrial exposure. Workers in factories, vinyl industry, paper mills, refineries, asbestos, etc.

⇒ Other. Mercury amalgams, electro-magnetic fields from cellular phone antenna, high voltage power lines.

>SOLUTION: DETOXIFICATION (EXCRETION) VIA:
* Urine. Increase intake of clean water, vitamin C, beans (sulfur amino acids are chelators), garlic, chelation EDTA therapy.
* Feces. 50 billion bacteria/lb fecal matter. 40% of lymphoid tissue is surrounding the GI tract. Common constipation leads to toxic buildup, dysbiosis. Increase fluid, fiber, psyllium seed husk, sena, cascara sagrada, buckthorn, fructo-oligosaccharides, probiotics (lactobacillus, yogurt). Appropriate use of enemas, coffee enemas (every other day during intensive detox).
* Sweat. Skin is the largest organ of body, 2000 pores/square inch skin. Increase sweating through exercise, hot tubs, jacuzzi, sauna.

Hyperthermia can be useful. Bring core body temperature up to 102 F for 10 minutes/day. Do not use anti-perspirants.

* Liver. Most significant detoxifying organ of body, using conjugase (put together), oxidase, reductase, and hydrolase enzymes to neutralize poisons. Increase intake of glutathione (dark green leafy veg), silymarin, garlic, vitamin E, selenium.

* Other. Some chose chelation therapy, mercury amalgam removal, magnets to neutralize EMF pollution.

-Get rid of the garbage.

Everyone is detoxifying their bodies all day throughout their lives--or they would die. But some people don't detox fast enough, and the toxins build up to encumber their bodily processes. One of the favored theories of aging says that eventually the accumulation of these cellular waste products overwhelms the cells and they begin to die. Similarly, fermenting yeast creates alcohol to a certain point and then dies in its own toxins. Cell cultures of living tissue that are kept in a fresh nutrient solution and changed daily to eliminate toxin buildup will experience slowed aging.

If I was forced to summarize the essence of good health into one simple sentence, it would be: "bring in the right groceries (nutrients) and take out the trash (toxins)." Each of the 60 trillion cells in your body is like a house in your neighborhood. You must bring in the right collection of essential groceries and remove the garbage often. Many cancer patients have erred at both ends of this equation: not enough essential nutrients coupled with an accumulation of poisons.

Fortunately, humans are not "virgins" at exposure to poisons. The human body, when properly nourished, has an enormous capacity to either excrete or neutralize a certain amount of poisons. Yet 20th century pollution has stretched the limits of our elaborate detoxification systems. We have physical means of eliminating waste products through urine, feces, exhaled air, sweat and tears. We also possess an elaborate system of chemical detoxification that is mostly concentrated in the liver, where a complex array of enzymes serve to neutralize poisons. Cytochrome P-450, catalase, mixed function oxidase, conjugase and other enzymes are constantly at work neutralizing and excreting poisons from the body. That is why the liver is often the secondary organ affected after some other part of the body becomes cancerous--like trying to break up a fight and, instead, getting beat up.

Not only do many people voluntarily consume poisons, such as tobacco, alcohol, prescription and "recreational" drugs; but we are also exposed to an alarming amount of involuntary poisons in our air, food, and water supply. Annually, America alone dumps 90 billion pounds of toxic waste into our 55,000 toxic waste sites, spray 1.2 billion pounds of pesticides on our food crops[7], spews forth 600 pounds of air pollutants for every person in America. Scientists have found residues of the lethal industrial solvent PCB (polychlorinated biphenyls) and the pesticide DDT in every human on earth, including mother's milk. And on it goes.

After looking at the toxic burden carried by the average American adult, the question is not "why do 1/3 of us get cancer?", but a more appropriate question might be "why do only 1/3 of us get cancer?" A noted professor at the University of Illinois, Dr. Sam Epstein has profound evidence showing that regardless of other measures taken, our cancer epidemic will not be abated until we get our environmental disaster cleaned up. By increasing the body's ability to purge poisons, detoxification may help the cancer recovery process for some individuals. Toxic burden blunts the immune system, erodes the delicate DNA, changes cellular functions and encourages cancer growth.

A word on coffee enemas. Enemas are one of the oldest healing modalities in human literature. Milk enemas are still used by noted surgeons and gastroenterologists to stem diarrhea that does not respond to medication. Coffee enemas have been in the Merck Medical Manual for decades, until 1977, when editors of the manual claimed that this revered therapy was eliminated for "lack of space" in the new manuscript. The reality is that coffee enemas became the focal point in criticizing alternative cancer therapies. Coffee enemas help to purge the colon and liver of accumulated toxins and dead tissue. Coffee enemas are prepared by brewing regular organic and caffeinated coffee, let cool to body temperature, then use enema bag as per instructions with 4 to 8 ounces of the coffee solution. Proponents of this therapy use it daily for very sick cancer patients, or weekly for recovering cancer patients.

As a by-product of living, we create our own waste products, which must be eliminated or we die in our own biological sewage. Urine contains a collection of worn out parts, filtered out toxins and potentially lethal ammonia. The intestines can become a distillation device like the old moonshiner "still", loaded with strange by-products as bacteria ferment food matter into an incredible array of chemicals and gases. Feces contains unabsorbed food matter, about 50 billion bacteria per pound and many toxins that could cause cancer if allowed to contact the intestinal wall long enough.

Detoxification includes:

-**Urine**. Increasing urinary output and dilution of urine poisons by drinking more clean water, 8-10 cups of fluid daily, which is enough to have urine that is light yellow in color and inoffensive in odor. Drink filtered water, preferably from reverse osmosis. Chelation therapy helps the body to gather up toxic minerals and excrete them via the urine.

-**Feces**. Improve fiber intake until feces are soft in consistency. Also, fix digestive problems, such as low output of hydrochloric acid or digestive enzymes. Take mild herbal purgatives, such as buckthorn, senna, and cascara sagrada. Some people use enemas and colonic irrigation. The typical American diet is low in fiber and loaded with poisons. Colon cleansing, through a variety of methods, is crucial for whole body detoxification.

-**Sweat**. Encourage purging of toxins through sweat glands by taking hot baths or steam baths, then scrubbing the skin with a natural sponge to scrape off the excreted poisons.

-**Mercury**. With more than 90% of the American population sporting at least a few mercury fillings in their teeth, the subject of mercury poisoning has become a hot topic. Lewis Carroll's classic book, Alice in Wonderland, showcased the "mad hatter" as representative of an industry that whimsically used mercury to give stiffness to formal felt hats. Mercury is a deadly poison, and putting it in the mouth to erode over the years and eventually be swallowed is just plain ridiculous. About 1% of the population, or 2 million people, are very sensitive to any exposure to mercury while most other people would be better off without any mercury in their mouth. Some people have found relief from a wide assortment of diseases, including cancer, by having their mercury fillings replaced with non-toxic ceramic or gold material.[8]

-**Chelation of heavy metals**. Lead poisoning is much more common than mercury poisoning. Though our use of lead is starting to be reduced, lead is a clearcut immune poison and has been targeted by the Environmental Protection Agency as a "top priority" cleanup item. Chelation therapy involves injecting chemicals (like EDTA) that put the heavy metal in a molecular "cage" and carry it out of the body in the urine. Chelation therapy may help to reduce heavy metal toxicity, which is assessed by mineral excretion in the urine or by hair/nail analysis.

-**Reduce intake of poisons**. Over a century after the evidence clearly pointed toward the harmful effects of smoking, 25% of Americans and up to 90% of males in other countries still smoke. In my work with hundreds of cancer patients, I have never seen a smoker get better. Ironically, smoking may have a minor benefit for some people, since smoking elevates basal metabolism, which is particularly noticeable in hypothyroid individuals. My hunch is that people who find smoking such an addiction are using nicotine to elevate basal metabolism as a crutch to support their sagging thyroid output. A way to ease the withdrawal for these people is to normalize thyroid output. See the "action" plan for more details on thyroid help.

According to the National Academy of Sciences, pesticide residues on food crops causes 14,000 new cases of cancer each year out of 1.3 million total cases. Which means that about 1% of our cancer comes from pesticide use and abuse. That estimate did not include the more recent findings that pesticides amplify each other's toxicity by 500 to 1000 fold!! That 1% is fairly insignificant, unless you are one of those 14,000 people.

> TO CLEAN YOUR FRESH COMMERCIAL PRODUCE. For those people who do not have easy access to organic produce, which is grown without pesticide use, peeling or washing produce is mandatory. For produce that you consume entirely, like broccoli and apples, soak it in a solution of one gallon of warm water per 2 tablespoons of vinegar for 5 minutes, then rinse and brush.

From tainted water, food and air; to exposure to carcinogens in the home and work place; to voluntary intake of poisons in drugs, alcohol and tobacco to showers of electromagnetic radiation falling on us-- Americans are constantly pushing the outer envelope for toxin tolerance. Too many of these common toxins both assault the fragile DNA and blunt immune functions. We need to be more responsible in dealing with our 20th century waste products. Cancer patients need to do everything possible to eliminate accumulated wastes and minimize intake of new toxins.

3) MALNUTRITION
MACRONUTRIENTS OF:
⇒ Carbohydrates (simple vs complex, glycemic index of foods, regulating prostaglandins through insulin & glucagon levels)
⇒ Fiber (soluble vs insoluble, adequate for regular bowel movements)
⇒ Fat: Useful include olive, canola, medium chain triglycerides, lecithin, fish oil, flax, borage, evening primrose, black current, hemp. Unhealthy fats include: too much fat (40% kcal vs 20%), hydrogenated, saturated, oxidized.
⇒ Protein: Proper quantity and quality necessary. Lean and clean protein found in chicken, fish, turkey, and beans. Vegetarians must match grains with legumes for complementary amino acids to create a high quality (biological value) protein.
⇒ Water. 2/3 of our body is water. Must consume high quality clean water throughout the day to improve hydration.
MICRONUTRIENTS OF:
⇒ Vitamins
⇒ Minerals
⇒ Ultra trace minerals
⇒ Minor dietary constituents (i.e., lycopenes from tomato, allicin from garlic, sulforaphane from cabbage)
⇒ Conditionally essential nutrients (i.e., Coenzyme Q-10, taurine, arginine, EPA).

> **Too much, too little, or an imbalance of any nutrient leads to malnutrition. Most malnutrition in US is via the cumulative effects of long term sub-clinical deficiencies.**

JUICING VERSUS PUREEING. Some of the earlier efforts at treating cancer with nutrition involved diets high in vegetables with regular fruit and vegetable juices offered throughout the day. Juicing has its advantages, because one glass of carrot juice is equal to about a pound of carrots, which few of us could eat. Unfortunately, much of the valuable anti-cancer nutrients in the vegetables get tossed out with the pulp that is discarded. That is why I recommend a complete liquification of the vegetable or fruit rather than just extracting juice from it. Vitamix (800-848-2649) is a unique blender device which keeps all the valuable nutrients in while allowing you to consume more vegetables in a liquid form. There are 10 times more cancer fighting agents in pureed whole vegetables than in juice extracted from vegetable pulp.

DR. QUILLIN'S ULTIMATE HEALTH TIPS

1) Eat God's food, not mankind's.
2) Maintain a healthy gut environment through fiber, fluid, and probiotics.
3) Take balanced supplements in addition to, rather than instead of, good eating.
4) Minimize fat, sweets, salt, and alcohol.
5) Exercise & eat to leanness--pinch an inch.
6) Drink lots of clean water.
7) Emphasize *vegetables, *whole grains, and *legumes with some lean fish & poultry, fruit, & nuts.
8) Tolerance--90% good food, 10% others.
9) Detoxify--cleanse the body & avoid poisons.
10) Live, love, laugh, learn, forgive, sing praises, & seek peace.

>The KISS (keep it simple, student) method of optimal nutrition.
     -Go natural. Eat foods in as close to their natural state as possible. Refining food often adds questionable agents (like food additives, salt, sugar and fat), removes valuable nutrients (like vitamins, minerals, and fiber) and always raises the cost of the food.
     -Expand your horizons. Eat a wide variety of foods. By not focusing on any particular food, you can obtain nutrients that may be essential but are poorly understood while also avoiding a buildup of any substance that could create food allergies or toxicities.

-Nibbling is better. Eat small frequent meals. Nibbling is better than gorging. Our ancestors "grazed" throughout the day. Only with the advent of the industrial age did we begin the punctual eating of large meals. Nibbling helps to stabilize blood sugar levels and minimize insulin rushes; therefore has been linked to a lowered risk for heart disease, diabetes, obesity and mood swings.

-Avoid problem foods. Minimize your intake of unhealthy foods which are high in fat, salt, sugar, cholesterol, caffeine, alcohol, processed lunch meats and most additives.

-Seek out nutrient-dense foods. Maximize your intake of life-giving foods, including fresh vegetables, whole grains, legumes, fruit, low fat meat (turkey, fish, chicken) and clean water. Low fat dairy products, especially yogurt, can be valuable if you do not have milk allergies or lactose intolerance.

-Monitor your quality of weight, rather than quantity of weight. Balance your calorie intake with expenditure so that your percentage of body fat is reasonable. Pinch the skinfold just above the hipbone. If this skin is more than an inch in thickness, then you may need to begin rational efforts to lose weight. Obesity is a major factor in cancer. For a more exact way to track your percent body fat, use the Futrex (phone 800-545-1950), a device based on research done at the United States Department of Agriculture. This device measures the thickness of fatty tissue in the biceps region, which is most representative of total body fat. How much you weigh is not nearly as crucial as the percent of fat in the body. Of all the controversies that plague the nutrition field, one issue that all nutritionists will agree on is to eat less fat in your diet and store less fat in your body.

-Eat enough protein. Cancer is a serious wasting disease. I have counseled far too many cancer patients who looked like war camp victims, having lost 25% or more of their body weight due to insufficient protein intake. Take in 1 to 2 grams of protein for each kilogram of body weight. Example: 150 pound patient. Divide 150 pounds by 2.2 to find 68 kilograms, multiply times 1 to 2, yields 68 to 136 grams of protein daily is needed to generate a healthy immune system. While a protein excess can have some harmful side effects, a protein deficiency is disastrous for the cancer patient.

-Use supplements in addition to, rather than instead of, good food. Get your nutrients with a fork and spoon. Do not place undo reliance on pills and powders to provide optimal nourishment. Supplements providing micronutrients (vitamins and minerals) cannot reverse the major influence of foods providing macronutrients (carbohydrate, fat, protein, fiber, water). Foods are top priority in your battle plan against cancer.

-Shop the perimeter of grocery store. On the outside of your grocery store you will find fresh fruits, vegetables, bread, fish, chicken and dairy. Once you venture into the deep dark interior of the grocery store, nutritional quality of the foods goes way down and prices go way up. Organic produce is raised without pesticides and may be valuable in helping cancer patients. However, organic produce is unavailable or unaffordable for many people. Don't get terribly concerned about having to consume organic produce. Any produce that cannot be peeled (like watermelon or bananas) should be soaked for 5 minutes in a solution of one gallon lukewarm clean water with 2 tablespoons of vinegar

-If a food will not rot or sprout, then don't buy it or throw it out. Your body cells have similar biochemical needs to a bacteria or yeast cell. Foods that have a shelf life of a millenia are not going to nourish the body. Think about it: if bacteria is not interested in your food, then what makes you think that your body cells are interested? Foods that cannot begin (sprouting) or sustain (bacterial growth) life elsewhere, will have a similar effect in your body.

-Dishes should be easy to clean. Foods that are hard to digest or unhealthy will probably leave a mess on plates and pots. Dairy curd, such as fondue, is both difficult to clean and very difficult for your stomach to process. Same thing with fried, greasy or burned foods.

>**Essential nutrient pyramid.**
We need to recognize the priority placed on essential nutrients. We can live weeks without food, a few days without water and only a few minutes without oxygen. Keep in mind the relative importance of these essential nutrients.

HIERARCHY OF NUTRIENT NEEDS

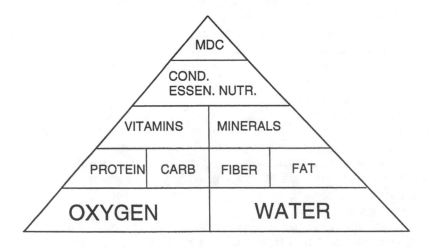

Oxygen and water form the basis of human life. Make sure that your quality and quantity of intake pay homage to this fact. Protein, carbohydrate, fiber and fat form the next level of importance. Vitamins and minerals are the essential micronutrients required for health.

Above these essential substances are two levels of quasi (meaning "as if it were") nutrients. Conditionally essential nutrients include Coenzyme-Q10, carnitine, EPA and GLA (fatty acids) and much more. Some people may require these nutrients in the diet during certain stressful phases of their lives. Minor dietary constituents (MDCs) include a wide variety of plant compounds that have shown remarkable anti-cancer abilities. Indoles in the cabbage family, lycopenes in tomatoes, allicin in garlic, immune stimulants in sea vegetables and others make up this new and exciting category. Eating a wide variety of unprocessed plant foods will help to insure adequate intake of these quasi-nutrients.

Can Nutrients Reverse the Cancer Process?

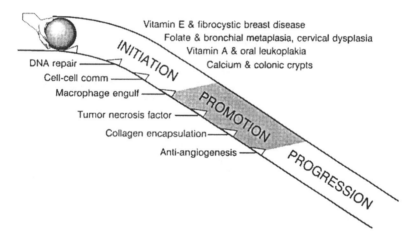

4) EXERCISE.

Humans evolved as active creatures. Our biochemical processes depend on regular exercise to maintain homeostasis. A well respected Stanford physician, Dr. William Bortz, published a review of the scientific literature on exercise and concluded: "our dis-eases may be from dis-use of the body."[9] Cancer patients who exercise have fewer side effects from oncology therapy. Exercise oxygenates the tissue, which slows the anaerobic cancer cell progress. Exercise stabilizes blood sugar levels, which selectively deprives cancer cells of their favorite fuel. Even if exercise is not a possibility for the cancer patient, deep breathing would be invaluable. The most essential nutrient in the human body is oxygen. Sheldon Hendler, MD, PhD has written an excellent book on the need for oxygenation of tissue in THE OXYGEN BREAKTHROUGH.[10] Westerners typically are sedentary and breath shallowly, which deprives the body of oxygen, which is a perfect environment for cancer.

Exercise is an absolutely essential ingredient for health. A primary tool for detoxification, stabilizing blood glucose levels, improving digestion and regularity, proper oxygenation of tissue, stress tolerance, improving hormone output (i.e. growth hormone & DHEA), burning fatty tissue, eliminating harmful by-products (i.e., estrogen, uric acid).

5) BLOOD GLUCOSE

The literature clearly points toward a substantial increase in glucose metabolism with the onset of cancer. Sugar has a number of ways in which it promotes cancer:

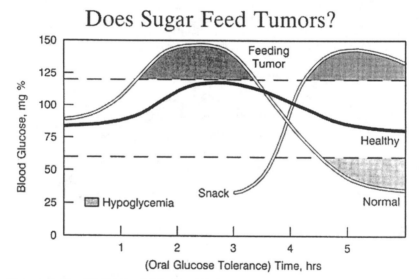

Does Sugar Feed Tumors?

Source: Rothkopf M, Nutrition Vol 6, #4, p 145, Aug 1990 supplement

1) Rises in blood glucose generate corresponding rises of insulin, which then pushes prostaglandin production toward the immune-suppressing and stickiness-enhancing PGE-2. While fish oil (EPA) and borage oil (GLA) have a favorable impact on cancer, these potent fatty acids are neutralized when the blood glucose levels are kept high. Refer back to the prostaglandin chart earlier in this chapter.

2) Cancer cells feed directly on blood glucose, like a fermenting yeast organism. Elevating blood glucose in a cancer patient is like throwing gasoline on a smoldering fire.

3) Elevating blood glucose levels suppresses the immune system
The average American consumes 20% of calories from refined white sugar, which is more of a drug than a food.

BLOOD GLUCOSE REGULATION
GLYCEMIC INDEX OF FOODS: prostaglandins

▲BEST: fats (oils, avocado, nuts, seeds) protein (chicken, fish)

BETTER:vegetables, legumes, dairy

GOOD: complex carbs (whole grains)

POOR: simple & refined carbs (sugars, fruits, juicing)

REGULATE BLOOD SUGAR TO SLOW CANCER GROWTH

>There is a long-standing well-accepted link between elevated insulin levels and risk of cancer.[11]

>Cancer cells demonstrate a 3 to 5 fold increase in glucose uptake compared to healthy cells.[12]

>Cancer thrives on glucose while also initiating gluconeogenesis and insulin resistance.[13] Lipid based parenteral solutions for cancer patients slow cancer growth.

>Modest ingestion of glucose (75 gm) caused a measurable decline in cell-mediated immunity in 7 healthy human volunteers. Mechanism of action is probably via elevated insulin, which competes with mitogens for binding sites on lymphocytes.[14]

>In animal studies, progressive increase in sucrose in the diet leads to a dose-dependent decline in antibody production.[15]

>Healthy human volunteers ingested 100 gram portions (average US daily intake) of simple carbohydrates from glucose, fructose, sucrose (white sugar), honey, and orange juice. While simple sugars signficantly impaired the capacity of neutrophils to engulf bacteria, starch ingestion did not have this effect.[16]

>In a study comparing 50 colorectal cancer patients to healthy matched controls, the cancer patients ate considerably more sugar and fat than the healthy people.[17]

>An epidemiological study of 21 countries suggests that high sugar intake is a major risk factor toward breast cancer.[18]

>Animals were fed isocaloric diets of carbohydrates. The group eating more sugar developed significantly more mammary tumors than the starch-fed group.[19]

>SOLUTION: Eat less sweet foods. Never eat anything sweet by itself. Choose fructose, honey, molasses, sucanat & colorful fresh fruit. Exercise, stress, alcohol and drug intake all relate to maintenance of healthy blood glucose.

6) REDOX

Life is a continuous balancing act between oxidative forces (pro-oxidants) and protective forces (antioxidants). We want to fully oxygenate the tissue, which generates pro-oxidants, but we also want to protect healthy tissue from excess oxidative destruction, using anti-oxidants. Anti-oxidants are a sacrificial substance, to be destroyed in lieu of body tissue. Anti-oxidants include beta-carotene, C, E, selenium, zinc, riboflavin, manganese, cysteine, methionine, N-acetylcysteine, and many herbal extracts (i.e. green tea, pycnogenols, curcumin).

Tumor tissue does not absorb anti-oxidants as effectively as healthy host tissue. Hence loading the patient with therapeutic levels of anti-oxidants is like giving the good cells bullet proof vests before you go in with a SWAT unit that opens fire (chemo and radiation), thus killing more cancer cells than healthy cells. Some recent research shows that the destruction of tumor tissue that occurs with administration of EPA fish oil is because the tumor cells do not have normal protection against the oxidation of fats. These highly polyunsaturated fats are like grenades going off in cancer cells, but have minimum impact on healthy cells which are able to protect themselves with fat soluble anti-oxidants, like vitamin E and CoQ.

>SOLUTION: Use an appropriate mix of mixed antioxidants along with adequate breathing and oxygenation of cells for optimal redox levels to fight cancer.

7) IMMUNE DYSFUNCTIONS

We have an extensive network of protective factors that circulate throughout our bodies to kill any bacteria, virus, yeast or cancer cells. Think of these 20 trillion immune cells as both your Department of Defense and your waste disposal company. The immune system of the average American is "running on empty". Causes for this problem include toxic burden, stress, no exercise, poor diet, unbridled use of antibiotics and vaccinations, innoculations from world travelers, and less breast feeding.

Most experts now agree to the "surveillance" theory of cancer. Cells in your body are duplicating all day every day at a blinding pace. This process of growth is fraught with peril. When cells are not copied exactly as they should be, then an emergency call goes out to the immune system to find and destroy this abnormal saboteur cell. This process occurs frequently in most people throughout their lives. Fortunately, only one in three people will actually develop detectable cancer, yet most experts agree that everyone gets cancer about 6 times per lifetime. It is the surveillance of an alert and capable immune system that defends most of us from cancer.

In the cancer patient, for a variety of reasons, the immune system has not done its work.

The immune system can be <u>shut down</u> by:
-toxic metals, like lead, cadmium and mercury
-volatile organic chemicals, from agriculture and industry
-sugar
-omega-6 fats, like soy and corn oil
-stress and worry, and more.
The immune system can also be <u>enhanced</u> by:
-vitamins, like A, beta-carotene, C, E, and B-6
-quasi-vitamins, like Coenzyme Q-10, EPA and GLA (special fats)
-minerals, like zinc, chromium, and selenium
-amino acids, like arginine and glutathione
-herbal extracts, like echinecea, ginseng, Pau D'arco, and astragalus
-nutrient factors, like yogurt, garlic, cabbage, enzymes and fresh green leafy vegetables.
-positive emotions, like love, forgiveness and creative visualization

We are going to bolster your immune army with improved:
-quantity by producing more Natural Killers cells, tumor necrosis factor, lymphocytes, interleukin and interferon.
-quality by
1) reducing the ability of cancer cells to hide from the immune system. A healthy immune system will attack and destroy any cells that do not have the "secret pass code" of host DNA. Both the fetus and cancer are able to survive by creating a hormone, HCG, which

allows the fetus to hide from the immune system. Tumor necrosis factor (TNF), which is specifically made by the immune system to kill cancer cells, is like a sword. TNF-inhibitor is produced in the presence of HCG and is like putting a sheath on the sword. Digestive enzymes and vitamins E and A help to clear away the deceiving "Stealth" coating on the tumor and improve tumor recognition by the immune system.

      2) providing anti-oxidants. We can put special shielding on the immune soldiers so that when they douse a cancer cell with deadly chemicals, the immune soldier is protected and can go on to kill other cancer cells. Otherwise, you seriously restrict the "bag limit" of any given immune soldier.

OUR HEALTH CARE "ARMAGEDDON"

IMMUNE DISORDERS	CAUSED BY
cancer	poor diet
bacterial infections	stress
(drug resistance)	toxins
allergies	innoculations
auto-immune	world travel
lupus, MS, arthritis	less breast feed.
AIDS	excess antibiotics
ebola, level 6 contagion	
	= 1/2 IMMUNITY.

>**Deal with your allergies**.

      If nutrition itself is a controversial subject, then allergies represent controversy to the cubed power. From 25% to 50% of the population suffer from allergies, which can come from foods that we eat (ingestant), air particles that we breath (inhalant) or substances on our skin (contact). Allergies can cause an amazing array of diseases, including immune problems, arthritis, diabetes, heart disease, mental illness and more. The reason allergies are so complicated to detect and treat is the limitless combinations of chemicals in the human body. You might react to wheat products only if you consume citrus at the same meal and are under stress. Otherwise, wheat may not create any problems. Some people have transient food allergies, that come and go along with the pollen seasons. Because of this trend, some allergists subscribe to the "rain barrel" theory, in which you only have allergic reactions when the rain barrel is overflowing, such as combined allergies with stress.

Allergies are generated by an over-reactive immune system. What happens is that small undigested particles (polypeptides and peptides) of food pass through the intestinal wall into the blood stream and are recognized by the immune system as an invading bacteria (since its DNA is not yours). Now, you may be thinking that an over-reactive immune system should help to fight cancer, yet the immunoglobulins that instigate allergies will depress the production of cancer-killing immune factors, like natural killer cells and tumor necrosis factor. Allergies create an imbalanced immune system. Correct the allergies and you can re-establish a balanced and vigorous immune attack on the cancer.

Detecting and correcting allergies is a challenge at the Sherlock Holmes level. There are many methods designed to determine allergies, including radio-allergo-sorbent test (RAST), skin patch, dietary food challenge and sub-lingual testing. Most accurate diagnostic tests for allergies require a blood sample to be sent to either Serammune Labs for the ELISA/ACT test (800-553-5472) or ImmunoLaboratories Elisa test (800-231-9197) or ALCAT (800-881-AMTL).

Another way to relieve and/or detect allergic reactions is to use the Ultra-Clear program distributed by Metagenics (800-692-9400) or its generic equivalent ProCleanse from Progressive Labs (800-527-9512). This product is composed of rice protein (hypoallergenic) coupled with vitamins, minerals and amino acids to help the body eliminate toxins. For the full program, you consume this powdered protein drink as your only food for 21 days. Once you have allowed your allergic reactions to subside on this diet, then you can detect the offending substances by methodically re-introducing foods to your diet. Once you determine what foods or inhalants that you are allergic to, then it requires diligence to avoid that substance for at least 2 weeks while you reset the switch on the immune system. Allergic reactions can be:

-Type I. Immediate reaction of less than 2 hours. It is estimated that less than 15% of all food allergies are of this easily-detected type.

-Type 2. Delayed cytotoxic reaction which may require days to develop into subtle and internal symptoms. It is estimated that 75% of food allergies involve this category of cell destruction. The ELISA/ACT test detects type 2 delayed reactions.

-Type 3. Immune complex mediated reactions. In this reaction, a "wrestling match" goes on between the antigen (offending factor) and antibody (immune factor trying to protect the body) which can easily slip through the permeable blood vessels due to large amounts of histamine release.

-Type 4. T cell dependent reactions. Within 36-72 hours after exposure to the offending substance, inflammation is produced by stimulating T-cells.

Allergies are common, complex to diagnose, difficult to treat and closely related to a variety of diseases, including cancer. A primitive and not terribly accurate way to find allergies involves the hypoallergenic diet. For 4 days, eat nothing but rice, apples, carrots, pears, lamb, turkey, olive and black tea. If you find relief from any particular symptoms, then add back a new food every four days and record the results. The most common allergenic foods are milk, wheat, beef, eggs, corn, peanut, soybeans, chicken, fish, nuts, mollusks and shellfish. Outside of humans, no other creature on earth consumes milk after weaning. Only 11-20% of Americans breast feed, which helps explain why the most allergenic food in the world is cow's milk.

Detecting and treating food allergies is a real challenge. I have found that any or all of the following can blunt allergic reactions: alfalfa (3-6 tablets daily), bee pollen (2-4 tablets daily), L-histidine (1000-1500 mg) and vitamin C (2-20 grams) .

8) GLAND OR ORGAN INSUFFICIENCY

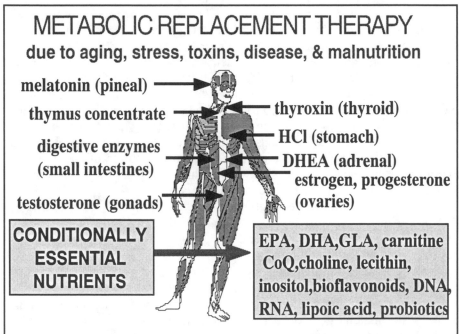

As we age, many glands and organs produce less vital hormones and secretions.
* Stomach (hydrochloric acid)
* Pancreas (digestive enzymes)
* Thyroid (thyroxin)
* Adrenals (DHEA, cortisol)
* Thymus (thymic extract)

* Spleen (spleen concentrate)
* Joints (glucosamine sulfate)
* Pineal (melatonin)
* Pituitary (growth hormone).

Replacing missing secretions often dramatically improves health.
>**Thyroid check**.

The second most common malnutritive condition in the world, after protein-calorie, is iodine deficiency, with about 400 million people suffering this condition. The mineral iodine feeds the thyroid gland, a small walnut-shaped gland in the throat region that produces a mere one teaspoon of thyroxin annually. But that thimble-full of thyroxin can make a huge difference in whether you will be bright or dull, fat or lean, healthy or sick, energetic or always tired. Like other organs, when the thyroid gland is deprived of its needed nutrients, it becomes enlarged. There are some regions of the world, particularly inland and mountainous areas, where iodine deficiency (goiter) is so common that the few people who do not have goiter are called "bottlenecks" for their abnormally slim necks. While the United States has made progress against goiter by adding iodine to salt, there are unsettling results from studies showing that about 33% of children consuming with seemingly adequate iodine intake still have goiter.[20]

What does all this have to do with cancer? There is compelling evidence that low thyroid output substantially elevates the risk for cancer.[21] Based upon the groundbreaking work by Broda Barnes, MD, PhD from 1930 through 1980, it is clear that about 40% of the population suffers from chronic hypothyroidism. Dr. Barnes earned his doctorate in physiology and medical degree from the University of Chicago. His primary interest was the thyroid gland. He found that people with a basal temperature of less than 97.8 F. were probably suffering from low thyroid. Symptoms include coldness; easy weight gain; constipation; sexual dysfunctions of infertility, frigidity, heavy periods, regular miscarriages or impotence; elevated serum lipids to induce heart disease; mental confusion and depression; hypoglycemia and diabetes; and cancer. This may sound like an improbable grocery list of diseases that can all stem from one simple cause. But realize that the thyroid gland regulates energy metabolism throughout the body, which is the basis for all other functions.

Work with your physician on this issue. Blood tests for thyroid function are not valid indicators of thyroid problems. Body temperature is the best way to detect hypothyroidism. Take your temperature first thing in the morning before getting out of bed. If your temperature is below 97.8 F., then you may have a problem that can be easily resolved. Dessicated thyroid supplements are inexpensive and non-toxic. For some people, raw thyroid (Premier Labs, available from U.S. Health 800-935-8743), ginseng, kelp, homeopathic preparations for stimulating thyroid function, exercise, chromium picolinate, L-carnitine and/or medium chain triglycerides (MCT) will slowly bring thyroid function up to normal. People who consume kelp, or sea vegetables, often have healthier thyroid functions, which indicates that sea vegetables or kelp tablets should be consumed by cancer patients. Here is another area of "simple solutions for major problems".

9) MALDIGESTION

After a lifetime of high fat, high sugar, overeating, too much alcohol, stress, drugs, indigestible foods (i.e., pizza); many Americans have poor peristalsis, insufficient stomach and intestinal secretions, damaged microvilli, imbalances of friendly (probiotic) vs unfriendly (anaerobic, pathogenic) bacteria. One must remove, repair, replace, re-inoculate. Food separation (combinations) may be of value for a brief time until the GI tract recuperates. Digestive enzymes and/or hydrochloric acid taken with meals may help.

As many people mature, they can lose their ability to produce hydrochloric acid in the stomach (hypochlorhydria), or digestive enzymes in the intestines (pancreatic insufficiency), or their intestines become inhabited by hostile bacteria (dysbiosis), or their intestines become more permeable to food particles which causes allergies to surface.

Charles Farr, MD, PhD has been a pioneer in many areas of comprehensive health care, including nutrition and computer diet analysis. Dr. Farr has noticed that humans seem to slide into an "involutional malnutrition", meaning a retrograde or degenerative change in health. The beginning of the problems may stem from low output of stomach acid or pancreatic enzymes, which leads to poor digestion. Also, pathogens can now survive the less hostile GI tract for absorption into the bloodstream. Since the cancer patient has a compromised immune system that is not firing on all cylinders, this problem leaves the patient open to infections, called opportunistic infections, which can only gain a foothold in that person when their host defenses are down. Among the key host defense mechanisms against infections are mucous, saliva, acid and enzymes that guard the GI tract.

To determine the health of the digestive tract, you will probably need the help of a holistically oriented physician. There are diagnostic companies, like Metametrix (800-221-4640) or Great Smokies Lab (800-522-4762), that are skilled at detecting the problem in a compromised GI tract. If you cannot find professional help, then here are some tips to help you determine if you have a problem with digestion. If your GI tract is working well, then you should have:

-a sensation of stomach emptying about 30-60 minutes after a meal.

-no excessive gas or discomfort.

-daily soft bowel movements that do not have greasy appearance or terribly offensive odor.

-bowel movements that do not have undigested food matter within.

If you do not have this "ideal" GI tract, then read on.

1) Hypochlorhydria. If you have a sense of stomach fullness for more than 30 minutes after eating, then you may be suffering from insufficient hydrochloric acid flow. To test this hypothesis, take 2

DEATH BEGINS IN THE COLON
Eli Metchnikoff, Nobel laureate 1908

WHY IT HAPPENS	WHAT IT CAUSES	HOW TO FIX IT
less breast feeding	change in colon pH	i.e. garden
high sugar, fat diet	putrefactive microorg.	1) cleanse
alcohol, drugs	parasites	enemas
antibiotics	yeast	2) re-acidify
too much meat	virus	whey wash
low whey intake	by-products	3) implant
whole grains (FOS)	living decay	human lact.
less fiber		4) maintenance
toxins		FOS, wh.gr.
		whey, diet

---

capsules of betaine hydrochloride (derived from beets), available at most health food stores, with your meal. If this therapy improves symptoms, then hypochlorhydria was indeed your problem. If this does not improve symptoms, then add 1 more pill with each meal until you get to five pills. If you have heartburn, then decrease dosage next time. If you find no relief, then discontinue altogether.

2) Pancreatic insufficiency. If you have cramps, heartburn or your food appears relatively undigested or greasy in the stools, then you may not be making enough digestive enzymes to break down your food. For enzyme replacement therapy, use digestive enzymes from Enzymatic Therapy (800-558-7372), called BioZyme. You may need 2-3 pills with each meal. If symptoms improve, then you may need to continue this therapy for the foreseeable future.

3) Parasites. Most of us have intestinal parasites. In some of us, these worms and bacteria are causing serious harm to the lining of the intestinal tract, such as a permeable gut which allows allergies to form. Our ancestors developed many de-worming techniques that they used seasonally, such as fasting while consuming purgative herbs or regular

flushing out with garlic. In order to confirm if you have a problem, you must send a stool sample to a lab (Metametrix, Great Smokies) capable of detecting the myriad of microorganisms that inhabit the GI tract.

10) CHRONIC INFECTIONS.

Candida albicans is very common in women, especially people who eat much sugar. Intestinal parasites and even liver flukes are common in the US. Use garlic, iodine, wormwood, walnut shell extract, cloves, and other purgatives with caution as vermifuge. The book, THE CURE FOR ALL CANCER by Hulda Clarke, ND, PhD is a wildly optimistic book that does not cure all cancer, but focuses solely on the elimination of liver flukes (parasites) from the body and isopropyl alcohol from the diet. These factors are among the many underlying causes of cancer, but not the only cause or even the most common cause. I have worked with many of the patients who failed therapy on THE CURE FOR ALL CANCER. This factor is only one small piece of the puzzle that causes cancer.

11) pH (potential hydrogens)

Acid alkaline balance (7.41 ideal in human veins) brought about by:
♦ proper breathing
♦ exercise (carbonic buffer from carbon dioxide in blood)
♦ diet (plant foods elevate pH, animal foods and sugar reduce pH)
♦ water (adequate hydration improves pH).
♦ other agents, such as cesium chloride, citric acid, sodium bicarbonate
Cancer is acidic (low pH) tissue.[22] It is clear from all human physiology textbooks that pH in the blood, saliva, urine and other areas is a critical factor for health. Blood pH is usually 7.35-7.45 with 7.41 thought to be ideal. Acceptable pH for saliva is 6.0-7.5, stomach 1.0-3.5, colon 5.0-8.4 and urine 4.5-8.4. Most foods influence pH--pushing toward either acid or alkaline. Clinicians will spend much time adjusting parenteral feedings to achieve a proper pH in the blood. Meanwhile, there have been many alternative health books that attempt to treat various diseases by adjusting the body pH via the diet.

Potential hydrogens, or pH, refers to the acid or alkaline nature of a chemical. If you mix a mild acid, like vinegar, with a mild alkaline substance, like baking soda, then the resulting reaction produces a salt-- they neutralize one another by exchanging hydrogens. Just about everything that goes in your mouth can alter pH, including oxygen. The acidic pH of cancer cells also decreases the oxygen-carrying capacity of the surrounding blood so that tissue can become somewhat anaerobic-- which are perfect conditions for cancer to thrive. Deep breathing has an alkalizing effect on the blood. An alkalizing diet of lots of plant food also helps to encourage removal of toxic heavy metals.

The macrobiotic book claims that pH adjustment is one of the more crucial objectives of their diet.[23] Yet, I have worked with a few cancer patients who got worse on the macrobiotic program. Remember our discussion of biochemical individuality--not everyone will thrive on the same diet. Nick Gonzales, MD sometimes uses a diet high in red meat to adjust the cancer patient's pH into a normal range. It appears that some people are prone toward extreme acid or alkaline metabolism. For these people on the edge of acceptable biological pH, diet provides a counterbalance to bring serum pH back toward normal. Think of sailing a small boat where you may have to use your body as a counterbalance to prevent the boat from being tipped over by the wind. If your metabolism is in jeopardy of "tipping over" toward extreme pH, then diet and breathing become your counterbalances that keep metabolism upright.

While this area may be absolutely essential for some cancer patients, a trial and error method may be the only way to find out which direction your pH needs adjusting. If your condition improves on the macrobiotic program, then you are pushing your pH in the right direction. If your condition worsens on the macrobiotic program, then you must push your pH in the opposite direction.

About 8% of the population must have acid forming foods to counterbalance their extremely alkalotic pH. Some people can eat anything they want and their internal mechanisms compensate to find an acceptable pH. For many people, an alkalizing diet (toward the left) will help to neutralize their acidifying tendencies, which can invite cancer.

Venous pH is the most accurate indicator of your overall body pH. Yet blood tests are invasive, expensive and not practical for regular use. A rough indicator of your body pH is your saliva and urinary pH. You can purchase Nitrazine paper from your local druggist and follow the directions for measuring saliva or urine pH. Test your saliva at least one hour after any food or drink. If your saliva is strongly acidic, then you may need to emphasize this part of my program.

12) HYPOXIA

Humans are aerobic organisms. All cells thrive when there is proper oxygenation to the tissue. Red blood cell production is dependent on iron, copper, B-6, folate, B-12, protein, & zinc. Adequate exercise and proper breathing help. Cofactors, like CoQ, B-vitamins improve aerobic energy metabolism in cell mitochondria. Fatty acids in diet dictate "membrane fluidity" of all cells and ability to absorb oxygen.

One of the most prominent differences between healthy cells and cancer cells is that cancer is an anaerobic cell, fermenting rather than metabolizing food and living in the absence of oxygen. Professor Otto Warburg received two Nobel prizes, in 1931 and 1944 for his work on cell bioenergetics, or how the cell extracts energy from food. In 1966, Professor Warburg spoke to a group of Nobel laureates regarding his work on cancer cells: "...the prime cause of cancer is the replacement of the respiration of oxygen in normal body cells by a fermentation of sugar."

Cancer cells are more like primitive yeast cells, extracting only a fraction of the potention energy from sugar by fermenting food substrates down to lactic acid.

This singular difference is both the strength and weakness of cancer. Cancer slowly destroys its host by using up fuel inefficiently and thus causing lean tissue wasting, in which the patient begins to convert protein to sugar in order to maintain a certain level of blood sugar. Cancer also hides in its oxygen deficit pockets. The denser and more anaerobic the tumor mass, the more resistant the tumor is to radiation therapy.

Aerobic-enhancing   nutrients. Yet, by oxygenating the tissue, you can exploit the "Achilles heel" of cancer. Cancer shrinks from oxygen like a vampire shrinking from daylight. Fuel is burned in the cellular furnaces, called mitochondria. As long as the mitochondrial membrane is fluid and permeable, oxygen flows in and carbon dioxide flows out and the cell stays aerobic. With a diet high in fat, saturated fat and cholesterol; the mitochondrial membrane becomes more rigid and less permeable to the flow of gases and electrons, which are essential to aerobic metabolism.

Nutrient factors that heavily influence aerobic metabolism include the B-vitamins, including biotin, B-1 thiamin, B-2 riboflavin and B-3 niacin. Numerous herbal extracts, including ginseng and ginkgo biloba, can enhance the aerobic capacity of the cell. Coenzyme Q-10 is a nutrient that is the rate-limiting step in aerobic metabolism, not unlike the bridge that ties up traffic going into the city during rush hour. Most people are low in their levels CoQ.

Breathing is a lost art in our modern world. Ancient scholars and spiritual teachers taught us that breath is the essence of life. Modern Americans breathe shallowly, or try the military breathing stance with chest thrust out and stomach sucked in--all of which leaves the tissue oxygen-starved. Proper breathing should include stomach and diaphragm deep breathing. Lay flat on your back on the floor. Place a book on your stomach. Begin inhaling through the nose and push out the stomach. Raise the book as high as you can, then complete inhalation by filling the chest with air. Exhale through the mouth slowly. This is diaphragm breathing, which more thoroughly oxygenates tissue and can be done by the most bed-ridden patient.

In another effort to oxygenate tissue, some physicians have been using hydrogen peroxide therapy given intravenously for cancer, AIDS, chronic fatigue and allergy patients. For more information on physicians in your area who can administer this safe and potentially helpful therapy, contact the International Oxidative Medical Association in Oklahoma City at 405-634-7855.

13) EFFECTS OF AGING.

By age 65, the average American has eaten 100,000 lb (50 tons) of food. Poor diet accumulates in chronic sub-clinical malnutrition; such as calcium & osteoporosis, chromium & diabetes, vitamin E & heart disease, vitamin C and cancer. Toxins accumulate in fatty tissue and liver. Chronic exposure to unchecked pro-oxidants eventually creates arthritis, Alzheimer's, heart disease, stroke, cancer, etc. Organ reserve is used up in stress and poor diet. The Hayflick principle tells us that we have 55 cell divisions maximum in a lifetime. Once your "bank account" is empty, it is difficult to recover from serious disease. Errors in DNA replication become more common as we age. Telomeres become shortened. The risk for cancer doubles with every 5 years of age. Although only 12% of US is over 65 yrs, 67% of US cancer patients are over 65. Gland/organ insufficiencies can be partially compensated. Ill health consequences of aging may be slowed down.

14) PHYSICAL ALIGNMENT

Spinal vertebrae must be in proper alignment. Chiropractic & osteopathic manipulations on spine, joints, skull plates can be helpful.

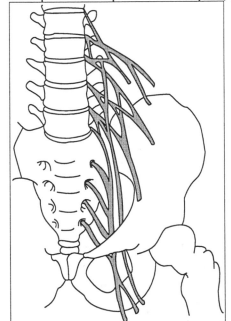

Accidents, poor muscle tone, and aging create alignment problems. Nerves and blood vessels radiate from the spinal column (see drawing), which can become misaligned and cause compression on these vital channels of energy. Exercise, inversion and physical manipulations from chiropractic or osteopathic physicians may solve these problems.

15) ENERGY ALIGNMENT

Meridians, shakras, and energy pathways were discovered by acupuncturists. Use magnets, acupuncture, electro-acupuncture, and acupressure to correct these problems. Homeopathy probably works on this level.

16) MECHANICAL INJURY

Chronic injury requires hyperplasia, or the growth of new cells. If not properly nourished, new cell growth can become erratic and error-prone, leading to arthritis, cancer, & Alzheimers.

CONQUERED BREAST CANCER

G.R. is a 48 year old female diagnosed in October of 1995 with advanced breast cancer. After her bilateral radical mastectomy, doctors discovered 14 positive lymph nodes. Prognosis: less than 2 years to live, even with medical therapy. Patient began 6 rounds of chemo in her home town. Became violently ill. "Camped out in the bathroom" with nausea and vomitting. In June of 1996, went to another hospital where she refused chemo, but received 6 weeks of radiation therapy twice daily to the chest and underarm lymph nodes that were positive. At same time began an aggressive nutrition program including lean and clean meat (elk, deer, fish), lots of vegetables and water, abundant prayer, and a wide assortment of nutrition supplements. As of July 1996, she was considered "disease free". Began taking combined nutrition supplements in September of 1996. As of January 1998, she continues to be healthy with no disease detectable and excellent quality of life. She offers these words of encouragement to anyone facing advanced cancer: "You need to have a determination and a will to live. Fight the cancer."

ENDNOTES

[1]. Selye, H, STRESS WITHOUT DISTRESS, JB Lippincott, NY, 1974
[2]. Newell, GR, Primary Care in Cancer, p.29, May 1991
[3]. Achterberg, J., IMAGERY IN HEALING, New Science, Boston, 1985
[4]. Cooper, CL (ed.), STRESS AND BREAST CANCER, John Wiley, NY, 1988
[5]. National Cancer Institute, NCI# NO1-CN-45133, National Institute of Health, Washington, DC 1977
[6]. Achterberg, J, IMAGERY IN HEALING, New Science Library, Boston, 1985, p. 177
[7]. Quillin, P, SAFE EATING, M. Evans, NY, 1990
[8]. Huggins, HA, IT'S ALL IN YOUR HEAD, Life Sciences Press, Colorado Springs, 1989
[9]. Bortz, WM, Journal American Medical Association, vol.248, no.10, p.1203, Sept.10, 1982
[10]. Hendler, SS, THE OXYGEN BREAKTHROUGH, Simon & Schuster, NY, 1989
[11]. Yam, D, Medical Hypothesis, vol.38, p.111, 1992
[12]. Demetrakopoulos, GE, et al., Cancer Research, vol.42, p.756S, Feb.1982
[13]. Rossi-Fanelli, F., et al., Journal Parenteral and Enteral Nutrition, vol.15, p.680, 1991
[14]. Bernstein, J., et al., American Journal Clinical Nutrition, vol.30, p.613, 1977
[15]. Nalder, BN, et al., Journal Nutrition, Apr.1972
[16]. Sanchez, A., et al., American Journal Clinical Nutrition, vol.26, p.180, 1973
[17]. Bristol, JB, et al., Proceedings American Association of Cancer Research, vol.26, p.206, Mar.1985
[18]. Horrobin, DF, Medical Hypotheses, vol.11, no.3, p.319, 1983
[19]. Hoehn, SK, et al., Nutrition & Cancer, vol.1, no.3, p.27, Spring 1979
[20]. Ziporyn, T., Journal American Medical Association, vol.253, p.1846, Apr.1985
[21]. Langer, SE, et al., SOLVED: THE RIDDLE OF ILLNESS, Keats, New Canaan, 1984
[22]. Newell, K, et al., Proceedings of National Academy of Sciences, vol.90, no.3, p.1127, Feb.1993
[23]. Aihara, H., ACID & ALKALINE, Macrobiotic Foundation, Oroville, CA, 1971

Chapter 13

RATIONAL CANCER TREATMENT

IF I HAD CANCER,
WHAT WOULD I DO?

FAMOUS EXPERT OPINION: "Space travel is utter bilge." Sir Richard vander Riet Wooley, renowned and knighted British scientist, 1956

I would use an appropriate combination of:

1) restrained cytotoxic therapies to reduce tumor burden

2) an aggressive collection of naturopathic (cell restorative) therapies to bolster host defense mechanisms.

The combination of changing the underlying conditions that brought on the cancer (naturopathic) and attacking the cancer with therapies that kill cancer but do not harm the host (cytotoxic) can be incredibly effective.

Chemotherapy, radiation and surgery may be appropriate in certain cancers and for certain people. But make sure that the physician understands the concept of "restrained" medical therapies against cancer. I have worked with cancer patients who were devastated by unrestrained chemo, radiation or surgery.

If you threw a hand grenade into your garage to get rid of the mice, then you may have accomplished to goal of killing the mice, but you don't have a garage anymore. Similarly, too many cancer patients are exposed to "maximum sub-lethal" therapies which may provide an initial "response" or tumor shrinkage, but in the end may reduce the quality and quantity of life for the cancer patient by suppressing immune functions, damaging the heart and kidneys and creating a tumor that is "drug resistant", or virtually bullet-proof.

There are other cancer therapies that may be more effective at killing cancer and less toxic to the cancer patients, such as Cell Specific

Cancer Therapy, Ukrain, Govallo's vaccine and others. See the referral agencies listed in the Appendix for more information on your options in cancer treatment.

RATIONAL CANCER TREATMENT
synergism between naturopathy & restrained allopathy

NATUROPATHY/cell restorative	ALLOPATHIC/cytotoxic
nutrients (essential & non-essential)	Cell Specific Cancer Therapy
oxygenation (exercise/breathing)	hydrazine sulfate (cachexia)
detoxification	Coley's toxins
psycho-neuroimmunology	ImmunoAugmentive Therapy
hormonal/glandular balancing	cesium chloride
probiotic establishment	laetrile/amygdalin
digestive improvements	clodronate
magnets/energy medicine/chakras	IV proteolytic enzymes
spinal & cranial subluxation	surgery or brachytherapy
homeopathy	Ukrain
massage therapy	Govallo's vaccine
botanicals (Essiac, Iscador)	Tributyrate/antineoplastons

PATIENT PROFILE: BEAT ENDSTAGE TUBERCULOSIS

Galen Clark went to Yosemite Valley to die of endstage tuberculosis. He was 42 years of age that fall of 1856. His doctor told him that coughing up chunks of his lungs meant he had up to 6 months to live. The first thing that Clark did was to carve his own tombstone, thus accepting his mortality, a ritual that would give us all a better appreciation of our finite time on earth. Next Galen Clark started eating what was available in Yosemite in those days, which means clean and lean wild game, nuts, berries, vegetables, etc. Thus, he made a quantum improvement in his diet. He then began doing what he wanted to do, hiking and creating trails, in the place he treasured the most, Yosemite Valley. He didn't die 6 months later, but rather 54 years later, just shy of his 96th birthday. Having bolstered his "host defense mechanisms" with good thoughts and good nutrition, he overcame an untreatable disease that was the number one cause of death in those days. Maybe you can do the same, if you are suffering with cancer.

Chapter 14

BEATING CANCER SYMPTOMS

"What cancer cannot do: It cannot cripple love, or shatter hope, or corrode faith, or destroy peace, or kill friendship, or suppress memories, or silence courage, or invade the soul, or steal eternal life, or conquer the Spirit." anonymous, from Ann Landers column

For many cancer patients, the side effects can be worse than facing a life-threatening disease. This concise guide may help to minimize many of the complications from cancer or the cytotoxic treatment. My humble gratitude to Marge Affleck, RN and Rebecca Wright, RD for their invaluable assistance in completing this chapter.

PATIENT PROFILE: MIND OVER NUTRIENTS

S.H. was a cute 33 year old Colorado farmer's wife and mother of 2 small children when she was diagnosed with breast cancer in the spring of 1992. She had a radical bilaterial mastectomy along with chemo and radiation at her nearby hospital. The cancer metastasized to her internal organs, liver and bone and she was told to "get her affairs in order." She failed therapy at an alternative clinic in Mexico. She came to a hospital that I worked at in such advanced state of disease that our doctors did not expect her to live 2 months. She began the nutrition program, coupled with detoxification, psycho-spiritual counseling, fractionated chemotherapy and radiation. In two months, she not only wasn't dead, she was off her pain medication. In 6 months, her hair had grown back, her disease was markedly diminished and she was having an excellent quality of life. After 14 months, the cancer has been reduced to tiny shadows on her CAT scans. By then, her husband thought she had beat the disease, and he had been supporting her throughout her 3 year battle with cancer. But he decided that he had enough, and he left her. And one month later, she died of coronary arrest, quite possibly a "broken heart." We need to pay homage to the importance and the majesty of our human spirit. A truckload of vitamins will not help a cancer patient who is suffering from a broken or troubled spirit.

	ALLOPATHIC RX	NATUROPATHIC RX
NAUSEA	Zofran, Compazine	enzymes, ginger, acupressure wrist band, acupuncture
VOMITING	Phenergan, Tigan	suck on ice cubes, yogurt, ginger tea or caps, ginger ale, acupuncture
ANOREXIA	Megace, Marinol	enzymes, small meals, ginger, dining with others, zinc, B vitamins
MALNUTRITION	TPN, Advera, Impact	hydrazine sulfate, Dragon slayer shake, enzymes, high protein meals
DIARRHEA	Lomotil, Imodium, Questran	milk enemas, Pepto Bismal, acupuncture, psyllium
MALDIGESTION	enzymes, Hcl, Pancrease	enzymes, probiotics, enemas, betaine HCl, ginger, mustard
CONSTIPATION	Senacote, Milk Magnesia, Mag Citrate, glycerin suppositories	probiotics, sena, buckthorn, cascara sagrada, epsom salts, high fiber
GAS	Phyzeme, Propulsid, Reglan, Zantac	enzymes (such as Beano), avoid beans & nuts, probiotics, soil based organisms, walking
ANEMIA	Epogen	liquid liver extract, B-12, chelated iron in small amounts, folate, copper, beet juice, shark liver oil
LEUKOPENIA	Newpogen	ImmunoPower, PCM4, bovine cartilage, garlic, ginseng, shark liver oil, echinecea, vit. C, E, A, betacarotene, selenium, zinc, magnesium, colloidal silver, astragalus, colostrum, golden seal, ginkgo, etc.
HAIR LOSS		1600 iu vit.E 1-2 weeks prior to beginning chemo, aloe, vit.D ointment
FATIGUE	Megace, antidepressants, i.e. Prozac	B vit., bee pollen, chromium, DHEA except for hormonal cancers, caffeine from tea, high protein diet
ORAL MUCOSITIS	Mylanta or Maalox, or Zylocaine with Benadryl	vit.E oil from capsule topically applied 3x daily with cotton swab
CANDIDA INFECTIONS	Diflucan, Vitrex, Nystatin	Australian tea tree oil topical in mouth region, garlic, undecylinic acid, caprylic acid, probiotics
DEPRESSION	Prozac, etc.	St. John's wort, sunlight, ginkgo, DHEA except for hormonal cancers
ANXIETY	Xanax, Ativan	hops, valerian, kava, homeopathic, 5HTP
INSOMNIA	Ambien, Xanax	melatonin, 5HTP
PAIN	Tylenol to morphine	acupuncture, biofeedback, hypnosis

Chapter 15

PARTING COMMENTS

"Unless we put medical freedom into the Constitution, the time
will come when medicine will organize itself into an undercover
dictatorship...To restrict the art of healing to one class of men
and deny equal privileges to others will constitute the Bastille of
medical science." Dr. Benjamin Rush, signer of the Declaration
of Independence

The "war on cancer" is far from over. We have spent an
extraordinary amount of money researching therapies that
hold little promise in preventing or curing cancer. Much
of our problem lies in our misconception about cancer: that blasting it out
of the system is more appropriate than changing the underlying causes of
the condition. That test tube studies with chemo drugs have anything to
do with humanely curing a cancer patient.

While the scope of the book is to offer helpful advice on using
nutrition to improve outcome in cancer treatment, there are some
fundamental flaws in the structure of our health care system and
governmental surveillance that impair our ability to investigate and use
rational cancer treatments. In the state of California, chemotherapy,
radiation and surgery are the only LEGAL options for cancer patients.
Physicians have lost their licenses and even gone to jail for venturing
outside the narrow confines of this allopathic model for cancer. There
are 7 states in the U.S. that have passed an AMTA bill, or Access to
Medical Treatment Act, meaning the licensed health care professional
can offer whatever therapies the doctor and the patient agree to be
appropriate. Such freedom is desperately needed if we are to truly win the
war on cancer. I strongly encourage all Americans to voice your opinion
with your representative in state and federal legislatures regarding the
need for more freedom and options in cancer treatment. Why do cancer
patients have to leave the country or visit some "underground" clinic to
seek alternative cancer treatment. How can we possibly consider the

FDA protecting cancer patients when much of what is FDA approved is either ineffective or barbaric?

Other changes that would radically improve cancer treatment and cost effectiveness of cancer care in this country:

FIXING U.S. HEALTH CARE SYSTEM
less government, more market freedom

1) AMTA. Access to Medical Treatment Act. Therapists & patients free to chose.

2) Medical Savings Account. Make the patient a "better steward"of their health care dollars.

3) Outcomes data. Let the more effective, less expensive therapies be highlighted.

4) Health insurance risk assessment. Calculated actuarial grid for likelihood of payout, i.e. cars,fires, floods.

5) Fewer government subsidies (hospitals, diagnostic equipment), which distort market place supply & demand.

6) Triage: system of assigning priorities of medical treatment based on urgency & chance of survival

7) Allocating limited funds. 50% of Medicare, die in 6 months. Restart heart 95% die within 6 months.

PARTING COMMENTS

Congratulations on having read this far. You are already half way toward a recovery, given your obvious motivation and new grasp of options for improving your cancer outcome. You are the pro-active and assertive cancer victor. You have been through some or all of the phases that come with the disease: anger, denial, rejection, isolation, withdrawal, and more. While the bulk of this book is spent providing nutritional facts to change the biochemistry of your body, my final parting comments are directed more at your soul. Because cancer is a disease of the mind, body and spirit.

I believe that cancer is far more than an individual physical disease. Cancer is also a symptom of modern society that is organically unsound, that needs metabolic healing. In every era, we try to identify the outside enemy. But we have met the enemy--and it is us. Today we wage full scale chemical warfare on ourselves with potent agricultural and industrial carcinogens, while stripping our once benevolent food supply of any vestige of nutritional value. We are subjected to intolerable stress from work and dissolving family structures, thousands of murders per year on TV and movies, and an endless procession of gut-wrenching stories on the nightly news.

This book is written for you, the cancer patient and soon-to-be victor. But it goes one step further. Since you are reading this section, we can safely assume that you have a mission on earth that is not yet accomplished. Once you beat your own person cancer, you may find a strong sense of purpose in spreading what you have learned or even addressing the "cancers" in society.

From my cancer patients I have learned of the incredible tenacity of the human body and spirit; of the immeasurable dignity and generosity that is waiting to be expressed by all of us; of the undying passion and commitment shown by a dedicated mate when a loved one is failing; and above all-of the preciousness of life. In our increasingly callous world, it is easy to drift away from the true pleasures in life: love, enthusiasm, laughter, freedom, meaningful work, skills developed, helping one another and savoring the beauty in this emerald paradise planet. For many people, cancer has become the ultimate "truth serum" in helping them to establish real priorities.

Nourish your body, mind and spirit. Take every opportunity to say: "I love you." Give away smiles with wreckless abandon. Practice random acts of kindness and beauty. Savor each day as though it may be your last, because the same holds true for all of us. You have the opportunity to be born again with a renewed vigor and purpose in life.

My prayer for you is the same thought that began this book; that you will soon be able to say: "Cancer is the best thing that ever happened to me." Since you have cancer, you might as well turn this ultimate challenge into the ultimate victory: to make your life into a masterpiece painting.

PATIENT PROFILE: SPIRIT OVER NUTRIENTS

H.G. was a fun-loving, guy who loved cigarettes, lots of wine and a good laugh. He developed prostate cancer with bone metastasis while in his mid 50s. His doctor said: "Get your affairs in order." H.G. went to a psycho-neuroimmunology clinic to help him use his mind as a healing tool in his advanced untreatable cancer. He felt that he had been burdened with an endless procession of responsibilities, from high school to the Marines, to a profession, family and more. He wanted to be free of all of this. He left his wife and his cancer went into remission. Meanwhile, his wife, B.G. was a non-smoker, drank very little, hiked, was in good shape, and ate a very good diet. One year after H.G. left her, B.G. developed advanced brain cancer and died within 6 weeks of diagnosis. Nutrition is an important factor in cancer outcome. But as a nutritionist, I must admit that what's eating you is at least as important as what you are eating. Feed your mind good thoughts. Feed your heart good feelings. Feed your body the right nutrients. And you will recover from this disease.

APPENDIX
✸
REFERRAL AGENCIES FOR CANCER TREATMENT & OTHER USEFUL INFORMATION

You just received the diagnosis of cancer and your whole world started spinning. There are many emotions that surface after such a diagnosis: why me?, anger, self-pity, stunned silence, depression and much more. All of these emotions are okay. Once you have surfaced from the depths of these emotions, your best strategy is to first get educated. But where do you start? There is so much information out there today! It has been said that getting information in today's information age is "like trying to get a drink from a fire hydrant". Maybe so.

But the following agencies can help to reduce the volume, complexity and confusion of the information available on your particular cancer. I strongly encourage everyone to get a second and third opinion before taking steps that are irreversible, such as surgery, chemotherapy and radiation. As I said at the beginning of this book, the best way for you to beat cancer is to first develop a sense of "can do"; others before you have beaten your form of cancer. Secondly, get educated. The following groups can be of great assistance. They charge for their services, but provide a rational and balanced analysis of the therapies that have demonstrated some effectiveness in your cancer.

INFORMATION SERVICES

-The Health Resource, 209 Katherine Drive, Conway, AR 72032, (501) 329-5272
-CanHelp, 3111 Paradise Bay Rd., Port Ludlow, WA 98365, (206) 437-2291, FAX (206) 437-2272
-People Against Cancer, P.O. Box 10, Otho, IO 50569, (515) 972-4444
-Center for Advancement in Cancer Education, P.O. Box 215, 200 East Lancaster Ave., Wynnewood, PA 19096, (215) 642-4810
-World Research Foundation, 15300 Ventura Blvd., Suite 405, Sherman Oaks, CA 91403, (818) 907-5483
-INTERNET USERS: www.healthy.com or www.onhealth.com

Some of the following charge fees for their services, which include providing information on a wide range of unconventional cancer therapies. You should ask at the outset what the total fees are. The value of each service may depend on what you are looking for. Some services run computer searches, and others do in-person or over-the-telephone consultations.

-The Arlin J. Brown Information Center, Inc., P.O. Box 251, Fort Belvoir, VA 22060, (703) 752-9511

-Cancer Control Society, 2043 North Berendo St., Los Angeles, CA 90027, (213) 663-7801

-Cancer Federation, P.O. Box 52109, Riverside, CA 92517, (714) 682-7989

-Center for Advancement in Cancer Education, P.O. Box 215, 200 East Lancaster Ave., Wynnewood, PA 19096, (215) 642-4810

-Foundation for Advancement in Cancer Therapy (FACT), P.O. Box 1242, Old Chelsea Station, New York, NY 10113, (212) 741-2790

-International Health Information Institute, 14417 Chase St., Suite 432, Panorama City, CA 91402

-International Holistic Center, Inc., P.O. Box 15103, Phoenix, AZ 85060, (602) 957-3322

-DATIC Health Resources, Inc. (Diagnostic Aides Therapeutic Information Computerized), Apt. 114, 1075 Bernard Ave., Kelowna, British Columbia V1Y 6P7, Canada, (604) 862-3228 or P.O. Box 218, Chilliwack, British Columbia V5P 6J1, Canada, (604) 792-7175

-National Health Federation, 212 West Foothill Blvd., P.O. Box 688, Monrovia, CA 91016, (818) 357-2181

-National Self-Help Clearinghouse, 25 West 43rd St., Room 620, New York, NY 10036

-Nutrition Education Association, Inc., 3647 Glen Haven, Houston, TX 77025, (713) 665-2946

-Patient Advocates for Advanced Cancer Treatments, Inc. (PAACT), 1143 Parmelee NW, Grand Rapids, MI 49504, (616) 453-1477

-Planetree Health Resource Center, 2040, Webster St., San Francisco, CA 94115, (415) 923-3680

REFERRALS ON ALTERNATIVE TREATMENTS

-American Assoc. of Orthomolecular Medicine, 7375 Kingsway, Burnaby, British Columbia, V3N3B5 Canada

-American College of Advancement in Medicine, 231 Verdugo Drive, Suite 204, Laguna Hills, CA 92653, Ph# 714-583-7666

-Arlin J. Brown Information Center, PO Box 251, Ft. Belvoir, VA 22060, Ph#703-451-8638

-Cancer Control Society, 2043 N. Berendo St., Los Angeles, CA 90027, Ph# 213-663-7801

-Comm. for Freedom of Choice in Medicine, 1180 Walnut Av., Chula Vista, CA 92011, Ph# 800-227-4473/Fax: 619-429-8004

-European Institute for Orthomolecular Sciences, PO Box 420, 3740 A.K., Baarn, Holland

-Found. for Advancement in Cancer Therapy, Box 1242, Old Chelsea Sta., New York, NY 10113, Fax: 212-741-2790
-Gerson Institute, PO Box 430, Bonita, CA 91908, Ph# 619-267-1150/Fax: 619-267-6441
-Intl. Academy of Nutrition and Preventive Medicine, PO Box 18433, Asheville, NC 28814, Ph# 704-258-3243/Fax: 704-251-9206
-Intl. Assn. of Cancer Victors & Friends, 7740 W. Manchester Ave., No.110, Playa del Rey, CA 90293, Ph#213-822-5032/Fax: 213-822-5132
-We Can Do!, 1800 Augusta, Ste.150, Houston, TX 77057, Ph# 713-780-1057

MIND & BODY CONNECTION: READING LIST
General
-Dossey, L., Meaning & Medicine, New York, Bantam, 1991
-Anderson, G., The Cancer Conquerer, Kansas City, Andrews & McMeel, 1988
-LeShan, L., Cancer as a Turning Point
Forgiveness
-Casarjian, R., Forgiveness: A Bold Choice for a Peaceful Heart, New York, Bantam, 1992
Healing
-Borysenko, J., Minding the Body, Mending the Mind, New York, Bantam, 1987
-Simonton, O.C., & Henson, R., The Healing Journey, New York, Bantam, 1992
-Myss, C., Why People Don't Heal and How They Can, Harmony, NY 1997
-Moyers, B., Healing the Mind, New York, Bantam Doubleday, 1993
Thought, Attitude, and Negativity
-Benson, H., Your Maximum Mind: Changing Your Life by Changing the Way You Think, New York, Random House, 1987
-Cousins, N., Head First: The Biology of Hope, New York, E.P. Dutton, 1989
-Martorano, J.T. & Kildahl, J., Beyond Negative Thinking: Reclaiming Your Life Through Optimism, New York, Avon, 1989
-Pennebaker, J.W., Opening Up: The Healing Power of Confiding in Others, New York, Avon Books, 1990
-Seligman, M.E.P., Learned Optimism: How to Change Your Mind and Your Life, New York, Pocket Books, 1990
Spirituality
-Borysenko, J., Fire in the Soul, New York, Warner, 1993

NUTRIENTS HAVE A PROFOUND IMPACT
ON THE IMMUNE SYSTEM

There is an abundance of scientific documentation linking nutrient intake with immune quality and quantity. This is a very crucial issue for the cancer patient.

Many nutrients taken orally can provide pharmacological changes in immune function in humans. Protein, arginine, glutamine, omega-6 and omega-3 fats, iron, zinc, vitamins E, C, and A have all been proven to modulate immune functions.[1]

Vitamin A deficiency causes reduced lymphocyte response to antigens and mitogens, while beta-carotene supplements stimulate immune responses.[2]

There is extensive literature supporting the importance of vitamin B-6 on the immune system. In one study, B-6 supplements (50 mg/day) provided a measurable improvement in immune functions (T3 and T4 lymphocytes) for 11 healthy well fed older adults.[3]

Various B vitamins have been linked to the proper functioning of antibody response and cellular immunity.

Folate deficiency decreases mitogenesis.

Deficiency of vitamin C impairs phagocyte functions and cellular immunity.

Vitamin E deficiency decreases antibody response to T-dependent antigens, all of which gets worse with the addition of a selenium deficiency. In test animals, normal vitamin E intake was not adequate to optimize immune functions.[4] Modest supplements of vitamin E have been shown to enhance the immune response.

While iron deficiency can blunt immune functions, iron excess can increase the risk for cancer.[5] Iron presents an interesting case; 1) because it is the most common nutritional problem world-wide, 2) because low levels of iron will depress the immune system, and 3) because high levels of iron will stimulate both bacterial and tumor growth. Iron intake needs to be well regulated...not too much, and not too little.

Zinc exerts a major influence on the immune system. Lymphocyte function is seriously depressed and lymphoid tissues undergo general atrophy in zinc-deficient individuals. The lymphocytes in zinc-deficient animals quickly lose their killing abilities (cytotoxicity) and engulfing talents (phagocytosis) for tumor cells and bacteria. Natural killer cell and neutrophil activity is also reduced. All of these compromised immune activities elevate the risk for cancer.

Copper plays a key role in the production of superoxide dismutase and cytochrome systems in the mitochondria. Hence, a deficiency of copper is manifested in a depressed immune system, specifically reduced microbicidal activity of granulocytes.

Selenium works in conjunction with vitamin E to shield host cells from lipid peroxidation. Humoral immune response is depressed in selenium deficient animals. Selenium and vitamin E deficiencies lead to increased incidence of enteric lesions. Lymphocyte proliferation is reduced in selenium deficiency. The theory is that selenium and vitamin E help to provide the host immune cells with some type of "bullet proof plating" against the toxins used on foreign cells. Hence, one immune body can live on to destroy many invaders if enough vitamin E and selenium allow for these critical chemical shields.

In magnesium deficiency, all immunoglobulins (except IgE) are reduced, along with the number of antibody forming cells. Magnesium is crucial for lymphocyte growth (involvement in protein metabolism) and transformation in response to mitogens. Prolonged magnesium deficiency in animals leads to the development of lymphomas and leukemia.

Iodine plays an important role in the microbicidal activity of polymorphonuclear leukocytes. Activated neutrophils may use the conversion of iodide to iodine to generate free radicals for killing foreign invaders.

Boron is an interesting trace mineral, since it is now recognized for its role in preventing osteoporosis, yet is still not considered an essential mineral. Boron deficiency in chicks creates immune abnormalities like arthritis.

Toxic trace minerals, like cadmium, arsenic and lead all blunt the immune system.

The quality and quantity of fat in the diet plays a major role in dictating the health of the immune system. A deficiency of the essential fatty acid (linoleic acid) will lead to atrophy of lymphoid tissue and a depressed antibody response. And yet excess intake of polyunsaturated fatty acids will also diminish T-cell immune responsiveness. Since fat directly affects prostaglandin pathways, and prostaglandins (depending on the pathway) can either depress or enhance immune function, fat intake is crucial in encouraging a healthy immune system. Oxidized cholesterol is highly immuno-suppressive. Cholesterol is less likely to oxidize while in the presence of anti-oxidants, like vitamin E, C, and beta-carotene.

-Alexander, JW, et.al., Nutritional immodulation in burn patients, Critical Care Medicine, voll.18, no.2, pg.149, 1990
-Alexander, JW, Nutrition and Infection, Archives of Surgery, vol.121, p.966, Aug.1986
-Alexander, JW., Nutrition and infection: new perspectives for an old problem, Archives of Surgery, vol.121, pg.966, 1986
-Baehner, RL, Autooxidation as a basis for altered function by polymorphonuclear Leukocytes, Blood, vol.50, no.2, p.327, Aug.1977
-Barone J, et.al., Dietary fat and natural-killer-cell activity, Americian Journal Clinical Nutrition, vol.50, no.4, pg.861, Oct.1989
-Beisel WR, Single nutrients and immunity, American Journal Clinical Nutrition, vol.35, (Suppl.), pg.417, 1982
-Beisel, WR, et al., Single-Nutrient effects on immunologic functions, Journal of the American Medical Association, vol.245, no. 1, p.53, Jan.2, 1981

-Beisel, WR, Single nutrients and immunity, American Journal Clinical Nutrition, vol.35, p.417, Feb. supp, 1982

-Beisel, WR, The history of nutritional immunology, Journal of Nutritional Immunology, vol.1(1), p.5, 1992

-Bendich, A., Anti-oxidant vitamins and immune responses, in NUTRITION AND IMMUNOLOGY, p.125, Liss, NY, 1988

-Bower, RH, Nutrition and immune function, Nutrition in Clinical Practice, vol.5, no.5, pg.189, 1990

-Bowman, TA, et.al., Vitamin A deficiency decreases natural killer cell activity and interfon production in rats, Journal Nutrition, vol.120, no.10, p.1264, Oct. 1990

-Carver, JD, et.al., Dietary nucleotide effects upon murine natural killer cell activity and macrophage activation, Journal of Parenteral and Enteral Nutrition, vol.14, no.1, pg.18, Jan.1990

-Cerra, FB, et.al., Effect of enteral nutrient on in vitro tests of immune function in ICU patients: a preliminary report, Nutrition, vol.6, no.1, pg.84, 1990

-Cerra, FB, Immune system modulation: nutritional and pharmacologic approaches, Critical Care Medicine, vol.18, no.2, Jan.1990

-Cerra, FB, Nutrient modulation of inflammatory and immune function, Americian Journal of Surgery, vol.161, p.230, Feb.1991

-Chandra RK, ed., Comtemporary issues in clinical nutrition, vol.11, NUTRITIONAL IMMUNOLOGY, New York, Alan R. Liss, Inc., 1988

-Chandra RK, Nutrition, immunity and outcome; past, present and future, Nutrition Research, vol.8, no.3, pg.225, 1988

-Chandra, RK, et.al., Effect of two feeding formulas on immune responses and mortality in mice challenged with listeria monoclytogenes, Immunology Letters, vol.27, pg.45, 1991

-Chandra, RK, Immunodeficiency in Undernutrition and Overnutrition, Nutrition Reviews, vol.39, no.6, pg.225, June 1981

-Chandra, RK, Nutrition and immunity-basic considerations. Part 1., Contemporary Nutrition, vol.11, no.11, 1986

-Chang, KJ, et.al., Comparison of the effect of lipoxygenase metabolites of arachidonic acid and eicosapentaenoic acid on human natural killer cell cytotoxicity, Prostaglandins Leukotrienes Essentially Fatty Acids, vol.38, no.2, pg.87, Nov.1989

-Chang, KJ, et.al., Role of 5-lipoxygenase products of arachidonic acid in cell-to-cell interaction between macrophages and natural killer cells in rat spleen, Journal Leucocyte Biology, vol.50, no.3, pg.273, Sept.1991

-Chang,l KJ, et.al., Effect of oral ingestion of eicosapentaenoic acid-ethyl ester on natural killer cell activity in rat spleen cells, Prostaglandins Leukotrienes Essential Fatty Acids, vol.37, no.1, pg.31, July 1989

-Chowdhury, BA, et.al., Effect of zinc administration on cadmium-induced suppression of natural killer cell activity in mice, Immunology Letters, vol.22, no.4, pg.287, Oct.1989

-Christou, N, Perioperative nutritional support: immunologic defects, Journal of Parenteral and Enteral Nutrition, vol.14, no.5, supp., Sept.1990

-Cifone, MG., et.al., In vivo cadmium treatment alters natural killer activity and large granular lymphocyte number in the rat, Immunopharmacology, vol.18,no.3, pg.149, Nov-Dec.1989

-Daly, JM, etl.al., Enteral nutrition with supplemental arginine, RNA and Omega-3 fatty acids: a prospective clinical trial, Journal of Parenteral and Enteral Nutrition, vol.15, no.1, pg19S, 1991

-Garre MA, et.al., Current concepts in immune derangement due to undernutrition, Journal of Parenteral and Enteral Nutrition, vol.11, no.3, pg.309, 1987

-Gershwin ME, et.al., NUTRITION AND IMMUNITY, Orlando, Academic Press, Inc., 1985

-Ghoneum, M., et.al., Suppression of murine natural killer cell activity by tributyltin: in vivo and in vitro assessment, Environmental Research, vol.52, no.2, p.178, Aug.1990

-Gottschlich MM, Differential effects of three enteral dietary regimens on selected outcome variables in burn patients, Journal of Parenteral and Enteral Nutrition, vol.14, no.3, pg.225, 1990

-Hallquist, NA, et.al., Maternal-iron-deficiency effects on peritoneal macrophage and peritoneal natural natural-killer-cell cytotoxicity in rat pups, Americian Journal Clinical Nutrition, vol.55, no.3, pg.741, March, 1992

-Halstead, BW, immune augmentation therapy, Journal International Academy Preventive Medicine, vol.9, no.1, pg.5, 1985

-Ilback, NG, Effects of methyl mercury exposure on spleen and blood natural killer (NK) cell activity in the mouse., Toxicocology, vol.25, no.1, pg.117, March 1991

-Immune system modulation: symposium on nutritional and pharmacologic approaches, Critical Care Medicine, vol.18, no.2, (S) pg.85, 1990

-Kafkewitz, D., et.al., Deficiency is immunosuppressive, American Journal Clinical Nutrition, vol.37, pg.1025, 1983

-Katz, DP, et.al., Enteral nutrition: potential role in regulating immune function, Current Opinion in Gastroenterology, vol.6, pg.199, 1990

-Kelly, Cathal, Immunosuppression in the surgical oncology patient, Nutrition and Immunology Digest, vol.1, no.2, 1991

-Kennes, B, et.al., Effect of vitamin C supplements on cell-mediated immunity in old people, Gerontology, vol.29, no.5, pg.305, 1983

-KINNEY, JM, et.al., NUTRITION AND METABOLISM IN PATIENT CARE,Philadelphia, W.B. Saunders Co., 1988

-Kulkarni, AD, etal., Influence of dietary glutamine and IMPACT, on in vivo cell-mediated immune response in mice, Nutrition, vol.6, no.1, pg.66, 1990

-Levy, JA., Nutrition and the immune system, in Stites DP et al., Basic and Clinical Immunology, 4th Edition, Los Altos, Ca., Lange Medical Publications, pg.297, 1982

-Lieberman, MD, Effects of nutrient substrates on immune function, Nutrition, vol.6, no.1, lpg.88, 1990

-Meadows GG,l et.al., Ethanol induces marked changes in lymphocyte populations and natural killer cell activity in mice, Alcohol Clinical Exp Research, vol.16, vol.3, p.47, June 1992

-Muzzioli, M., et.al., In vitro restoration by thymulin of NK activity of cells from old mice, International Journal of Immunopharmacol, vol.14, no.1, pg.57, Jan.1992

-Nair, MP, et.al., Immunoregulation of natural and lymphokine-activated killer cells by selenium, Immunopharmacology, vol.19, no.3, pg.177, May-June, 1990

-Nutrition and the immune response, Dairy Council Digest, vol.56, no.2, March-April, 1985

-Nuwayri-Salti, N., et.al., Immunologic and anti-immunosuppressive effects of vitamin A, Pharmacology, vol.30, no.4, pg.181, 1985

-Palombo, JD, et.al., (Collective Review), Endothelial cell factors and response to injury, Surgery, Gynecology & Obstetrics, Vol.173, p.505, Dec. 1991

-Petrie, HT, et.al., Selenium and the immune response: 2. Enhancement of murine cytotoxic T-lymphocyte and natural killer cell cytotoxicity in vivo, Journal Leucocyte Biology, vol.45, no.3, pg.215, March 1989

-Petrie, HT, Selenium and the immune response: 2. Enhancement of murine cytotoxic T-lymphocyte and natural killer cell cytotoxicity in vivo, Journal Leucocyte Biology, vol.45, no.3, p.215, March, 1989

-Randall, HT, Enteral nutrition: tube feeding in acute and chronic illness, Journal of Parenteral and Enteral Nutrition, vol.8, no.2, pg.113, 1984

-Reynolds, JV, The influence of protein malnutrition on T cell, natural killer cell, and lymphokine-activated killer cell function, and on biological responsiveness to high-dose interleukin-2, Cellular Immunology, vol.128, no.2, pg.569, July 1990

-Riley, ML, et.al., Failure of dietary restriction to influence natural killer activity in old rats, Mechanisms of Ageing and Development, vol.50, no.1, pg.81, Oct.1989

-Roth, JA, et.al., In vivo effect of ascorbic acid on neutrophil function in healthy and dexamethasone-treated cattle, American Journal Veterinary Research, vol.46, no.12, Dec., 1985

-Schlichter, LC, et.al., Interactive effects of Na and K in killing by human natural killer cells, Experimental Cell Research, vol.184, no.1, pg.99, Sep.1989

-Schriever, MM, et.al., Natural killer cells, vitamins, and other blood components ofvegetarian and omnivorous men, Nutrition Cancer, vol.12, no.3, p.271, 1989

-Spear, AT, et.al., Iron deficiency alters DMBA-induced tumor burden and natural killer cell cytotoxicity in rats, Journal Nutrition, vol.122, no.1, pg.46, Jan.1992

-Talbott, MC, et.al., Pyridoxine supplementation: effect on lymphocyte responses in elderly persons, Journal of Clinical Nutrition, vol.46, p659, 1987

-Update on Immunonutrition symposium, Nutrition, vol.6, no.1, pg.1, 1990

-Vijayaratnam, V., et.al., The effects of malnutrition on lymphoid tissues, Nutrition, vol.3, no.3, pg.213, 1987

-Wagner, PA, et.al., Zinc nutriture and cell-mediated immunity in the aged, International Journal Vitamin Nutrition Research, vol.53, no.1, pg.94, 1983

-Wan, JMF, et.al. Symposium on the interaction between nutrition and inflammation, Proceedings of the Nutrition Society, vol.48, p.315, 1989

-Watson, RR, Immunological enhancement by fat-soluble vitamins, minerals, and trace metals,Cancer Detection and Prevention, vol.9, p.67, 1986

-Wollschlager, C, et.al., A lipid, arginine and RNA supplemented enteral formula (IMPACT) alters airway colonization in intubated patients, Americian Review of Respiratory Diseases, 141:334A, 1990

-Yamashita, N. et.al., Effect of eicosapentaenoic and docosahexaenoic acid on natural killer cell activity in human peripherlal blood lymphocytes, Clinical Immunology Immunopathology, vol.59, lno.3, pg.335, June 1991

-Yirmiya, R., et.al., Ethanol increases tumor progression in rats: possible involvement of natural killer cells, Brain Behavior Immun, vol.6, no.1, pg.74, March 1992

ENDNOTES

[1]. Alexander, JW, et al., Critical Care Medicine, vol.18, p.S159, 1990

[2]. Rhodes, J., and Oliver, S., Immunology, vol.40, p.467, 1980

[3]. Talbott, MC, et al., American Journal of Clinical Nutrition, vol.46, p.659, 1987

[4]. Bendich, A., et al., Journal of Nutrition, vol.116, p.675, 1986

[5]. Cerutti, PA, Science, vol.227, p.375, 1985

APPENDIX

MAIL ORDER NUTRITION PRODUCTS

If you have a health food store nearby, then it would be a good idea to develop a relationship with a knowledgeable salesperson. If you do not have a health food store nearby, or do not have the time to shop, then the following companies can give you good service and value.

BULK FOODS

Organic produce sent overnight: Diamond Organics 800-922-2396

Allergy Resources Inc., 195 Huntington Beach Dr., Colorado Springs, CO 80921, ph 719-488-3630

Deer Valley Farm, RD#1, Guilford, NY 13780, ph. 607-674-8556

Diamond K Enterprises, Jack Kranz, R.R. 1, Box 30, St. Charles, MN 55972, ph. 507-932-4308

Gravelly Ridge Farms, Star Route 16, Elk Creek, CA 95939, ph. 916-963-3216

Green Earth, 2545 Prairie St., Evanston, IL 60201, ph. 800-322-3662

Healthfoods Express, 181 Sylmar Clovis, CA 93612, ph. 209-252-8321

Jaffe Bros. Inc., PO Box 636, Valley Center, CA 92082, ph. 619-749-1133

Macrobiotic Wholesale Co., 799 Old Leicester Hwy, Asheville, NC 28806, ph. 704-252-1221

Moksha Natural Foods, 724 Palm Ave., Watsonville, CA, 95076, ph. 408-724-2009

Mountain Ark Co., 120 South East Ave., Fayetteville, AR, 72701, ph. 501-442-7191, or 800-643-8909

New American Food Co., PO Box 3206, Durham, NC 27705, ph. 919-682-9210

Timber Crest Farms, 4791 Dry Creek, Healdsburg, CA, 95448, ph. 707-433-8251, FAX -8255

Walnut Acres, Walnut Acres Road, Penns Creek, PA 17862, ph. 717-837-0601

STORES THAT SELL VITAMINS, MINERALS, & HERBS

Bronson, 800-235-3200

NutriGuard, 800-433-2402

Health Center for Better Living, 813-566-2611

Vitamin Research Products, 800-877-2447

Vitamin Trader, 800-334-9310

Terrace International, 800-824-2434

U.S. Health Distributors, 800-935-8743, or 407-722-2900

Willner Chemists, 800-633-1106

STORES THAT SPECIALIZE IN SELLING HERBS

Gaia Herbals, 800-994-9355

Frontier Herbs 800-786-1388; fax 319-227-7966

Blessed Herbs 800-489-HERB; fax 508-882-3755

Trout Lake Farm 509-395-2025

San Francisco Herb Co. fax 800-227-5430

Star West 800-800-4372

APPENDIX

NUTRITION AND CANCER BOOKS

If you cannot obtain these books from your local book store, try the following mail order stores: Tattered Cover Bookstore, Denver, CO, 800-833-9327; or Mail Order Books 800-233-5150; or Discount Books 800-833-0702 or the Internet via www.amazon.com.

-Balch, JF, and Balch, PA, PRESCRIPTION FOR NUTRITIONAL HEALING, Avery Publ, Garden City, NY, 1990, ISBN 0-89529-429-x

-Bendich, A., and Chandra, RK, MICRONUTRIENTS AND IMMUNE FUNCTION, Annals of New York Academy of Sciences, vol.587, ISBN 0-89766-575-9

-Boik, J., CANCER & NATURAL MEDICINE, Oregon Medical Press, Princeton, MN, 1995, ISBN 0-9648280-0-6

-Cilento, R., HEAL CANCER, Hill Publishers, Melbourne, Australia, 1993, ISBN 0-85572-213-4

-Congress of United States, Office of Technology Assessment, UNCONVENTIONAL CANCER TREATMENTS, U.S. Government Printing Office, Washington, DC, 1990, GPO # 052-003-01208-1, (ph. 800-336-4797)

-Diamond, WJ, et al, DEFINITIVE GUIDE TO CANCER, Future Medicine, Tiburon, CA, 1997, ISBN 1-887299-01-7

-Jacobs, M., VITAMINS AND MINERALS IN THE PREVENTION AND TREATMENT OF CANCER, CRC Press, Boca Raton, FL, 1991, ISBN 0-8493-4259-7

-Kaminski, MV, HYPERALIMENTATION, Marcel Dekker Press, NY, 1985, ISBN 0-8247-7375-6

-Laidlaw, SA, and Swendseid, ME, VITAMINS AND CANCER PREVENTION, Wiley & Sons (ph.800-225-5945), 1991, ISBN 0-471-56066-9

-Machlin, LJ, HANDBOOK OF VITAMINS, Marcel Dekker, NY, 1991, ISBN 0-8247-8351-4

-Meyskens, FL, and Prasad, KN, MODULATION AND MEDIATION OF CANCER BY VITAMINS, S. Karger Publ., Basel, Switzerland, 1983, ISBN 3-8055-3526-0

-Meyskens, FL, and Prasad, KN, VITAMINS AND CANCER, Humana Press, Clifton, NJ, ISBN 0-89603-094-6
-National Academy of Sciences, DIET, NUTRITION, AND CANCER, National Academy Press (ph.800-624-6242), 1982, ISBN 0-309-03280-6
-Poirier, LA, et al., ESSENTIAL NUTRIENTS IN CARCINOGENESIS, Plenum Press, NY, 1986; ISBN 0-306-42471-1
-Prasad, KN, and Meyskens, ML, NUTRIENTS AND CANCER PREVENTION, Humana Press, Clifton, NJ, 1990, ISBN 0-89603-171-3
-Prasad, KN, VITAMINS AGAINST CANCER, Healing Arts Press, Rochester, VT, 1984, ISBN 0-89281-294
-Quillin, P and Williams, RM (eds), ADJUVANT NUTRITION IN CANCER TREATMENT, Cancer Treatment Research Foundation, Arlington Heights, IL, 1994, ISBN 0-9638263-0-1
-Quillin, P, BEATING CANCER WITH NUTRITION, Nutrition Times Press, Tulsa, OK 1994, ISBN 0-9638372-0-6
-Simone, CB, CANCER AND NUTRITION, Avery Publ., Garden City, NY, 1992, ISBN 0-89529-491-5
-U.S. Dept. Health & Human Services, SURGEON GENERAL'S REPORT ON NUTRITION AND HEALTH, U.S. Government Printing Office (ph. 800-336-4797), 1988, GPO # 017-011-00465-1
-Werbach, MR, NUTRITIONAL INFLUENCES ON ILLNESS, Third Line Press, Tarzana, CA, 1996, ISBN 0-9618550-5-3

GOOD NUTRITION REFERENCES:

Anderson, WELLNESS MEDICINE, Keats, 1987
Balch & Balch, PRESCRIPTION FOR NUTRITIONAL HEALING, Avery, 1993
Eaton, PALEOLITHIC PRESCRIPTION, Harper & Row, 1988
Grabowski, RJ, CURRENT NUTRITIONAL THERAPY, Image Press, 1993
Haas, STAYING HEALTHY WITH NUTRITION, Celestial, 1992
Hausman, THE RIGHT DOSE, Rodale, 1987
Hendler, DOCTOR'S VITAMIN AND MINERAL ENCYCLOPEDIA, Simon & Schuster,1990
Lieberman, S. et al., REAL VITAMIN & MINERAL BOOK, Avery, 1990
Murray, M, et al., ENCYCLOPEDIA OF NATURAL MEDICINE, Prima, 1990
National Research Council, RECOMMENDED DIETARY ALLOWANCES, Nat Academy, 1989
Price, NUTRITION AND PHYSICAL DEGENERATION, Keats, 1989
Quillin, P., HEALING NUTRIENTS, Random House, 1987
Shils, ME, et al., MODERN NUTRITION IN HEALTH & DISEASE, Lea & Febiger, 1994
Werbach, M, NUTRITIONAL INFLUENCES ON ILLNESS, Third Line, 1997

APPENDIX

NUTRITIONALLY-ORIENTED DOCTORS

PHYSICIANS WHO USE NUTRITION AS PART OF CANCER TREATMENT

ZIP CODE, NAME, CREDENTIALS, ADDRESS, CITY, STATE, PHONE, FAX

08648 Charles Simone MD, 123 Franklin Corner Rd, Lawrenceville, NJ 609-896-2646
10019 Emanuel Revici MD, 200 W. 57th St., #402, New York, NY 212-246-5122
10022 Robert Atkins MD, 152 E. 55th St. New York, NY 212-758-2110
10901 Michael Schachter MD, Two Executive Blvd, #202, Suffern NY 914-368-4700
23507 Vincent Speckhart MD, 902 Graydon Ave, #2, Norfolk, VA 804-622-0014
30342 Stephen Edelson MD, 3833 Roswell Rd #110, Atlanta, GA 404-841-0088
33133 Victor Marcial-Vega MD, 4037 Poinciana Av, Coconut Grove,FL 305-442-1233
60008 Jack Taylor DC, 3601 Algonquin Rd, #801, Rolling Meadows, IL 847-222-1192
60201 Keith Block MD, 1800 Sherman Ave, #515, Evanston, IL 847-492-3040
80303 Robert Rountree MD, 4150 Darley Ave, #1, Boulder, CO 303-499-9224
85712 Jesse Stoff MD, 2122 N Craycroft Rd, #112, Tucson, AZ 520-290-4516
89502 Douglas Brodie MD, 309 Kirman Ave, #2, Reno, NV 702-324-7071
89502 James Forsythe MD, 75 Pringle Way, #909, Reno, NV 702-826-9500
89502 John Diamond MD, 4600 Kietzke Ln, M-242, Reno, NV 702-829-2277
91910 Lawrence Taylor MD, 1000 Cordova Court, Chula Vista, CA 888-422-7434
92143 Ernesto Contreras MD, P.O. Box 43-9045, San Ysidro, CA 800-700-1850
92154 Geronimo Rubio MD, 555 Saturn Blvd,Bld B, M/S 432, San Diego,CA 619-267-1107
97209 Tori Hudson ND, 2067 NW Lovejoy, Portland, OR 503-222-2322
97214 Martin Milner ND, 1330 SE 39th Ave, Portland, OR 503-232-1100
98105 Patrick Donovan ND, 5312 Roosevelt Way NE, SeattleWA 206-525-8015
98199 Dan Labriola ND, P.O. Box 99157, Seattle, WA 206-285-4993
V8T 4E5 Abram Hoffer MD, 2727 Quadra, #3, Victoria, BC CANADA 250-386-8756
W1N1AA Etienne Callebout MD, 10 Harley St., London CANADA 44-171-467-8312

HEALTH CARE PROFESSIONALS WHO USE NUTRITION AS PART OF THEIR PRACTICE

01002, Amherst Family Health Ctr., 12 Dickinson St., Amherst, MA, ph. 413-253-2300, fax 256-0464
01060, Northampton Wellness Assoc., 52 Maplewood, Northampton, MA, ph. 413-584-7787, fax -7778
01370, Teri Kerr, RD, 304 Shelburne Center Rd., Shelburne Falls, MA, ph. 413-625-2745, -9619
01506, Robert F. Barnes, DO, 3489 E. Main Rd., Fredonia, NY, ph. 716-679-3510, fax -3512
01523, Maharishi Med Ctr., 679 George Hill Rd., Lancaster, MA, ph. 800-290-6702, fax 508-368-0674
01583, Thomas LaCava, MD, 360 W. Boylston St. #107, W Boylston, MA, ph. 508-854-1380, fax -1377
01583, Vera Jackson, MD, 360 W. Boylston St. #107, West Boylston, MA, ph. 508-854-1380
01852, Svetlana Kaufman, MD, 24 Merrimack St. #323, Lowell, MA, ph. 508-453-5181
01950, Barbara S. Silbert, DC, 172 State St. #1, Newburyport, MA, ph. 508-465-0929
02062, Comp Psychiatric Res, Inc., 49 Walpole St. #2, Norwood, MA, ph. 617-551-8181, 332-9936

02134, Commonwealth Chelation Ctr., 39 Brighton Ave., Allston, MA, ph. 617-254-2500, fax 783-1519
02134, Ruben Oganesov, MD, 39 Brighton Ave., Boston, MA, ph. 617-783-5783, fax, -1519
02140, Marino Ctr. for Health, 2500 Massachusetts Ave., Cambridge, MA, ph. 617-661-6225, fax -492-2002
02146, Judith K. Shabert, MD, 125 Rockwood St., Brookline, MA, ph. 617-738-0370
02161, Carol Englender, MD, 1126 Beacon St., Newton, MA, ph. 617-965-7770
02339, Richard Cohen, MD, 51 Mill St #1, Hanover, MA, 617-829-9281, fax -0904
02630, Center for Preventive Medicine, 275 Millway, Barnstable, MA, ph. 508-362-4343, fax -1525
02879, Peter Himmel, MD, 321 Main St., Wakefield, RI, ph. 401-783-6777, fax -6752
03038, Keith D. Jorgensen, MD, 44 Birch St. #304, Derry, NH, ph. 603-432-8104
03257-1999, Savely Yurkovsky, MD, 12 Newport Rd., New London, NH, ph. 603-526-2001
03264, Inst Naturopathic Health, 572 Tenney Mt. Hwy., Plymouth, NH, ph. 603-536-4888, fax 927-4309
03431, Michele C. Moore, MD, 103 Roxbury St. #302, Keene, NH, ph. 603-357-2180
03903, Dayton Haigney, MD, 46 Dow Hwy., Eliot, ME, ph. 207-384-2828
03908, Dayton Haigney, MD, 21 Liberty St., South Berwick, ME, ph. 207-384-2828
04096, Women to Women, One Pleasant St., Yarmouth, ME, ph. 207-846-6163
04281, Kenneth E. Hamilton, MD, PA, 52 High St., South Paris, ME, ph. 207-743-9295, fax -0540
04785, Joseph Cyr, MD, 47 Main St., Van Buren, ME, ph. 207-873-7721, fax -7724
04901, Arthur B. Weisser, DO, 184 Silver St., Waterville, ME, ph. 207-873-7721, -7724
05301, Grace Urological, Inc., 194 Canal St., Brattleboro, VT, 802-257-4265
05452, Charles Anderson, MD, 175 Pearl St., Essex Junction, VT, ph. 802-879-6544
06040, Optimum Health, 483 West Middle Turnpike #309, Manchester, CT, ph. 860-643-5101
06410, Central Connecticut Chiropractic, 391 Highland Ave. Rt. 10, Cheshire, CT, ph. 203-272-3239
06450, Meriden Chiropractic Group, 74 South Broad St., Meriden, CT, ph. 203-235-0171, fax 630-3611
06460, Harmony Health Care, 67 Cherry St. Harmony Pl., Milford, CT, ph. 203-877-1936, fax -2228
06470, Deep Brook Center, 46 West St., Newtown, CT, ph. 203-426-4553
06477, Mark A. Breiner, DDS, 325 Post Road #3A, Orange, CT, ph. 203-799-6353, fax 795-2749
06477, Robban Sica, MD, 325 Post Rd., Orange, CT, ph. 203-799-7733, fax -3650
06610, Tadeusz A. Skowron, MD, 50 Ridgefield Ave. #317, Bridgeport, CT, ph. 203-368-1450
06757, Kent Chiropractic Health Ctr., PC, 25 N Main St. #6, Kent, CT, ph. 860-927-4455, fax -4463
06790, Jerrold N . Finnie, MD, 333 Kennedy Dr., Torrington, CT, ph. 860-489-8977
06851, Ahmed N. Currim, 148 East Ave. #1L, Norwalk, CT, ph. 203-853-1339, fax -866-4616
06880, Marie A. DiPasquale, MD, 29 Old Hill Farms Rd., Westport, CT, ph. 203-226-1719
06880, Sidney M. Baker, MD, 40 Hillside Rd., Weston, CT, ph. 203-227-8444, fax -8443
06880, Thomas T. Brunoski, MD, 4 Ivy Knoll, Westport, CT, ph. 203-454-5963, fax 221-1522
07003, Majid Ali, MD, 320 Belleville Ave., Bloomfield, NJ, ph. 201-586-4111
07003, R. Russomanno, MD, 350 Bloomfield Ave. #1, Bloomfield, NJ, ph. 201-748-9330, fax -6985
07024, Gary Klingsberg, DO, 1355 15th St. #200, Fort Lee, NJ, ph. 201-585-9368
07041, James Neubrander, MD, 96 Millburn Ave. #200, Millburn, NJ, ph. 201-275-0234, fax -1646
07042, Plastic Surgery Ctr., Montclair, NJ, ph. 201-746-3535, fax -4385
07052, Faina Munits, MD, 51 Pleasant Valley Way, West Orange, NJ, ph. 201-736-3743
07055, Jose R. Sanchez-Pena, MD, 124 Gregory Ave. #201, Passaic, NJ, ph. 201-471-9800, fax -9240
07065, Dr.'s Choice, 1082 St. George Ave., Rahway, NJ, ph. 908-388-4787, fax -4380
07080, Mark Friedman, MD, PA, 2509 Park Ave. #2D, S. Plainfield, NJ, ph. 908-753-8622, fax -0141
07450, Constance Alfano, MD, 104 Chestnut, Ridgewood, NJ, ph. 201-444-4622
07470-3493, Homeopathy Ctr. of New Jersey, 746 Valley Rd., Wayne, NJ, ph. 201-694-7711
07512, Boro Chiropractic, 79 Union Boulevard, Totowa, NJ, ph. 201-904-0997, fax -9055
07601, Robin Leder, MD, 235 Prospect Ave., Hackensack, NJ, ph. 201-525-1155
07675, Joseph Spektor, MD, 54 Indian Dr., Woodcliff Lake, NJ, ph. 201-307-0633
07701, Family Chiro Ctr, 746 Sycamore Ave., Shrewsbury/Tinton Fa, NJ, ph. 908-530-0405, fax -4195
07702, David Dornfeld, DO, 167 Ave. at the Common #1, Shrewbury, NJ, ph. 908-389-6455, fax -6365
07702, Neil Rosen, DO, 167 Avenue at the Common #1, Shrewsbury, NJ, ph. 908-389-6455, fax -6365
07748, David Dornfeld, DO, 18 Leonardville Rd., Middletown, NJ ph. 908-671-3730, fax 706-1078
07748, Neil Rosen, DO, 18 Leonardville Rd., Middletown, NJ, ph. 908-671-3730, fax 706-1078
07840, Robert A. Siegel, MD, 2-B Doctors Park, Hackettstown, NJ, ph. 908-850-1810
07940, Howard C. Weiss, MD, 28 Walnut St., Madison, NJ, ph. 201-301-1770, fax -9445
07962, New Health Initiatives, 95 Mt. Kemble Ave., Morristown, NJ, ph. 973-971-4610, fax 290-7582
08003, Magaziner Medical Ctr., 1907 Greentree Rd., Cherry Hill, NJ, ph. 609-424-8222, fax -2599
08034, Brian Karlin, DO, 1916 Old Cuthbert Rd. #A-1, Cherry Hill, NJ, ph. 609-429-3335
08043, Lifeline Medical Ctr., 1600 S. Burntmill Rd., Voorhees, NJ, ph. 609-627-5600
08092, Robert D. Miller, DO, 196 Main St., West Creek, NJ, ph. 609-296-4643, fax -3393

08203, Michael J. Dunn, Jr., MD, Brigantine Town Ctr., Brigantine, NJ, ph. 609-266-2473
08225, Barry D. Glasser, MD, Rt. 9 & Mill Rd., Northfield, NJ, ph. 609-646-9600
08234, E.Andujar, MD, 3003 English Cr Ctr. #210, Egg Harbor Township, ph. 609-646-2900, fax -3436
08332, Charles H. Mintz, MD, 10 E. Broad St., Millville, NJ, ph. 609-825-7372, fax 327-6588
08502, Amwell Health Ctr., 450 Amwell Rd., Belle Mead, ph. 908-359-1775
08540, Leonid Magidenko, MD, 212 Commons Way #2, Princeton, NJ, ph. 609-921-1842, fax -6092
08540, Princeton Total Health, 212 Commons Way #2, Princeton, NJ, ph. 609-921-1842, fax -6092
08648, C. Simone, MD, 123 Franklin Corner Rd., Lawrenceville, NJ, ph. 609-896-2646, fax 883-7173
08701, Ivan Krohn, MD, 117 E. County Line Rd., Lakewood, NJ, ph. 908-367-2345, fax -2727
08753, Ivan Krohn, MD, 2008 Rt. 37 E #1, Toms River, NJ, ph. 908-506-9200
08816, P. Gilbert, DDS, 123 Dunhams Corner Rd, East Brunswick, NJ, ph. 732-754-7946, fax 254-0287
08837, C. Y. Lee, ME, 952 Amboy Ave., Edison, NJ, ph. 908-738-9220, fax -1187
08837, Dr. Richard B. Menashe, 15 S. Main St., Edison, NJ, ph. 732-906-8866, fax -0124
08837, Ralph Lev, MD, 15 S. Main St., Edison, NJ, ph. 908-738-9220, fax -1187
08854, Laurence Rubenstein, DO, 10 Plainfield Ave., Piscataway, NJ, ph. 908-469-1155, fax 457-9420
08873, Marc Condren, MD, 15 Cedar Grove Lane #20, Somerset, NJ, ph. 908-469-2133
08879, Center for Head & Facial Pain, 2045 Rt. 35 S., South Amboy, NJ, ph. 908-727-5000, fax -5497
10001, Sheila George, MD, 226 W. 26th St. 5th Floor, New York, NY, ph. 212-924-5900, fax -7600
10011, Scott Gerson, MD, 13 W. Ninth St., New York, NY, ph. 212-505-8971, fax 677-5397
10016, Michael Teplitsky, MD, 31 E. 28th St., New York, NY, ph. 212-679-3700, fax -9730
10016, Nancy Weiss, MD, 109 E. 36th St., New York, NY, ph. 212-683-8105
10016, Place for Achieving Total Health, 274 Madison Ave. #402, NY, NY, ph. 212-213-6155, fax -6188
10016, Robert Faylor, MD, 377 Park Ave. S. #33, New York, NY, ph. 212-679-6717, fax -6714
10016, Ronald Hoffman, MD, 40 E. 30th St. 10th Floor, New York, NY, ph. 212-779-1744, fax -0891
10019, Carol Goldstein, DC, 850 7th Ave. #602, New York, NY, ph. 212-489-9396, fax -8164
10019, Physicians For Complementary Med, 24 W. 57th St. #701, NY, NY, ph. 212-397-5900, fax -6054
10019, Robin Leder, MD, 159 W. 53rd St. #18-D, New York, NY, ph. 212-333-2626
10021, Jay Lombard, DO, 133 E. 73rd St., New York, NY, ph. 212-861-9000
10021, Leo Galland, MD, 133 E. 73rd St., New York, NY, ph. 212-861-9000
10021, Martin Feldman, MD, 132 E. 76th St., New York, NY, ph. 212-744-4413, fax 249-6155
10021, Richard N. Ash, MD, 860 Fifth Ave., New York, NY, ph. 212-628-3113, fax 249-3805
10021, Strang Cancer Prevention Ctr., 428 E. 72nd St., New York, NY, ph. 212-410-3820, fax 794-4958
10021, Tom Bolte, MD, 133 E. 73rd St., New York, NY, ph. 212-861-9000, fax 516-897-8386
10022, Frederick Mindel, DC, 133 E. 58th St. #505, New York, NY, ph. 212-223-8683, fax -8687
10022, Robert C. Atkins, MD, 152 E. 55th St., New York, NY, ph. 212-758-2110, fax 751-1863
10022, The Atkins Centre, 152 E. 55th St., New York, NY, ph. 212-758-2110, fax 755-2859
10023, Tristate Healing Ctr., 175 W. 72nd St., New York, NY, ph. 212-362-9544, fax 769-3566
10024, Edward S. Cheslow, MD, 107 W. 82nd St. #103, New York, NY, ph. 212-362-0449
10024, Katherine H. Leddick, 25 Central Park West, New York City, NY, ph. 212-875-1770
10025, Holistic Health Center, 229 W. 97th St., New York, ph. 212-932-2381, fax -1363
10025, Ostrow Inst. for Pain Mgmt., 250 W 100th St. #317, NY, NY, ph. 212-838-8265, fax 752-5140
10038, Carol O. Ellis, MD, 11 John St. #603, New York, NY, ph. 212-227-2462, fax 809-6549
10128, Firshein Ctr. Comprehensive Med, 1230 Park Ave. #1B, NY, NY, ph. 212-860-0282, fax -0276
1018, Sally Ann Rex, DO, 1343 Easton Ave., Bethlehem, PA, ph. 215-866-0900
10312, Napoli Chiropractic Office, 611 Lamoka Avenue, Staten Island, NY, ph. 718-967-0300, fax -0300
10458, Shashikant Patel, MD, 405 E. 187th St., Bronx, NY, ph. 718-365-7777, fax -1179
10459, Richard Izquiredo, MD, 1070 Southern Blvd. Lower Level, Bronx, NY, ph. 212-589-4541
10460, Uttam L. Munver, MD, 1963-A Daly Ave., Bronx, NY, ph. 718-991-8300
10509, J. C. Kopelson, MD, 221 Clock Tower Commons, Brewster, NY, ph. 914-278-6800, fax -6897
10543, Healing Partners, 921 W. Boston Post Rd., Mamaroneck, NY, ph. 914-381-7687, fax -0942
10543, Monica Furlong, MD, 921 W. Boston Post Rd., Mamaronerck, NY, ph. 914-381-7687, fax -0942
10566, Joel Edman, 2 Rence Fate, Courtlandt Manor, NY, ph. 914-528-7878, fax -7991
10597, Found. for Cartilage & Immun. Research, 104 Post Office Rd., Waccabuc, NY, ph. 800-947-8482
10597, John Prudden, MD, 104 Post Office Rd., Waccabuc, NY, ph. 914-763-6195
10901, Bruce Oran, DO, DC, Two Executive Blvd. #202, Suffern, NY, ph. 914-368-4700, fax -4727
10901, M. Schachter, MD, DIPL, 2 Executive Blvd. #202, Suffern, NY, ph. 914-368-4700, fax -4727
10941, Optimal Health Medical Assoc., P.L.L.C., 825 Rt. 211 East, Middletown, NY, ph. 914-344-3278

10962, Neil L. Block, MD, 14 Prel Plaza, Orangeburg, NY, ph. 914-359-3300
11024, Mary F. DiRico, MD, 1 Kingsport Rd., Great Neck, NY, ph. 516-466-5245
11040, Sun F. Pei, DO, 1 Fairfield Lane, New Hyde Park, NY, ph. 516-775-5285
11042, Lakeville OB-Gyn, 2001 Marcus Ave., Lake Success, NY, ph. 516-488-2757, fax -3940
11106, Albert W. Winyard III, MD, 23-35 Broadway, Astoria, NY, ph. 212-249-0903
11204, Pavel Yutsis, MD, 1309 W. 7th St., Brooklyn, NY, ph. 718-259-2122, fax -3933
11204, Yelena Shvarts, MD, 1309 W. 7th St., Brooklyn, NY, ph. 718-259-2122, fax -3933
11210, Brooklyn Ctr. of Holistic Med, 2515 Avenue M, Brooklyn, NY, ph. 718-258-7882, fax 692-4175
11218, A. F. Chu-Fong, MD, 185 Prospect park SW #102, Brooklyn, NY, ph. 718-438-6565, fax -1361
11219, Tova Rosen, MD, 5001 - 14th Ave. #A-7, Brooklyn, NY, ph. 718-435-9695
11228, Morris Westfried, 7508 15th Ave., Brooklyn, NY, ph. 718-837-9004
11229, Asya Benin, MD, 2116 Avenue P, Brooklyn, NY, ph. 718-338-1616
11230, Tsilia Sorina, MD, 2026 Ocean Ave., Brooklyn, NY, ph. 718-375-2600
11235, Michael Telpistky, MD, 415 Oceanview Ave., Brooklyn, NY, ph. 718-769-0997, fax 646-2352
11358, Ronald B. keys, 43-06 159th St., Flushing, NY, ph. 718-460-3966, fax -3966
11377, Fire Nihamin, MD, 39 - 65 52nd St., Woodside, NY, ph. 718-429-0039, fax -6965
11548, D'Brant Chiropractic Clinic, 55 Northern Blvd., Greenvale, NY, ph. 516-484-4897, fax -1964
11554, C. L. Calapai, DO, 1900 Hempstead Turnpike, East Meadow, NY, ph. 516-794-0404, fax -0332
11559, Mitchell Kurk, MD, 310 Broadway, Lawrence, NY, ph. 516-239-5540, fax 371-2919
11577, Rachlin Centre, 10 Power House Rd., Roslyn Heights, NY, ph. 516-625-6884, fax -6294
11590, Savely Yurkovsky, MD, 309 Madison St., Westbury, NY, ph. 516-333-2929
11717, Juan J. Nolasco, MD, 78 Wicks Rd #1, Brentwood, NY, ph. 516-434-4840
11743, Serafina Corsello, MD, FACAM, 175 E. Main St., Huntington, NY, ph. 516-271-0222, fax -5992
11746, Michael Fass, MD, A-Plaza 680 East, Huntington Station, NY, ph. 516-549-4607
11777, Steve Nenninger, ND, 109 Randall Ave., Port Jefferson, NY, ph. 516-331-0161
11784, Pernice Chiropractic, 301 Mooney Pond Rd., Seldem, NY, ph. 516-736-1000, fax -1023
11787, Michael Jardula, MD, 60 Terry Road, Smithtown, NY, ph. 516-361-3363
11788, Vincent C. Parry, DO, 236 Northfield Rd., Hauppauge, NY, ph. 516-724-2233
11797, Nutrition Works, 814 Woodbury Rd., Woodbury, NY, ph. 516-364-4441, fax -2602
11803, Thomas K. Szulc, MD, 720 Old Country Rd., Plainview, NY, ph. 516-931-1133, fax -1167
11959, Lewis S. Anreder, MD, 33 Montauk Hwy. Quogue, NY, ph. 516-653-6000, fax 288-8208
12203, K. A. Bock, MD, FACAM, 10 McKown Road #210, Albany, NY, ph. 518-435-0082, fax -0086
12572, Janet Draves, ND, 8 Knollwood Rd., Rhinebeck, NY, ph. 914-876-3993, fax -5365
12572, K. A. Bock, MD, FACAM, 108 Montgomery St., Rhinebeck, NY, ph. 914-876-7082, fax -4615
12572, Rhinebeck Health Ctr., 108 Montgomery St., Rhinebeck, NY, ph. 914-876-7082, fax -4615
12901, Adirondack Preventive Center, 50B Court St., Platsburgh, NY, ph. 518-561-2023, fax 561-2042
13039, ADIO Health Systems, 8129 Rt. 11, Cicero, NY, ph. 315-699-5000
13662, The Wellness Institute, 284 Andrew Street Rd., Massena, NY, ph. 315-764-7328, fax -5699
13820, Richard J. Ucci, MD, 521 Main St., Oneonta, NY, ph. 607-432-8752
13850, Acup & Chinese Herbal Med, 1020 Vestal Pkwy East, Vestal, NY, ph. 607-754-6043, fax -6150
14092, Donald M. Fraser, MD, 5147 Lewiston Rd., Lewiston, NY, ph. 716-284-5777
14217, Doris J. Rapp, MD, 2757 Elmwood Ave., Buffalo, NY, ph. 716-875-5578, fax -5399
14225, Allergy & Environmental Health Ctr., 65 Wahrie Dr., Buffalo, NY, ph. 716-833-2213, fax -2244
14301, Paul Cutler, MD, FACAM, 652 Elmwood Ave., Niagra Falls, NY, ph. 716-284-5140
14733, Reino Hill, MD, 230 W. Main St., Falconer, NY, ph. 716-665-3505
15203, Pain Release Clinic, 1320 E. Carson St., Pittsburgh, PA, ph. 412-431-7246, fax 488-3039
15237, Paul Del Bianco, MD, 9401 McKnight Rd. #301-B, Pittsburg, PA, ph. 412-366-6780
15317, Dennis J. Courtney, MD, 4198 Washington Road #1, McMurray, PA, ph. 412-941-1193
15522, Bill Illingwirth, DO, 120 W. John St., Bedford, PA, ph. 814-623-8414
15601, Alfonso S. Arevalo, MD, 100 W. Point Dr., Greensboro, PA, ph. 412-836-6041
15601, Ralph A. Mirando, MD, Road 12 - Box 108, Greensburg, PA, ph. 412-838-7632, fax 836-3655
15644, R. Christopher Monsour, MD, 70 Lincoln Way East, Jeannette, PA, ph. 412-527-1511
15666, Mamduh El-Attrache, MD, 20 E. Main St., Mt. Pleasant, PA, ph. 412-547-3576
16125, Roy E. Kerry MD, 17 Sixth Ave., Greenville, PA, ph. 412-588-2600
16146, Andrew Baer, MD, 92 West Connelly Blvd., Sharon, PA, ph. 412-346-6500
16335, Total Health Med, 505 Poplar St. Room PG02, Meadville, PA, ph. 814-337-7429, fax -5476
17022, Dennis Gilbert, DO, 50 N. Market St., Elizabethtown, PA, ph. 717-367-1345, fax -6616
17055, John M. Sullivan, MD, 1001 S. Market St. #B, Mechanicsburg, PA, ph. 717-697-5050, fax -3156
17403, Kenneth E. Yinger, DO, 1561 E. Market St., York, PA, ph. 717-848-2544
17701, Francis M. Powers, Jr., MD, 1100 Grampian Blvd., Williamsport, PA, ph. 717-326-8203

17837, George C. Miller II, MD, 3 Hospital Dr., Lewisburg, PA, ph. 717-524-4405, fax 523-8844
18013, Francis J. Cinelli, DO, 153 N. 11th St., Bangor, PA, ph. 610-588-4502, fax -6928
18103, Frederick Burton, MD, 321 E. Emmaus Ave., Allentown, PA, ph. 610-791-2452, fax -9974
18104, D. Erik Von Kiel, DO, Liberty Square Med. Ctr. #200, Allentown, PA, ph. 610-776-7639
18104, Von Kiel Ctr., Liberty Square Med. Ctr. #200, Allentown, PA, ph. 610-776-7639, fax 434-7090
18201, Arthur L. Koch, DO, 57 West Juniper St., Hazleton, PA, ph. 717-455-4747
18235, P. Jayalakshmi, MD, 330 Breezewood Rd., Lehighton, PA, ph. 215-473-7453
18253, K.R. Sampathachar, MD, 330 Breezewood Rd., Lehighton, PA, ph. 215-473-7453
18335, Healthplex Medical Center, Rt. 209, Marshalls Creek, PA, ph. 800-228-4673, fax 717-223-7355
18644, 8th St. Family Chiropractic Center, 131 W. 8th St., Wyoming, PA, ph. 717-693-9393, fax -2703
18702, William N. Clearfield, DO, 318 S. Franklin St., Wilkes Barre, PA, ph. 717-824-0953
18923, Harold H. Byer, MD, PhD, 5045 Swamp Rd. #A-101, Fountainville, PA, ph. 215-348-0443
18951, Harold Buttram, MD, 5724 Clymer Rd., Quakertown, PA, ph. 215-536-1890
18951, William G. Kracht, DO, 5724 Clymer Rd., Quakertown, PA, ph. 215-536-1890
18966, Suvarna Hannah, ND, 3463 Norwood Place, Holland, PA, ph. 215-579-0409, fax 504-1094
19020, Robert J. Peterson, DO, 2169 Galloway Road, Bensalem, PA, ph. 215-579-0330
19023, Health Achievement Ctr., 112 S. 4th St., Darby, PA, ph. 610-461-6225, fax 583-3356
19040, Bartley L. Stein, 38 Maurice Lane, Hatboro, PA, ph. 800-213-6331, fax 215-674-3857
19041, C. G. Maulfair Jr., DO, FACAM, 600 Haverford Rd. #200, Haverford, PA, ph. 800-733-4065
19047, George Danielewski, MD, 142 Bellevue Ave., Penndel, PA, ph. 215-757-4455
19056, Joseph A. Maxian, DO, 56 Highland Park Way, Livittown, PA, ph. 215-945-0707, fax -9120
19064, Joseph Bellesorte, DO, 930 W. Sproul Rd., Springfield, PA, ph. 610-328-3000
19067, Center for Natural Medicine, 303 Floral Vale Blvd., Yardley, PA, ph. 215-860-1500
19072, Andrew Lipton, DO, 822 Montgomery Ave #315, Narbeth, PA, ph. 610-667-4601
19087, Joan Michelland, Lac, 700 Knox Road, Wayne, PA, ph. 610-687-8595
19095, Preventive medicine Group, 1442 Ashbourne Rd., Wyncote, PA, ph. 215-886-7842, 887-1921
19102, Robert A. Smith, MD, 1420 Locust St. #200, Philadelphia, PA, ph. 215-545-2828
19111, Quinlan Alternative Medicine Ctr., 7301 Hasbrook Ave., Philadelphia, PA, ph. 215-722-7200
19115, Larry S. Hahn, DO, 9892 Bustleton Ave. #301, Philadelphia, PA, ph. 215-464-4111
19116, Maura Galperin, MD, 824 Hendrix St., Philadelphia, PA, ph. 215-677-2337
19118, Brij Srivastava, MD, 3309 N. Friend St., Philadelphia, PA, ph. 215-634-1920
19144, Frederick Burton, MD, 69 W. Schoolhouse Ln., Philadelphia, PA, ph. 215-844-4660
19147, Sarah M. Fisher, MD, 706 S. Second St., Philadelphia, PA, ph. 215-627-8401, fax -7227
19148, Brian Karlin, Do, 2500 S. Sheridan St., Philadelphia, PA, ph. 215-465-5583
19148, Joseph Steingard, MD, 2601 S. 12th St., Philadelphia, PA, ph. 215-389-6461
19148, Mark Tests, DO, 2601 S. 12th St., Philadelphia, PA, ph. 215-389-6461
19151, K.R. Sampathachar, MD, 6366 Sherwood Rd., Philadelphia, PA, ph. 215-473-4226
19348, Nicholas D'Orazio, MD, 100 E. State St. 2nd Floor, Kennett Square, PA, ph. 610-444-7224
19562, C. G. Maulfair Jr., DO, 403 N. Main St., Topton, PA, ph. 800-733-4065, fax 610-682-9781
19562, Maulfair Medical Center, 403 N. Main St., Topton, PA, ph. 610-682-2104, fax -9781
19808, Chrysalis Natural Medicine, 1008 Milltow Rd., Wilmington, DE, ph. 302-994-0565, fax 995-0653
19810, Vincent Vinciguerr, DC, 1800 Naamans Road, Wilmington, DE, ph. 302-475-3200
19966, G. Yossif, MD, PhD, 559 E. Dupont Hwy., Millsboro, DE, ph. 800-858-3370, fax 302-934-7949
20008, Andrew Baer, MD, 4123 Connecticut Ave., N.W., Washington, DC, ph. 202-363-8770
20008, G. H. Mitchell, MD, 2639 Connecticut Ave., N.W. #C-100, Washington, DC, ph. 202-265-4111
20015, A Rosemblat, MD, 5225 Wisconsin Ave., N.W. #401, Wash, DC, ph. 202-237-7000, fax -0017
20016, Inner Health, 4801 Wisconsin Ave., Washington, DC, ph. 202-244-1310, fax -1340
20016, Susan McConnell, 3006 Arizona, Washington, DC, ph. 202-966-3061
20164, Oscar G. Rasussen, Ph. 118 Avondale Dr., Sterling, VA, ph. 703-450-1640, fax -1630
20165-5843, Joan Walters, ND, 277 Terrie Dr., Sterling, VA, ph. 703-430-2310, fax -3405
20808, Paul V. Beals, MD, 9101 Cherry Lane #205, Laurel, MD, ph. 301-490-9911
20850, David G. Wember, MD, 26 Guy Ct., Rockville, MD, ph. 301-424-4048, fax 294-0854
20852, Bruce Rind, MD, 11140 Rockville Pike #520, Rockville, MD, ph. 301-816-3000, fax -0011
20852, Norton Fishman, MD, 11140 Rockville Pike #520, Rockville, MD, ph. 301-816-3000
20895, Dana Godbout Laake, 11223 Orleans Way, Kensington, MD, ph. 301-933-5919
20895, Healing Matters, 3700 Washington St., Kensington, MS, ph. 301-942-9024, fax 946-9035
21133, Arnold Brenner, MD, 8622 Liberty Plaza Mall, Randalistown, MD, ph. 410-922-1133, fax -9740
21146, Linda Ciotola, 692 Ritchie Hwy. #100, Severna Park, MD, ph. 410-544-6168
21207, Univ. of Maryland Compl Med, 2200 Kernan Dr., Baltimore, MD, ph. 410-448-6871, fax -6875
21208-3905, Ronald Parks, MD, 3655B Old Court Rd #19, Baltimore, MD, ph. 410-486-5656

21209, Binyamin Rothstein, DO, 2835 Smith Ave. #203, Baltimore, MD, ph. 410-484-2121, fax -0338
21209-2023, Acupuncture Clinic, 6719 Newstead Lane, Baltimore, MD, ph. 410-823-7793, fax -7793
21211, Lisa P. Battle, MD, 3100 Wyman Park Dr., Baltimore, MD, ph. 410-338-3059
21403, Cheryl Brown-Christopher, MD, 1419 Forest Dr. #202, Annapolis, MD, ph. 410-268-5005
21903, A.P. Cadous, MD, 2324 W. Joppa Rd. #100, Baltimore, MD, ph. 410-296-3737, fax -0650
22001, E. Abdelhalim, MD, Rt. 40 W, 39070 John Mosby Hwy. Aldie, VA, ph. 703-327-2434, fax -2729
22001, N. W. Levin, MD, Rt. 50 W. 39070 John Mosby Hwy. Aldie, VA, ph. 703-327-2434, fax -2729
22003, Andrew Baer, MD, 7023 Little River Turnpike, Annandale, VA, ph. 703-941-3606
22041, Sophini P. Patel, MD, 5201 Leesburg Pike #301, Falls Church, VA, ph. 703-845-8686, fax -2661
22044, A.M. Rosemblat, MD, 6316 Castle Pl. #200, Falls Church, VA, ph. 703-241-8989, fax 532-6247
22831, Harold Huffman, MD, P.O. Box 197, Hinton, VA, ph. 703-867-5242
23093, David G. Schwartz, MD, P.O. Box 532, Louisa, VA, ph. 540-967-2050
23112, Peter C. Gent, DO, 11900 Hull St., Midlothian, VA, ph. 804-379-1345
23185, The HEALTH. Center, 487 McLaws Circle #1A, Williamsburg, VA, ph. 757-656-6363, fax -
6363
23452, Nelson M. Karp, MD, 460 S. Independence Blvd., Virginia Beach, VA, ph. 704-497-3439
23454, Robert A. Nash, MD, 921 First Colonial Rd. #1705, Virginia Beach, VA, ph. 804-422-1295
23507, Vincent Speckhart, MD, 902 Graydon Ave., Norfolk, VA, ph. 804-622-0014
23518, Med Acupuncture Clinic, 3607 N. Military Hwy., Norfolk, VA, ph. 757-853-7434, fax 855-5215
23970, Frederick C. Sturmer, Jr., MD, 416 Durant St., South Hill, VA, ph. 804-447-3162
24378, E. M. Cranton, MD, Ripshin Rd. - Box 44, Trout Dale, VA, ph. 540-677-3631, fax -3843
24378, Mount Rogers Clinic, Inc., 799 Ripshin Road, Trout Dale, VA, ph. 540-677-3631, fax -3843
24378, W. C. Douglass, Jr. MD, Ripshin Rd. - Box 44, Trout Dale, VA, ph. 540-677-3631, fax -3843
25301, Steve M. Zekan, MD, 1208 Kanawha Blvd. E, Charleston, WV, ph. 304-343-7559
25601, R.L. Toparis, DO, 20 Hospital Dr. Doctors Park, Logan, WV, ph. 304-792-1662
25601, Thomas A. Horsman, MD, 20 Hospital Dr. Doctors Park, Logan, WV, ph. 304-792-1624
25801, Michael Kostenko, DO, 114 E. Main St., Beckley, WV, ph. 304-253-0591
25801, Prudencio Corro, MD, 251 Stanaford Rd., Beckley, WI, ph. 304-252-0775
26651, John R. Ray, DO, 3029 Webster Road, Summersville, WV, ph. 304-872-6583
27103, Walter Ward, MD, 1411 B Plaza West Rd., Winston Salem, NC, ph. 910-760-0240
27510, Community Wholistic Health Ctr., 103 Weaver St., Carrboro, NC, ph. 919-933-4354, fax -4303
27513, Loghman Zaiim, MD, 1817 N. Harrison Ave., Cary, NC, ph. 919-677-8383, fax -8380
27607, John Pittman, MD, 4505 Fair Meadow Lane #211, Raleigh, NC, ph. 919-571-4391, fax -8968
27609, NC Prev & Wellness Med Ctr., 4016 Barrett Dr. #210, Raleigh, NC, ph. 919-787-0084, fax -0170
27705, Integrated Health Care, 112 Smoft Ave., Ourham, NC, ph. 919-286-7755, fax -7754
27820, Bhaskar D. Power, MD, 1201 E. Littleton Road, Roanoke Rapids, NC, ph. 919-535-1411
27870, Gen. Hlth Ctr., 1201 E. Littletown Rd., Roanoke Rapids, NC, ph. 919-535-1412, fax 567-5000
28210, S. Charlotte Chiro. Center, Inc. 10701 - G Park Rd., Charlotte, NC, ph. 704-544-8844, fax -8631
28315, Keith E. Johnson, MD, 1111 Quewhiffle, Aberdeen, NC, ph. 919-281-5122
28604, Charles Wiley, MD, P.O. Box 307, Banner Elk, NC, ph. 704-898-6949, fax -6950
28677, John W. Wilson, MD, Plaza 21 North, Statesville, NC, ph. 704-876-1617
28677, Ron Rosedale, MD, Plaza 21 North, Statesville, NC, ph. 704-876-1617
28711, James Biddle, MD, 465 Crooked Creed Rd., Black Mountain, NC, ph. 704-669-7762, fax -4255
28801, Caroline Ctr. for Metabolic Med., 49 Zillicoa St., Asheville, NC, ph. 704-252-5545, fax 281-3055
28801, Greenspan Chiropractic Clinic, 261 Asheland Ave., Asheville, NC, ph. 704-252-1882, fax -1417
28806, John Wilson, MD, 1312 Patton Ave., Asheville, NC, ph. 800-445-4762, fax 704-876-0640
28806, Ron Rosedale, MD, 1312 Patton Ave., Asheville, NC, ph. 800-445-4762, fax 704-876-0640
29169, James M. Shortt, MD, SC, 2228 Airport Road, Columbia, SC, ph. 800-992-8350
29169, Theodore C. Rozema, MD, 2228 Airport Rd., Columbia, SC, ph. 800-992-8350
29304, Ctr. for Compl.Health & Ed., 404 Hope Mills Rd., Fayetteville, NC, ph. 910-423-4086, fax -2930
29340, William King, DDS, 715 Logan St., Gaffney, SC, ph. 864-489-8921
29356, Scott Brand, DC,103 S. Poplar Ave., Landrum, SC, ph. 864-457-5124
29406, Arthur M. LaBruce, 9275-G Medical Plaza Dr., Charleston, SC, ph. 803-572-1771
29407, Palmetto Orthod & TMJ, 712 St. Andrews Blvd., Charleston, SC, ph. 803-556-8930, fax -0742
29418, Judy Kameoka, MD, 3815 W. Montague Ave. #200, Charleston, SC, ph. 803-760-0770
29420, Ctr. Occup & Env Med. 7510 Nortforest Dr., N. Charleston, SC, ph. 803-572-1600, fax -1795
29566, David Croland, DO, 4326 Baldwin Ave., Little River, SC, ph. 803-249-6755, fax -3323
29575, Donald W. Tice, DO, 4301 Dick Pond Rd., Myrtle Beach, SC, ph. 803-215-5000, fax -5005
29687, Albert S. Anderson, MD, 3110 Wade Hampton Blvd., Taylors, SC, ph. 864-244-9020, fax -9044
30014, Gloria Freundlich, DO, 4122 Tate St., Covington, GA, ph. 770-787-0880

30060, Ralph C. Lee, MD, 110 Lewis Dr. #B, Marietta, GA, ph. 770-423-0064, fax -9827
30080, M. Truett Bridges, Jr., 1751 Point Pleasant, Smyrna, GA, ph. 770-436-0209, fax 444-9596
30120, Steven Garber, DC, 861 JFH parkway, Cartersville, GA, ph. 770-386-7707, fax 387-2414
30130, James L. Bean, MD, 4575 Piney Grove Dr., Cuming, GA, ph. 770-887-9418
30240, CliniCare Medical Center, 302 S. Greenwood St., LaGrange, GA, ph. 706-884-8360
30247, Pleasant Hill Chiropractic Ctr, 830 Pleasant Hill Rd., Lilburn, GA, ph. 770-925-9955, 923-0200
30303, Lavonne M. Painter, MD, 99 Butler St. S.E., Atlanta, GA, ph. 404-730-1491
30307, David Epstine, DO, 427 Moreland Ave. #100, Atlanta, GA, ph. 404-525-7333, fax, 521-0084
30309, Piedmont Hospital, 1968 Peachtree Road, NW, Atlanta, GA, ph. 404-605-3319, fax -1702
30309, William E. Richardson, MD, 1718 Peachtree St. NW #552, Atlanta, GA, ph. 404-607-0570
30337, D. Robert Howard, MD, 1650 Virginia Ave., College Park, GA, ph. 404-761-9500, fax -6995
30338, Bernard Miaver, MD, 4480 N. Shallowford Rd., Atlanta, GA, ph. 770-395-1600
30342, Stephen Edelson, MD, 3833 Roswell Rd #110, Atlanta, GA, ph. 404-841-0088
30360, Milton Fried, MD, 4426 Tilly Mill Rd., Atlanta, GA, ph. 770-451-4857, fax 404-451-8492
30503, Kathryn Herndon, MD, 530 Spring St., Gainesville, GA, ph. 404-503-7222
30525, William J. Lee, MD, P.O. Box 229, Clayton, GA, ph. 706-782-4044
30701, Patricia Tygrett, DO, P.O. Box 1988, Calhoon, GA, ph. 706-625-5204
31088, Terril J. Schneider, MD, 205 Central Dr. #19, Warner Robins, GA, ph. 912-929-1027
31201, James T. Alley, MD, 380 Hospital Dr. #125, Macon, GA, ph. 912-745-1575, -1974
31322, Carlos Tan, MD, 4 Pooler Prof. Plaza, Pooler, GA, ph. 912-748-6631
31416-0306, Joseph Marshall, DC, 411 Stephenson Ave., Savannah, GA, ph. 912-352-4832, fax -4833
31701-1875, Thomas C. Paschal, MD, 715 W. Third Ave., Albany, GA, ph. 912-438-9002
31730, Olive Gunter, MD, 24 N. Ellis St., Camilla, GA, ph. 912-336-7343, fax -7400
32084, St. Augustine Phys As. 419-A Anastasia Blvd., St. Augustine, FL, ph. 904-824-8353, fax -5705
32134, George Graves, DO, 11512 Country Road 316, Ft. McCoy, FL, ph. 352-236-2525, fax -8610
32159, Nelson Kraucak, MD, 8923 N.E. 134th Ave., Lady Lake, FL, ph. 904-750-4333
32174, Hana T. Chaim, DO, 595 W. Granada Blvd. #D, Ormond Beach, FL, ph. 904-672-9000
32216, John Mauriello, MD, 4063, Salisbury Road #206, Jacksonville, FL, ph. 904-296-0900, fax -8346
32216, Stephen Grable, MD, 4205 Belfort Rd. #3075, Jacksonville, FL, ph. 904-296-4977
32244, Psychotherapy Center, 6037 Longchamp Dr., Jacksonville, FL, ph. 904-771-8934
32250, Beaches Healthcare Center, 831-C N. Third St., Jacksonville Beach, FL, ph. 904-241-9680
32257, Mandarin Chiro. Ctr, 9891-2 San Jose Blvd. #2, Jacksonville, FL, ph. 904-262-8600, fax -3899
32308, Anti-Aging Medicine, 1630-A N. Plaza Dr., Tallahassee, FL, ph. 904-656-8846, fax 224-5594
32317, Royce V. Jackson, MD, 1630-A N. Plaza Dr., Tallahassee, FL, ph. 904-656-8846, fax 671-2921
32405, James W. DeRuiter, MD, 2202 State Ave #311, Panama City, FL, ph. 904-747-4963, fax -1271
32405, Naima Abdel-Ghany, MD, PhD, 340 W. 23rd St. #E, Panama City, FL, ph. 904-763-7689
32524, Ward Dean, MD, P.O. Box 11097, Pensacola, FL, ph. 904-484-0595
32570, William Watson, MD, 5536 Stewart St. N.W., Milton, FL, ph. 904-623-3863, fax -2201
32605, G. G. Feussner, MD, 6717 N.W. 11th Pl. #D, Gainesville, FL, ph. 352-331-7303, fax 332-8732
32605, Leonard Smith, MD, 720 SW 2nd Ave. #202, Gainesville, FL, 352-378-6262, fax -0779
32646, Carlos F. Gonzales, MD, 7991 S. Suncoast Blvd., Homosasso, FL, ph. 352-382-8282
32708, Peter D. Hsu, DO, 116 W. SR 434, Winter Springs, FL, ph. 407-327-3322, fax -3324
32714, W. Clinic, 195 S. Westmonte Dr. #'s H I J, Altamonte Springs, FL, ph 407-862-8834, fax -5951
32716, Peter D. Hsu, DO, 1650 Ocean Shore Blvd., Ormond, Beach, FL, ph. 904-441-1477
32750, Bixon Chiropractic Center, 242 W. Hwy 434, Longwood, FL, ph. 407-834-2226
32750, Donald Colbert, MD, 1908 Boothe Cl., Longwood, FL, ph. 407-331-7007, fax -5777
32751, Eileen M. Wright, MD, 340 N. Maitland Ave. #100, Maitland, FL, ph. 407-740-6100
32751, Jack E. Young, MD, 341 N. Maitland Ave. #200, Maitland, FL, ph. 407-644-2729, fax -1205
32751, Joya Lynn Schoen, MD, 341 N. Maitland Ave. #200, Maitland, FL, ph. 407-644-2729, fax -1205
32763, Travis L. Herring, MD, 106 W. Fern Dr., Orange City, FL, ph. 904-775-0525, fax -3911
32765, Roy Kupsinel, 1325 Shangri-La Lane, Oviedo, FL, ph. 407-365-6681, fax 1834
32778, James Coy, MD, 204 Texas Ave., Tavares, FL, ph. 904-742-7344
32789, James Parsons, MD, 8303 2699 Lee Rd., Winter Park, FL, ph. 407-528-3399
32792, Center Altern. Therapies, 305 N. Lakemont Ave., Winter Park, FL, ph. 407-647-0077, fax -1923
32803, Inst. Pain Care & Fmly Hlth, 2224 E. Concord St., Orlando, FL, ph. 407-896-3005, fax -3066
32803, Way to Natural Health, 500 N. Mills Ave., Orlando, FL, ph. 407-841-4581, fax 843-2342
32804, Kenneth Hoover, MD, 2909 N. Orange Ave. #108, Orlando, FL, ph. 407-897-6002
32903, Glen Wagner, MD, 121 6th Ave., Indialantic, FL, ph. 407-723-5915, fax 724-0287
32907, Neil Ahner, MD, 1663 Georgia St., Palm Bay, FL, ph. 407-729-8581, fax -6079

32953, James Parsons, MD, 5 Minna Lane #201, Merritt Island, FL, ph. 407-452-0332
32958, C. Health Innovations, P.A., 600 Schumann Dr., Sebastian, FL, ph. 561-388-5554, fax -2410
32958, Peter Holyk, MD, 680 Jordan Ave., Sebastian, FL, ph. 407-388-1222
32960, John Song, MD, 1360 U.S. 1 #1, Vero Beach, FL, ph. 407-569-3566
33009, Phys Med S, 1140 E. Hallandale Beach Blvd. #A, Hallandale, FL, ph. 954-456-1311, fax -1473
33020, Herbert Padell, DO, 210 S. Federal Hwy. #302, Hollywood, FL, 954-922-0470, fax 921-5555
33020, S. Marshall Fram, MD, 1425 Arthur St. #211, Hollywood, FL, ph. 954-925-3140
33026, Eric Rosenkrantz, MD, 1551 N. Palm Ave., Pembroke Pines, FL, ph. 954-432-8511
33063, Keith Latham, Lac, 2650 Aloe Avenue, Coconut Creek, FL, ph. 954-973-7880
33064, Anthony J. Sancetta, DO, 3450 Park Central Blvd. N., Pompano Beach, FL, ph. 954-977-3700
33064, D Roehm, MD, 3400 Park Central Blvd. N. #3450, Pompano Bch, FL, ph. 305-977-3700, -0180
33064, Fariss D. Kimbell, Jr., MD, 3450 Park Central Blvd. N., Pompano Beach, FL, ph. 305-977-3700
33133, Victor A. Marcial-Vega, MD, 4037 Poinciana Ave., Miami, FL, ph. 305-442-1233, fax 445-4504
33134, Maria Vega, MD, 2916 Douglas Rd., Coral Gables, FL, ph. 304-442-1233
33139, Perfect Health Center, 901 Pennsylvania Ave. #203, Miami Beach, FL, ph. 305-538-1064
33155, Herbert Pardell, DO, 7980 Coral Way, Miami, FL, ph. 305-267-5790, fax -5855
33160, Dayton Medical Center, 18600 Collins Ave., N. Miami Beach, FL, ph. 305-931-8484, fax -5042
33160, Martin Dayton, MD, 18600 Collins Ave., N. Miami beach, FL, ph. 305-931-8484, fax 936-1845
33162, S DiMauro, MD, 16666 N.E. 19th Ave. #101, N. Miami Bch, FL, ph. 305-940-4848
33176, Joseph G. Godorov, DO, 9055 S.W. 87th Ave. #307, Miami, FL, ph. 305-595-0671
33176, Ear, Nose & Throat, 9805 WE 87th Ave., Stanley Cannon, MD, ph. 305-279-3020, fax -1751
33179, Don S. Poster, MD, 1380 NE Miami Gardens Dr. #235, N. Miami Beach, FL, ph. 954-432-4518
33179, Hemato. Med, 1380 NE Miami Gardens Dr. #225, N. Miami Beach, FL, ph 305-949-4259, fax -947-2713
33180, Ntrl Hlth Institutes America, 19044 NE 29th Ave., Aventura, FL, ph. 305-705-0345, fax -0437
33304, Adam Frent, DO, 2583 E. Sunrise Blvd., Ft. Lauderdale, FL, ph. 313-425-0235, fax -9003
33316, Bruce Dooley, MD, 500 S.E. 17th St., Fort Lauderdale, FL, ph. 305-527-9355, fax -4167
33319, Arthritis Consuling Serv, Inc., 4620 N. State St. Rd 7 #206, Ft. Lauderdale, FL, ph. 800-327-3027,
33319, Insti A Med, 7200 W. Commercial Blvd. #210, Fort Lauderdale, FL, ph. 954-748-4991, fax -
5022
33319, Richard Frieberg, Lac, 5467 Gate Lake Road, Tamarac, FL, ph. 954-494-2903
33334, Bern. Chiro Ctr., 997 E. Oakland Park Blvd., Ft. Lauderdale, FL, ph. 954-565-4440, fax -5312
33406, J Medlock, DDS, 2326 S. Congress Ave. #1D, W. Palm Beach, FL, ph. 561-439-4620, fax -6704
33409, A. Court, MD, 2260 Palm Bch Lakes Blvd. #213, W Palm Bch, FL, ph. 561-684-8137,
33432, R. Willix, Jr. MD, 1515 S. Federal Hwy. #306, Boca Raton, FL, ph. 561-362-0724, fax -9924
33461, S. Pinsley, DO, 2290 - 10th Ave. N. #605, Lake Worth, FL, ph. 407-547-2264, fax 220-7332
33477, Neil Ahner, MD, 1080 E. Indiantown Rd., Jupiter, FL, ph. 407-744-0077, fax -0094
33486, Eric Hermansen, MD, 951 N.W. 13th St. #4B, Boca Raton, FL, ph. 407-392-4920, fax -4979
33487, A. Sancetta, DO, 7300 N. Federal Hwy. #104, Boca Raton, FL. ph. 800-995-9453
33487, L. Haimes, MD, 7300 N. Federal Hwy. #107, Boca Raton, FL, ph. 407-994-3868, fax 997-8998
33510, Carol Roberts, MD, 1209 Lakeside Dr., Brandon, FL, ph. 813-661-3662
33556, Bay Area Psy. Consultants, 13949 Friendship Ln, Odessa, FL, ph. 813-920-3014, fax 376-0078
33606, Eugene Lee, MD, 1804 W. Kennedy Blvd. #1, Tampa, FL, ph. 813-251-3089, fax -5668
33613, J. Ethridge, MD, 13615 Bruce Downs Blvd. #113, Tampa, FL, ph. 813-971-9850, fax -9817
33629, D. Carrow, MD, 3902 Henderson Blvd. #206, Tampa, FL, ph. 813-832-3220, fax 282-1132
33702, Wunderlich Center, 1152 94th Ave. N., St. Petersburg, FL, ph. 813-822-3612, fax -578-1370
33733, Intl Institute Reflexology, 5650-1st Ave. N., St. Petersburg, FL, ph. 813-343-4811, fax 381-2807
33743, Daniel S. Stein, MD, P.O. Box 49072, St. Petersburg, FL, ph. 813-864-6116
33803, S. Todd Robinson, MD, 4406 S. Florida Ave. #30, Lakeland, FL, ph. 941-646-5088
33813, Robinson Family Clinic, 4406 S. Florida Ave., Lakeland, FL, ph. 941-646-5088, fax -7534
33907, Alters Chiro. & Natural Health Ctr., 33 Barkley Cl., Ft. Myers, FL, ph. 941-939-7645, fax -2644
33937, Richard Saitta, MD, 1010 N. Barfield Dr., Marco Island, FL, ph. 813-642-8488
33940, Myron B. Lezak, MD, 800 Goodlette Road N. #270, Naples, FL, ph. 941-649-7400, fax -6370
33940-5461, David Perlmutter, MD, 800 Goodlette Road N. #270, Naples, FL, ph. 813-262-8971
33948, James Dussault, ND, 1720 El Jobean Rd., Port Charlotte, FL, ph. 941-255-3988
33980, Health Altern. Inc., 22959 Bayshore Road, Port Charlotte, FL, ph. 941-766-1800, fax 255-0009
34205, J. Ossorio, MD, 101 River Front Blvd. #150, Bradenton, FL, ph. 941-748-8704, fax 741-8066
34207, Center for Holsitic Medicine, 810 53d Ave. West, Bradenton, FL, ph. 941-727-7722, fax -7711
34208, Eteri Melinikov, MD, 116 Manatee Avenue E, Bradenton, FL, ph. 941-748-7943
34236, Holistic Health Care, 1521 Dolphin St., Sarasota, FL, ph. 941-365-6273, fax -4269
34236, Thomas McNaughton, MD, 1521 Dolphin St., Sarasota, FL, ph. 941-965-6273, 365-4269

34239, Joseph Ossorio, MD, 2345 Bee Ridge Rd #5, Sarasota, FL, ph. 941-921-1412
34429, Azeal Borromeo, MD, 700 S.E. 5th Terrace #7, Crystal River, FL, 904-795-4711, fax -7559
34601, Holistic Health Clinic of Brooksville, 10443 N. Broad St., Brookville, FL, ph. 352-544-0047
34652, Michael H. Beilan, DO, 5211 U.S. Hwy. 19 N #200, New Port Richey, FL, ph. 813-842-3111
34683, Palm Harbor Ctr for Funct. Med, 2939 Alt. 19 N., Palm Harbor, FL, ph. 813-787-0706, fax -0734
34684, Glenn Chapman, MD, 34621 U.S. Hwy. #19-N, Palm Harbor, FL, ph. 813-786-1661
34695, Ctr. Holistic Medicine, 105 N. Bayshore Dr., Safety Harbor, FL, ph. 813-724-0135, fax -0129
34952, Ricardo V. Barbaza, MD, 1874 SE Port St. Lucie Blvd., Port St. Lucie, FL, ph. 561-335-4994
34977, Sherri W. Pinsley, DO, 7000 SE Federal Hwy #302, Stuart, FL, ph. 407-220-1697
34994, Jason P. Schwartz, DC, 915 E. Ocean Blvd. #2, Stuart, FL, ph. 800-749-3651, fax 561-286-2649
34994, Neil Ahmer, MD, 705 N. Federal Hwy., Stuart, FL, ph. 407-692-9200, fax -9888
35226, Gus J. Prosch, Jr., MD, 759 Valley St., Birmingham, AL, ph. 205-823-6180, fax -6000
35801, George Gray, MD, 521 Madison St. #100, Huntsville, AL, ph. 205-534-1676, fax -0926
36251, Robert B. Andrews, Jr., DO, 544 E. First Ave., Ashland, AL, ph. 205-354-2131
36547, New Beginnings Med. Grp., 1404 W. 1st St., Gulf Shores, AL, ph. 334-968-6515, fax -6756
36818, Pravinchandra Patel, MD, P.O. Drawer DD, Coldwater, MS, ph. 601-622-7011
37205, Stephen L. Reisman, MD, 28 White Bridge Rd., Nashville, TN, ph. 615-356-4244, fax -9741
37303, H. Joseph Holliday, MD, 1005 W. Madison Ave., Athens, TN, ph. 423-744-7540
37311, Cleveland Care First, 1995 Keith St, NW, Cleveland, TN, ph. 423-472-2273
37404, William B. Findley, MD, 1404 Dodds Ave., Chattanooga, TN, ph. 423-622-5113
37405, Robert Burkich, MD, 707 Signal Mtn. Rd., Chattanooga, TN, ph. 423-266-4474, fax -4464
37862, Ratcliff Chiropractic Office, 826 Middle Creek Rd., Sevierville, TN, ph. 615-453-1390
37923, James Carlson, DO, 509 N. Cedar Bluff Rd., Knoxville, TN, ph. 423-691-2961
38024, Lynn A. Warner, Jr., MD, 503 E. Tickel #3, Dyersburg, TN, ph. 901-285-4910
38119, Jerre Minor Freeman, MD, 6485 Poplar Ave., Memphis, TN, ph. 901-278-4432
38774, Robert Hollingsworth, MD, 901 Forrest St., Selby, MS, ph. 601-398-5106
39128, Internal Med Specialists, 201 N. Buffalo Dr., Las Vegas, NV, ph. 702-242-2737, fax 255-3170
39564, James H. Waddell, MD, 1520 Government St., Ocean Springs, MS, ph. 601-875-5505
40059, Kirk D. Morgan, MD, 9105 US Hwy 42, Prospect, KY, ph. 502-228-0156, fax -0512
40207, Eye Disease Prevention Task Force, 902 Dupont Rd. #200, Louisville, KY, ph. 800-852-7540
40222, Inner Light Consultants, Inc., 305 N. Lyndon Lane, Louisville, KY, ph. 502-429-8835, fax -8835
40403, Edward K. Atkinson, MD, 448 Calico Rd., Berea, KY, ph. 606-925-2252
42025, 42025, Charles Leon Bolton, DC, 200 E. 12th St., Benton, KY, ph. 502-527-0994, fax -0994
42101, John C. Tapp, MD, 414 Old Morgantown Rd., Bowling Green, KY, ph. 502-781-1483
42501, Stephen S. Kiteck, MD, 1301 Pumphouse Rd., Somerset, KY, ph. 606-678-5137
42501, Stephen S. Kiteck, MD, 600 Bogle St., Somerset, KY, ph. 606-677-0459
43065, Physicians Care Ctr., Inc., 10401 Sawmill Pkwy., Powell, OH, ph. 614-761-0555, fax -8937
43068, Active Life Family Chiro. Center, 7509 E. Main St. #104, Reynoldsburg, OH, ph. 614-866-5158
43220, M. Ayur-Veda, 3250 W. Henderson Rd. #202, Columbus, OH, ph. 614-451-0677, 293-5984
43224, David C. Korn, DO, 3278 Maize Rd., Columbus, OH, ph. 614-268-6170
43230, P. Chiro, Hunter's Ridge Mall, 336 S. Hamilton Rd, Gahanna, OH, ph. 614-471-5442, fax -5462
43348, Paul Bonetzky, DO, One Aries Ctr., Russels Point, OH, ph. 513-843-5000
43537, Elizabeth C. Christenson, MD, 219 W. Wayne St., Maymee, OH, ph. 419-893-8438, fax -1465
43623, James C. Roberts, Jr., MD, 4607 Sylvania Ave., Toledo, OH, ph. 419-882-9620, fax -9628
44052, Robert Stevens, DO, 2160 Reid Ave., Lorain, OH, ph. 216-246-3993
44060, Concord Chiropractic, 9841 Johnnycake Ridge Road, Mentor, OH, ph. 216-354-6767, fax -6919
44094, L. M. Porter, MD, 36001 Euclid Ave. #A-10, Willoughby, OH, ph. 216-942-5838, fax -1337
44113, Robert B. Casselberry, MD, 2132 W. 25th St., Cleveland, OH, ph. 216-771-5855, fax -4534
44124, Pain Relief & Med. Health Ctr., 5576 Mayfield Rd., Lyndhurst, OH, ph. 216-460-1880, fax -1832
44130, Radha Baishnab, MD, 7225 Old Oak Park Blvd. #2B, Cleveland, OH, ph. 216-234-8080
44131, John M. Baron, DO, 4807 Rockside #100, Cleveland, OH, ph. 216-642-0082
44145, D. Lonsdale, MD, 24700 Center Ridge Rd., Cleveland, OH, ph. 216-835-0104, fax 871-1404
44145, Douglas Weeks, MD, 24700 Center Ridge Road, Cleveland, OH, ph. 216-835-0104, fax 871-1404
44145, Prev Med Group, 24700 Center Ridge Rd #317, Cleveland, OH, ph. 216-835-0104, fax 871-1404
44313, Josephine C. Aronica, MD, 1867 W. Market St., Akron, OH, ph. 330-867-7361, fax 869-7392
44320, Francis J. Waickman, MD, 544 "B" White Point Dr., Akron, OH, ph. 216-867-3767, fax -4857
44410, John L. Baumeier, DO, Inc., 1645 State Rte. 5, Cortland, OH, ph. 330-638-3026, fax -3704
44425, James P. Dambrogio, DO, 212 N. Main St., Hubbard, OH, ph. 216-534-9737, fax -9739
44460, William Z. Kolozsi, MD, 2380 Southeast Blvd., Salem, OH, ph. 216-337-1152

44511, J. Ventresco, Jr., DO, 3848 Tippecanee Road, Youngstown, OH, ph. 330-792-2349, fax -6415
44718, Jack E. Slingluff, DO, 5850 Fulton Rd., NW, Canton, OH, ph. 330-494-8641
45231, Holistic Health Ctr., 800 Compton Rd #24, Cincinnati, OH, ph. 513-521-5333, fax -5334
45241, Ted Cole, DO, 9678 Cincinnati-Columbus Rd., Cincinnati, OH, ph. 513-779-0300
45241, W Chester Fmly Practice, Inc. 9678 Cinti-Cols Rd., Cincinnati, OH, ph. 513-779-0300, fax -6805
45244, David C. Black, DC, 502 Old St. Rt. 74, Cincinnati, OH, ph. 513-528-6112, fax -6112
45246, Leonid Macheret, MD, 375 Glensprings, Dr. #400, Cincinnati, OH, ph. 513-851-8790
45380, Charles W. Platt, MD, 552 South West St., Versailles, OH, ph. 513-526-3271
45410, Gary A. Dunlop, DO, 2640 St. Charles Ave., Dayton, OH, ph. 937-253-6741, fax -2431
45459, John H. Boyles, Jr., MD, 7076 Corporate Way, Centerville, OH, ph. 937-434-0555
45505, Narinder K. Saini, MD, 1911 E. High St., Springfield, OH, ph. 513-325-1155
45742, Essence of Life Ministries, Rt. 1, Box 172, Little Hocking, OH, ph. 614-989-2300
45817, Celebration of Health, 122 Thurman St. #248, Bluffton, OH, ph. 419-358-4627, fax -1855
45817, Jay Nielsen, MD, 122 Thurman St. #248, Bluffton, OH, ph. 419-358-4627, fax -1855
45879, Don K. Snyder, MD 11573 State Route 11, Paulding, OH, ph. 419-399-2045
46077-0700, Robert C. Brooksby, DO, 1500 W. Oak St. #400, Zionsville, IN, ph. 317-873-3321
46131, Merrill Wesemann, MD, 251 E. Jefferson, Franklin, IN, ph. 317-736-6121
46158, Norman E. Whitney, DO, 492 S. Indiana St., Mooresville, IN, ph. 317-831-3352
46208, Gary L. Moore, MD, 3351 N. Meridian St. #202, Indianapolis, IN, ph. 317-923-8978, fax -8982
46220, Laurence Webster, MD, 6801 Lake Plaza Dr. #B-208, Indianapolis, IN, ph. 317-841-9046
46227, David A. Darbo, MD, 2124 E. Hanna Ave., Indianapolis, IN, ph. 317-787-7221
46236-8923, Kevin Cantwell, MD, 11715 Fox Rd. #400-227, Indianapolis, IN, ph. 317-870-9360
46322, Cal Streeter, DO, 9635 Saric Ct., Highland, IN, ph. 219-924-2410, fax -9079
46383, Myrna D. Trowbridge, DO, 850 - C Marsh St., Valparaiso, IN, ph. 219-462-3377
46404, Family Medicine & Wellness Ctr., 3300 W. 15th Ave., Gary, IN, ph. 219-944-3100, fax, 3110
46514, Douglas W. Elliott, MD, 1506 Osolo Rd. #A, Elkhart, IN, ph. 219-264-9635
46601, Anne L. Kempf, DC, 1202 Lincoln Way East, South Bend, IN, ph. 219-232-5892, fax 237-0910
46601, Keim T. Houser, MD, 515 N. Lafayette, Blvd., South Bend, IN, ph. 219-232-2037
46616, David E. Turner, DO, 336 W. Navarre St., South Bend, IN, ph. 219-233-3840
46703, Tri-State Chiropractic Clinic, 2014 N. Wayne St., Angola, IN, ph. 219-665-3106
46750, Huntington General Practice, 941 E. Etna Ave., Huntington, IN, ph. 219-356-9400, fax 356-4254
46805, Joseph P. Fiacable, MD, 2426 Lake Avenue, Fort Wayne, IN, ph. 219-423-3304
46962, Marvin D. Dziabis, MD, 300 W. Seventh St., North Manchester, IN, ph. 219-569-2274
47130, George Wolverton, MD, 647 Eastern Blvd., Clarksville, IN, ph. 812-282-4309
47355, David Chopra, MD, P.O. Box 636, Lynn, IN, ph. 317-874-2411
47394, Oscar Ordonex, MD, 400 S. Oak, Winchester, IN, ph. 317-584-6600
47714, Harold T. Sparks, DO, 3001 Washington Ave., Evansville, IN, ph. 812-479-8228, fax -7327
48017, Gurudarshan S. Khalsa, MD, 450 S. Main St., Clawson, MI, ph. 248-288-9200
48018, Albert J. Scarchilli, DO, 30275 13 Mile Rd., Farmington Hills, MI, ph. 810-626-7544
48043, June DeStefano, DO, 263 5B Gratiot, Mt. Clemens, MI, ph. 810-465-7514
48080, Adam Frent, DO, 23550 Harper Ave., St. Clair Shores, MI, ph. 810-779-5700, fax -9296
48094, James Ziobron, DO, 58060 Van Dyke, Washington, MI, ph. 810-781-6523
48103, Lynn J. Chandler, PhD, 3599 Delhi Overlook, Ann Arbor, MI, ph. 313-663-7616
48104, Glenn Miller, DC, 1054 S. Main St., Ann Arbor, MI, ph. 313-995-2124
48176, John G. Ghuneim, MD, 420 Russell #204, Saline, MI, ph. 313-429-2581, fax -3955
48188, Jarmina Ramirez-Salcedo, MD, 2038 Otter Pond Ln., Canton, MI, ph. 313-397-5842
48203, E. M. Gidney, MD, 12850 Woodward Ave., Highland park, MI, ph. 313-869-5070, fax -5072
48304, Alzheimers.Ctr.,1520 N. Woodward Ave. #210, Bloomfield Hills, MI, ph. 888-264-8211, fax 810-203-0321
48310, AlternaCare, PC, 37300 Dequindre #201, Sterling Heights, MI, ph. 810-268-0228
48322, Ellen Kahn, PhD, 7001 Orchard Lake Road #330A, West Bloomfield, MI, ph. 248-737-8780
48331, Farmington Med Ctr., 30275 W. 13 Mile Rd., Farmington Hills, MI, ph. 810-626-7544, fax -9698
48334, FHFP, 23910 W. Thirteen Mile Rd #C-301, Farmington Hills, MI, ph. 810-851-1600, fax -0421
48334, Mary E. Short, DO, 30275 13 Mile Rd., Farmington Hills, MI, ph. 810-626-7544
48345, Wahagn Agbabian, DO, PC, 28 N. Saginaw #1105, Pontiac, MI, ph. 248-334-2424, fax -2924
48346, Nedra Downing, DO, 5639 Sashabaw Rd, Clarkston, MI, ph. 248-625-6677, fax -5633
48451, Marvin D. Penwell, DO, 319 S. Bridge St., Linden, MI, ph. 313-735-7809
48451, Thomas A. Padden, DO, 16828 Bridge St., Linden, MI, ph. 313-432-1010, fax -9080
48532, Preventive and Family Care Ctr., 1044 Gilbert St., Flint, MI, ph. 810-733-3140, fax -5623
48532, The Fatigue Clinic of Michigan, G-3494 Beecher Rd, Flint, MI, ph. 810-230-7855
48532, William M. Bernard, DO, 1044 Gilbert St., Flint, MI, ph. 810-733-3140

48706, Parveen A. Malik, MD, 808 N. Euclid Ave., Bay City, MI, ph. 517-686-3760
48838, Longevity Ctr. of W. Michigan, 420 S. Lafayette, Greenville, MI, ph. 616-754-3679, fax -8968
48910, Dallas Chiropractic Clinic, 1505 W. Holmes Rd., Lansing, MI, ph. 517-882-0251
49004, Eric Born, DO, 100 Maple St., Parchment, MI, ph. 616-344-6183
49201, J. Daniel Clifford, MD, 300 W. Washington #270, Jackson, MI, ph. 517-787-9510
49240, Grass Lake Medical Ctr., 12337 E. Michigan Ave., Grass Lake, MI, ph. 517-522-8403, fax -4275
49512, Grant Born, DO, 2687 - 44th St. SE, Grand Rapids, MI, ph. 616-455-3550, fax -3462
49512, Tammy Geurkink-Born, DO, 2687 44th St. SE, Grand Rapids, MI, ph. 616-455-3550, fax -3642
49709, Atlanta Medical Clinic, 12394 State St., Atlanta, MI, ph. 517-785-4254, fax -2273
49709, Atlanta Medical Clinic, 12394 State St., Atlanta, MI, ph. 517-785-4254
49870, F. Michael Saigh, MD, 411 Murray Rd W. U.S. 2, Norway, MI, ph. 906-563-9600
50124, Ballard Chiropractic Office, 602 Main St. #370, Huxley, IA, ph. 515-597-3636
50314, Jacqueline Stoken, MD, DO, 411 laurel #3300, Des Moines, IA, ph. 515-247-8400
50314, Jacqueline Stoken, MD, DO, 411 Laurel #3300, Des Moines, IA, ph. 515-247-8400
50501, Calisesi Chiropractic Clinic, 24 S. 14th St., Ft. Dodge, IA, ph. 515-576-2183, fax -2336
51105, Horst G. Blume, MD, 700 Jennings St., Sioux City, IA, ph. 712-252-4386
52402, Robert J. Klein, DO, 1652 42nd St. NE, Cedar Rapids, IA, ph. 319-395-0223
52807, David Nebbeling, DO, 622 E. 38th St., Davenport, IA, ph. 319-391-0321, fax -5741
53018, Carol Uebelacker, MD, 1760 Milwaukee St., Delafield, WI, ph. 414-646-4600, fax -4215
53027, Edward G. Holtman, DC, 315 S. Sumner St., Hartford, WI, ph. 414-673-5650
53186, Donald Bergman, DC, 161 W. Sunset Dr., Waukesha, WI, ph. 414-549-0606, fax -9121
53218, Milwaukee Pain Clinic, 6529 W. Fond du Lac Ave., Milwaukee, WI, ph. 414-464-7246
53226, J. Robertson, Jr. DO, 1011 N. Mayfair Rd. #301, Milwaukee, WI, ph. 414-302-1011, fax -1010
53226, Jerry N. Yee, DO, 2505 N. Mayfair Rd., Milwaukee, WI, ph. 414-258-6282
53226, Robert R. Stocker, DO, 2505 N. Mayfair Rd., Milwaukee, WI, ph. 414-258-5522
53965, R. Waters, MD, Race & Vine Streets, Wisconsin Dells, WI, ph. 608-254-7178, fax 253-7139
54022, Diane Diegel, Lac, 186 County Road U, River Falls, WI, ph. 715-425-0333, fax -2273
54311, Eleazar M. Kadile, MD, 1538 Bellevue St., Green Bay, WI, ph. 920-468-9442, fax -9714
54456, Bahri O. Grungor, MD, 216 Sunset Pl., Neillsville, WI, ph. 715-743-3101
54601, Lifespring Health Service, 216 S. 23rd St., La Crosse, WI, ph. 608-785-0038, fax -0038
55102, Phyllis Goldin, MD, 311 Ramsey, St. Paul, MN, ph. 612-227-3067
55441, J. Eckerly, MD, 10700 Old Country Rd 15 #350, Minneapolis, MN, ph. 612-593-9458, fax -0097
55441, M. Dole, MD, 10700 Old Country Rd 15 #350, Minneapolis, MN, ph. 612-593-9458, fax -0097
55805, Duluth Clinic, 400 E. 3rd St., Duluth, MN, ph. 218-722-8364, fax 725-3067
56379, Sauk Rapids Chiropractic, 220 N. Benton Dr., Sauk Rapids, MN, ph. 320-255-1309, fax -0464
56716, Biermaier Chiro Clinic, 1226 University Ave., Crookston, MN, ph. 218-281-6311, fax -6312
57069, Harold J. Fletcher, MD, 28 E. Cherry, Vermillion, SD, ph. 605-624-2222
57201, Mary Goepfert, MD, P.O. Box 513, Watertown, SD, ph. 605-882-4664
57301, Harvey & Associates, 409 E. 11th, Mitchell, SD, ph. 605-996-4533
57325, Theodore R. Matheny, MD, 1005 S. Sanborn St., Chamberlain, SD, ph. 605-734-6958
57730-9703, Dennis R. Wicks, MD, HCR 83, Box 21, Custer, SD, ph. 605-673-2689
58201, Richard H. Leigh, MD, 2134 Library Cl., Grand Forks, ND, ph. 701-775-5527, fax -2539
58701, Brian E. Briggs, MD, 718 - 6th St., SW, Minot, ND, ph. 701-838-6011, fax -5055
59068, Oliver B. Cooperman, MD, P.O. Box 707, Red Lodge, MT, ph. 406-446-3055
59101, Arthritis & Osteoporosis Ctr., 1239 N. 28th St., Billings, MT, ph. 800-648-6274
59102, David C. Healow, MD, 1242 N. 28th #1001, Billings, MT, ph. 406-252-6674
59108, Richard A. Nelson, MD, 1001 S. 24th West #202, Billings, MT, ph. 406-656-7416
59474, Robert Stanchfield, MD, 925 Oilfield Ave., Shelby, MT, ph. 406-434-5595, fax -2701
59601, Bruce T. Smith, MD, 111 N. Jackson #4J, Helena, MT, ph. 406-449-3636
59645, Daniel J. Gebhardt, MD, 12 E. Main, White Sulphur Spring, MT, ph. 406-547-3384
59729, Michael Lang, ND, Box 1473, Ennis, MT, ph. 406-682-5040
59801, M. Public Health Partners, 1637 S. Higgins, Missoula, MT, ph. 406-542-3400, fax 728-1830
60004, Kingsley Medical Center, 3401 N. Kennicott Ave., Arlington Heights, IL, ph. 800-255-7030
60005, Terrill K. Haws, DO, 121 S. Wilke Rd #111, Arlington Heights, IL, ph. 847-577-9457, fax -8601
60008, Center BioEnergetic Med, 1811 Hicks Rd., Rolling Meadows, IL, ph. 847-934-1100, fax -0548
60013, Michael Shery, PhD, 121 Brookbridge, Cary, IL, ph. 800-736-5424, fax 847-639-0869
60013, Michael Shery, PhD, 121 Brookbridge, Gary, IN, ph. 800-516-1445, fax 847-639-0869
60025, Edward R. Karp, 1969 John's Drive, Glenview, IL, ph. 847-998-6611, fax 564-4162
60067, Busse Wellness Ctr., Ltd., 909 E. Palatine Rd #F, Palatine, IL, ph. 847-776-2111, fax -1711

60076, John H. Olwin, MD, 9631 Gross Point Rd., Skokie, IL, ph. 817-676-4030
60098, John R. Tambone, MD, 102 E. South St., Woodstock, IL, ph. 815-338-2345
60108, Old Town Chiro Ctr, 125 S. Bloomingdale Rd #7, Bloomingdale, IL, ph. 630-893-7313, fax -7453
60134, Midwest Ctr.Envir. Medicine, 302 Randall Rd. #206, Geneva, IL, ph. 630-232-1900, fax -7971
60194, Joseph Mercola, MD, 1443 W. Schaumburg Rd., Schaumburg, IL, ph. 847-985-1777, fax -0693
60201, Evanston Holistic Ctr., 1629 Orrington Ave., Evanston, IL, ph. 847-733-9900, fax -0105
60301, Caring medical & Rehab. Svcs., 715 lake St. #600, Oak Park, IL, ph. 708-848-7789, fax -7763
60301, Ctr. Integ. Trest. Biochem. Nutr, 715 Lake St #106, Oak Park, IL, ph. 708-383-3800, fax -3445
60301, Ross A. Hauser, MD, 715 Lake St. #600, Oak Park, IL, ph. 708-848-7789, fax -7763
60402, Cameo Chiropractic, Inc., 6929 Roosevelt Rd., Berwyn, IL, ph. 708-788-4950, fax -4953
60408, Braidwood Family Medical, 233 E. Reed St., Braidwood, IL, ph. 815-458-6700, fax -6705
60423, Briar House, 8504 Stuenkel Rd., Frankfort, IL, ph. 815-469-8385
60430, Frederick Weiss, MD, 3207 W. 184th St., Homewood, IL, ph. 708-334-7000
60477, Holistic Health Chiropractic, 16543 Oak Park Ave., Tinley Park, IL, ph. 708-429-1670
60506, Thomas Hesselink, MD, 888 S. Edgelawn Dr. #1743, Aurora, IL, ph. 630-844-0011, fax, -0500
60554, H.B. De Bartolo, Jr., MD, 11 DeBartolo Dr., Sugar Grove, IL, ph. 708-859-1818, fax -2021
60563, Naperville Holistic Health, 1280 Iroquois Ave. #200, Naperville, IL ph. 630-369-1220, fax -1639
60603, Alan F. Bain, MD, 104 S. Michigan Ave. #705, Chicago, IL, ph. 312-236-7010
60611, Cancer Prevention Coalition, Inc., 520 N. Michigan #410, Chicago, IL, 0ph. 312-467-0600
60614, David Edelberg, MD, 990 W. Fullerton Ave. #300, Chicago, IL, ph. 773-296-6700, fax -1131
60659, Razvan Rentea, MD, 3525 W. Peterson #611, Chicago, IL, ph. 773-583-7793, fax -7796
61008, M. Paul Dommers, MD, 554 S. Main St., Belvidere, IL, ph. 815-544-3112
61101, Maculan Chiropractic Clinic, 1005 S. Main St., Rockford, IL, ph. 815-965-3212, fax 969-8110
61252, Terry W. Love, DO, 2610 - 41st St., Moline, IL, ph. 309-764-2900
61548, Midwest Hlth Renewal Ctr., 205 S. Englewood Dr., Metamora, IL, ph. 309-367-2321, fax -2324
63033, Tipu Sultan, MD, 11585 W. Florissant, Florissant, MO, ph. 314-921-7100
63080, Ronald H. Scott, DO, 131 Meredith Lane, Sullivan, MO, ph. 314-468-4932
63084, Clinton C. Hayes, DO, 100 W. Main, Union, MO, ph. 314-583-8911
63105, H Walker, Jr., MD, PhD, 138 N. Meramec Ave., St. Louis, MO, ph. 314-721-7227, fax -7247
63122, N. Neeb, DO, 12166 Old Big Bend Rd #104, Kirkwood, MO, ph. 341-984-0033, fax -0020
63127, Generations Health Care, Inc., 9701 Landmark Pkwy. #207, St. Louis, MO, ph. 314-842-4802
63127, Octavio R. Chirino, MD, 9701 Landmark Pkwy. Dr. #207, St. Louis, MO, ph. 314-842-4802
63131, Garry A. Johnson, MD, 1926 Firethorn Dr., Des Peres, MO, ph. 314-821-7616
63136, Russell C. Forbes, DC, 10501 Halls Ferry Road, St. Louis, MO, ph. 314-869-5591, fax 653-2181
63141, Simon M. Yu, MD, 11709 Old Ballas Rd. #200, St. Louis, MO, ph. 314-605-5111, fax 991-5200
64052, Applewood Med Ctr, Inc., 9120 E. 35th St., Independence, MO, ph. 816-358-2712, fax 229-6696
64111, James F. Holleman, DO, 3100 Main St. #201, Kansas City, MO, ph. 816-561-6555, fax -6777
64111, Lisa Humbert, DC, 4301 Main St. #12, Kansas City, MO, ph. 816-531-5645
64114, James Rowland, DO, 8133 Wornall Rd., Kansas City, MO, ph. 816-361-4077
64118, H. Hlth Systems, 8002 N. Oak Trafficway #108, Kansas City, MO, ph. 816-436-9355, fax -1441
64119, C Rudolph,DO,PhD,2800-A Kendallwood Pkwy.,Kansas City, MO, ph 816-453-5940,fax-1140
64119, McD, Med Ctr., 2800-A Kendallwood Pkwy., Kansas City, MO, ph. 816-459-5940, fax -1140
64804-0929, Ralph D. Cooper, DO, 1608 E. 20th St., Joplin, MO, ph. 417-624-4323
65711, Doyle B. Hill, DO, 600 N. Bush, Mountain Grove, MO, ph. 417-926-6643
65803, The Shealy Institute, 1328 E. Evergreen, Springfield, MO, ph. 417-865-5940, fax -6111
65803, William C. Sunderwirth, DO, 2828 N. National, Springfield, MO, ph. 417-869-6260
66102, John Gamble, Jr., DO, 1606 Washington Blvd., Kansas City, KS, ph. 913-321-1140
66604, John Toth, MD, 2115 S.W. 10th, Topeka, KS, ph. 913-232-3330, fax -4066
67212, Frank Smith, DC, 9505 W. Central #104, Wichita, KS, ph. 316-729-1633
67219, Ctr. Improve Human Funct, 3100 N. Hillside Ave., Wichita, KS, ph. 316-682-3100, fax -5054
67337, J.E. Block, MD, 1501 W. 4th, Coffeyville, KS, ph. 316-251-2400
67601, Roy N. Neil, MD, 105 W. 13th, Hays, KS, ph. 913-628-8341
68114, Jeffrey Passer, MD, 9300 Underwood Ave., #520, Omaha, NE, ph. 402-398-1200, fax -9119
68144, Eugene C. Oliveto, MD, 10804 Prairie Hills Dr., Omaha, NE, ph. 402-392-0233
68154, Richard J. Holcomb, MD, 248 N. 129th St., Omaha, NE, ph. 402-334-7964, fax 391-6818
68739, SACRAD Heart Clinic, 405 W. Darlene St., Hartington, NE, ph. 402-254-3935, fax -2393
68862, Otis W. Miller, MD, 408 S. 14th St., Ord, NE, ph. 308-728-3251
69001, Kenneth W. Ellis, MD, 1401 E. H St. #3A, McCook, NE, ph. 308-345-8376
70006, Wallace Rubin, 3434 Houma Blvd. #201, Metairie, LA, ph. 504-888-8800, fax -455-6796

70043, Saroj T. Tampira, MD, 800 W. Virtue St. #207, Chalmette, LA, ph. 504-277-8991
70053, Diana Betancourt, MD, 522 3rd St., Gretna, LA, ph. 504-363-0101
70065, Maria Hernandez-Abril, MD, 3814 Williams Blvd., Kenner, LA, ph. 504-443-4306, fax -4547
70112, James Carter, MD, 1430 Tulane Ave., New Orleans, LA, ph. 504-588-5136, fax 584-3540
70118-3761, Janet Perez Chiesa, MD, 360 Millaudon St., New Orleans, LA, ph. 504-484-6655
70121, Charles C. Mary Jr., MD, 1201 S. Clearview Pkwy. #100, Jefferson, LA, ph. 504-737-4636
70448, James Carter, MD, 800 Hwy 3228, Mandeville, LA, ph. 504-626-1985
70471, Roy M. Montalbano, MD, 120 Century Oaks Lane, Mandeville, LA, ph. 504-626-1985
70503, Sydney Crackower, MD, 701 Robley Dr. #100, Lafayette, LA, ph. 318-988-4116
70508, John Jester, PhD, 3 Flagg Pl. #B4, Lafayette, LA, ph. 318-984-3770, fax -1202
70560, Adonis J. Domingue, MD, 602 N. Lewis #600, New Iberia, LA, ph. 318-365-2196
70607, Am. Wellness Center, 3501 5th Ave. #A, Lake Charles, LA, ph. 800-566-7360, fax 318-479-2099
70809, Chiropractic Sports & Injury Center, 5207 Essen Lane #5, Baton Rouge, LA, ph. 504-766-3031,
71357, Joseph R. Whitaker, MD, P.O. Box 458, Newelton, LA, ph. 318-467-5131
71369, Steve Kuplesky, MD, 296 Christine Lane, Simmesport, LA, ph. 318-941-2671
71603-6352, Pine Bluff Allergy Clin., 3900 Hickory St., Pine Bluff, AR, ph. 501-535-8200
71913, William Wright, MD, 1 Mercy Dr. #211, Hot Springs, AR, ph. 501-624-3312
71953, David P. Bowen, MD, 622 Mena St. #A, Mena, AR, ph. 501-394-7570
72201, Norbert J. Becquet, MD, 613 Main St., Little Rock, AR, ph. 501-375-4419
72450, Len Kemp, MD, One Medical Dr., Paragould, AR, ph. 501-239-8504, fax 3204
72601, Carol Chaney, MD, P.O. Box 1254, Harrison, AR, ph. 870-427-6462, fax 741-3949
72601, Clearsprings Health Center, P.O. Box 2195, Harrison, AR, ph. 870-427-6462, fax 741-3949
72653, Merl B. Cox, DO, 126 South Church, Mountain Home, AR, ph. 501-424-5025
72654, Melissa Taliaferro, MD, Cherry St. P.O. Box 400, Leslie, AR, ph. 501-447-2599, fax -2917
72756, Back to Health Chiropractic, 302 N. 8th St. #1, Rogers, AZ, ph. 501-936-8300
72766, G. Howard Kimball, MD, 900 Dorman, #E, Springdale, AR ph. 501-756-3251, fax -9186
73069, TCM Health Center, 2233 W. Lindsey #118, Norman, OK, ph. 405-579-7888, fax -7890
73102, Paul Wright, MD, 608 N.W. 9th St. #1000, Oklahoma City, OK, ph. 405-272-7494
73109, Genesis Med R. Inst. 5419 S. Western Ave., Oklahoma City, OK ph. 405-634-1310, fax -7320
73118, Charles D. Taylor, MD, 4409 Classen Blvd., Oklahoma City, OK, ph. 405-525-7751, fax -0303
74037, Leon Anderson, DO, 121 Second St., Jenks, OK, ph. 918-299-5039
74058, Gordon P. Laird, DO, 304 Boulder, Pawnee, OK, ph. 918-762-3601
74105, Ruth Miller, DO, 1710B E. 51st St., Tulsa, OK, ph. 918-742-1996, fax -5995
74105, Springer Clinic, Inc., 3233 E. 31st St., Tulsa, OK, ph. 918-749-8000, fax 742-6401
74134, Donna S. Hathaway, DC, 3151 S. 129th E. Ave. #R, Tulsa, OK, ph. 918-665-1120
74136, Planter Naturopathic Clinic, 5711 E. 71st St. #100, Tulsa, OK, ph. 918-488-6100, fax -6112
74764, Ray E. Zimmer, DO, 602 N. Dalton, Valliant, OK, ph. 405-933-4235
75023, Charles W. Sizemore, DDS, 3020 Legacy Dr. #210, Plano, TX, ph. 972-491-1434, fax -1261
75038, Francis, J. Rose, MD, 1701 W. Walnut Hill #200, Irving, TX, ph. 214-594-1111, fax 518-1867
75061, Irving Medical Ctr., 620 N. O'Connor, Irving, TX, ph. 972-259-3541, fax 254-1019
75075, Applied Nutrition Concepts, 2828 W. Parker Rd. #208, Plano, TX, ph. 972-612-5505, fax -5505
75075, Cornelius Matwijecky, MD, 3900 W. 15th St. #305, Plano, TX, ph. 214-964-8889, fax -0026
75075, Linda martin, Do, 1524 Independence #C, Plano, TX, ph. 214-985-1377, fax 612-0747
75208, James M. Murphy, MS, 400 S. Zang #1218, Dallas, TX, ph. 214-941-3100, fax -1979
75227, Theodore J. Tuinstra, DO, 7505 Scyene Rd. #302, Dallas, TX, ph. 214-275-1141, fax -1370
75231, Donald R. Whitaker, DO, 8345 Walnut Hill Lane #230, Dallas, TX, ph. 214-373-3016
75231, Peter Rivera, MD, 7150 Greenville Ave. #200, Dallas, TX, ph. 214-891-0466
75234, Martha Jo Taylor, 2925 LBJ Freeway, Dallas, TX, ph. 972-488-2533, fax -2533
75234, Natural Wellness Center, 2880 LBJ Freeway #219, Dallas, TX, ph. 972-247-4500, fax -1412
75244, Stephen Sporn, 1`3612 Midway Rd. #333-16, Dallas, TX, ph. 972-490-3703, fax 980-6850
75248, J. Robert Winslow, DO, 5025 Arapaho #550, Dallas, TX, ph. 214-702-99777
75251, Michael G. Samuels, DO, 7616 LBJ Freeway #230, Dallas, TX, ph. 214-991-3977, fax 788-2051
75503, T. Overlock, MD, 2700 Richmond Rd. #14A, Texarkana, TX, ph. 903-832-6565, fax -5120
75956, John L. Sessions, DO, 1609 S. Margaret, Kirbyville, TX, ph. 409-423-2166, fax -5496
76011, Acupuncture & Herb Center, 2301 N. Collins #118, Arlington, TX, ph. 817-261-5577, fax -5577
76011, Alan Rader, DC, 2301 N. Collins #190, Arlington, TX 76011, ph. 817-461-6119, fax 226-1162
76012, R.E. Liverman, DO, 1111 San Juan Ct., Arlington, TX, ph 817-469-1266
76017, Dept. Omm, Unthsc-fw, 3500 Camp Bowie Blvd., Ft. Worth, TX, ph. 817-735-2235, fax -2480
76054, Antonio Acevedo, MD, 729 W. Bedford-Euless Rd., Hurst, TX, ph. 817-595-2580

76095, Nutr. Direction for Total Wellness, P.O. Box 210633, Bedford, TX, ph. 817-685-6304, fax -0078
76107, Gerald Harris, DO, 1002 Montgomery #3-103, Ft. Worth, TX, ph. 817-732-2878, fax -9315
76111, R. Tan, MD, PA, 3220 North Freeway #106, Ft. Worth, TX, ph. 817-626-1993, fax -2310
76112, C. Hawed, DO, 6451 Brentwood Stair Rd. #115, Ft. Worth, TX, ph. 817-446-8416, fax -8413
76112, J. Mahoney, DO, 6451 Brentwood Stair Rd. #115, Ft. Worth, TX, ph. 817-446-8416, fax -8413
76308, T. Roger Humphrey, MD, 2400 Rushing, Wichita Falls, TX, ph. 940-766-4329, fax 767-3227
76801, Larry Doss, MD, 1501 Burnett Dr., Brownwood, TX, ph. 915-646-8541
76903, B. Thurman, MD, 102 N. Magdalen #290, San Angelo, TX, ph. 915-653-3562, fax 994-1162
77027, Kenneth W. O'Neal, MD, 1800 W. Loop S. #1650, Houston, TX, ph. 713-871-8818
77042, Wholistic & Psychosomatic Medicine, 10714 Briar Forest, Houston, TX, ph. 713-789-0133
77055, Jerome L. Borochoff, MD, 8830 Long Point #504, Houston, TX, ph. 713-461-7517
77055, Robert Battle, MD, 9910 Long Point, Houston, TX, ph. 713-932-0552, fax -0551
77057, Moe Kakvan, MD, 3838 Hillcroft #415, Houston, TX, ph. 713-780-7019, fax -9783
77058, Stephen O. Rushing, MD, 16856 Royal Crest Dr., Houston, TX, ph. 713-286-2195, fax -2197
77063, Balanced Bodies Chiropractic 9099 Westheimer #501, Houston, TX, ph. 713-977-0005
77076, Stephen Weiss, MD, 7333 North Freeway #100, Houston, TX, ph. 713-691-0737
77089, Biotech Chiro Clinic, 11003 Resource Parkway #103, Houston, TX, ph. 281-481-9299, fax -9286
77098, Ctr. Integrated Med, 3120 Southwest Freeway #415, Houston, TX, ph. 713-523-4181, fax -4184
77338, Life Center Houston, 9816 Memorial #206, Humble, TX, ph. 800-349-7249, fax 281-540-4329
77459, Eric K. Tondera, 52 Wellington Ct., Missouri City, TX, ph. 713-988-3223, fax -5643
77480, Elisabeth-Anne Cole, MD, 1002 Brockman St., Sweeny, TX, ph. 409-548-8610, fax -8614
77504, Carlos Nossa, MD, 4010 Fairmont Pkwy. #274, Pasadena, TX, ph. 713-768-3151
77520, Ronald L. Cole, MD, 1600 James Bowie Dr. #C-104, Baytown, TX, ph. 281-422-2229, fax -8064
78041, Ruben Berlanga, MD, 649-B Dogwood, Laredo, TX, ph. 210-733-0424
78064, Gerald Phillips, MD, 111 Smith St., Pleasanton, TX, ph. 210-569-2118, fax -5958
78229, Pain & Stress Management Clinic, 5282 Medical Dr. #160, San Antonio, TX, ph. 800-669-2256,
78240, J. Archer, DO, 8637 Fredericksburg Rd. #150, San Antonio, TX., ph, 210-697-8445, fax -0631
78240, R. Nelms, DO, 8637 Fredericksburg Rd. #150, San Antonio, TX, ph. 210-697-8445, fax -0631
78550, Robert R. Somerville, MD, 712 N. 77 Sunshine Strip #21, Harlingen, TX, ph. 210-428-0757
78613, Ron Manzanero, MD, 201 S. Bell #104, Cedar park, TX, ph. 512-258-1645, fax -2586
78681, Natural Healing Clinic, 405 Old West Dr., Round Rock, TX, ph. 512-255-3631, fax -3972
78704, The Pain Mgmt. Ctr., 4303 Victory #300, Austin, TX, ph. 512-444-7246, fax -0832
78735, Stephen C. Ahrens, 6108 Highway 290 W., Austin, TX, ph. 512-892-2635, fax -7460
78757, Vladimir Rizov, MD, 911 W. Anderson Ln. #205, Austin, TX, ph. 512-451-8149, fax -0895
79109, Gerald Parker, DO, 4717 S. Western, Amarillo, TX, ph. 806-355-8263
79109, Health by Design Chiropractic, 6110 Canyon Dr., Amarillo, TX, ph. 806-352-3330, fax 467-0003
79109, John T. Taylor, DO, 4714 S. Western, Amarillo, TX, ph. 806-355-8263
79119, Roby D. Mitchell, MD, 3501 Soncy Rd. #129, Amarillo, TX, ph. 806-467-9824, fax 354-9823
79410, Mark R. Wilson, MD, 4002 - 21st St. #A, Lubbock, TX, ph. 806-795-9494
79603, William Irby Fox, MD, 1227 N. Mockingbird Lane, Abilene, TX, ph. 915-672-7863
80122, Milt Hammerly, MD, 5161 E. Arapahoe Rd. #290, Littleton, CO, ph. 303-693-2626, fax 796-8174
80206, Lauren E. Mitchell, DO, 2222 E. 18th St., Denver, CO, ph. 303-333-3733, fax -1351
80218, Philip Incao, MD, 1624 Gilpin St., Denver, CO, ph. 303-321-2100, fax -3737
80228, Frontier Medical Institute, 255 Union St. #400, Lakewood, CO, ph. 303-986-9455, -0892
80302, Arlene Kellman, DO, 2150 Pearl St., Boulder, CO, ph. 303-444-8337, fax -8393
80304, Michael Z. Zeligs, MD, 1000 Alpine #211, Boulder, CO, ph. 303-442-5492
80631, Pathways, 3211 20th St. #D, Greeley, CO, ph. 970-356-3100, fax -4827
80903, William Nelson, ND 1422 N. Hancock Ave. #5-S, Colorado Springs, CO, ph. 719-635-4776
80907, James R. Fish, MD, 3030 N. Hancock, Colorado Springs, CO, ph. 719-471-2273
80910, M. Martin Hine, MD, 303 S. Circle #202, Colorado Springs, CO, ph. 719-632-7003
80918, Carl Osborn, DO, 6050 Erin Park #200, Colorado Springs, CO, ph. 719-260-8122
80918, George J. Juetersonke, DO, 5455 N. Union Blvd. #200, Colorado Springs, CO, ph. 719-528-1960
81001, Ron Concialdi, DDS, 2037 Jerry Murphy Rd. #202, Pueblo, CO, ph. 719-545-3070, fax -3071
81301, Miclene A. Fecteau, DO, 1911 Main Ave. #101, Durango, CO, ph. 970-247-1160
81401, Columbia Naturopathic Health Ctr, 700 E. Main #5, Montrose, CO, ph. 970-240-2082, fax -8677
81505, William L. Reed, MD, 2700 G Rd. #1-B, Grand Junction, CO, ph. 970-242-1417
81622, Rob Krakovitz, MD, 430 W. Main St., Aspen, CO, ph. 970-927-4394
82001, Jonathan Singer, DO, 1805 E. 19th St. #202, Cheyenne, WY, ph. 307-635-4362

82580, Abram Ber, 5011 N. Granite Reef Rd., Scottsdale, AZ, 602-941-2141, fax -4114
82604, Preventive Health Resources, 2300 Mulberry, Casper, WY, ph. 307-234-2044
82717, Rebecca Painter, MD, 201 West Lakeway, Gillette, WY, ph. 307-682-0330, fax 686-8118
83440, Dana Miller, DC 19 N. Center St., Rexburg, ID, ph. 208-356-6772, fax -8658
83651, Integrated Medical Arts Ctr., 824 17th Ave. S., Nampa, ID, ph. 208-466-5517, fax -3172
83651, Nampa Chiropractic Center, 1003 7th Street S., Nampa, ID, ph. 208-466-5459
84047, Meridian Health Ctr, 1225 E. Fort Union Blvd. #200, Midvale, UT, ph. 801-561-4804, fax -5078
84088, Cordell Logan, PhD, ND, 9265 S. 1700 W #A, West Jordan, UT, ph. 801-562-2211, fax -0063
84098, Kenneth Wolkoff, MD, 3065, W. Fawn Dr., Park City, UT, ph. 801-655-8214
84107, Dennis Harper, DO, 5263, S. 300 W #203, Murray, UT, pg. 801-288-8881, fax 262-4860
84604, Dennis Remington, MD, 1675 N. Freedom Blvd. #11-E, Provo, UT, ph. 801-373-8500, fax -3426
84604, Judith S. Moore, DO, 1675 N. Freedom Blvd. #11-E, Provo, UT, ph. 801-373-8500, fax -3426
85012, Ralph F. Herro, MD, 5115 N. Central Ave., Phoenix, AZ, ph. 602-266-2374, fax 264-2172
85015, Sam Schwart, DO, DSC, 1822 W. Indian School Rd., Phoenix, AZ, ph. 602-277-8911
85018, Bruce H. Shelton, MD, 2525 W. Greenway Rd. #300, Phoenix, AZ, ph. 602-993-1200, fax -0160
85018, Royal Orthoped & Pain Rehab, 3610 N. 44th St. #210, Phoenix, AZ, ph. 602-912-4996, fax -5635
85018, S. Olsztyn, MD, 4350 E. Camelback Rd. #B-220, Scottsdale, AZ, ph. 602-840-8424, fax -8545
85022, H.C. Purtzer, DO, 13825 N. 7th St. #H, Phoenix, AZ, ph. 602-942-6944, fax -6945
85032, J Sherman, DO, 1222 Paradise Vill. Pkwy. S. #328-A, Phoenix, AZ, ph. 602-494-1735, fax -1735
85201, Gracey Chiropractic Clinic, 1530 N. Country Club Drive #18, Mesa, AZ, ph. 602-964-4407
85206, William W. Halcomb, DO, 4323 E. Broadway #109, Mesa, AZ, ph. 602-832-3014
85224, Carol Cooper, Lac, 3417 N. Evergreen St. #A, Chandler, AZ, ph. 602-777-9045
85251, Kathleen Dry, MD, 4020 N. Scottsdale Rd. #300, Scottsdale, AZ, ph. 602-947-1545, fax -2392
85254, T. Friedmann, MD, 10565 N. Tatum Blvd. #B115, Phoenix, AZ, ph. 602-381-0800, fax 0054
85258, Allergy Disease Ctr., 9699 N. Hayden Rd. #108, Scottsdale, AZ, ph. 602-951-9090, fax -9270
85260, Gordon Josephs, MD, 7315 E. Evans Rd., Scottsdale, AZ, ph. 602-998-9232
85308, Gen. Practice, Assoc., PC, 4901 W. Bell Rd. #2, Glendale, AZ, ph. 602-939-8916, fax 978-2817
85308, Lloyd D. Arnold, DO, 4901 W. Bell Rd. #3, Glendale, CA, ph. 602-939-8916, fax 978-2817
85331, F. George II, DO, 38425 N. Spur Cross Rd., Cave Creek, AZ, ph. 602-488-6331 fax -0297
85344, S.W. Meyer, DO, 322 River Front Dr. P.O. Box 1870, Parker, AZ, ph. 520-669-8911
85374, Natural Healthcare Alt., 12211 West Bell Road #205B, Surprise, AZ, ph. 602-583-9180, fax -9180
85541, Gary Gordon, MD, 901 Anasazi Rd., Payson, AZ, ph. 520-472-9086
85712, Jesse Stoff, MD, 2122 N. Cracroft Rd. #112, Tucson, AZ, ph. 520-290-4516, fax -6403
85712-2501, Alan K. Ketover, MD, 10752 N. 89th Pl. #C-134m, Scottsdale, AZ, ph. 602-880-4700
85712-2501, Gene D. Schmutzer, DO, 2425 N. Alvernon Way, Tucson, AZ. ph. 802-795-0292
85718, Nutritional & Matabolic Medicine, 1840 E. River Rd., Tucson, AZ, ph. 520-577-1940, fax -1743
85742, Gregg G. Libby, DC, 4811 W. Daphne Lane, Tucson, AZ, ph. 520-579-9775
85749, Alzheimer's Prev. Found., 11901 E. Coronado, Tucson, AZ, ph. 520-749-8374, fax -2669
85750, Alexander P. Cadoux, MD, 5655 E. River Rd., #151, Tucson, AZ, 520-529-9668, fax -9669
86001, Natureworks Medical Center, 516 N. Humphreys, Flagstaff, AZ, ph. 520-779-1016
86326, Darrel Parry, DO, 1699 E. Cottonwood St., Cottonwood, AZ, ph. 602-639-2200
86334, Eric D. Bower, NMD, P.O. Box 404, Paulsen, AZ, ph. 520-771-3740
86336, John J. Adams, MD, 299 Van Deren, #3, Sedona, AZ, ph. 520-282-3014
86336, Lester Adler, MD, 40 Soldiers Pass Rd. #11-14, Sedona, AZ, ph. 520-282-2520
86336, Welch Medical Clinic, 2301 W. Hwy. 89A, Sedona, AZ, ph. 520-282-0609
86351, Cheryl Harter, MD, 80 Raintree Rd., Sedona, AZ, ph. 520-284-9777
87110, Ralph J. Luciani, DO, 2301 San Pedro NE #G, Albuquerque, NM, ph. 505-888-5995
87111, Gerald Parker, DO, 9577 Osuna NE, Albuquerque, NM, ph. 505-271-4800
87111, John T. Taylor, DO, 9577 Osuna NE, Albuquerque, NM, ph. 505-271-4800
87501, Bert A. Lies, Jr., MD, 539 Harkle Road #D, Santa Fe, NM, ph. 505-982-4821
87504, Shirley B. Scott, MD, P.O. Box 2670, Santa Fe, NM, ph. 505-986-9960
87505, John L. Laird, MD, 1810 Calle de Sebastian #H-4, Santa Fe, NM, ph. 505-989-4690
87532, LaMesilla Clinic, 116 Rt. 399, Esponola, NM, ph. 505-753-4466
87544, Los Alamos Pediatric Clinic, 3917 W. Road #136, Los Alamos, NM, ph. 505-662-9620
88005, Adex Cantu, MD, 301 Perkins Dr., Albuquerque, NM, ph. 505-524-4858
88201, Annette Stoesser, MD, 112 S. Kentucky, Roswell, NM, ph. 505-623-2444, fax -9693
88201, Mark Danforth, DOM, 1114 S. Union, Roswell, NM, ph. 505-627-7164
89040, William O. Murray, MD, P.O. Box 305, Overton, NV, ph. 702-397-2677, fax -2420
89104, M. Michael Robertson, MD, 1150 S. Eastern Ave., Las Vegas, NV, ph. 702-385-4429, fax -1383

89106, Milne Medical Center, 2110 Pinto Lane, Las Vegas, NV, ph. 702-385-1393, fax -4170
89119, Ji-Zhou Kang, MD, 5613 S. Eastern, Las Vegas, NV, ph. 702-798-2992
89121, F. Fuller Royal, MD, 3663 Pecos McLeod, Las Vegas, NV, ph. 702-732-1400
89128, Desert Shores Medical Opt, 2620 Regatta Dr. #211, Las Vegas, NV, ph. 702-360-5000
89410, Frank Shallenberger, MD, 1524 Hwy. 395, Gardnerville, NV, ph. 702-782-4164
89410, Steven Holper, MD, 3233 W. Charleston #2, Las Vegas, NV, ph. 702-878-3510, fax -1405
89501, Donald E. Soli, MD, 708 N. Center Dr., Reno, NV, ph. 702-786-7101
89502, W. Douglas Brodie, MD, 309 Kirman Ave. #2, Reno, NV, ph. 702-324-7071
89509, Biomedical Health Ctr., 6490 S. McCarran Blvd. #C-24, Reno, NV, ph. 702-827-1444, fax -2424
89509, C. Ibarra-Ilarina, MD, 6490 S. McCarran Blvd. #C24, Reno, NV, ph. 702-827-1444, fax -2424
89509, Michael L. Gerber, MD, 3670 Grant Dr., Reno, NV, ph. 702-826-1900
90006, Hans D. Gruenn, MD, 12732 Washington Blvd., Los Angeles, CA, ph. 310-822-4614
90025, Yancey R. Rousek, 12021 Wilshire Blvd. #802, West Los Angeles, CA, ph. 310-478-5301
90025, M. Olsen, MD, Inc., 11600 Wilshire Blvd. #306, Los Angeles, CA, ph. 310-473-0911, fax -0311
90028, James J. Julian, MD, 1654 Cahuenga Blvd., Hollywood, CA, ph. 213-467-5555
90031, Marc R. Rose, MD, 3325 N. Broadway, Los Angeles, CA, ph. 213-221-6121, fax -225-6120
90031, Michael R. Rose, MD, 3325 N. Broadway, Los Angeles, CA, ph. 213-221-6121, 225-6120
90064, Joseph Sciabbarasi, MD, 2211 Corinth Ave. #204, Los Angeles, CA, ph. 310-477-8151
90064, R. Grossman, Lac, 11500 West Olympis Blvd. #635, Los Angeles, CA, ph. 310-358-6125
90211, C. Lippman, MD, 291 La Cienega Blvd. #207, Beverly Hills, CA, ph. 310-289-8430, fax -8165
90212, Larrian Gillespie, MD, 505 S. Beverly Dr. #233, Beverly Hills, CA, ph. 310-471-2375
90265, Malibu Health, 22917 Pacific Coast Hwy., Malibu, CA, ph. 310-456-9393, fax -9482
90272-0306, Joe D. Goldstrich, MD, P.O. Box 306, Pacific Palisades, CA, ph. 310-454-1212
90401, Bridget O'Bryan, ND, 1437 7th St. #301, Santa Monica, CA, ph. 310-458-8020
90401, Cynthia Watson, MD, 530 Wilshire Blvd. #203, Santa Monica, CA, ph. 310-393-0937
90401, David Y. Wong, MD, 1431 7th St. #20, Santa Monica, CA, ph. 310-450-9998
90403, Charles Marcus, Lac, 1821 Wilshire Blvd. #570, Santa Monica, CA, ph. 310-586-9737
90403, DeOrio Med Grp., 1821 Wilshire Blvd. #100, Santa Monica, CA, ph. 310-828-3096, fax 453-1918
90403, M. Susser, MD, 2730 Wilshire Blvd. #110, Santa Monica, CA, ph. 310-453-4424, fax 828-0261
90403, Santa Monica Well. Ctr, 1137 Second St. #116, Santa Monica, CA, ph. 310-451-7170, fax -4044
90404, Chi H. Yang, MD, 1260-15th St. #1119, Santa Monica, CA, ph. 310-587-2441
90404, Sports Med., 1454 Cloverfield Blvd. #200, Santa Monica, CA, ph. 310-829-1990, fax -5134
90505, David Y. Wong, MD, 3250 Lomita Blvd. #208, Torrance, CA, ph. 310-326-8625, fax -1735
90680, William Goldwag, MD, 7499 Cerritos Ave., Stanton, CA, ph. 714-827-5180
90804, H. Casdorph, MD, PhD, 1703 Termino Ave. #201, Long Bch, CA, ph. 310-597-8716, fax -4616
90804, Michael E. Lieppman, MD, Inc., 1760 Termino Ave. #10, Long Beach, CA, ph. 562-597-5511
91010, Robert Banever, OMD, Lac, 2961 Royal Oaks Drive, Duarte, CA, ph. 318-514-5756
91024, Keenan Chiropractic, 90 N Baldwin Ave. #2, Sierra Madre, CA, ph. 818-355-9884, fax -9837
91208, Joseph Lee Filbeck, Jr., MD, 1812 Verdugo Blvd., Glendale, CA, ph. 818-952-2243
91316, I. Abraham, MD, 17815 Ventura Blvd., #'s 111, 113, Encino, CA, ph. 818-345-8721
91324, Richard Creitz, DC, 19401 Parthenia St. #10, Northridge, CA, ph. 818-700-9600, fax -1314
91345, Sion Nobel, MD, 10306 N. Sepulveda Blvd., Mission Hills, CA, ph. 818-361-0155
91361, E. Hanzelik, MD, 1240 Westlake Blvd. #231, Westlake Village, CA, ph. 805-446-4444, fax -4448
91361, J. Horton, MD, 1240 Westlake Blvd. #231, Westlake Village, CA, ph. 805-446-4444, fax -4448
91361, Phillip H. Taylor, MD, Inc., 3180 Willow Lane #104, Thousand Oaks, CA, ph. 805-497-3839
91362, Med Altern & Pain Center, 1864 Orinda Ct., Thousand Oaks, CA, ph. 805-942-1881, fax -1881
91364, Community Chiro. Health Center, 23317 Mulholland Dr., Woodland Hills, CA, ph. 818-591-8847
91401, Salvacion Lee, MD, 14428 Gilmore St., Van Nuys, CA, ph. 818-785-7425
91406, Donald Getz, OD, 7136 Haskell Ave. #125, Van Nuys, CA, ph. 818-997-7888, fax -0418
91436, A. L. Klepp, MD, Inc., 16311 Ventura Blvd. #845, Encino, CA, ph. 818-981-5511, 907-1468
91436, Tony Perrone, PhD, 15720 Ventura Blvd. #508, Encino, CA, ph. 818-783-2881, fax -2886
91472, Whitaker Wellness Inst., 4321 Birch St. #100, Newport Beach, CA, ph. 800-340-1550
91505, Douglas Hunt, MD, 2625 W. Alameda #326, Burbank, CA, ph. 818-566-9889, fax -9879
91506, David J. Edwards, MD, 2202 W. Magnolia, Burbank, CA, ph. 800-975-2202
91602, David C. Freeman, MD, 11311 Camarillo St. #103, N. Hollywood, CA, ph. 818-985-1103
91604, C. Law, Jr., MD, 3959 Laurel Canyon Blvd. #1, Studio City, CA, ph. 818-761-1661, fax -0482
91702, William C. Bryce, MD, 400 N. San Gabriel Ave., Azusa, CA, ph. 818-334-1407
91723, James Privitera, MD, 105 N. Grandview Ave., Corvina, CA, ph. 818-966-1618, fax -7226

91730, John B. park, MD, 9726 Foothill Blvd., Rancho Cucamonga, CA, ph. 909-987-4262
91780, H.Q. Hoang, MD, 9700 Las Tunas Dr. #340, Temple City, CA, ph. 818-286-3686, fax -9617
91780, Leo Milner, DC, 5814 Temple City Blvd., Temple City, CA, ph. 818-285-4142, fax 291-2017
91786, B. Chan, MD, 1148 San Bernadino Rd. #E-102, Upland, CA, ph. 909-920-3578, fax 949-1238
92008, Cynthia Leeder, DC, 800 Grand Ste. C-2, Carlsbad, CA, ph. 760-434-4615, fax -7191
92008, Mark Drucker, MD, 4004 Skyline Rd., Carlsbad, CA, ph. 619-729-4777
92008, S. Lawrence, DDS, 785 Grand Ave. #206, Carlsbad, CA, ph. 760-729-9050, fax 439-1624
92014, Ronald M. Lesko, DO, 13983 Mango Dr. #103, Del mar, CA, ph. 619-259-2444, fax -8925
92021, William J. Saccoman, MD, 505 N. Mollison Ave. #103, El Cajon, CA, ph. 619-440-3838
92024, Asano Acupuncture Assoc., 543 Encinitas Blvd., Encinitas, CA, ph. 760-753-8857
92028, Erhardt Zinke, MD, 2131 Winter Warm Rd, Fallbrook, CA, ph. 619-728-4901
92037, Charles A. Moss, MD, 8950 Villa Jolla Dr. #2162, La Jolla, CA, ph. 619-457-1314, fax -3615
92037, Longevity Clinic of LaJolla, 5580 La Jolla Blvd. #113, LaJolla, CA, ph. 619-456-1996, fax -1955
92037, Pierre Steiner, MR, 1550 Via Corona, La Jolla, CA, ph. 619-657-8333
92069, William C. Kubitschek, DO, 1194 Calle Maria, San Marcos, CA, ph. 619-744-6991
92083, Health & Longevity Inst. 2598 Fortune Way #K, Vista, CA, ph. 760-598-7042, fax 727-4554
92102, John L. May, MD, 458 - 26th St., San Diego, CA, ph. 619-685-6900, fax -6901
92105, David Getoff, CNC, 2128 Ridgeview Dr., San Diego, CA, ph. 619-262-2232
92109, Stephen Kaufman, DC, 2443 Wilbur Ave., San Diego, CA, ph. 619-581-1795, fax -9043
92110, The Livingston Found. Med. Ctr., 3232 Duke St., San Diego, CA, ph. 619-224-3515, fax -6253
92111, Dragon West Family Health Center, 4683 Mercury St., San Diego, CA, ph. 619-607-3806
92118, Capt. D.E. Sprague, MD, USS Constellation CV 64, Coronado, CA, ph. 619-545-5655
92234, Arianne Kloven, ND, 34464 Calle Las Palmas, Cathedral City, CA, ph. 760-328-1070
92262, David C. Freeman, MD, 2825 Tahquitz McCallum #200, Palm Springs, CA, ph. 619-320-4292
92262, Edmund Chein, MD, 2825 Tahquitz Way Bldg. A, Palm Springs, CA, ph. 619-327-8939
92262, Sean Degnan, MD, 2825 Tahquitz McCallum #200, Palm Springs, CA, ph. 619-320-4292
92270, Charles Farinella, MD, 69-730 Hwy. 111 #106A, Rancho Mirage, CA, ph. 619-324-0734
92324, Hiten Shah, MD, 22807 Barton Rd., Grand Terrace, CA, ph. 714-783-2773
92373, Jeannette M. McKee, DC, 1150 Brookside Ave. #L, Redlands, CA, ph. 714-793-5226, fax -2787
92405, First Chiropractic, 1947 N. E. Street, San Bernadino, CA, ph. 909-882-0575, fax -3965
92544, Health and Growth Assoc., 28195 Fairview Ave., Hemet, CA, ph. 909-927-1768, fax -1548
92587, John V. Beneck, MD, 22107 Old Paint Way, Canyon Lake, CA, 909-244-3866, fax -0109
92626, Advanced Bio Institute, 1530 Baker #J, Costa Mesa, CA, ph. 714-540-0727, fax -0873
92646, Francis Foo, MD, 10188 Adams Ave., Huntington Beach, CA, ph. 714-968-3266, fax -6408
92653, D. Calabrese, MD, 24953 Passo De Valencia #3A, Laguna Hills, CA, ph. 714-454-0509, fax -2033
92660, Allen Green, MD, 4019 Westerly Pl. #100, Newport Beach, CA, ph. 714-251-8700, fax -8900
92660, J. W.Thompson, MD, 4321 Birch St. #100, Newport Beach, CA, ph. 714-851-1550, fax -9970
92660, Joan Resk, DO, 4063, Birch St. #230, Newport Beach, CA, ph. 714-863-1110
92660, Ctr.Personal Develop, 4299 MacArthur Blvd. #106, Newport Bch, CA, ph. 714-756-1642, fax -8618
92660, Whitaker Wellness Inst., 4321 Birth St. #100, Newport Beach, CA, ph. 714-851-1550, fax -9970
92660, Whitaker Well Inst, 4321 Birch Street #100, Newport Beach, CA, ph. 714-851-1550, fax -9970
92667, Ntrl Hlth Women, 30100 Town Centre Dr. #0-117, Laguna Niguel, CA, ph. 714-249-1612, fax -4911
92677-5185, Joseph A. Ferreira, MD, 23 Redondo, Laguna Niguel, CA, ph. 714-249-2091, fax -2091
92691, Crown Vlly Chiro, 27652 Crown Valley Pkwy. Mission Viejo, CA, ph. 714-364-1901, fax -4437
92691, David A. Steenbock, DO, 26381 Crown Valley Pkwy. #130, Mission Veijo, CA, ph. 800-300-1063,
92691, Duke D. Kim, MD, 27800 Medical Ctr. Rd. #116, Mission Vijeo, CA, ph. 714-364-6040, -0502
92706, Felix Praklasam, MD, 415 Brookside Ave., Redlands, CA, ph. 909-798-1614
92720, Ronald R. Wempen, MD, 14795 Jeffrey Rd. #101, Irvine, CA, ph. 714-551-8751, fax -1272
92780, Marjorie Moore-Jones, 1034 Irvine Blvd., Tustin, CA, ph. 714-528-0216
92804, Schwartz Chiropractic, 504 S. Brookhurst Street, Anaheim, CA, ph. 714-533-1813
92821, Edgar A. Lucidi, MD, 410 W. Central #101, Brea, CA, ph. 714-256-8458, fax 990-5724
92843, Dr. Jeremy E. Kaslow, 12665 Garden Grove Blvd. #604, Garden Grove, CA, ph. 714-530-5691
93018, H.J. Hoegerman, MD, 101 W. Arrellaga #D, Santa Barbara, CA, ph. 805-963-1824
93023, Richard Hiltner, MD, 169 E. El. Roblar, Ojai, CA, ph. 805-646-1495
93023, The Natural Medicine Ctr., 1434 E. Ojai Ave., Ojai, CA, ph. 805-640-1100, fax -8020
93041, Knight Chiro Health, 521 W. Channel Islands Blvd. #4, Port Hueneme, CA, ph. 805-984-1500
93065, Derrick D'Costa, MD, 2816 Sycamore Dr. #101, Simi Valley, CA, ph. 805-522-1344, fax -2074
93101, Kenneth J. Frank, MD, 831 State St. #280, Santa Barbara, CA, ph. 805-730-7420, fax -7434
93108, Las Aves Fmly Hlth , 1805 D. E. Cabrillo Blvd., Santa Barbara, CA, ph. 805-565-3959, fax -3989

93111, Michael Hergenroet, 5290 Overpass Road #101, Santa Barbara, CA, ph. 805-681-7322
93301, A. Laser & Prev. Med., 500 Old River Rd. #170, Bakersfield, CA, ph. 805-663-3099, fax -3095
93301, Carmelo A. Palteroti, DO, 606 34th St., Bakersfield, CA, ph. 805-327-3756
93301, Ralph G. Seibly, MD, 2123-17th Ave., Bakersfield, CA, ph. 805-631-2000, fax -0914
93313, John B. Park, MD, 6501 Schirra Ct. #200, Bakersfield, CA, ph. 805-833-6562, fax -3498
93465, Richard A. Hendricks, MD, 1050 Las Tablas Rd., Templeton, CA, ph. 805-434-1836
93527, John B. Park, MD, 200 N. G. St., Porterville, CA, ph. 209-781-6224, fax -0294
93534, Mary Kay Michelis, MD, 1739 W. Avenue J, Lancaster, CA, ph. 805-945-4502, fax -4841
93534, Richard P. Huemer, MD, 1739 West Ave. J, Lancaster, CA, ph. 805-945-4502, fax -4841
93551, Vitality Health, 4505 Talento Way, Palmdale, CA, ph. 805-722-0612, fax 943-0792
93727, David J. Edwards, MD, 360 S. Clovis Ave., Fresno, CA, ph. 209-251-5066, -5108
93923, Gerald A. Wyker, MD, 25530 Rio Vista Dr., Carmel, CA, ph. 408-625-0911, fax -0467
93940, Howard Press, MD, 172 Eldorado St., Monterrey, CA, ph. 408-373-1551, -1140
94022, Claude Marquetta, MD, 5050 El Camino Real #110, Los Altos, CA, ph. 415-964-6700
94022, Robert F. Cathcard III, MD, 127 2nd St. #4, Los Altos, CA, ph. 415-949-2822
94022, Women's Hlth Care & Prev. Med, 101 1st St. #441, Los Altos, CA, ph. 415-941-5905, fax -2175
94025-1244, Jeffry L. Anderson, MD, 45 San Clemente Dr. #100-B, Corte Madera, CA, ph. 415-927-7140,
94061, Rajan Patel, MD, 1779 Woodwide Rd. #101, Redwood City, CA, ph. 415-365-2969
94061, Springer Homeopathic Care, 1244 Crompton Road, Redwood City, CA, ph. 415-365-2023
94070, Ciro Chiropractic, 1701 Laurel St., San Carlos, CA, ph. 415-508-9111, fax 591-8800
94102, Gary S. Ross, MD, 500 Sutter #300, San Francisco, CA, ph. 415-398-0555
94102-1114, Alan S. Levin, MD, 500 Sutter St. #512, San Francisco, CA, ph. 415-677-0829, fax -9745
94107, Bruce Wapen, MD, P.O. Box 77007, San Francisco, CA, ph. 415-696-4500
94109, Gene Pudberry, DO, 2000 Van Ness Ave. #414, San Francisco, CA, ph. 415-775-4448
94114, Larry Forsberg, Lac, 1201 Noe Street, San Francisco, CA, ph. 415-207-9878
94114, Rosemary Rau-Levine, MD, 690 Church St. #1, San Francisco, CA, ph. 414-522-0250, fax -0250
94115, Richard Kunin, M.D., 2698 Pacific Ave., San Francisco, CA, ph. 415-346-2500, fax -4991
94121, Laurens N. Garlington, MD, 56 Scenic Way, San Francisco, CA, ph. 415-751-9600, fax 750-0466
94127, Denise R. Mark, MD, 345 W. Portal Ave. 2nd Floor, San Francisco, CA, ph. 415-566-1000
94127, Paul Lynn, MD, 345 W. Portal Ave. 2nd Floor, San Francisco, CA, ph. 415-566-1000
94127, Scott V. Anderson, MD, 345 West Portal Ave., San Francisco, CA, ph. 415-566-1000
94133, Wai-Man Ma, MD, DC, 728 Pacific Ave. #611, San Francisco, CA, ph. 415-397-3888
94134, Leo Bakker, MD, 830 Felton St., San Francisco, CA, ph. 415-239-4954
94520, John P. Toth, MS, 2299 Bacon St. #10, Concord, CA, ph. 510-682-5660, fax -8097
94523, Alternatives in Psychiatry, 1224 Contra Costa Blvd., Concord, CA, ph. 510-945-1447
94533, Edward J. Noa, DC, 3045 Travis Blvd., Fairfield, CA, ph. 707-426-6135, fax -6135
94538, Klein Chiropractic, 39201 Liberty St., Freemont, CA, ph. 510-790-1000, fax -1000
94549, Ezra Clark, MD, 3772 Happy Valley Rd., Lafayette, CA, ph. 510-284-4845, fax -2820
94550, Geraldine P. Donaldson, MD, 1074 Murietta Blvd., Livermore, CA, ph. 510-443-8282
94577, Steven H. Gee, MD, 595 Estudillo St., San Leandro, CA, ph. 510-483-5881
94596, Alan Shifman Charles, MD, 1414 Maria Lane, Walnut Creek, CA, ph. 510-937-3331
94609, Thaleia Li'Rain, Lac, 6355 Telegraph Avenue #305, Oakland, CA, ph. 510-848-0937
94705, Wellmed, 3031 Telegraph Ave. #230, Ber Valley, CA, ph. 510-548-7384
94706, Ross B. Gordon, MD, 405 Kains Ave., Albany, CA, ph. 510-526-3232, fax -3217
94903, Scott V. Anderson, MD, 25 Mitchell Blvd. #8, San Rafael, CA, ph. 415-472-2343
94920, Tiburon Chiro. Wellness Center, 1640 Tiburon Blvd., Tinuron, CA, ph. 415-435-7420, fax -7421
94925, M Rosenbaum, MD, 45 San Clemente Dr. #B-130, Corta Madera, CA, ph. 415-927-9450
95003, Jade Mtn. Health Ctr., 8065 Aptos St., Aptos, CA, ph. 408-685-1800, fax -0108
95008, Carl L. Ebnother, M.D., 621 E. Cambell Ave. #11A, Campbell, CA, ph. 408-378-7970, fax -4908
95032, Los Gatos Longevity Inst., 15215 National Ave. #103, Los Gatos, CA, ph. 408-358-8855
95032, Cecil A. Bradley, MD, 14981 National Ave. #6, Los Gatos, CA, ph. 408-358-3663
95070, John C. Wakefield, MD, 18998 Cox Ave. #D, Saratoga, CA, ph. 408-366-0660, fax -0665
95134, F.T. Guiliford, MD, 2674 N. First St. #101, San Jose, CA, ph. 408-433-0923
95202, Luigi Pacini, MD, 1307 N. Commerce St., Stockton, CA, ph. 209-464-7757
95207, Walter S. Yourchek, MD, 4553 Quail Lakes Dr., Stockton, CA, ph. 209-951-1133
95401, Ron Kennedy, MD, DC, 2460 W. third St. #225, Santa Rosa, CA, ph. 707-576-0100, fax -1700
95404, Terri Su, MD, 95 Montgomery Dr. #220, Santa Rosa, CA, ph. 707-571-7560, fax -8929
95405, James Seeba, OMD, Lac, 3861 Montgomery Dr., Santa Rosa, CA, ph. 707-546-9628, fax -0403
95437, Peter Glusker, MD, 442 M. Merherson St., Fort Bragg, CA, ph. 707-964-6624, fax -6624

95567, JoAnn Vipond, MD, 12559 Hwy. 101 N., Smith River, CA, ph. 707-487-3405
95616, Bill Gray, MD, 413 F St., Davis, CA, ph. 916-756-0567, fax -0567
95662, David M. McCann, 8880 Greenback Lane #B, Orangevale, CA, 916-988-7275, fax -0782
95669-0790, William A. Lockyer, MD, P.O. Box 790, Plymouth, CA, ph. 209-267-5620
95823, Health Associates Med Group, 3391 Alta Arden #3, Sacramento, CA, ph. 916-489-4400, fax -1710
95825, Martin Mulders, MD, 3301 Alta Arden #3, Sacramento, CA, ph. 916-489-4400, fax -1710
95825, Michael Kwiker, DO, 3301 Alta Arden #3, Sacramento, CA, ph. 916-489-4400, fax -1710
96001, Bessie J. Tillman, MD, 2054 Market St., Redding, CA, ph. 916-246-3022
96028, Charles K. Dahlg, MD, Hwy. 299, E. Hosp. Annex, Fall River Mills, CA, ph. 916-335-5354
96701, Center for Holistic Med, 99-128 Aiea Heights Dr. #501, Aiea, HI, ph. 808-487-8833, fax -8859
96740, Michael Traub, ND, 75-5759 Kuakini Hwy. #202, Kailua Kona, HI, ph. 808-329-2114
96750, Clifton Arrington, MD, P.O. Box 649, Kealakekua, HI, ph. 808-322-9400
96813, Frederick Lam, MD, 1270 Queen Emma St. #501, Honolulu, HI, ph. 808-537-3311
96816, Linda A. Fickes, DC, 3728 Lurline Dr., Honolulu, HI, ph. 808-377-1811, fax 737-7486
96826, David Miyauchi, MD, 1507 S. King St. #407, Honolulu, HI, ph. 808-949-8711, fax -988-2188
96826, Wendell K.S. Foo, MD, 2357 S. Beretania St. #A-349, Honolulu, HI, ph. 808-373-4007
97005, George F. Wittkopp, MD, 5040 S W Griffith Dr. #102, Beaverton, OR, ph. 503-643-0049
97201, OHSU Dept. Surg, 3181 SW Sam Jackson Park Rd., Portland, OR, ph. 503-494-5300, fax -8884
97201, Stanley Jacob, MD, Oregon Health Sciences Univ., Portland, OR, ph. 503-494-8474
97216, J. Stephen Schaub, MD, 9310 S.E. Stark St., Portland, OR, ph. 503-256-9666, fax 253-6139
97220, Jeffrey Tyler, MD, 163 N.E. 102nd Ave., Portland, OR, ph. 503-255-4256
97220, Northwest Ctr. for Environm Med, 177 N.E. 102nd Bldg. V, Portland, OR, ph. 503-261-0966
97302, Chiropractic Physicians PC, 705 Ewald SE, Salem, OR, ph. 503-378-0068, fax -0069
97302, James Auerbach, MD, 235 Salem Heights Ave, SE, Salem, OR, ph. 503-363-0524
97304, Terrence Howe Young, MD, 1205 Wallace Rd., N.W., Salem, OR, ph. 541-371-1588
97321, Monty Ross Ellison, MD, 909 Elm Street, Albany, OR, ph. 541-928-6444
97330, Acupuncture Clinic of Corvallis, 2021, NW Grant Ave., Corvallis, OR, ph. 541-753-5152
97420, Joseph T. Morgan, MD, 1750 Thompson Rd., Coos Bay, OR, ph. 541-269-0333, fax -7389
97520, Integrated medical Services, 1607 Siskiyou Blvd., Ashland, OR, ph. 541-482-7007, fax -5123
97520, Partners for Health, 3206 Linda Ave., Ashland, OR, ph. 541-488-0478, fax -5509
97520, Ronald L. Peters, MD, 1607 Siskiyou Blvd., Ashland, OR, ph. 541-482-7007
97527, James Fitzsimmons, Jr., MD, 591 Hidden Valley Rd., Grants Pass, OR, ph. 541-474-2166
97914, George Gillson, MD, 915 SW 3rd Ave., Ontario, OR, ph. 541-889-9121, fax -5302
98004, Bellevue Chiropractic Center, Inc., 1530 Bellevue Way SE, Bellevue, WA, ph. 206-455-2225
98004, David Buscher, MD, 1603 116th Ave., NE #112, Bellevue, WA, ph. 206-453-0288
98008, Leo Bolles, MD, 15611 Bel Red Rd., Bellevue, WA, ph. 206-881-2224
98020, NW Center for Homeopathic Medicine, 131 Third Avenue N., Edmonds, WA, ph. 206-774-5599
98023, Thomas A. Dorman, MD, 515 W. Harrison St. #200, Kent, WA, ph. 206-854-4900
98026, The Evergreen Clinic, 22200 Edmonds Way #A, Edmonds, WA, ph. 206-542-5595
98032, Jonathan Wright, MD, 515 W. Harrison St. #200, Kent, WA, ph. 206-854-4900, fax 850-5639
98034, Jonathan Collin, MD, FACAM, 12911 120th Ave. NE #A-50, Kirkland, WA, ph. 206-820-0547
98034, Michelle N. Ramauro, ND, 12040 98th Ave. #205-A, Kirkland, WA, ph. 425-821-3006
98102, Cathy Lindsay, DO, 914 E. Miller St., Seattle, WA, ph. 206-325-5430
98103, R. Wood Wilson, ND, P.O. Box 31205, Seattle, WA, ph. 206-673-2437
98109, Barbara Kreemer, ND, 311 Blaine St., Seattle, WA, ph. 206-281-4282, fax 283-1146
98110, C. Brown, MD, 25995 Barber Cut-off Rd NE #B-1, Kingston, WA, ph. 360-297-8700, fax -8777
98112, Rainbow Natural Health Clinic, 409 - 15th Avenue E., Seattle, WA, ph. 206-726-8450
98115, Fernando Vega, MD, 420 NE Ravenna Blvd., Seattle, WA, ph. 206-522-5646
98115, Ralph T. Golan, MD, 7522 20th Ave. NE, Seattle, WA, ph. 206-524-8966
98115, Steven Hall, MD, 420 NE Ravenna #A, Seattle, WA, ph. 206-523-8580, fax 524-5054
98119, Linda Luster, MD, 200 West Mercer #E-114, Seattle, WA, ph. 206-284-6907
98125, Mitchell Marder, DDS, 822-A Northgate Way, Seattle, WA, ph. 206-367-6453, fax -4971
98125, NW Ctr.Compl Med, 10212 5th Ave. NE #200, Seattle, WA, ph. 206-282-6604, fax -9631
98155, Health & Wellness Institute, 3521 NE 148th St., Seattle, WA, ph. 206-440-1526, fax -8511
98188, Health Balances, 4109 S. 179th St., Seattle, WA, ph. 206-244-1383, fax 244-1383
98236, Brad Weeks, MD, 6456 S. Central Ave., Clinton, WA, ph. 360-341-2303, fax -2313
98368, J. Douwe Rienstra, MD, 242 Monroe St., Port Townsend, WA, ph. 360-385-5658, fax -5142
98368, Townsend Letter for Doctors, 911 Tyler St., Port Townsend, WA, ph. 360-385-4555, fax -0699
98405, Health Enhancement Corporation, 3315 S. 23rd #200, Tocoma, WA, ph. 253-566-1616

98466, A Calpeno, DC, 4111-A Bridgeport Way, W, University Place, WA, ph. 206-565-2444
98506, All Ways Chiropractic Center, 1401 Forth Ave. East, Olympia, WA, ph. 360-351-8896
98597, Carol Knowlton, MD, 503 1st St. S. #1, Yelm, WA, ph. 360-458-1061, fax -1661
98597, Elmer M. Cranton, MD, FACAM, 503 1st St. S. #1, Yelm, WA, ph. 360-45801061, fax -1661
98663, Richard P. Huemer, MD, 3303 N.E. 44th St., Vancouver, WA, ph. 360-696-4405
98665, Harry C.S. Park, MD, 1412 N.E. 88th St., Vancouver, WA, ph. 360-574-4074
98683, Steve Kennedy, MD, 406 S.E. 131st Ave. #202-B, Vancouver, WA, ph. 360-256-4566
98902, Randell E. Wilkinson, MD, 302 S. 12th Ave., Yakima, WA, ph. 509-453-5507, fax 575-0211
98902, Richard S. Wilkinson, MD, 302 S. 12th Ave., Yakima, WA, ph. 509-453-5506, fax 575-0211
99009, High Road Clinic, 42207 N. Sylvan Rd., Elk, WA, ph. 509-292-2748, fax -2748
99203, Holistic Family Medicine, 2814 S. Grand Blvd., Spokane, WA, ph. 509-747-2902
99203, William Corell, MD, South 3424 Grand, Spokane, WA, ph. 509-838-5800, fax -4042
99206, Burton B. hart, DO, E. 12104 Main, Spokane, WA, ph. 509-927-9922, fax -9922
99352, Stephen Smith, MD, 1516 Jadwin, Richland, WA, ph. 509-946-1695
99503, Denton, MD, 3201 C St. #306, Anchorage, AK, ph. 907-056-3620, fax 561-4933
99518, Robert Rowen, MD, 615 E. 82nd St. #300, Anchorage, AK, ph. 907-344-7775, fax 522-3114
99567, Peters Creek Chiropractic, P.O. Box 367, Chugiak, AK, ph. 907-688-7676
99577, Omni Medical Ctr., 615 E. 82nd Ave. #300, Anchorage, AK, ph. 704-344-7775
99645, D. Lynn Mickleson, MD, 440A W. Evergreen, Palmer, AK, ph. 907-745-3880, fax -2631
99687, Robert E. Martin, MD, P.O. Box 870710, Wasilla, AK, ph. 907-367-5284
99801, Maureen Longworth, MD, 16295 Point Lena Loop, Juneau, AK, 907-789-0266

IN CANADA
B0J 1J0, J.W. LaValley, MD, 227 Central St., Chester, NS, ph. 902-275-4555
K7A 1C3, Clare McNeilly, MD, 33 Williams St. E., Smith Falls, Ontario, ph. 613-283-7703
K8A 5T3, Naturopathic Outreach, 360 Renfrew Street, Pembroke, Ontario, ph. 613-732-9298
L4N 8K2, Barrie Holistic Centre, 127 Golden Meadow Rd, Barrie, Ontario, ph. 705-721-9932
L8N 3Z5, A. Fargas-Babjek, MD, 1200 Main St. W, Hamilton, Ontario, ph. 905-521-2100, fax 523-1224
M1E 3E6, L. Direnfeld, MD, 256 Morningside Ave. #325, W. Hill, Ontario, ph. 416-282-5773
M2N 6L4, Pain Clinic, 5 Park Home #620, North York, Ontario, ph. 416-221-2118
M4K 3T1, Paul Jaconello, MD, 751 Pape Ave, #201, Toronta, Ontario, ph. 416-463-2911, fax 469-0538
M4T 1Y7, K. Kerr, MD, 401 - 1407 Yonge St. #401, Toronto, Ontario, ph. 416-927-9502, fax 929-1424
N0B 2N0, Woolwich Health Ctre, 10 Parkside Drive, Saint Jacobs, Ontario, ph. 519-664-3794
N0M 1H0, Richard W. Street, MD, Bo 100 - Gypsy Lane, Blythe, Ontario, ph. 519-523-4433
N3H 3Y7, Complementary Healing Arts, 401 Laurel St., Cambridge, Ontario, ph. 519-653-3731
N3H 3Y7, Complementary Healing Arts, 401 Laurel St., Cambridge, ON, ph. 519-653-3731
P6B 1R4, Healing Arts Center, 426 Bruce St., Sault Ste. Marie, Ontario, ph. 705-256-8112
T0A `T0, Richard Johnson, MD, Box 96 - 4818 - 51st St., Grand Centre, Alberta, ph. 403-594-7574
T0G 1E0, P.V. Edwards, MD, Box 449, High Prairie, Alberta, ph. 403-523-4501, fax -4800
T0G 1E0, R. Laughlin, MD, Box 449, High Prairie, Alberta, ph. 403-523-4501, fax -4800
T0H 1L0, A Cooper, MD, Box 283, Fairview, Alberta, ph. 403-835-2525
T2G 1A2, F. Logan Stanfield, MD, 206 - 25 12th Avenue SE, Calgary, Alberta, ph. 403-265-6171
T2L 1V9, W.J. Mayhew, MD, 102 - 3604 52 Ave NW, Calgary, Alberta, ph. 403-284-2261, -9434
T3B 0M3, Bruce Hoffman, MD, 202-4411 16th Ave. NW, Calgary, Alberta, ph. 403-286-7311
T5E 1N8, Andrew W. Serada, MD, 10 - 4936 - 87th, Edmonton, Alberta, ph. 403-450-1991, fax -1990
T5E 1N8, Northgate medical Center, 9535-135 Avenue, Edmonton, Alberta, ph. 403-476-3344
T5L 4X5, White Oaks Sqr, 12222 - 137 Ave #116, Edmonton, Alberta, ph. 403-423-9355, fax 473-2856
T5P 4J5, K.B. Wiancko, MD, 205-9509 156 St., Edmonton, Alberta, ph. 403-483-2703, fax 486-5674
T6E 4G6, Tris P. Trethart, MD, 8621 - 104 St., Edmonton, Alberta, ph. 403-433-7401, fax -0481
V0H 2C0, Alex A. Neil, MD, 216 - 3121 Hill Road, Winfield, BC, ph. 604-766-0732
V1R 4C2, Hunt Naturopathic Clinic, 1338A Cedar Avenue, Trail, BC, ph. 250-368-6999, fax -6995
V2A 6J9, Dietrich Wittell, MD, P.O. Box 70, Penticton, BC, ph. 604-492-9849
V2G 1G6, D. Loewen, MD, 177 Yorkston St, #202, Williams Lake, BC, ph. 604-398-7777, fax -7734
V3S 2P1, Zigurts Strauts, MD, 304 - 16088 - 84th Ave., Surrey, BC, ph. 604-543-5000, fax -5002
V4V 1H8, Health Trek Research Inc., 11270 Highway 97, Winfield, BC, ph. 250-766-3633, fax -3633
V6K 2E1, D. Stewart, MD, 2184 W. Broadway #435, Vancouver, BC, ph. 604-732-1348, fax -1372
V6K 3C4, Saul Pilar, 205-2786 W. 16th Avenue, Vancouver, BC, ph. 604-739-8858, fax -8858
V9Y 4T9, John Cline, MD, 3855 - 9 Ave., Port Alberni, BC, ph. 604-723-1434

INDEX

A

1, 25 D-3, 160
5FU (fluorouracil), 55, 61, 165, 168
714X, 45
Abdullah, Tariq, 89
Abel, Ulrich, 26
Abnormal growth, 6, 15, 22, 30
Abravanel, Elliott, 99
Access to Medical Treatment Act, 243
Accessory factors, 185-210
Acemannan, 190
Acetyl Coenzyme A, 176, 185
Achterberg, Jean, 213
Acidity-basicity, 15, 20, 40, 44, 75-76, 234-235: table, 76
Active ingredients (cartilage), 195
Active-culture foods, 78
Acupuncture, 237
Adaptogens, 137-139, 144-145, 192, 196
Adenocarcinoma, 21
Adenylate cyclase, 157
Adjuvant nutrition, 5, 8, 49, 51
Adrenal gland, 148, 230
Adrenal metabolism, 101
Adrenaline, 169
Adriamycin, 6, 28, 54-55, 147, 164-165, 171, 175, 192
Aerobic metabolism, 73, 78-79, 147, 174-175, 235-236
Aerobic tissue, 73, 79, 147
Aerobic-enhancing nutrients, 236
Aflatoxin, 90, 147, 188
Aging effects, 25, 237
AIDS, 36, 38, 149, 170, 195-196, 198
Air pollution, 74, 215
Alcohol, 65, 74, 81, 163, 175
Allergic reactions, 229
Allergies, 6, 10, 16, 64, 71, 135, 148, 169, 192, 196, 200, 203-204, 220, 228-231
Allicin, 146
Allopathy, 7, 31, 128, 240, 242
Aloe powder, 189-191: safety issues, 191
Aloe vera, 75, 133, 189, 195
Alpha carotene, 157-158
Alpha tocopheryl acetate, 162
Alpha-linolenic acid (ALA), 73, 135
Alpine barley, 106
Alternative cooking styles, 86
Alternative therapies, 9-10, 27, 29, 36-46
Alzheimer's disease, 9, 36, 162, 205, 237
American Cancer Society, 17, 27, 37, 45
American College of Nutrition, 8
American diet, 65, 72

American Dietetic Association, 65
American Heart Association, 165
American Holistic Medical Association, 196
American Medical Association, 42, 65
Ames, Bruce, 18, 72
Amino acids, 56, 68, 72, 146, 204, 206
Amygdalin, 43
Amylase, 40, 179
Anablast, 45
Anaerobic tissue, 13, 15, 20, 44, 48, 75, 78, 164-165, 175, 186, 235-236
Analgesics, 16, 43
Ancestral diet, 40, 73-74, 99-100, 102, 149-150
Anemia, 242
Angina, 9
Angiogenesis, 146, 192, 195, 202, 206
Anorexia, 242
Anthocyanins, 134-135
Anthraquinones, 189
Antibiotics, 7, 18, 29, 49, 56, 88, 190, 204
Antigens, 249
Antimony trisulfide, 42
Antioxidants, 9, 48, 54-55, 78-79, 81, 134, 136-138, 142-144, 147, 157-158, 161, 163-164, 168, 171, 185-187, 200-202, 207, 226, 250, 228
Anti-cancer activity, 155-159, 161, 163-164, 167-168, 171-173, 175, 178, 190, 196, 200-201, 205-206
Anti-cancer diets, 91-127
Anti-clotting agent, 140
Anti-coagulants, 54, 167-168
Anti-diuretic hormone, 79
Anti-fungals, 146, 190
Anti-inflammatory, 144, 190, 193, 196, 201, 203
Anti-mitotic, 192, 196
Anti-neoplastic activity, 38, 42, 82, 201
Anti-proliferative factors, 57, 79
Anti-viral, 138-139, 145, 189-190, 202
Anxiety, 242
Apathy, 66
Apoptosis, 188, 201, 206
Appetite/food intake, 15, 66, 91
Apple walnut gelatin, 116
Apple bread pudding, 124
Arabinogalactan, 136
Arginine, 68, 198, 249
Arsenic, 250
Arterial blockage, 16-17
Arthritis, 16, 36, 54, 148, 162, 179, 196, 211, 237, 250
Asbestos, 81
Ascorbic acid, 82, 168, 174
Aspirin, 55, 175

Assessment component, 61
Astragalus, 41, 56, 60, 133, 138
ATP, 147, 175-176, 185‹j ‹åAtrial fibrillation, 46
Attitude, 8, 10, 14, 248
Autoimmunity, 71, 144, 196
Autonomic bodily functions, 38
Ayurvedic status, 102
AZT, 190

B

Bacillus Calmette-Guerin (BCG), 146
Bacon/tomato/spinach sandwich, 123
Bacteria, 7, 35, 44, 49, 70, 74, 78, 88, 163, 180, 199
Bacterial fermentation, 74, 180
Bacterial translocation, 70, 78, 163, 199
Bailar, John, 24-26
Baked apples, 107
Banana dessert, 112
Banana salad, 115
Barberry, 42
Barbiturates, 81
Barley, 96
Barnes, Broda, 231
Barnes, Stephen, 141
Basal cell carcinoma, 145
Basil pesto, 126
Basil, 133
Baxter Diagnostics pH Indicator Strips, 75
BBQ tempeh, 111
Bean dip, 114-115
Bedell, Berkley, 37
Bee pollen, 204
Benzopyrene, 135
Beri-beri, 174
Beta carotene, 54-55, 75, 79, 82, 88, 129, 154, 156-159, 164, 187-188, 249-250,: chart, 82; safety issues, 158-159
Beta cryptoxanthin, 157
Beta glucans, 90, 144
Beta glucuronidase, 207
Betain hydrochloride, 233
Betatene, 158
Bifidobacteria, 199-200
Bile salts, 136
Biochemical vaccinations, 38
Biochemistry, 10, 15-16, 19, 38, 48, 66, 81, 138-139, 141, 148-149, 222
Bioenergetics (aerobic vs. anaerobic), 78
Bioflavonoids, 31, 41, 57, 71, 81, 88-90, 134-135, 151, 201, 203-205
Biological dualism, 44
Biological response modifiers, 51-52, 70-84, 146
Biological therapies, 29, 35
Biologically-guided chemotherapy, 38

Biopsy, 27, 127, 208
Biostatistics, 26
Biotin, 78, 180, 199, 236
Bircaglu, Arsinur, 198
Birth defects, 27-29, 179
Birth place (immune system), 70
Bjorksten, Johan, 26
Black tea, 142
Bladder cancer, 55, 58, 83, 146, 155, 173, 175, 177
Bladder ulcers, 27
Bleeding, 29, 156
Blood clotting, 166
Blood filtration, 45
Blood glucose, 139, 224-226
Blood pressure, 213
Blood sugar, 89, 138, 141, 145-146, 163, 177, 185, 224-226
Blood testing (allergy), 229
Bloodroot, 41-42
Body fat, 77
Body shape, 101
Body weight, 66
Bolus delivery, 28, 30, 34
Bone cancer, 11, 25, 50, 168, 241, 245
Bone immune system cells, 28, 33, 70
Bone marrow suppression, 28, 33
Bone marrow transplant, 55, 151, 164, 199
Bone marrow, 28, 33, 55, 70, 149, 151, 155, 164, 190, 199
Books (nutrition and cancer), 255-256
Borage oil, 147, 163, 224
Boron, 250
Bortz, William, 223
Botanicals (herbs), 31, 38, 41, 60, 130, 133-147
Bovine cartilage, 45, 60, 79, 192-197
Bovine tracheal cartilage (BTC). SEE Bovine cartilage.
Bowman Birk Inhibitor, 141, 206
Brachytherapy, 31, 34
Brain cancer, 42, 164-165, 171, 245
Brain, 35, 42, 164-165, 171, 245
Braunwald, E., 17
Braverman, Albert, 26
Breakfast muffins, 109
Breast cancer, 11, 20, 23, 26-28, 41, 59, 77, 79-80, 140-143, 147, 150, 155, 158-160, 167, 173, 180, 193, 199, 205-207, 213, 238, 241
Breast disease reversal, 163
Breathing, 75, 78, 234, 236
Brekhman, I., 138
Broccoli, 106, 115
Bromelain, 150
Bronchial metaplasia, 155
Brown rice delight, 122
Brown rice muffins, 123
Buckthorn, 42

Bulk cooking, 95
Bulk foods (mail order), 254
Burdock, 42‹j   ‹àBurton, Lawrence, 44-45
Burzynski, Stanislaw R., 42
Butter, 98
Button mushrooms, 116
Butyric acid, 199
Bypass surgery, 16-17, 212
Byproducts, 15

C

Cabbage pecan salad, 121
Cachexia, 43, 53-54, 66-67, 150, 196, 198
Cadmium, 250
Caffeine, 65, 142, 163
Caisse, Rene, 41-42
Calcification, 12, 21
Calcitonin, 160
Calcium D-glucarate (CDG), 74, 77, 141, 207
Calcium gluconate, 191
Calcium receptor, 159
Calcium, 64, 73-74, 77, 81, 88, 100, 128, 141, 147, 159-160, 191, 194, 207
Calorie deficiency, 15, 66-68
Camellia sinensis, 142
Cameron, Ewan, 44
Camphor, 45
Cancell (Entelev), 45
Cancer conditions, 6-7, 13-15, 17, 30-31, 66-68, 75, 201-202, 211-238: chart, 6
Cancer costs, 10, 26, 37-38
Cancer patient malnourishment, 66-68
Cancer prevention/treatment options, 11-12, 14, 37, 171
Cancer process reversal (chart), 223
Cancer symptoms (relief of), 241-242
Candida infections, 242
Canthaxanthin, 88, 157-158
Carbohydrates, 67, 77, 86, 224-226
Carboxylase enzymes, 180
Carcinogens, 18-19, 28, 72, 74, 78, 89-90, 135, 147, 157, 163, 198, 201-202, 218-219
Carcinoma, 155
Cardiomyopathy, 147
Cardiotoxins, 28, 55, 171
Carnitine, 55, 147-148, 176, 192, 223
Carotenoids, 41, 54, 81, 88-90, 134, 156-159, 187
Carpal tunnel syndrome, 177
Carrot and cabbage salad, 126
Carrot brownies, 118
Carrots with bean sprouts, 110
Cartilage, 45
Cascara, 42

CAT scan x-rays, 12, 46, 61, 69, 208, 241
Cat's claw, 56, 79, 133, 144
Catalase, 172‹j   ‹àCatalysts, 149
Cataracts, 9, 162
Catechins, 134, 142
Catechol, 45
Catecholamines, 213
Catheter, 34
Catrix/cicatrix, 193
Cauliflower salad, 117
Causes (cancer), 15-21: toxic overload, 18-19; stress, 19-20
Caveman diet, 39
Cell differentiation, 71
Cell division, 154-155
Cell membrane, 73-74, 78-79, 81, 138
Cell physiology, 73-74
Cell respiration, 78
Cell-specific cancer therapy (CSCT), 14, 45, 239-240
Cellular communication, 75-76, 155-156, 189, 191
Cellular treatment, 38, 42
Center for Disease Control, 65, 179
Central nervous system stimulant, 139
Certified Nutrition Specialist, 8, 49
Cervical cancer, 55, 59, 77, 155, 165, 173, 179, 199, 213
Cervical dysplasia, 155, 179
Chaparral, 41
Chelation/chelators, 135, 186, 202, 216, 218
Chemical resistance, 7, 30
Chemical structure (vitamin K), 167
Chemotherapy, 6-7, 12-14, 21, 23, 25-28, 30-31, 33-34, 36, 38, 43, 48, 51, 53-55, 58, 66-69, 83, 90, 128, 134, 138, 145-146, 149, 157-158, 164-165, 180, 186, 188, 199, 208, 211, 238-239, 241, 243: history, 26, 33-34
Chicken and sweet potato dinner, 125
Chicory, 133
Chinese medicine, 138-139 et passim
Chiropracty, 40, 237
Chlorinated hydrocarbons, 141
Chlorophyll, 88, 134
Cholecalciferol, 159-161
Cholesterol, 65, 73, 129, 146, 169, 204-205, 211, 250
Choline, 157, 204-205
Chondroitan sulfate, 148, 194
Chop suey, 113
Chromium GTF, 78
Chromium, 56-57, 64, 78
Chromosomes, 71
Chronic fatigue syndrome, 36
Chronic infections, 234
Cinnamon, 133

Cirrhosis, 162
Cisplatin, 28, 55-56, 188, 202
Clinical setting, 8, 12, 49
Clinical syndromes, 66
Clotting factor, 167
Coagulation, 167
Cobalt ascorbate, 80, 82, 172, 178
Cobalt, 82, 172, 178
Codonopsis, 145
Coenzyme Q-10, 60, 78-79, 81, 135, 147-148, 176, 223, 236
Coffee enemas, 40, 208, 217
Coley, William D., 35
Colitis, 27
Collagen, 31, 203, 206-207, 214
Collagenase, 135, 143
Colon cancer, 12, 23, 26-27, 39, 46, 61, 64, 69, 88, 136, 155, 159-160, 164, 173-174, 179, 190, 211
Colon, 12, 23, 26-27, 39, 46, 61, 64, 69, 78, 88, 136, 155, 159-160, 163-164, 173-174, 179, 190, 211, 217, 233: chart, 233
Colorectal cancer, 136, 164, 179
Colostomy, 46
Confusion, 29
Conjugase, 149
Connective tissue, 169
Consema, 145
Constipation, 40, 200, 242
Conventional therapies, 33-36, 47-50
Cookbook, 91-127
Cooking classes, 86
Coping, 215
Copper, 128, 130, 249
Cori cycle, 75
Corneal cancer, 195
Cortisone, 16, 190, 193
Cottage cheese, 125
Coumadin, 54
Coumarin, 167-168
Couscous with nuts, 109-110
Cousins, Norman, 19, 214
Creatine kinase, 165
Crock pots, 98
Crohn's disease, 144
Cruciferous vegetables, 65, 90, 143
Cruciferous 400 (sulfurophane), 77, 143
Cryptoxanthin, 158
Curaderm, 145
Curcumin (curcuma longa), 79, 136-137
Cure rates, 25
Curie, Marie, 34
Curry, 136-137
Cyanide compound, 43
Cyanocobalamin, 178
Cysteine, 187
Cytochrome P-450, 163
Cytokines, 198
Cytoma, 208

Cytotoxic therapies, 7, 13, 31, 48-50, 54, 56, 165, 239
Cytoxan, 28-29

D

D-alpha-tocopherol, 201
D-calcium pantothenate, 176
D-mannose, 190
D'Amore, Patricia, 195
Dairy products, 10, 89, 200
Dam, Henrik, 166
Dandelion greens, 133
Daunomycin, 55, 164
Death rate, 5, 11, 13, 18, 23, 25, 27, 30, 53, 66-68, 80: graph, 23
Degenerative diseases, 9, 16-17, 30, 65
Demographics, 24
Dentition, 72
Department of Health and Human Services, 65
Depression, 11, 56, 149-150, 213-215, 242
Detoxification, 10, 19, 21, 31, 40, 60, 74, 135-136, 139, 142-143, 147, 163, 169, 187, 192, 204, 206-208, 215-219, 241: chart, 74
Deviled eggs, 120
Diabetes, 139, 150, 180, 191
Diarrhea, 27, 64, 200, 242
Dicumarol, 167
Dietary food challenge, 229
Dietary guidelines, 17
Dietary program, 40, 99-102
Dietary requirement, 51-52
Diethylstilbestrol, 171
Digestive enzymes, 12, 149-151, 230
Digestive functions, 64
Dimethylglycine (DMG), 191-192, 207
Disaccharides, 200
Disease maintenance, 11
Dithiolethiones, 143
Diuresis, 79
Diuretics, 212
DMBA, 55, 82-83, 89, 147, 163-164, 188
DMSO, 38
DNA damage, 18-19, 34, 55, 67, 71-74, 78-79, 134-135, 138, 140, 142, 144, 147, 155, 157-158, 161, 175, 237
DNA, 15, 18-19, 34, 55, 67, 71-74, 78-79, 134-135, 138, 140, 142, 144, 147, 155, 157-158, 161, 175, 197-198, 204, 237
Doctors (nutritionally oriented), 257-276: Canada, 276
Dosage in combination, 80
Dose-dependent response, 51, 67
Doxorubicin, 54-55, 164, 167

Dragon-slayer shake, 93-95, 107, 118
Drip infusion, 34
Drug interactions, 64
Drug resistance, 7, 13, 15, 23, 49, 202, 239
Drugs, 74, 128
Duke, James, 41
Dunaliella algae, 158‹j   ‹âDurie, Brian, 197
Dyspepsia, 156

E

Early detection, 25-26
Eating out, 93
Echinacin, 136
Echinecea (purpurea), 41, 60, 133, 136
Education, 14, 61
Eicosapentaenoic acid (EPA), 54, 73, 135
Einstein, Albert, 170
Eisenberg, David, 36
Elastase, 135
Electrolytes, 39, 73-74, 86
Electromagnetic radiation, 18, 45
Electrons, 78, 89
Eleutherococcus senticosus, 139
Ellagic acid, 134
Emphysema, 46
Emulsifier, 81
Encapsulated cancer, 27, 31, 35, 171
Endometrial cancer, 27, 141, 177
Endorphins, 19, 213-214
Enemas, 40, 208, 217
Energy alignment, 237
Enkephalins, 214
Entelev (Cancell), 45
Environmental factors, 18, 25, 30, 74, 215-219
Enzyme therapy, 149-151
Enzymes, 40, 52, 64, 66, 72, 74, 79, 90, 135, 142, 149-151, 175-176, 180, 204, 232-234
Epicatechin, 142
Epidemiology, 157, 164, 226
Epigallocatechin gallate, 134, 142
Episomes, 71, 159-160
Epithelial tissue, 155
Epithelial cancer, 26
Epstein, Samuel, 19
Ergosterol, 160
Escharotics, 42
Eskimos, 10
Esophageal cancer, 24, 136, 142, 146, 175, 187
Esophagus, 163
Essential nutrients, 83-84, 200, 223, 230
Essential vitamins, 78, 81
Essiac, 41, 133, 145
Estradiol, 140, 171
Estriol, 140
Estrogen binder, 27, 141
Estrogen damage, 143

Estrogen receptors, 77, 140-141, 203
Estrogen safety issues, 140-141
Estrogen, 27, 77, 140-141, 143, 203, 206-207
Estrogen-dependent tumors, 143, 203
Estrone, 140
Ethnic diet (chart), 102
Eumetabolic therapy, 38
Evening primrose oil, 12, 73, 77
Excretion, 64
Exercise, 8, 10, 17-18, 20-21, 31, 36, 75, 78, 101, 223-224, 234, 237
External medicine, 10
Eye damage, 27, 141

F

Faith healing, 38
False hope, 47
Farr, Charles, 232
Fast food, 91
Fasting, 20
Fat cells, 77
Fat content (diet), 65, 250
Fat digestion, 149
Fat solubility, 70, 162
Fat, 70, 77, 65, 100, 149, 162, 250, et passim
Fatigue, 11, 208, 242
Fatty acids, 44, 48, 57, 64, 70, 73, 80, 130, 141, 149, 172, 186, 189, 197, 200, 203, 205, 223-224, 250
Fatty liver, 140
Feces, 215, 217-218
Feeding the cancer, 48. SEE ALSO Sugar feeding (cancer).
Feline leukemia, 190
Fertility, 162
Fever/chills, 29
Fiber intake, 57 et passim
Fibrocystic breast disease, 163
Filtering (immune system), 71
Fish oil, 54-55, 68, 73, 77, 79, 135, 147, 162-163, 167, 198, 224, 226
Fistulas, 27
Flavanols, 134
Flavanones, 135
Flavin adenine dinucleotide, 175
Flavones, 134
Flavonoids, 135
Flax oil, 73, 135, 163
Flaxseed, 133
Fleming, Alexander, 29
Floressence, 133
Fluorouracil. SEE 5FU.
Folacin, 52, 57, 64, 72178-180
Folate, 67, 71, 178-180, 205, 249
Folic acid, 48, 54, 178-180: antagonists, 4
Folinic acid, 72, 178
Folkman, Judah, 195
Food additives, 65

Food and Drug Administration, 37-38, 42, 45, 81, 157, 190, 244
Food as medicine, 85-127
Food digestion/absorption, 28, 78
Food extracts, 130
Food habits/choices, 60, 63-64, 74, 85-86, 219-223
Food ratings (chart), 87
Forgiveness, 248
Forgotten cancers, 26
FOS (fructo-oligosaccharides), 198-200
Foster Study, 73
Fractionated delivery, 28, 31, 34, 241
Framingham Study, 66
Free radicals, 9, 44, 78-79, 81-82, 89, 137, 143-144, 158, 163, 169, 172, 175, 186, 203, 250
French fries (baked), 110
Freund, E., 150
Fructo-oligosaccharides, 78
Fructose, 200
Fruit and sprout salad, 114
FUDR, 208
Fungi, 144-145
Fungus conditions, 6-7, 13, 75

G

Gaby, Alan, 196
Gall stones, 46
Gamma linolenic acid (GLA), 54, 73
Garlic, 41, 74, 79, 89, 133, 138, 146-147: recipes, 114, 125
Gas, 242
Gastrointestinal cancer, 53, 68, 138, 149
Gastrointestinal tract, 70, 78, 88, 144, 190-191, 199, 232-234
Gayelords, 91
Gelatin extracts, 148
Genetics/genetic expression, 30, 57, 71-73, 150, 159, 164, 186, 197-198
Genistein, 71, 79, 205-206
Geopathogenic zones, 44
Gerson, Max, 17, 20, 39-40, 73, 88: Gerson program, 39, 73, 88
Gey, Fred, 9
Ginger tea, 106
Ginger, 106, 133
Gingersnap-baked apples, 120
Ginkgo biloba, 79, 137-138, 236
Ginkgoflavonglycosides, 137
Ginseng, 41, 56, 133, 138-141, 206, 236: safety issues, 140-141
Ginsenosides, 139
Gland/organ insufficiency, 230-232
Glandular therapy, 148-149, 197
Glandulars, 130, 148-149, 197
Glazed carrots, 112
Glucans, 190
Glucaric acid (calcium D glucarate), 207

Glucokinase, 180
Glucosamine sulfate, 148, 231
Glucose tolerance factor, 78
Glucose, 6, 20-21, 43, 55, 57, 78, 164, 224: tolerance factor, 78
Glucosinolates, 143
Glutamine, 187, 249
Glutathione peroxidase (GSH-Px), 81, 90, 175, 187, 191
Glutathione S-transferase, 143
Glutathione, 74, 79, 81, 90, 136, 143, 175, 186-189, 191, 207
Glycation/glycosylation, 185-186
Glycemic index, 14, 56-57, 206, 225: chart, 225
Glycerol, 149
Glycine, 187, 191
Glycogen, 206
Glycoproteins, 75, 149, 191
Glycosaminoglycans, 194
Goiter, 231
Golacin, 72
Gold, Joseph, 42-43
Goldenseal, 60, 145
Gonadal metabolism, 101
Gonads, 77, 101: gonadal metabolism, 101
Gonzales, Nicholas, 40, 235
Govallo's vaccine, 240
Grandfather clause/tradition, 37
Granola, 112
Grant, John, 30
Granulocytes, 71
Grape seed extract, 79, 133
Grapefruit salad, 118
Green tea, 41, 79, 133, 142-143: polyphenols, 142-143
Grocery popularity (chart), 64
Growth phase (cancer cell), 34
Guided imagery, 38
Guidelines (food), 88-89
Gut bacteria, 78, 198-200
Gut mucosa, 78

H

Haelan 851, 141, 206
Hair loss, 11, 54, 145, 156, 165, 242
Harkin, Tom, 37
Harmon, Denom, 9
Hathcock, John, 156
Hayflick principle, 237
Head cancer, 163-164, 203
Healing, 30, 248
Health care system, 243-245: chart, 244
Health costs, 25-26
Health insurance, 11, 26, 36-37, 244
Health tips, 220
Heart damage, 28, 55, 66, 147, 164-165, 171, 192, 239
Heart disease, 9-10, 16-17, 19, 23, 27, 34, 141, 162-163, 169, 178, 201, 237

Heat therapy, 31, 34-36, 54, 56, 202-203
Heavy metals, 216, 218
Heidelberg Tumor Center, 26
Hemangiopericytoma, 208
Hemolytic anemia, 161
Hepatotoxins, 28
Herbal escharotics, 145
Herbal medicine, 41-42, 56, 133-147
Herbal Veil Tonic, 145
Herbicides, 7, 141
Herbs (mail order), 254
Herpes zoster, 195
Hesperidin, 135
Hexanicotinate, 175-176
Highlight cake, 119
High-risk body parts, 26
Hippocrates, 35, 38, 143, 147, 189
Histamine, 203
HIV, 155, 190
Hodgkins disease, 33
Hoffer, Abram, 83
Homocysteine, 178
Honey-baked onions, 108
Hormone ablation, 84
Hormon independence, 7, 13
Hormone-dependent cancers, 140-141
Hormones, 7, 13, 18, 77, 84, 86, 140-141, 176, 207, 224
Host defense mechanisms, 7-8, 10, 31, 47, 51, 75, 139, 178, 239-240
Hot peppers, 133
Hoxsey, Harry, 41-42, 133, 145: Hoxsey formula, 145
Hughes, Howard, 63
Human chorionic gonadotropin (HCG), 79
Human genome, 71
Human papilloma virus, 155
Hyaluronidase, 135, 203
Hydrazine sulfate, 38, 42-43, 54, 168
Hydrochloric acid, 64, 212, 230
Hydrogen peroxide, 21, 44, 136, 172
Hydrogenated fats, 73
Hydrolase, 149-150
Hydroxyl radicals, 135
Hypercalcemia, 194
Hyperplasia, 195
Hypertension, 145, 159
Hyperthermia. SEE Heat therapy.
Hypoallergenic diet, 230
Hypochlorhydria, 233
Hypocholesterolemic agent, 51
Hypothyroidism, 231
Hypoxia, 55, 175, 235-236
Hypoxic cancer cells, 55, 175

I

Ihde, Daniel, 29
Imagery, 19

Immune dysfunctions/disorders, 226-232: chart, 228
Immune factors, 35, 78, 196
Immune functions, 51-52, 56, 67, 70-71, 74, 130, 135-139, 142-144, 146-149, 155-156, 161-163, 168-169, 171, 176-178, 187, 192, 198-199, 226-232, 239, 249-250
Immune response, 35, 53, 67, 189-192, 197, 200-201, 204, 227, 249-250
Immune suppression, 6-7, 9, 12-17, 19, 21, 26, 28, 30, 44, 49, 54, 79, 138, 160, 179, 204, 213-215, 225
Immune system, 6-7, 9, 12-17, 19, 21, 26, 29, 35, 44-45, 52, 56-57, 66, 68, 70-71, 77-79, 89-90, 136-137, 144, 149, 179, 189, 197, 203-204, 212-214, 226-232, 249-250: chart, 56
Immuno-augmentative therapy, 38, 44
Immunoglobulin A, 148
Immunoglobulins, 70, 148, 166, 197, 229, 250
Immunologic vaccines, 44
ImmunoPower, 14, 60, 78-79, 130-132: ingredients, 131-132
Immunotherapy, 174
Incidence rates, 5, 11, 13, 18, 23, 25-26: graph, 23, 25
Individualized treatment, 10
Indole-3-carbinol, 143
Indoles, 90, 143
Infection, 7, 16, 19, 26, 35, 64, 68, 151, 155, 199, 234
Infertility, 27
Information services, 246-247
Inositol hexanicotinate, 79
Insomnia, 66, 242
Insulin, 6, 43, 57, 150, 169, 186
Intact women, 26-27
Interferon, 29, 35, 138, 227
Interleukin, 2, 29, 35, 144-145, 174, 227
Internal medicine, 10
International Oxidative Medical Association, 236
Interstitial radiation, 34
Intestinal absorption, 188-189
Intestinal bacteria/microflora, 199, 207
Intestinal tract, 78, 88, 144
Intra-arterial infusion, 31, 34
Intravenous vitamins, 14
Investigative New Drug (IND), 45
Iodine, 231, 250
Ionizing radiation, 34
Iron, 55, 64, 88, 128, 130, 161-163, 171, 192, 249
Irritability, 66
Iscador, 12, 42
Ishizuka, Sagen, 40
Isoflavones, 90, 205

Isoleucine, 146
Isothiocyanates, 143

J

Jacobs, Maryce, 39-40
Janov, Arthur, 8
Jansson, Birger, 39
Japanese diet, 40-41
Johns Hopkins University, 90
Joint pain, 150
Juicing, 20, 220
Junk food, 64

K

Kandaswami, Chithan, 202
Kelley, Donald, 150
Kelley, William D., 40: Kelley program, 40
Kennedy, Ann, 90, 206
Kidney cancer, 172, 208
Kidney damage, 28, 165, 239
Killer cell activity, 68
Kitchen tips, 98
Krebs, Ernst, 43, 191
Kupffer cells, 139
Kushi, Michio, 40
Kushner, Rose, 28
Kyolic, 146

L

L-carnitine, 192
L-glutathione (GSH), 187-189
L-glycine, 206-207
La Costa Spa, 8
Label reading, 98
Lactic acid, 75
Lactobacillus acidophilus, 199
Laetrile, 38, 43, 191
Lamm, Richard, 11
Lane, I. William, 193-195
Langer, Robert, 195
LaPacho, 41, 56, 133, 145
Laryngeal papillomatosis, 155
Larynx cancer, 20, 214
Lawrence, J.H., 44
Laxative, 189-190
Lead, 250
Leaky gut, 64
Lecithin (phosphatidycholine), 204-205
Lectin, 42, 64, 73, 98, 135, 147, 162, 205
Lee, Anne, 195
Leg pain, 9
Legumes, 90
Lentil chili, 118
Lentil soup, 106-107‹j ‹àLentils (baked), 115
Lentinan, 144
Lentz, Rigdon, 45, 203
Leprosy, 44
Leucine, 146
Leucovorin, 55, 165, 168, 178

Leukemia, 22, 26-29, 34, 45, 54-55, 59, 150, 155, 168, 172-173, 179, 250
Leukocytes, 250
Leukopenia, 145, 242
Levamisol, 69
Licorice, 42, 133, 145
Life style, 18, 30, 41, 57, 150
Life insurance, 26
Lifespan, 11-12, 23, 26, 28, 52, 54, 59, 83
Lind, James, 134, 169
Linoleic acid, 48, 250
Lipase, 40, 149
Lipid bilayer, 73
Lipid peroxidation, 135, 138, 156, 161, 203
Lipid peroxides, 135, 161
Lipids, 73, 133, 135, 138, 156, 161, 203
Lipoic acid, 78-79, 81, 148, 185-186: safety issues, 186
Liver cancer, 11, 24, 50, 59, 140, 173, 188, 205, 208, 241
Liver damage, 27-28, 129, 135-136, 140-141, 146-147, 156, 163, 188, 192, 198
Liver function, 139-140, 200
Liver, 11, 24, 27-28, 35, 39, 50, 59, 74, 81, 89, 129, 135-136, 139-141, 146-147, 156, 163, 173, 188, 192, 198, 200, 205, 208, 216-217, 241
Livingston diet/program, 20, 88
Livingston-Wheeler, Virginia, 43-44
Lobectomy, 21
Low fat diet, 88, 100
Lumpectomy, 180
Lung cancer, 11, 21, 26, 53-54, 57-60, 68, 81-82, 148-150, 155-159, 168, 173, 208: graph, 58
Lupron, 127
Lutein, 88, 157-158
Lycopenes, 79, 88, 157-158, 187
Lyme disease, 37
Lymph system, 21, 33, 45, 70-71, 84, 127, 180, 199, 203, 238
Lymphocytes, 27, 52, 149, 162-163, 191-192, 227, 249-250
Lymphoid tissue damage, 33
Lymphokine-activated killer cells (LAK), 35, 174
Lymphoma, 28, 33, 155, 250
Lysine, 192
Lysosomes, 150

M

M.D. Anderson Hospital, 67, 138, 165
Macrobiotics, 10, 20, 40-41, 60, 73, 88, 99-100, 141, 206, 234-235ʝ ‹åMacronutrients, 64, 86, 219 Macrophages, 139, 190, 196

Magic bullet, 10, 27, 29-31, 44
Magnesium, 64, 73, 81-82, 128, 212, 250
Mail order products, 254
Maitake D-fraction, 79-80, 144-145
Maitake mushrooms, 79-80, 90, 133, 144-145, 195
Malabsorption, 64, 161-162, 212
Maldigestion, 6, 232-234, 242
Malnourishment, 30, 48, 50, 53, 60
Malnutrition, 5-6, 15-16, 30, 48, 51, 53-54, 63-69, 91, 165, 219-223, 232-234, 242: chart, 63
Mammary cancer, 207
Manganese, 130
Mannans, 190-191
MAO inhibitor, 54
Maple-baked pears, 110-111
Marinated vegetables, 119
Mastocytoma, 193
Maturation (immune system), 70
Mayo Clinic, 43
Measles, 155
Mechanical injury, 72, 237
Medical freedom, 36-38, 243-245
Medical savings account, 244
Medicare, 26
Medium chain triglycerides (MCT), 203-204
Megavitamins, 58, 173
Melanoma, 80, 145, 157, 164, 172, 174, 177
Melatonin, 159, 231
Membrane barrier, 73-74
Menadiol, 168
Menadione, 166, 168
Menaquinone, 166
Menopause symptoms, 141
Mental illness, 36
Menus, 103-105
Mercury, 218
Metabolic replacement therapy (chart), 230
Metabolic type, 40, 99, 101: table, 101
Metabolism, 15, 30, 40, 66-67, 74, 99, 101, 147, 174-176, 180, 185, 192, 200, 224-226, 230, 236: table, 101; replacement therapy (chart), 230
Metaphysical link, 20, 38, 212-215, 248: reading list, 248
Metastasis, 21, 39, 43, 46, 50, 67, 72, 74, 77, 135-136, 138, 140, 143, 145-146, 150, 160, 167-168, 171-172, 202-203, 206, 208, 241, 245
Metavitamin functions, 167
Metchnikoff, Eli, 78, 198, 233
Methione, 205
Methionine, 192
Methotrexate, 28, 48, 54-55, 67, 72, 168, 178-179

Methyl donors, 178-179, 205
Methylxanthines, 163ʝ ‹åMevalonate, 147
Mexican beans, 113
Micronutrients, 219
Microwave, 36
Middleton, Elliott, 202
Milk enemas, 217
Milk thistle, 74, 133, 135-136, 205
Mind/body connection (reading list), 248
Minerals, 56, 73, 128, 133, 254: mail order, 254
Miso rice, 107
Misonidazole, 171
Mistletoe (Iscador), 12, 41-42
Mitchell, J.S., 167
Mitchell, Peter, 147
Mitochondria, 79, 147, 161, 192, 236
Mitogens, 52
Mitomycin, 54, 56, 80, 140, 145
Mock turkey, 111-112
Moerman diet/program, 20, 88
Moertel, Charles, 43, 173
Molecular biology, 27, 35
Molybdenum, 64
Monoamine oxidase inhibitor, 43
Monoclonal antibodies, 35
Monosaccharides, 190, 200
Morphine, 29
Moss, Ralph, 26, 43
Mouth cancer, 55, 155, 158, 164, 168
Mouth sores, 11, 27
Mucopolysaccharides, 195
Multiple cancers, 69
Multiple myeloma, 151
Multiple sclerosis, 36, 159
Muscle contractions, 29
Muscular dystrophy, 36
Mushroom extract (PSK), 12
Mushrooms, 12, 41, 90, 144-145: extract, 12, 41
Mustard gas, 26, 33
Mutagens, 28
Myocardial toxin, 28
Myopathy, 52
Myricetin, 134

N

N-acetyl-cysteine, 187
Naessens, Gaston, 45
Naphthoquinone, 167
Naringen, 135
National Academy of Sciences, 24, 65, 170, 218
National Cancer Advisory Board, 28
National Cancer Institute, 13, 19
National Library of Medicine, 8
Native Americans, 148ʝ ‹åNatural foods, 220
Natural predators, 7

Naturopathy, 7, 10, 31, 212, 239, 242
Nausea/vomiting, 11, 30, 37-38, 54, 64, 145, 161, 238, 242
NCI, 23-25, 27, 29, 35, 40-41, 43, 82, 90, 142, 158, 165, 194, 202, 207, 214
Neck cancer, 163-164, 203
Necrosis, 12
Negative synergism (toxins), 81
Neoplasia, 48, 195
Nephrotoxins, 28
Neurological stimulation, 40
Neuropathy, 177
Neutraceutical, 66
New York Academy of Sciences, 8
Niacin, 31, 51, 55, 67, 78-79, 129, 147, 167, 175-176, 192
Nicotinamide adenine dinucleotide, 175
Nicotinic acid, 129
Niehans, Paul, 42
Nieper, Hans, 44
NIH, 19, 37, 51, 129, 170, 213
Nitric oxide, 71, 190
Nitrilosides, 43
Nitrogen, 45, 68
Nitrosamines, 143, 146, 163
Nixon, Richard, 11, 22
No cooking week diet, 102-105: menus, 103-105
No work diet, 99-100, 102
Non-small-cell lung cancer, 28, 155-156
Normal nutrient status, 66-68
Nucleic acids, 176, 197-198
Nucleotides, 197-198
Nutrient deficiencies, 51, 64-67, 73, 161: syndromes, 51; chart, 66; graph, 161
Nutrient density, 87, 221
Nutrient digestion/absorption, 78
Nutrient excretion/loss, 64
Nutrient intake, 249-250
Nutrient need during recovery, 174
Nutrient requirements, 64, 77, 222-223: pyramid chart, 222
Nutrient toxicity, 48, 129-130
Nutritional oncology, 5, 8, 12, 17-18, 20-21, 47, 60-61
Nutritional supplements, 9, 14, 20, 40, 60, 77, 128-132
Nutritional synergism, 70-84: graph, 83
Nutritional therapy, 5, 8-9, 12, 14, 17-18, 20-21, 28, 32, 38-40, 44, 46-50, 60-61, 66, 69, 70-84, 127-132, 151, 180, 208, 238, 241: functions (chart), 66

O

Oat raison scones, 120-121
Oatmeal raisin cookies, 126-127
Oatmeal, 214

Obesity, 57, 204-205‹j ‹àObligate glucose metabolizers, 48, 57
Office of Alternative Medicine, 8, 37
Office of Technology Assessment, 20, 37
Oligomeric proanthocyanidins, 71, 79, 134-135
Oligosaccharides, 200
Omega-3 fats, 249
Omega-6 fats, 56, 249
Omnivore week diet, 99-100, 102, 117-127: menus, 117-127
Oncogenes, 164
Oncology, 5, 7-8, 10, 12, 17-18, 20-21, 26, 28, 31, 34, 47-51, 53-54, 60-61, 173, 199. SEE ALSO Nutritional oncology.
Onions, 78, 89, 133, 200
OPC, 135
Oral leukoplakia, 155, 157
Oral mucositis, 165, 242
Orchiectomy, 84
Organ failure, 16, 30, 54
Organic produce (mail order), 254
Oriental diet, 10, 40, 100
Ornish, Dean, 17
Osteoporosis, 159, 250
Outcome improvement, 51-62
Ovarian cancer, 26, 55, 59, 77, 140-141, 159, 165, 173, 188, 199
Ovaries, 26, 55, 59, 77, 140-141, 159, 165, 173, 188, 199
Oxidation (jewelry), 75
Oxygen lack, 6, 13, 15, 44, 78-79
Oxygen respiration, 78
Oxygen supply, 8, 20-21, 38, 73, 78-79, 222-224, 235-236
Oxygen therapy, 38
Oxygenation, 38, 73, 78-79, 222-224, 235-236
Ozone, 21, 44

P

P-450, 143
Packer, Lester, 186
Pain, 242
Paleolithic diet, 57, 100: vs. modern diet (graph), 100
Palm oil, 201
Palmitate, 154-156
Panax ginseng. SEE Ginseng.
Panax japonicum, 139
Panax quinquefolium, 139
Panax pseudoginseng, 139
Panax trifolium, 139
Pancreas, 11, 24, 39-40, 59-60, 151, 173, 187, 208, 230, 233
Pancreatic cancer, 11, 24, 40, 59-60, 173, 187, 208
Pancreatin, 39
Pangamic acid, 191
Pantothenic acid, 64, 176
Paranormal psychology, 38
Parasite characteristics, 15

Parasites, 6, 233-234
Parathyroid, 160
Parsley, 133
Pasteur, Louis, 7-8, 89, 198
Pasteurization, 7
Pathogens, 44-45
Patient profiles, 12, 21, 32, 46, 50, 61, 69, 84, 127, 151, 180, 208, 238, 240-241, 245
Pau D'Arco (LaPacho), 41, 56, 133, 145
Pauling, Linus, 44, 83, 169-171
Pediatric oncology, 25, 67
Pellagra, 51
Pelletier, Kenneth, 19
Peptides, 42, 148-149
Peripheral neuropathy, 165, 180, 186
Periwinkle, 41
Pernicious anemia, 178
Personality factors, 19
Pert, Candace, 19, 213
Pesticides, 7, 18, 43, 81, 141, 218
pH, 6, 15, 75, 78, 86, 180, 234-235
Phagocytes, 249
Phagocytosis, 139
Pharmacologic therapies, 44, 66
Phenols, 143
Phenylalanine, 68
Phosphatidylcholine, 73, 135
Phospholipids, 147
Photosynthesis, 89, 134
Phylloquinone, 166
Physical alignment, 237
Physical therapies, 38
Phytochemicals, 137-138, 143
Phytoene, 157
Phytoestrogens, 90, 140, 206
Phytofluene, 157
Piecrust, 96
Pigmentation, 158
Pineal gland, 231
Pioneers (alternative therapy), 38-45
Pirodoxal-5-phosphate, 176
Pita bread sandwich, 119-120
Pita pizza, 121
Pituitary gland, 231
Pituitary metabolism, 101
Plant extracts, 41
Plasma cytoma, 151
Plasma protein synthesis, 66
Platelets, 77, 137, 140, 143, 151, 163, 166: activating factor, 137
Pleomorphism, 45
Pneumonia, 68, 191
Pokeroot, 42
Poly A/Poly U, 198
Polymerase, 72
Polypeptides, 148‹j ‹àPolyphenols, 41, 134, 142-143
Polysaccharides, 90, 189, 200
Polyunsaturated fats, 81, 204, 250

Positive synergism (nutrients), 81-82
Post-menopausal patients, 28
Potassium, 39, 64, 73, 81, 89, 212: ratio to sodium, 73
Potato celery soup, 114
Preleukemia, 155
Prenylamine, 165
Pressure cooker, 98
Pressure-cooked beef, 126
Prevention of cancer, 23
Preventive agent, 27
Preventive surgery, 26
Primal therapy, 38
Proanthocyanidins, 134-135
Probiotics, 78, 199-200, 232
Prodifferentiation, 201-202, 206
Progenitor cryptocides (PC), 43-44
Progesterone, 206
Promyelocytic leukemia, 154
Pro-oxidants, 78-79, 158, 161-162: vs. antioxidants, 78-79
Propolis, 204
Prostaglandin metabolism, 147
Prostaglandin PGE-1, 77, 137, 141
Prostaglandin PGE-2, 77
Prostaglandin synthesis, 77
Prostaglandins, 57, 77, 86, 137-138, 141, 147, 157, 162-163, 187, 189, 203, 250: chart, 77
Prostate cancer, 23, 26-27, 37, 41, 50, 69, 77, 84, 127, 141, 155, 159-160, 164, 175, 187, 190, 205-206, 245
Prostatectomy, 27, 127
Protease inhibitors, 90, 205-206
Protease, 40, 79, 90, 149, 205-206: inhibitors, 90, 205-206
Protein digestion, 179
Protein synthesis, 139
Protein, 14, 41, 48, 53, 64, 66-68, 81, 86, 100, 139, 179, 204, 221, 249-250
Prothrombin, 167-168
Prudden, John, 45, 193-197
PSA level, 50, 84, 127, 144
PSK (mushroom extract), 12
Psoriasis, 205
Psychology, 20, 31, 56
Psychoneuroimmunology (PNI), 38, 245
Psychospiritual problem, 213-215, 241
PUFA, 100
Pumpkin cake, 125
Pureeing, 220
Purgatives, 39, 234
Putrefaction, 78, 199
Pycnogenol, 135
Pyridoxal, 176
Pyridoxamine, 176
Pyridoxine, 176
Pyruvate, 185

Q

Quasi-vitamins, 56
Quercetin, 31, 56, 79, 134-135, 201-203: safety issues, 203
Questionable practitioners, 47
Quillin, Patrick, 8

R

Radiation poisoning, 143, 157, 163, 190
Radiation therapy, 6, 13-15, 19, 21, 23, 25, 27, 31, 34, 36, 48, 51, 53-55, 58, 66, 79, 83, 90, 127, 134, 147, 151, 157-158, 164-165, 168, 171, 175-177, 190, 199, 208, 238-239, 241, 243
Radical mastectomy, 180, 238, 241
Radioactivity hazard, 34
Radio-allergo-sorbent test, 229
Radium, 34
Raffinose, 200
Raspberry couscous cake, 115
Rational treatment plan, 239-240
Raw foods, 149-150
RDA, 65, 67-68, 84, 166, 169, 174: graph, 65
Reaction rate, 52
Reactive oxygen species, 78-79
Receptor site (DNA), 71
Recipes, 91-127
Recommended dietary allowance. SEE RDA.
Rectal ulcers, 27
Recurrence, 21, 27, 32, 50, 58, 83, 155-156, 163-164, 167-168, 171-172, 177, 203: graph, 58
Red blood cells, 52, 208: hemolysis, 52
Red clover, 42, 133
Red dye, 81
Red pepper and zucchini saute, 122
Redox, 226
Referrals, 246-253: agencies, 246-253; alternative treatments, 247-248
Regression (graph), 60
Regularity, 89
Rei-shi mushrooms, 90
Relaxation therapy, 38
Remission, 6, 12, 33, 49, 68, 83, 147, 172
Research, 27, 29, 39, 61: models, 29; results, 39
Response rate, 30
Reticuloendothelial system, 139
Reticulum cell sarcoma, 172
Retinoid, 207
Retinol palmitate, 156
Revici, Emmanuel, 44
Rhymid concentrate, 148-149

Rhymosins, 148‹j   ‹åRiboflavin, 64, 67, 78, 175
Rice bran, 201
Rice milk, 109
Rice porridge, 108
Rickets, 51, 160-161, 163
Risk increase (conventional therapy), 12, 25-26, 28-29
Risk vs. benefit (food), 87
Risks of nutrition therapy, 129-130
RNA, 68, 197-198, 204
Roasted rice/barley tea, 97
Roentgen, Wilhelm, 34
Roma beverage, 111
Royal bee jelly, 204
Royal salad dressing, 99
Rutin, 135, 151

S

Safety issues (vitamins), 140-141, 156, 158-161, 166, 168, 174, 178, 186, 191, 203
Sage, 133
Salad dressing, 99
Salad, 117
Saliva, 75
Salk, Jonas, 29
S-allyl cysteine, 146
Salmon dinner, 120
Sarcoma, 32, 72, 155, 172
Sattilaro, Anthony, 41
Saturated fats, 73, 201
Schweitzer, Albert, 39
Scorbutic, 53, 68, 174
Scrambled corn-tofu, 114
Scrambled eggs with rice, 126
Screening tests, 27
Scripps Clinic, 8
Scurvy, 44, 51-52, 134, 148, 161, 169, 174
Secondary malignancy, 28-29
Seed foods, 90
Selective toxins, 6, 31, 48, 51, 54, 56, 89, 164-166, 172
Selenium, 44, 54-57, 64, 74, 79, 81, 128, 130, 146, 249-250
Selye, Hans, 19-20, 213
Senility, 163, 165, 179
Serotonin, 169
Serum albumin, 53, 60, 67
Serum ascorbate, 53, 68
Sesame chicken, 117
Sesame seeds, 133
Shake recipe, 93-95
Shark cartilage, 193-194
Shark oil, 147
Shark vs. bovine cartilage, 193-194: chart, 194
Sheridan, Jim, 45
Shiitake mushrooms, 90, 144
Shingles, 195
Shock, 29
Shute brothers, 9
Sickle-cell anemia, 191

Side effects, 11-12, 28-29, 35, 49, 58, 61, 69, 84, 90, 129-130, 166, 174, 180, 241-242
Siegel, Bernie, 19, 214
Silymarin (milk thistle), 74, 133, 135-136, 205
Simonton, Carl, 19, 214
Skin cancer, 137, 145
Skin patch test, 229
Skin tumor, 89
Sloan Kettering Cancer Hospital, 26, 43, 207
Small-cell lung cancer, 58
Sneak, Eva Lee, 43
Sodium ascorbate, 168, 174
Sodium cyclamate, 81
Sodium, 39-40, 73-74, 81, 89, 100, 168, 174
Sodium-potassium ratio, 39-40, 73-74
Somatids, 45
Somnolence, 66
Sopcak, Ed, 45
Soy pilaf, 106
Soy spread, 112-113
Soy, 71, 106, 112-113, 133, 140-141, 205-206
Soybeans, 57, 90, 205
Soyburgers, 110
Spanish rice, 113-114
Spanish tomato salad, 111
Spice beets, 116
Spices, 133-134
Spicy beans, 95-96
Spicy ginger snaps, 122-123
Spicy turkey loaf, 118-119
Spike, 91
Spina bifida, 179
Spinach and Mandarin orange salad, 122
Spiritual healing, 20, 212-215, 248
Spleen, 71, 148-149, 163: concentrate, 149, 231
Sprouts, 95
Squamous cancer, 137, 145, 157
Squash, 111
Stabilized disease, 46
Stachyose, 200
Starch digestion, 179
Steiner, Rudolph, 42
Steroid hormone activity, 77
Sterols, 44
Stir-fried spinach with ginger, 125
Stomach acid, 44
Stomach cancer, 24, 89, 146, 188
Stomach, 24, 44, 89, 146, 188, 230
Stress, 17, 21, 72, 56-57, 176, 212-215, 224: reduction, 17
Succinate, 161-162
Succinic acid, 164
Sucrose, 100
Sugar and cancer (chart), 57
Sugar feeding (cancer), 6, 13-14, 48, 57, 73, 78, 103, 139, 164,

224: sugar and cancer (chart), 57; graph, 224
Sugar fermentation, 78
Sugar substitute, 99
Sugiura, Kanematsu, 43
Sulforaphane, 141
Super Enzyme Caps, 151
Superfoods, 89-91
Superoxide dismutase (SOD), 81
Supplements against cancer, 128-132
Surgeon General, 65
Surgery, 6, 12-14, 16, 21, 31-32, 35, 37, 54-55, 66, 68, 84, 127, 145, 157, 165, 198, 239, 243
Survival rate, 13, 23, 26-27, 52, 60, 67, 80, 136, 140, 149-150, 172: graph, 23
Surviving vs. thriving (graph), 52
Sweat, 74, 215-216, 218
Sweet potatoes, 112, 119
Sweet essene bread, 114
Sweet foods, 14. SEE ALSO Sugar feeding (cancer).
Sweet potatoes, 112, 119
Symptoms vs. cause (treatment), 16-17
Synergism, 31, 36, 49, 51, 54-55, 70-84, 88, 157, 159, 162, 164-165, 167, 170-172, 207, 240
Synergistic toxicity, 81
Synkavite, 166
Syracuse Cancer Research Institute, 42
Szent-Gyorgy, Albert, 134

T

T cells, 70, 149, 196, 214
Tabouli, 116
Tachycardia, 46
Tamoxifen, 27, 141, 206
Tardive dyskinesia, 205
Taxol, 12
Tea (roasted rice/barley), 97
Teratogens, 28, 129, 156
Teriyaki ginger tofu, 108
Terminal indicator, 66
Testicular cancer, 28, 33
Testis degeneration, 52
Testosterone, 77
Thalidomide, 37-38
Therapeutic benefits, 66
Therapeutic dosages, 52
Therapeutic nutrition (graph), 59
Thermogenesis, 203-204
Thiamin mononitrate, 174-175
Thiamin pyrophosphate, 174-175ςj ‹âThiamin, 67, 78, 174-175236
Thioctic acid, 185-186
Thompson, Stephen, 39
Thoracotomy, 46
Thought/attitude/negativity, 248
Three-bean salad, 108, 124-125
Thyme, 133
Thymidine, 176

Thymus gland, 19, 70, 148-149, 163, 230: extract, 149
Thyroid metabolism, 101
Thyroid, 10, 39-40, 101, 148, 218, 230-231: metabolism, 101
Thyroxin, 230
Time-out factor, 45
Tissue pathology, 66
Tissue wasting, 43
T-lymphocytes, 135
Tobacco, 74, 81, 218
Tocopherols, 161-162, 200-201
Tocotrienols, 79, 135, 162, 200-201
Tofu scrambled eggs, 115
Tofu with swiss chard, 109
Tolerance to therapy, 6, 13-14, 17, 31, 38, 49-61, 66-68, 79-80, 138, 145-146, 151, 158, 164-165, 171-172, 195, 223
Tomato and red onion salad, 120
Tomato sauce with pasta, 124
Topical ointments, 42
Total parenteral nutrition (TPN), 48, 53, 60, 67-68, 85, 151, 174
Toxic substances, 18-19, 24, 56, 215
Toxicity, 12, 34, 49, 51, 54, 81
Toxin overload, 6, 13, 18-19, 73-74, 81, 171, 188, 215-219, 237
Toxin processing (liver), 74
Trace minerals, 73, 148
Trans-fatty acids, 73
Transferrin, 67
Transfusion, 29
Treatment history/status, 33-46
Trend evidence, 25
Triglycerides, 203, 205
Triterpenoid saponins, 139
Tuberculosis, 44, 159, 240
Tulane University, 60
Tumor burden, 6, 10, 13, 31, 34-35, 68, 239
Tumor growth, 73, 195, 225: chart, 73
Tumor immunity, 157
Tumor necrosis factor inhibitors, 45, 203
Tumor necrosis factor, 35, 45, 158, 176, 197-198, 203, 227-228
Tumor promoters, 143
Tumor recurrence (graph), 58
Tumor response, 23, 30, 34-35, 42, 48-49, 54-56, 66-68, 80, 82, 136-137, 140, 145, 155-156, 160, 164-165, 168, 172-173, 177, 208, 239
Tumor starvation, 51, 53, 57, 67
Tumor-protective mechanisms, 79
Tuna cakes, 123-124ςj ‹âTuna-stuffed potatoes, 117
Tunnel vision, 10
Turkey feast, 121-122
Turmeric, 133, 136-137
Tyramine, 54
Tyrosine, 68, 147

U

U.S. Army Breast Cancer Research Project, 8
U.S. Department of Agriculture, 41, 165
Ubiquinone, 147
Ukrain, 14, 240
Ulcers, 19, 27, 213
Uncaria tomentosa, 144
Unconventional treatments, 20, 36
United States Pharmacopeia (USP), 151
University of Rochester, 27
Unprocessed foods, 88
Unproven/experimental therapies, 37
Uracil, 198
Urine, 44, 66, 74, 215, 217
Uterine cancer, 59, 173

V

Vaccine, 29
Vanadium, 64
Vascularization, 195
Vasodilators, 51, 77, 137
Vegans, 10
Vegetable burgers, 116
Vegetable color, 14
Vegetable platter, 118
Vegetable protein drink, 112
Vegetarian week diet, 102, 106-116: menus, 106-116
Vegetarians, 10, 20, 50, 60, 73, 99-100, 102
Vinblastine, 171
Vincristine, 41, 171
Virus neutralization, 136
Vitamin A, 54-58, 64-65, 71, 75, 82-83, 128-129, 154-156, 158, 162, 164-165, 167-168, 249: safety issues, 156
Vitamin B, 56, 58, 64, 71, 79-83, 128-129, 174-179, 191-192, 205, 236, 249
Vitamin B-1 (thiamine mononitrate), 174-175, 236
Vitamin B-2 (riboflavin), 175, 236
Vitamin B-3 (hexanicotinate), 79, 175-176, 236
Vitamin B-5 (D-calcium pantothenate), 176
Vitamin B-6, 56, 58, 64, 81, 83, 129, 176-178, 192, 249: safety issues, 178
Vitamin B-12 (cyanocobalamin), 71, 80, 82, 178-179, 205
Vitamin B-15, 191
Vitamin B-17, 191
Vitamin C, 10, 14, 16, 39, 44, 51-56, 58, 65, 68, 79, 81-83, 88, 100, 128-129, 134, 142, 148, 161-162, 166-174, 178, 186, 188,

192, 201, 204, 212, 214, 249-250: dosage (chart), 170; safety issues, 174
Vitamin D, 51, 57, 64, 71, 128, 158-161
Vitamin D-2, 160
Vitamin D-3, 158-161: safety issues, 160-161
Vitamin E succinate, 57, 79, 164-165
Vitamin E, 9, 51-52, 54-58, 64, 74, 79, 81, 83, 129, 135, 142, 147, 156, 158, 161-166, 168, 186, 188, 200-201, 249-250: safety issues, 166
Vitamin K (menadione), 55, 57, 67, 78-80, 82, 165-168, 172, 199: safety issues, 168
Vitamin K-1, 167-168
Vitamin K-2, 168
Vitamin K-3, 80, 167-168
Vitamin K-4, 168
Vitamin supplements, 128, 154-184, 221, et passim
Vitamin toxicity, 156, 158-159, 160-161, 166, 168, 174, 178
Vitamins (mail order), 254
Vitamix, 220
Volatile organic compounds, 56
Vulnerabilities by type, 101

W

War on cancer, 11-13, 17, 22-32, 243
Warburg, Otto, 44, 78, 235
Warfarin, 167
Waste expulsion, 73-74
Wasting diseases, 68, 196
Water quality, 74, 215
Water solubility, 73, 162
Wattenburg, Lee, 90, 143
Weakness, 66
Weeds, 7
Weight control, 221
Weight gain, 92: diet, 92
Weight loss, 66-68, 92, 149: diet, 92
West Virginia Medical School, 58
Wheat balls, 107-108
White blood cells, 12, 28, 89, 208
Whole wheat piecrust, 96
Window of efficacy (chart), 128
Wisdom teeth, 72
With organs (women), 26-27
Wobenzym, 151
World Health Organization, 142
Wound healing, 45

X

Xenoestrogens, 141

Y

Yeast infections, 75
Yeast, 190
Yew tree bark, 12
Yin-yang balance, 40

Z

Zeaxanthin, 157-158
Zinc chloride, 42
Zinc, 42, 56, 58, 64, 72, 83, 130, 162, 212, 249

shows you how to have all those valuable assets PLUS consume foods that nourish our ability to prevent and reverse many diseases.

In this fast-paced and entertaining video you will learn how to prepare a salad dressing that is both delicious and very good for you; how to cut your time in the kitchen by 50% to 80%; not all salt is bad, learn the secrets of balancing your "electrolyte soup" with healthy salts in the kitchen; too much sugar is killing many Americans; how to substitute healthier sweeteners; quick and easy breakfasts that get your day started right; 10 easy-to-follow guidelines for dramatically improving your health today; a simple technique for making garlic easy to cook, delicious-tasting and without the usual garlic "dragon breath" after effects; not all fats are bad for you; learn the healthy fats to use in the kitchen and as supplements; how to switch from the ever-present fat, salt, and sugar seasonings to healthy & delicious herbs that spice up your foods while making your body a "Fort Knox" against disease; how losing and gaining your health is much like tending a garden, both in effort and waiting time till the harvest.

HEALING SECRETS FROM THE BIBLE, 171 pages, $14.95
SIMPLE SOLUTIONS FOR COMPLEX MODERN HEALTH PROBLEMS

Thousands of years ago, God spoke to us through the Bible with timeless advice on a better life. Today, science has come to the independent conclusion that the Biblical lifestyle was far healthier than our modern lifestyle. Today, millions of good Christians suffer unnecessarily with poor health and die prematurely. Why? Because we are not following the basic principles of health that are taught in the Bible. "My people are destroyed from lack of knowledge (Hosea 4:6) Yet, God wants us to live a long, happy, healthy, and productive life. "I have come that they may have life, and have it to the full." John10:10

In this landmark book you will learn superfoods with extraordinary healing properties, the need for detoxification and how to do it, value of herbs in healing, importance of proper breath and water intake, exercises to tone the body, techniques for spiritual strenghtening and stress reduction.

Also included are the A, B, Cs of healing; a concise guide to using vitamins, minerals, herbs, and other nutrition supplements for specific ailments; a directory of foods and their healing properties; and much more.

Since our body is a "temple of the Holy Spirit" (1Corinthians 6:19), to claim our Divine inheritance of good health, we must follow the elegantly simple yet scientifically endorsed prescriptions in the Bible. God's food is more nourishing than man's food and God's healing is more effective than man's healing.

HONEY, GARLIC AND VINEGAR, 231 pages, $14.95

Discover the legendary healing powers found in these humble ingredients. Honey, garlic and vinegar have special scientifically-proven healing powers, and have been prized for thousands of years by the ancient Egyptians, Greeks and Romans. This book contains hundreds of remedies and delicious recipes to enrich your life. Learn scores of easy household cleaning formulas to keep your home sparkling for only pennies. Discover dozens of proven beauty preparations you can make in your own kitchen. These inexpensive, natural ingredients possess astounding properties discovered by health researchers at leading universities. Honey, garlic and vinegar have the following remarkable attributes: they lower blood pressure and cholesterol, improve circulation, and combat arthritis, prostate inflammation, muscle aches, help you sleep and improve digestion. They can also fight age spots, help speed weight loss, kill bacteria, disinfect wounds, ease pain, calm nerves, induce sleep, help fight fatigue, and more. Learn how to make compresses, liniments, tonics, ointments, teas, and more; all in the kitchen.

IMMUNOPOWER, 112 pages, $9.95

conquering your illness with the help of nutritional synergism

SYNERGISM: the action of two or more substances to achieve an effect of which each is individually incapable; meaning that 1+1=much more than 2

The good news is that "a well-nourished cancer patient can better manage and beat the disease". The bad news is that "we have lost the war on cancer." After spending $37 billion in drug research at the National Cancer Institute and over $1 trillion in hospital therapies, our 27 year old "war on cancer" has brought us an increase in the incidence and death rate from cancer with 5 year survival virtually unchanged at 50%. We cannot buy a magic bullet cure for cancer. Yet, optimal nutrition feeds the body's host defense mechanisms while empowing the mind of the cancer patient with the awareness that "I can do something about my condition." Many studies support the use of optimal nutrition as part of comprehensive cancer treatment.

Once convinced of the value of nutrition supplements, the cancer patient is faced with a "life and death scavenger hunt" to source out exotic nutritional ingredients, paying high prices for buying everything "a la carte" and suffering tremendous inconvenience in opening too many jars and taking too many pills full of too many impurities. Now there is a solution to this problem: ImmunoPower, which was designed by a world reknowned clinical nutritionist who worked with hundreds of cancer patients over the course of 8 years. ImmunoPower provides the supplemental nutrients that are specifically needed by the cancer patient, with a 75% savings in cost, reducing the pill consumption by 90% and providing nutrients in their most bioavailable and potent form. ImmunoPower is in a class by itself.

In this book, you will find all the information you need to know about ImmunoPower:

-what is in ImmunoPower and why

-the impact of an aggressive nutrition program on the cancer process

-the explanation of "nutritional synergism"

-harnessing the incredible healing power of Nature

-how to prepare ImmunoPower, with some clever recipes to give you good taste and variety

-the importance of a proper diet for the cancer patient, including the fact that "sugar feeds cancer"

-reasons why your insurance company may reimburse for ImmunoPower

-true stories from successful users of ImmunoPower. Remember, every case is different. Results may vary with the individual.

KITCHEN HEALTH TIPS

videotape, 56 minutes in length, retail price $19.95

Come into the kitchen of Patrick and Noreen Quillin and learn some of the clever and simple tips that can dramatically improve your diet. KITCHEN HEALTH TIPS is an easy and fun instructional video that takes out the confusion and adds back the fun in cooking nutritious foods. Noted nutritionist, Dr. Patrick Quillin, and his talented wife, Noreen Quillin will share some of their lifelong accumulated secrets on making the transition from the typical "white bread and bologna" American cooking to low fat, low sugar, unprocessed foods that are jam-packed with flavor. While most Americans chose their foods because of taste, cost, convenience, and emotional satisfaction; this video